LITERACY AND SCHOOLING

Edited by

David Bloome

University of Michigan

Ablex Publishing Corporation
Norwood, N.J. 07648

Printed in the United States of America.

Library of Congress Cataloging-in-Publication Data

Literacy and schooling.

  Bibliography: p.
  Includes index.
  1. Literacy. 2. Reading. 3. Literacy—Social
aspects. I. Bloome, David.
LC149.L4965 1987   372.4   86-20642
ISBN 0-89391-331-6

Ablex Publishing Corporation
355 Chestnut Street
Norwood, New Jersey 07648

Table of Contents

CHAPTER 2 THE DEVELOPMENT OF LITERACY: ACCESS, ACQUISITION AND INSTRUCTION   35

Scott Paris and Karen Wixson

CHAPTER 3 ILLITERACY AS A SOCIAL FAULT   55

David Smith

PART TWO—ACCESS AND DEFINITIONS OF LITERACY IN SCHOOL 65

CHAPTER 4 USING COHESION ANALYSIS TO UNDERSTAND ACCESS TO KNOWLEDGE 67

James Collins

CHAPTER 5 SULKING, STEPPING AND TRACKING: THE EFFECTS OF ATTITUDE ASSESSMENT ON ACCESS TO LITERACY 98

Perry Gilmore

PART THREE—LITERACY
AND INSTRUCTION   121

CHAPTER 6 READING AS A SOCIAL PROCESS IN A MIDDLE SCHOOL CLASSROOM   123

David Bloome

CHAPTER 7 CLASSROOM INTERACTION AND CURRICULAR CONTENT   150

Rebecca Barr

PART 4—LITERACY AT SCHOOL AND AT WORK   223

CHAPTER 10 LITERACY AT SCHOOL AND LITERACY AT WORK   225

Barbara Hutson

CHAPTER 11 WORKBOOKS: WHAT THEY CAN TEACH CHILDREN ABOUT FORMS   258

Deborah Keller-Cohen and Janet Heineken

Introduction
David Bloome

STUDYING LITERACY IN THE REAL WORLD

One of the most important developments in the study of literacy has been the movement of reading and writing out of the laboratory and into the real world. From a broad range of perspectives, researchers have been studying reading and writing as it occurs in classrooms, businesses, communities, and families, among other settings.

There are numerous reasons for the movement of readiing and writing from laboratory to real world. In part, the findings of experimental psycholinguistics and experimental cognitive psychology fostered a move to the real world. Psycholinguists such as Danks (Danks & Fears, 1979; Danks & Glucksberg, 1980; Danks & Hill, 1979), ᴜoodman (1976, 1982; Goodman & Goodman, 1979), Harste (Harste, Burke, & Woodward, 1982), Ruddell (1976), and Snow (1978, 1983; Snow, deBlauw, & Dubber, 1982) and cognitive psychologists such as Anderson (1977; Anderson & Pearson, 1984; Anderson, Spiro, & Montague, 1977), Brown (Brown & French, 1979), Cole (Cole, Gay, Glick, & Sharp, 1971), Ferreiro (Ferreiro & Teberosky, 1982); Frederiksen (1981), Kintsch (1977), Meyer (1977), Pearson (Pearson & Campbell, 1982; Pearson, Barr, Kamil, & Mosenthall, 1984), Rumelhart (1981; Rumelhart & Ortony, 1977), among others, provided a new view of reading and writing processes. Readers and writers were viewed as central actors within reading and writing, constructing meaning and modifying cognitive and linguistic processes to accommodate communicative purposes.

In part the movement from laboratory to real world was the result of pressure from educators who demanded that researchers produce findings applicable to classrooms. To do so, reading and writing researchers needed to identify and understand how classroom factors affected the cognitive and linguistic processes identifiedd in experimental settings. In so doing, researchers learned more about basic reading and writing processes and generated both findings and questions for basic research and classroom practice.

A third influence on the movement of reading and writing from laboratory to real world came from changes within the fields of anthropology, linguistics, sociology, and literary theory. In each of these fields, recent theory and technologies provided a means for exploring everyday events. The development of sociolinguistic ethnography, for example, provided a new view of everyday events and face-to-face interaction (cf. Gumperz, 1976, 1982; Gumperz & Hymes, 1972; Hymes, 1974, 1982). While still recognizing that the face-to-face interactions of everyday events were part of broad social and cultural structures, researchers emphasized the central role that people played within face-to-face interaction. People mutually establish, negotiate, and define face-to-face interaction (Erickson & Shultz, 1981). They jointly and concertedly construct an interpretation of what they are doing and what each is trying to communicate. Sociolinguistic ethnographers have provided a way to capture and talk about everyday events that emphasizes the local meaning and interpretations of the event without losing either the participants' perspectives or the essential social and cultural nature of everyday events.

Similar developments have occurred in linguistics, sociology, and literacy theory. Although each field brings a different set of definitions and history, within each field, the everyday activities of people—and how people view these activities—have become a central focus of research and theory-building.

In linguistics, the development of ethnomethodology (e.g., Garfinkel, 1967, 1972; Heap, 1977, 1982; Mehan, 1979; Sacks, 1972; Schegloff, 1972), sociolinguistics (e.g., DeStefano, 1978; Fishman, 1972; Halliday, 1973; Labov, 1972; Stubbs, 1980; Trudgill, 1974), the study of child language development (e.g., Bates, 1976; Bloom, 1975; Ervin-Trip & Mitchell-Kernan, 1977; Lindfors, 1980; Snow & Ferguson, 1977), among other related fields, moved the study of language from the study of idealized forms to the study of language in use. Language was redefined as a tool people use to accomplish social and communicative purposes. By definition, the study of language could not be isolated from the social and functional purposes for which people used language. From this perspective of language, researchers emphasized both the description of language in use (i.e., how people actually used language to accomplish their social and communicative goals) and the potentials of language (i.e., how language could be used to create meanings and structure situations).

In sociology, one direction researchers have recently taken focuses on how the everyday events of classrooms and schools are related to social structures (e.g., Borman & Spring, 1984; Dreeban, 1968) as well as how classroom social structures affect everyday events and interpersonal relationships (e.g., Bossert, 1979). Teachers and students are viewed as prime actors in the creation of social structures. Although researchers recognize that teachers and students react to larger social forces and constraints—community values, school district policies, and socioeconomic class structures—through their everyday face-to-face interactions, teachers and students are viewed as creating, constructing, negotiating, and maintaining both broad and situation-specific social forces and structures (e.g., Corsaro, 1980).

Within literary theory, as Robinson (Chap. 14, this volume) stated, texts had been viewed as having a single meaning. A reader's job was to uncover *the* meaning of the text. However, recent work in literary theory places the reader in a central role to determine what meaning a text may have (e.g., Eco, 1979; Golden, 1983; Ong, 1977). The reader's job is to derive a meaning from a broad range of potential meanings of the text (e.g., reader-response theory). The reader is only bounded by the cues and information provided by the text and by the norms for interpreting meaning associated with one's community. That is, readers are expected to make sense of a text in ways consistent with how others make sense of texts within their professional community (e.g., engineering, law, medicine, mechanics) or social community (e.g., church, neighborhood, family).

STANDARDS AND EMERGING DIRECTIONS FOR THE STUDY OF LITERACY

As the study of literacy moved from laboratory to real world, researchers had to concern themselves not only with methods and findings but with standards for studying literacy in the real world. Familiar standards for studying reading and writing had emphasized laboratory, experimental, or other isolated research settings. Although these standards provided a starting place, they were not directly applicable to the study of literacy in the real world. Other sets of standards needed to be developed.

For example, consider the ethnographic study of literacy. Although standards, procedures, and theoretical constructs for conducting ethnographies and ethnographic studies have been discussed for over 75 years, because of the topic of study (reading and writing within the face-to-face interactions of everyday events), the level of study (classrooms, lessons, homes, schools), and underlying assumptions about everyday events (e.g., that events and their meanings are actively constructed by the face-to-face interactions of people), a new set of standards for the ethnographic study of literacy needed to be articulated. During the late 1970s and early 1980s, numerous articles and books outlined standards for the ethnographic study of literacy both within and outtside of school settings (e.g., McDermott, Gospodinoff, & Aron, 1979; McDermott & Hood, 1982; Erickson, 1979; Green & Bloome, 1983; Spindler, 1982; Szwed, 1981). What these articles and books offered was a theoretical frame (or, perhaps, more accurately, a set of theoretical heuristics) for looking at literacy both in and out of classrooms (for a discussion of these theoretical heuristics, see Green, 1983; Wilkinson, 1982; Hymes, 1981; Cook-Gumperz & Gumperz, 1982). While these constructs have primarily emphasized the study of classroom processes, as Green and Weade (Chap. 1, this volume) illustrate, these constructs also provide a means of studying literacy, especially classroom literacy (as well as literacy events outside of the school related to classrooom literacy).

Similarly, in linguistics, sociology, and literary criticism, the need for reviewing and articulating standards for the study of literacy in the real world have led to emerging fields or redirections of established fields (for further discussion, with regard to linguistics, see Labov, 1972; Heap, 1977; Halliday, 1973; with regard to sociology, see Corsaro, 1980; Dreeban, 1968; Circourel, 1973; with regard to literary theory, see Eco, 1979; Golden, 1983).

THE UNIVERSITY OF MICHIGAN CONFERENCE

In February 1984, the Horace Rackham School of Graduate Studies and the School of Education, both of the University of Michigan, brought together researchers from across North America to explore emerging perspectives and fields in the study of literacy. Researchers represented a broad range of disciplines: anthropology, sociolinguistics, cognitive psychology, administration and policy studies, English and literary criticism, linguistics, educational sociology, special education, and developmental psychology.

A Focus on Upper Elementary Through Secondary School Levels

Of special importance at the conference was the study of literacy at the upper elementary, middle, and secondary school level. From a theoretical perspective, this focus was based on the need to develop a model of literacy and schooling that went beyond issues of initial access.

Models of literacy and schooling have emphasized young students and issues of access and issues of home-school continuity and discontinuity (e.g., Au, 1980; Cook-Gumperz & Gumperz, 1981; Hymes, 1981; Cazden, John & Hymes, 1972). However, there has been little discussion of models of literacy and schooling beyond beginning reading and writing. While factors such as access and home school difference may be important components of a model or frame for looking at literacy at the upper elementary through secondary school level, the central components can be assumed to be the roles, functions, and ways of "doing literacy" in school that students have learned over time. Simply put, because the students' relationships to school have changed and because the school's relationship to students has changed (as a result of both having attended school for several years and of changes in curriculum, instruction, and social and academic expectations), the issues that need to be explored with regard to literacy and schooling change as well (Knott, Chap. 15 this volume).

A second need to look at literacy at the upper elementary through secondary school levels, comes from educators who have increasingly called for new perspectives for looking at reading and writing at these levels. They have found that they cannot validly look at literacy and schooling at the upper elementary through secondary school level in the same way they have looked at early elementary school reading and writing.

Multiple Perspectives

The University of Michigan conference had been designed both to promote discussion among researchers and to identify bridges and links across the perspectives they brought to the study of literacy. A small number of research studies were read by participants prior to the conference and provided a common referent for discussion (Smith, Chap. 3, this volume; Collins, Chap. 4, this volume; Gilmore, Chap. 5, this volume; Bloome, Chap. 6, this volume; Barr, Chap. 7, this volume; Golden, Chap. 8, this volume; and Moll & Diaz, Chap. 9, this volume). The studies read for the conference were chosen because each combined multiple perspectives in the study of literacy *and* because each represented an emerging direction in the study of literacy.

An inherent danger in bringing together researchers from different disciplinary perspectives is that they might be unable to talk to one another (Cole & Scribner, 1976). Each disciplinary approach tends to have its own language and underlying assumptions. Hence there is the potential for participants to either ignore one another or to engage each other at a superficial level.

Through both the formal and informal conference discussions, it became clear that the potential danger of researchers not being able to understand each other's language had been resolved not only among conference participants but also among large segments of the research community. It also became clear at the conference that language differences across disciplines are not resolved by finding a common language. The language of each disciplinary approach is an important vehicle for communicating that approach's perspective and findings. Rather than finding a common language, researchers need to develop the "communicative competence" to use multiple research languages. At the same time, researchers must also be careful in constructing the language they use to describe their research: It must be made accessible to "outsiders."

Beyond Sharing Perspectives

A second purpose of the conference went beyond the sharing of perspectives and research on literacy. Of special importance was the identification of questions and issues that needed to be addressed by the study of literacy. Among the questions and issues identified were:

1. *How can researchers approach the study of literacy in school? How can issues of classroom processes, cultural processes, and social processes be framed to provide principled approaches to the study of literacy and literacy learnings?* Especially in Western societies, literacy and schooling seem inseparable. Thus, approaches to the study of literacy need to account for both the nature of schooling and the nature of classroom learning.

2. *What is the relationship between "access" to literacy and literacy?* There are many ways to define access to literacy. On one hand, access to literacy may be defined as institutional gatekeeping: Only a selected group of students is allowed to participate in one set of a school's literacy activities (e.g., book reading in the library). On the other hand, access to literacy may be defined as obtaining the requisite instruction to become literate. How access to literacy is defined by those people who control access to literacy, by those people who are denied access, and by researchers studying access has important implications for how literacy itself gets defined both in the field and in research endeavors.

3. *How does instruction define literacy?* When teachers and students engage in literacy lessons, they negotiate a definition of literacy. In part, the definition they negotiate is based on the nature of the interaction between teacher and students, the texts they use, how they use the texts, and the curricular constraints under which they work.

4. *What is the relationship between literacy at school and literacy at work?* Throughout school, students learn ways of "doing literacy." It is assumed that these ways of "doing" reading and writing are transferable to and consistent with the ways of "doing literacy" at work. Yet, how schools define literacy and how work defines literacy may be very different, if, for no other reason, because school and work are different kinds of social systems (see Kirsch & Guthrie, 1983).

5. *What are the policy implications of the newly emerging directions in the study of literacy?* Simply put, researchers are examining the implications of research on literacy conducted within a broad range of emerging directions for school policy and

practice. In part, the examination of policy and literacy research requires an examination of how policy is constituted, what the goals of policy are, and what research can contribute to policy formation and implementation. In part, the examination of policy and literacy research requires a review of the substantive assumptions underlying school literacy policy.

6. *What are the definitions of literacy and literacy instruction being offered by the new emerging directions in the study of literacy?* Literacy and literacy instruction always occur within a context (or, perhaps more accurately, within multiple contexts). The ways in which literacy and literacy instruction are contextualized need to provide both educators and researchers with a means for manipulating and exploring literacy.

These six questions above correspond to the six parts of the book: "Approaching Literacy and Schooling"; "Access and Definitions of Literacy in School"; "Literacy and Instruction"; "Literacy at School and Literacy at Work"; "Policy Implications"; and "Contexts of Literacy Revisited."

A MODEL OF EMERGING DIRECTIONS IN THE STUDY OF LITERACY AND SCHOOLING

Researchers have cautioned about creating static models of literacy and schooling (e.g., Scribner & Cole, 1978; 1981). Both literacy and schooling are dynamic concepts, defined as much by the perspectives with which they are viewed as by the social, political, historical, cultural, communicative, and psychological contexts within which they take place. Thus, rather than generating a model of literacy, what is needed are models of how to approach literacy. How to approach literacy is an issue for both educational practitioners and researchers, since both must account for shifting definitions and contexts of literacy activity. Both educators and researchers must continuously make principled decisions about how to define and contextualize literacy activity.

The model that follows is intended to integrate issues highlighted in the study of literacy and schooling; thus, it presents a visual summary of core substantive issues involved in approaching literacy and schoooling. The model builds on the approaches to literacy and schooling described in this volume by Green and Weade, Paris and Wixson, Smith, Robinson, and Knott.

Among the key issues considered are (a) the nature and location of access to literacy within school and classroom contexts and how definitions of access define literacy itself (Paris & Wixson; Collins; Gilmore; Moll & Diaz; Knott); (b) how instruction defines literacy events (e.g., who does what, with whom, when, where, and how) including texts (Golden; Moll & Diaz; Barr; Bloome), social and communicative goals of literacy behavior (Smith; Barr; Moll & Diaz; Bloome; Green & Weade; Knott), and the meanings of author-reader, teacher-student-text, and student-student-text interactions (Golden; Barr; Bloome; Moll & Diaz; Robinson; Knott); (c) the relationship of school literacy to literacy in the postschool world of work and public institutions (Hutson; Keller-Cohen & Heineken; Guthrie); (d) how policy at

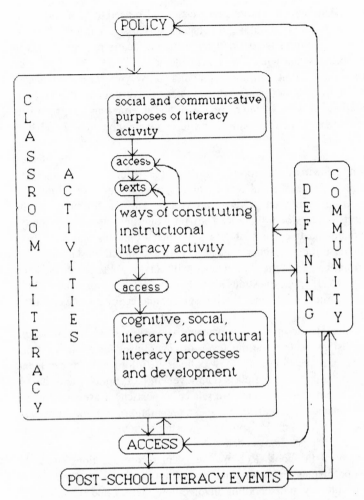

Figure 1. Core substantive issues involved in approaching literacy and schooling.

broad governmental levels and at school district and school levels influences definitions of literacy and structures classroom literacy events (Wallat; Guthrie); and (e) how literacy defines community and how community defines literacy (Robinson; Moll & Diaz; Green & Weade; Smith; Knott).

In brief, the model shows how various perspectives contribute to a picture of emerging directions in the study of literacy and schooling. The core of the model is everyday classroom literacy events, a theme or emphasis common to a broad range of emerging perspectives. From an anthropological and sociolinguistic perspective, questions need to be asked about how schools and communities differentiate access to different sets of classroom literacy experiences (Gilmore, Chap. 5, this volume; Smith, Chap. 3, this volume). Smith also raises questions about how school literacy provides access to postschool social status. Questions also need to be asked about access to literacy but from a psychological perspective (Paris & Wixson, Chap. 2, this volume). How do cultural factors and instructional factors provide access to those cognitive processes that constitute school literacy?

The questions Smith, Collins, Gilmore, and Paris and Wixson raise about access are, in part, reflections of how literacy communities are constituted. If literacy is viewed as a shared set of ways of interacting with and interpreting text, then it is appropriate to explore how people gain access to a literacy community and how communities limit access.

Beyond issues of access, grounded descriptions are needed of how literacy events are constituted within classroom instruction (see Bloome, Barr, Golden, Moll & Diaz, Green & Weade, and Knott, this volume). From a sociolinguistic ethnographic perspective, Bloome, Green and Weade, and Knott emphasize the interactional aspects of classroom literacy. They raise questions about the underlying social and communicative goals of classroom literacy events and how these goals get constituted through teacher-student-text interaction. Barr, Golden, and Moll and Diaz, from the perspectives of educational sociology, literary theory, and ethnography, respectively, raise questions about how the nature of texts involved in classroom literacy instruction influence teacher-student interaction and the construction of meaning.

The ways in which classroom literacy events are constituted are, in part, structured by policy decisions made at various levels of government and administration. Guthrie and Wallat raise questions about how policies are informed by research and how policies get implemented at the classroom level. In part, policies and the explicit goals of classroom literacy events are related to postschool uses of literacy. After all, school is intended, at least in part, as a preparation for work. However, Keller-Cohen and Heineken and Hutson raise questions about the relationship of schooling, literacy, and postschool endeavors.

In the last section of the book, Robinson and Knott pose questions about the future of research on literacy and schooling. Both scholars suggest that the key issues in research on literacy and schooling involve how literacy and schooling get contextualized. As such, they reject attempts to isolate literacy from everyday activity. Rather, they insist, it is through juxtaposing multiple perspectives of how everyday school literacy events are constituted that foundations are built for emerging directions in the study of literacy and schooling.

REFERENCES

Anderson, R. (1977). The notion of schemata and the educational enterprise: General discussion of the conference. In R. Anderson, R. Spiro, & W. Montague (Eds.), *Schooling and the acquisition of knowledge*. Hillsdale, NJ: Erlbaum.

Anderson, R., & Pearson, P. (1984). A schema-theoretic view of basic processes in reading comprehension. In P. Pearson, R. Barr, M. Kamil, & P. Mosenthal (Eds.), *Handbook of reading research*. New York: Longman.

Anderson, R., Spiro, R., & Montague, W. (Eds.). (1977). *Schooling and the acquisition of knowledge*. Hillsdale, NJ: Erlbaum.

Au, K. (1980). Participation structures in a reading lesson with Hawaiian children. *Anthropology and Education Quarterly, 11*(2), 91-115.

Bates, E. (1976). *Language and context: The acquisition of pragmatics.* New York: Academic Press.

Bloom, L. (1975). Language development review. In F. Horowitz (Ed.), *Review of child development research* (Vol. 4). Chicago: University of Chicago Press.

Borman, K., & Spring, J. (1984). *Schools in central cities.* New York: Longman.

Bossert, S. (1979). *Social relationships and classroom tasks.* New York: Cambridge University Press.

Brown, A., & French, L. (1979). The zone of potential development: Implications for intelligence testing in the year 2000. *Intelligence, 3,* 255-273.

Cazden, C., John, V., & Hymes, D. (Eds.). (1972). *Functions of language in the classroom.* New York: Teachers College Press.

Cicourel, A. (1973). *Cognitive sociology: Language and meaning in social interaction.* London: Penguin.

Cole, M., Gay, J., Glick, J., & Sharp, D. (1971). *The cultural context of learning and thinking: An exploration in experimental anthropology.* New York: Basic.

Cole, M, & Scribner, S. (1976). Theorizing about socialization of cognition. In T. Schwartz (Ed.), *Socialization as cultural communication.* Berkeley: University of California Press.

Cook-Gumperz, J., & Gumperz, J. (1982). Communicative competence in educational perspective. In L. Wilkinson (Ed.), *Communicating in the classroom.* New York: Academic Press.

Corsaro, W. (1980). Communicative processes in studies of social organization: Sociological approaches to discourse analysis. *Text.*

Danks, J., & Glucksberg, S. (1980). Experimental psycholinguistics. *Annual Review of Psychology, 31,* 391-417.

Danks, J., & Fears, R. (1979). Oral reading: Does it reflect decoding or comprehension? In L. Resnick & P. Weaver (Eds.), *Theory and practice of early reading* (Vol. 3). Hillsdale, NJ: Erlbaum.

Danks, J., & Hill, G. (1979). An interactive analysis of oral reading. In A. Lesgold & C. Perfetti (Eds.), *Interactive processes in reading.* Hillsdale, NJ: Erlbaum.

DeStefano, J. (1978). *Language, the learner and the school.* New York: Wiley.

Dreeban, R. (1968). *On what is learned in school.* Cambridge, MA: Harvard University Press.

Eco, U. (1979). *The role of the reader: Explorations in the semiotics of text.* Bloomington: Indiana University Press.

Erickson, F. (1979). *On standards of descriptive validity in studies of classroom activity* (Occasional paper #16). East Lansing, MI: Institute for Research on Teaching.

Erickson, F., & Schultz, J. (1981). When is a context? Some issues and methods in the analysis of social competence. In J. Green & C. Wallat (Eds.), *Ethnography and language in educational settings.* Norwood, NJ: Ablex.

Ervin-Tripp, S., & Mitchell-Kernan, C. (Eds.). (1977). *Child discourse.* New York: Academic Press.

Ferreiro, E., & Teberosky, A. (1982). *Literacy before schooling.* Exeter, NH: Heinemann.

Fishman, J. (1972). Domains and the relationship between micro and macro sociolinguistics. In J. Gumperz & D. Hymes (Eds.), *Directions in sociolinguistics.* In J. Gumperz & D. Hymes (Eds.) New York: Holt, Rinehart & Winston.

Frederiksen, C. (1981). Inference in preschool children's conversations—a cognitive perspective. In J. Green & C. Wallat (Eds.), *Ethnography and language in educational settings.* Norwood, NJ: Ablex.

Garfinkel, H. (1967). *Studies in ethnomethodology.* Englewood Cliffs, NJ: Prentice-Hall.

Garfinkel, H. (1972). Remarks on ethnomethodology. In J. Gumperz & D. Hymes (Eds.), *Directions in sociolinguistics.* New York: Holt, Rinehart & Winston.

Golden, J. (1983). If a text exists without a reader, is there a meaning? Insights from literary theory for reader-text interaction. In B. Hutson (Ed.), *Advances in reading/language research* (Vol. 2). Greenwich, CT: JAI.

Goodman, K. (1976). Behind the eye: What happens in reading. In H. Singer & R. Rudell (Eds.), *Theoretical models and processes of reading.* Newark, DE: International Reading Association.

Goodman, K. (1982). *Language and literacy: The selected writings of Kenneth S. Goodman* (Vol. 1). Boston: Routledge & Kegan Paul.

Goodman, K., & Goodman, Y. (1979). Learning to read is natural. In L. Resnick & P. Weaver (Eds.), *Theory and practice of early reading (Vol. 1). Hillsdale, NJ: Erlbaum.*

Green, J. (1983). Exploring classroom discourse: Linguistic perspectives on teaching-learning processes. *Educational Psychologist, 18*(3), 180–199.

Green, J., & Bloome D. (1983). Ethnography and reading: Issues, approaches, criteria and findings. In J. Niles (Ed.), *Thirty-second Yearbook of the National Reading Conference.* Rochester, NY: National Reading Conference.

Gumperz, J. (1976). Language, communication and public negotiation. In P. Sanday (Ed.), *Anthropology and the public interest: Fieldwork and theory.* New York: Academic Press.

Gumperz, J. (1982) *Discourse strategies.* London: Cambridge University Press.

Gumperz, J., & Hymes, D. (Eds.). (1972). *Directions in sociolinguistics,* New York: Holt, Rinehart, & Winston.

Halliday, M. (1973). Language as a social semiotic: Towards a general sociolinguistic theory. In M. Makkai & L. Heilman (Eds.), *Linguistics at the crossroads.* The Hague: Mouton.

Harste, J., Burke, C., & Woodward, V. (1982). Children's language and world: Initial encounters with print. In J. Langer & M. Smith-Burke (Eds.), *Reader meets author/bridging the gap: A psycholinguistic and socialinguistics perspective.* Newark, DE: International Reading Association.

Heap, J. (1977). Toward a phenomenology of reading. *Journal of Phenomenological Psychology,* 103–114.

Heap, J. (1982). Understanding classroom events: A critique of Durkin, with an alternative. *Journal of Reading Behavior, 14,* 391–412.

Hymes, D. (1974). *Foundations in sociolinguistics: An ethnographic approach.* Philadelphia: University of Pennsylvania Press.

Hymes, D. (Project director). (1981). *Ethnographic monitoring of children's acquisition of reading and language arts skills in and out of the classroom.* Final report to the National Institute of Education. Washington, D.C: U.S. Department of Education.

Kinstch, W. (1977). The representation of meaning in memory. New York: Academic Press.

Kirsch, I., & Guthrie, J. (1983). *Reading competencies and practices: Reading practices of adults in one high technology company.* (Technical Report #6). Newark, DE: International Reading Association.

Labov, W. (1972). *Sociolinguistic patterns.* Philadelphia: University of Pennsylvania Press.

Lindfors, J. (1980). *Children's language and learning.* Englewood Cliffs, NJ: Prentice-Hall.

McDermott, R., Gospodinoff, K., & Aron, J. (1979, December). *Criteria for an ethnographically adequate description of concerted activities and their contexts.* Paper presented at the meeting of the American Anthroppology Association, Washington, D.C.

McDermott, R., & Hood, L. (1982). Institutionalized psychology and the ethnography of schooling. In P. Gilmore & A. Glatthorn (Eds.), *Children in and out of school.* Washington, DC: Center for Applied Linguistics.

Mehan, H. (1979). Learning lessons: Social organization in the classroom. Cambridge, MA: Harvard University Press.

Meyer, B. (1977). The structure of prose: Effects on learning and memory and implications for educational practice. In R. Anderson, R. Spiro, & Montague (Eds.), *Schooling and the acquisition of knowledge.* Hillsdale, NJ: Erlbaum.

Ong, W. (1977). *The interfaces of the word: Studies in the evolution of consciousness and culture.* Ithaca, NY: Cornell University Press.

Pearson, P., Barr, R., Kamil, M., & Mosenthal, P. (Eds.). (1984). *Handbook of reading research.* New York: Longman.

Pearson, P., & Camperell, K. (1981). Comprehension of text structures. In J. Guthrie (Ed.), *Comprehension and Teaching: Research reviews.* Newark, DE: International Reading Association.

Rudell, R. (1976). Psycholinguistic implications for a system of communication model. In H. Siknger & R. Ruddell (Eds.), *Theoretical models and processes of reading.* Newark, DE: International Reading Association.

Rumelhart, D. (1981). Schemata: The building blocks of cognition. In J. Guthrie (Ed.), *Comprehension and teaching: Research reviews*. Newark, DE: International Reading Association.

Rumelhart, D., & Ortony, A. (1977). The representation of knowledge in memory. In R. Anderson, R. Spiro, & W. Montague (Eds.) *Schooling and the acquisition of knowledge*. Hillsdale, NJ: Erlbaum.

Sacks, H. (1972). An initial investigation of the useability of conversational data for doing sociology. In D. Sudnow (Ed.), *Studies in social interaction*. New York: Free Press.

Schegloff, E. (1972). Sequencing and conversational opening. In J. Gumperz & D. Hymes (Eds.), *Directions in sociolinguistics*. New York: Holt, Rinehart & Winston.

Scribner, S., & Cole, M. (1978). Literacy without schooling: Testing for intellectual effects. *Harvard Educational Review, 48*(4), 448–461.

Scribner, M, & Cole, M. (1981). *The psychology of literacy*. Cambridge, MA: Harvard University Press.

Snow, C. (1978). The conversational context of language acquisition. In R. Cambell & P. Smith (Eds.), *Recent advances in the psychology of language: Social and interactional factors* (Vol. 2). New York: Plenum.

Snow, C. (1983). Literacy and language in the preschool years. *Harvard Educational Review, 53*(2), 165–187.

Snow, C., deBlauw, A., & Dubber, C. (1982). Routines in parent-child interaction. In L. Feagans & D. Farran (Eds.), *The language of children reared in poverty*. New York: Academic Press.

Snow, C., & Ferguson, C. (Eds.). (1977). *Talking to children*. Cambridge, England: Cambridge University Press.

Spindler, G. (1982). General introduction. In G. Spindler (Ed.), *Doing the ethnography of schooling: Educational anthropology in action*. New York: Holt, Rinehart, & Winston.

Spiro, R. (1977). Remembering information from text: The "state of schema" approach. In R. Anderson, R. Spiro, & W. Montague (Eds.) *Schooling and the acquisition of knowledge*. Hillsdale, NJ: Erlbaum.

Spiro, R. (1980). Accommodative reconstruction in prone recall. *Journal of Verbal Learning and Verbal Behavior, 19*, 84–95.

Stubbs, M. (1980). Language & Literacy: The sociolinguistics of reading and writing. London: Routledge & Kegan Paul.

Szwed, J. (1981). The ethnography of literacy. In M. Whiteman (Ed.), *Variation in writing: Functional and linguistic-cultural difference*. Hillsdale, NJ: Erlbaum.

Trudgill, P. (1974). *Sociolinguistics: An introduction*. Middlesex, England: Penguin.

Wilkinson, L. (Eds.). (1982). *Communicating in the classroom*. New York: Academic Press.

PART ONE

APPROACHING LITERACY AND SCHOOLING

1 In Search of Meaning: A Sociolinguistic Perspective on Lesson Construction and Reading*

Judith Green
The Ohio State University

Regina Weade
University of Florida

The way in which reading is defined influences how reading will be approached in both schools and research. In schools as well as in the research community, reading has been viewed as both an object of instruction and a medium for instruction in other curriculum areas. This view has led to a focus on the skills, strategies, and processes individual readers acquire and use as they interact with a book in order to learn to read in formal instructional activities and read to learn in content area lessons. This approach, while productive, has provided a tightly focused view of reading, a view of the intrapersonal context of reading (Bloome & Green, 1984; Cazden, 1983).

This perspective tends to decontextualize the activity of reading/literacy from the social and instructional conversation in which it is embedded and to ignore reading that occurs as part of the everyday activities of daily life in classrooms (e.g., menu reading, interpretation of test items) (Bloome & Green 1982; Griffin, 1977). That is, it ignores the interpersonal nature of reading in classrooms and thus the ways in which instructional and communicative processes influence what occurs as well as how it occurs. When viewed from an interpersonal perspective, the acquisition of reading skills, strategies, and processes is not seen as an event that occurs in isolation of other classroom events and processes, instructional intentions of teachers, or resources students use to interpret the content and demand of the reading task (e.g., prior knowledge and experience, abilities, beliefs, expectations). Rather, reading is viewed as a process that is embedded in and influenced by instructional and communicative processes and events. These processes serve as a broader context for reading. As such, reading, like other aspects of classroom life, is defined as a product of the interactions among teacher, students, and material and thus is the result of interpersonal processes as well as intrapersonal ones.

No one research method can capture all aspects of reading; however, a general perspective has emerged that provides a conceptual framework through which the

*The research reported in this chapter was partially supported by a grant from the National Institute of Education, U.S. Department of Education (Grant # NIE-G-83-0063). However, the opinions and statements made in the chapter do not necessarily reflect the opinions or policies of the National Institute of Education, U.S. Department of Education.

3

interpersonal and intrapersonal aspects of reading/literacy in educational settings can be explored. This perspective is associated with a variety of methodological approaches each with its own set of questions and literature (e.g., ethnomethodology, ethnography of communication, sociolinguistics, teaching as a linguistic process). Regardless of the label, however, these approaches share a common focus: the systematic exploration of (a) everyday events of classroom life as they are constructed and interpreted by participants during social interactions, and (b) the ways in which participants use language to negotiate everyday life in classrooms.

The purpose of this chapter is two-fold: (a) to highlight the conceptual base of a social interation perspective to the study of educational processes, and (b) to demonstrate how this approach can be used to explore reading in the everyday contexts in which it is embedded. The analysis of a representative lesson from a junior high school English class is presented to illustrate the constructs to be discussed as well as demonsttrate what can be learned by adopting a social interaction perspective.

A LINGUISTIC PERSPECTIVE ON CLASSROOM PROCESSES: AN OVERVIEW

In the last decade, research from a social interaction (linguistic) perspective has explored everyday life of classrooms. This work seeks to understand the social and academic demands for participation and learning from the perspective of the participants (i.e., the teacher and the students). That is, it seeks to understand what members of a classroom need to know, understand, produce, predict, and evaluate in order to participate appropriately and gain access to learning (e.g., Bloome, this volume; Bloome & Green, 1984; Cazden, 1986; Cazden, John, & Hymes, 1972; Cochran-Smith, 1984; Collins, 1983; Cook-Gumperz, in press; Edwards & Furlong, 1978; Erickson, 1982; Erickson & Wilson, 1982; Gilmore & Glatthorn, 1982; Green, 1983a, 1983b; Green & Harker, 1982; Green & Wallat, 1981b; Hammersley & Atkinson, 1983; Heap, 1980; 1983; Heath, 1982; Mehan, 1979; Merritt & Humphrey, 1981; Morine-Dershimer, 1985; Spindler, 1982; Wallat & Green, 1982; Wilkinson, 1982).

Grounded in principles and constructs from anthropology, educational research, linguistics, and sociology, among others, this work focuses on a variety of aspects of everyday life in classrooms and other educational settings (e.g., home, community) including: (a) the ways in which social and academic life in educational settings is conducted and constructed through the social interactions of participants; (b) what is learned from such participation; and (c) how participation influences performance and assessment of student ability. Researchers from a social interaction perspective use analytic approaches such as conversational analysis, discourse analysis, ethnography of communication, and sociolinguistics to explore the nature of the classroom as a social system and to understand how teaching and learning are realized through face-to-face interactions among participants (e.g., Bloome, this volume; Cazden, 1986; Cook-Gumperz, 1985; Gilmore & Glatthorn, 1982; Green, 1983b; Green & Wallat, 1981a; Spindler, 1982; Stubbs, 1983).

From this body of research, a set of constructs can be extracted that provide a framework for understanding the nature of the classroom as a communicative environment and teaching and learning as linguistic processes. These constructs also form the basis of a language that can describe unfolding educational events and tasks; identify the regularities and routines in educational settings and tasks; explore multiple levels of classroom context; and examine ways in which social and academic context of lessons influence what occurs and what is learned. In addition, these constructs lay the foundation for understanding how this perspective differs from other approaches to the study of classroom processes (e.g., input-output models; process-product models; see Amidon & Hough, 1967; Dunkin & Biddle, 1974/1984; Evertson & Green, 1986; Gage, 1977; Koehler, 1978; Medley & Mitzel, 1963; Rosenshine & Furst, 1973, Shulman, 1986, for a discussion of representative examples of these perspectives). In the following discussions a representative set of constructs underlying a social interaction perspective will be presented. To facilitate discussion, the constructs will be grouped under three general constructs: (a) classrooms are communicative environments; (b) multiple contexts co-occur in classrooms; and (c) inferencing is required for conversational participation.

Classrooms Are Communicative Environments
One way to consider what is involved in defining the classroom as a communicative environment is to view the classroom as a setting in which specific kinds or sets of situations are represented by communicative events (cf. Goffman, 1981). In classrooms, particular types of communicative events are undertaken for instructional purposes (e.g., math, drill, spelling pretest, spelling definition, letter writing, essay writing, rule setting in volleyball, reading instruction, etc.). These events help to define the classroom as a setting which differs in specific ways from other types of communicative settings (e.g., church, home, supermarket). Classroom communication viewed in this way is a subset of general communication. What differs is the type of communication events, the goals for communication, and the demands on communicative abilities (cf. Hymes, 1974) and conversational inferences (cf. Gumperz, 1982) required for appropriate participation and access to learning in classroom events.

    The Classroom Is a Differentiated Communicative Environment. The nature of the classroom as a communicative environment becomes clearer when the social and academic demand for participation and the participation structures (cf. Erickson & Shultz, 1981; Philips, 1972, 1982) of events in a classroom are considered over time both within and across days. From an exploration of the various activities that make up everyday life in the classroom, an understanding of the classroom as a differentiated communicative environment can be obtained (e.g., Cazden, 1986; Bloome, this volume; Cochran-Smith, 1984; Erickson & Shultz, 1981; Florio, 1978; Green & Harker, 1982; Merritt & Humphrey, 1981; Philips, 1982). For example, as participants move from activity to activity, the rights and obligations for participation shift (cf. Erickson & Shultz, 1981; Philips, 1972, 1982), even when the physical setting (e.g., discussion circle) and the physical organization does not change (e.g., whole group sitting on the edge of the rug) (Green & Harker, 1982; Wallat & Green, 1979).

In other words, activity can shift without participants physically shifting from one space to another. Table 1 provides an example of such a shift in an English lesson. This lesson occurred during a 50-min period in November in a ninth grade junior high school English lesson. The students were reviewing a test with the teacher. The physical setting remained stable (all students sat at their desks), the general expectation for turn distribution (speak when called on) remained stable, but the nature of content and the way in which a response was to be given varied by phase. For example, in phase 1 students were to give the past and past participle for the verb provided in section 1 of the test. In phase 2, students were to identify the given verb. In phase 3, they were to determine the correct form of the missing verb and read the sentence, inserting the correct form of the verb in the appropriate place. In phase 4, the students were to identify the verb that was used incorrectly, correct the verb, and then read the sentence aloud when called on by the teacher. Finally, in phase 5, the students were to listen as the teacher gave the answers. In each phase of the lesson, different expectations for appropriate participation and presentation of information existed; each phase, therefore, formed a different context for what was occurring, even though the general organizational structure of the classroom (e.g., teacher and whole class structure) did not change. Changes in context were signaled by changes in activity, content, and manner of communication and not by changes in the overall physical structure.

These shifts were not random; rather, they reflected shifts in factors such as instructional activity, curriculum demands, teacher goals, degree of conversational cooperation provided by participants, and institutional constraints such as time and materials.

Lessons Are Constructed During Interaction. Viewed from a social interaction perspective, lessons are constructed and negotiated during interactions between teacher and students. Lessons are not scripts to be followed. Plans are general frameworks; they show what was intended, not what was delivered (Green & Harker, 1983). Changes in plans occur throughout lessons as *teachers orchestrate activity* to teach instructional goals and student needs. What is required for participation is signaled throughout the lesson and is reflected in the actions of participants as they interact with and build on their own messages and behaviors and those of other participants. For example, in the lesson described in Table 1, shifts in context followed the structure of the test under review. While the parts of the lesson might be predictable in that they follow the parts of the test, the way in which the teacher reviewed the test was not. The view of lessons as dynamic, evolving phenomena means that participants must attend to what is occurring and how it is occurring, if they are to participate appropriately. Decision-making, therefore, occurs both during planning and during lesson delivery.

Multiple Levels of Contexts Are Constructed

The differentiated and dynamic nature of classroom communication both within and across events and tasks requires participants to monitor continually what is

Table 1. Task by Lesson Phase by Content by time by ISU by IU

phase in Phase	N of Task	Length of of ISU s	N of ISUs	$\overline{M}$ Length M (S)	IUs	IU/ISU
1	Give past and past participle of verb when called on	527.8	20	26.4	88	4.4
2	Given a verb, identify the tense when called on	514.7	32	16.1	98	3.1
3	Given a verb in the present tense and a sentence with the word missing, read the sentence with the correct verb (verb in context) when called on	324.2	22	14.7	49	2.2
4	Given a sentence with the verb used incorrectly or an incorrect verb, correct the sentence and read it aloud when called on	618.1	18	34.3	86	4.8
5	Listen as the teacher gives the answer to the task—given a verb, identify whether the verb is active or passive. Check paper against the answer given the teacher. Ask questions when teacher is finished giving answers if there are any questions.	179.4	10	17.9	24	2.4

occurring, how it is unfolding, and who is participating or required to participate. In addition, if more than one activity is occurring at a time, the teacher must monitor not only the activity under construction but the other activities in which students are working. Students not involved with the teacher must also monitor what is required to complete the task in which they are engaged and the group with whom the teacher is working, if they are to know when to ask for help from the teacher (Merritt, 1982). Each of these activities is a separate context with its own rights and obligations for participation, spatial configuration, roles and relationships, and topics. Classrooms, therefore, have differentiated contexts, some of which may co-occur.

One way to conceptualize this process is as a set of interlocking and interdependent processes and levels of communication. Viewed in this way, lessons have a social structure (who can speak when, where, in what ways, about what, for what purpose), an academic content structure (academic content themes and task demands), and an activity (context) structure (what type of activity is occurring at any given point in the lesson—we're discussing how to do news and views; we are not doing news and views) (Erickson, 1982; Green & Harker, 1982). That is, as the teacher interacts with students or students work together without the teacher to reach instructional goals, the social and activity structures of the evolving event are being signaled simultaneously with the presentation of academic content. Therefore, in order to participate appropriately and to gain access to learning, students must not only provide the appropriate information but must do it in ways that match the social expectations and activity structure (e.g., raise one's hand rather than call out; give an answer in a complete sentence; tell a story that has a beginning, a middle, and an end) (Bloome, 1983; Cook-Gumperz, Gumperz, & Simons, 1981; Garnica, 1981; Green & Harker, 1982; Michaels, 1981; Scollon & Scollon, 1984). Context defined in this way is a constructed process, a product of social interaction, in which social, academic, and activity structures influence and/or support one another. In other words, contexts are not given in the setting (e.g., spelling lesson, arrival time, test) but are constructed by participants as they work together (cf. Erickson & Shultz, 1981; McDermott, 1976).

Recent work has shown that contexts can overlap. For example, whether a student will participate or not and what the manner of that response may be are partially due to peer standing and relationships as well as teacher or task demands (Cook-Gumperz et al., 1981; Bloome & Theodorou, in press). In other words, students are part of two different systems at the same time: the instructional system of teacher-student interaction and the peer interaction system (cf. Bloome & Theodorou, in press). These systems can be thought of as different contexts, contexts which overlap and influence what is occurring and how a performance is delivered. Context defined in this way is both a locally constructed activity and a phenomenon in which the local activity is embedded. Context, therefore, can be defined in a variety of ways at a variety of levels (see Bloome & Green, 1982, for further discussion of contexts from different perspectives).

The varied nature of context in classrooms can be further understood when the general classroom organization is considered (e.g., multitask, recitation format). In a classroom, if more than one event is occurring at a time, each event will have its own context, and thus, its own set of rights and obligations for participation and configuration of participants. Such contexts are primarily nonoverlapping. However, if a participant from one context (e.g., a small group, student-directed lesson) gains access to someone from the second context (e.g., the teacher), a third context can be formed or an existing context can be modified to include the new participant. If the latter occurs, the context which is entered will be altered to some degree since a new participant has entered. However, if the teacher slots out or leaves the context in a way that does not disrupt the activity (e.g., continue reading, excuse me for a second) to provide help, a new context is formed between the teacher and the student seeking help, and the earlier context is maintained in modified form (Merritt & Humphrey, 1981). Each context has an activity that has its own roles, relationships, topics, rights, and obligations for participation. Such contexts can co-occur; together they form a larger context, the organizational context of the classroom.

Some contexts may transcend events (e.g., peer network). These contexts, however, will also be signaled in the local event; therefore, on one level, they, too, will be reconstructed during the local activity. Contexts, viewed from this framework, are dynamic, evolving phenomena. In classrooms, shifts in context are signaled by shifts in cues such as physical space, participants, activity, rights and obligations for participation, and roles and relationships. To determine what context means in any given situation, it is necessary to select a locus of observation (e.g., teacher-student interaction). This locus will provide one view of context. However, by shifting lenses (e.g., view the lesson from the students' perspectives), different contexts can be identified and therefore different definitions of meaning and activity can be obtained for different participants (Bloome & Theodorou, in press; Mishler, 1984). Thus, definition of context is a principled phenomenon, one which depends on the theoretical question being explored and the locus of observation selected as well as on the way in which context is defined.

Inferencing Is Required for Participation

The multifaceted, evolving nature of lessons can be further understood when factors involved in the process of meaning construction and interpretations are considered. To meet the instructional goals of the lesson, the teacher must simultaneously coordinate the presentation of information with the participation of students. The teacher must decide who can talk when, where, about what, and for what purpose; weigh the effect of student participation on the forward flow of the lesson, provide feedback to students, meet individual student neeeds, and maintain group and lesson direction. Students are coparticipants in the construction of classroom lessons. As such, they must also monitor the teacher expectations as signaled during delivery; determine when, how, and whether to participate; monitor the academic, social, and activity demands; construct, interpret, and reconstruct text (e.g., read, write); observe teacher responses to others as well as to self to determine expectations for what to know and what to do (e.g., Bloome & Theodorou, in press; Cochran-Smith, 1984; Erickson, 1982; Frederiksen, 1981; Green, Harker, & Golden, 1986; Morine-Dershimer, 1986; Morine-Dershmer & Tenenberg, 1981; Wallat & Green, 1979, 1982).

At any given point in the lesson under construction, in order to interpret what is meant, participants must process both the content of the message and its delivery. That is, they must interpret *contextualization cues* (cf. Gumperz, 1982) including paralinguistic cues (e.g., pitch, stress, intonation, pause, rhythm), nonverbal: proxemic cues (e.g., distance between participants; shifts in distance), nonverbal: kinesics (e.g., gestures, body movements, facial expression, eye gaze), and verbal cues (e.g., syntax, phonology, semantics). Given that the meaning of any lexical item or message depends on how it is delivered and on what surrounds it at the point of use in the conversation, contextualization cues become critical to consider when exploring meaning construction and possible reasons for miscommunication (Gumperz, 1982; Gumperz & Herasimchuk, 1973). For example, the meaning of the term *OK* can provide feedback about the accuracy of a message or about the appropriateness of an action. It can also mean "Get ready; listen" as in "OK, now" said quickly as a unit. It can also be said slowly while a person who has the floor looks about; this use can be interpreted as a place holder, meaning "Don't go away." In each instance, the lexical item is the same in form but not in meaning.

The only way to determine meaning is to consider the meaning in context (e.g., Cazden, 1986; Corsaro, 1981, 1985; Gumperz, 1982; Green & Wallat, 1981b; Mishler, 1984; Sinclair & Coulthard, 1975). Meaning, therefore, is situation specific.

Contextualization cues are only one set of factors that contribute to the interpretation of messages and activity. A participant's frame of reference (e.g., Frederiksen, 1981; Green, 1983a;b; Green & Harker, 1982; Heap, 1980; Tannen, 1979) and interpretation of unfolding frames of reference within and across events (Green et al., 1986) also influence interpretation of meaning. Frames of reference, viewed from this perspective, are multifaceted. That is, different types of frames of reference are used by participants to "read" the academic, social, and activity demands of lessons and participation in classroom life. Some frames are brought to the activity by participants: personal frames and materials frames. Some are constructed during the lesson: academic frame, social frame, local frame; and some are developed over time: historical frames or frames from previous lessons (Green et al., 1986).

Personal frames can be equated with the lens a person brings to a lesson. This lens is composed of the past experiences, beliefs, and expectations a person brings about the activity as well as the person's abilities (e.g., physical, perceptual, linguistic, cognitive, social). The lens influences how the person perceives what is occurring and guides the actions the person takes. Because of the role teachers play in classrooms, a curriculum dimension (e.g., goals, content expectations, repertoire of instructional and organization strategies) is added to their personal frames. In addition, *materials* (e.g., books, physical objects, programs) bring frames of reference to instructional events. The frame of reference reflected in the organization and format of these materials contributes to the construction of meaning. That is, materials were written by someone, in specific ways, for specific purposes. Thus, material frames can influence how things come to mean in teacher and materials, students and materials, and teacher-student-material interactions. Each frame interacts in a lesson; each contributes to the meanings constructed during the interactions within lessons; and each participant's personal frame of reference guides interpretation and participation.

The frames brought to the task are only one type of frames used to interpret meaning and guide participation and decision-making. From the interactions among teacher, students, and curriculum materials, frames are also generated: that is, from the way in which turns are distributed, answers are accepted or rejected, or initiations are accepted, ignored, or redirected. Students extract a *social frame*, or pattern of expectation for how to be a student in the given event. From the way in which content is structured, questions are asked, or content presented, the *academic frame*, or expectations for what one is to know, is extracted by students. Both frames evolve as part of the unfolding lesson. Students, therefore, must monitor both what is occurring and how it occurs to know how to participate academically and socially within and across different phases or contexts of a lesson. Teachers must also monitor what is occurring and how it occurs in order to maintain the lesson and to make decisions about the future direction of the lesson and the type of student participation required. In addition, as discussed previously, how any message is interpreted depends on the *local frame*, the expectations and contextual information at the specific point in the lesson under consideration (e.g., the teacher asks a question, and students are expected to respond with an answer from the immediately preceding story segment). Viewed in this way, frames generated in lessons are evolving and are used to guide actions and interpret subsequent messages and actions. In other words, local frames at any given point are embedded in the history of what has occurred in prior parts of the lessons. Lessons themselves have histories. Interpretation of meaning, therefore, requires participants to monitor what is occurring and to consider this in light of past history in similar contexts within the classroom history.

Different phases of lessons can have different social and academic frames, or the frames in one can support those in another phase. When the frames support each other, the lesson proceeds toward the goal. However, if the frames are not consistent or if the teacher shifts frames without overtly signaling the shift, participation and learning can be affected (Green et al., 1986; Harker & Green, 1985). For example, a student can use a frame from the introduction to guide behavior during another phase of the lesson. This action can lead to inappropriate participation (Green et al., 1986). Frames can also clash (e.g., Erickson & Mohatt, 1982; Florio & Shultz, 1979; Green, 1983a; Mehan, 1979; Mehan, Cazden, Coles, Fisher, & Maroules, 1976; Scollon & Scollon, 1984; Philips, 1972, 1982; Wallat & Green, 1982). A teacher's expectations for performance (e.g., sharing, reading) may not match the way students perform. For example, a student may share a story in a culturally patterned way; this way of sharing, however, may not meet the teacher's expectation and thus lead to a negative assessment of ability (Michaels, 1981, 1984; Michaels & Cook-Gumperz, 1979). These frame clashes are often tacit and may or may not influence the overall lesson flow. Overt frame clashes influence the fluidity of lessons. They are points in which the flow of the lesson is interrupted. At such points the expectations for participation and information are made visible. These become points at which repair is needed. Observation of what occurs at such points permits extraction of norms or expectations for appropriate participation.

From participation in recurrent events and different contexts within the classroom, students extract a set of expectations for what will occur, when, and in what ways. These expectations can be thought of as an *historical frame* or *frame from previous lessons*. Such frames become part of the personal frame of a participant. That is, they help the participant predict what will occur, evaluate what is occurring, and participate in a given event. Frames of reference viewed in this way are dynamic, evolving entities that are both brought to lessons and generated in lessons.

These issues and constructs may help to define the nature of teaching and learning from a social interaction perspective. The constructs presented are illustrative, not all-inclusive. Taken together, they provide a picture of classrooms as dynamic environments in which both teachers and students must be continually active and monitor and interpret a complex set of cues as they work together to construct instructional activities and meet curricular goals.

In the remainder of this chapter, an example of a specific application of these constructs to the analysis of a ninth-grade English lesson will be presented. To frame the study and findings, an overview of the specific analytic approach to the study of classroom discourse will be provided.

A SOCIAL INTERACTION PERSPECTIVE: AN APPLICATION AND ANALYSIS

In the sections that follow, an analysis of a ninth-grade English lesson will be presented. The lesson was audiotaped during a study of classroom management (Evertson, 1985). The present analysis, therefore, involves secondary analysis of data. The lesson was analyzed using a system of discourse analysis that is grounded in the social interaction perspective. The system (Green & Wallat, 1981b) provides a principled, systematic means of freezing and reconstructing the evolving instructional conversation between teacher, students, and materials. The lesson is reconstructed in the form of a map of the unfolding lesson. The map serves as the basis for exploration of patterns of interactions. The analysis, however, is only one part of the analysis phase of a cycle of inquiry. Therefore, before presenting the results of the microanalysis of this lesson, the steps involved in this analytic approach will be provided.

The Cycle of Inquiry: Steps in Analysis
The general approach used in the study involved a type case analysis (cf. Erickson & Shultz, 1981; Green & Harker, 1982). In this approach, one class session of an effective teacher was selected from seven lessons collected during the school year. The teacher was both an effective manager and had high student achievement (Evertson, 1985; Weade, 1985). External validation of the teacher's effectiveness came from the fact that she was a runner-up to teacher of the year in her state. The lesson under consideration was a grammar test review that occurred on the third month of the school year. This lesson was selected as representative of the general classroom organization and teacher-student instructional activity.

The lesson was subjected to in-depth microanalysis to explore the way in which the teacher delivered instruction and the influence of instruction on student participation and performance. Special attention was given to the nature of the frames of reference constructed during the lesson and the influence of these frames on student performance. This lesson was used to identify recurrent patterns of interaction and to generate hypotheses about the way in which the teacher orchestrated instructional events. The patterns and hypotheses identified were then used to develop a descriptive model of patterns in the lesson. This model is currently being applied to the analysis of lessons on other days across the school year to explore questions of stability of instructional patterns, the nature of classroom social and academic demands, and ways in which instruction influences student participation and performance. In this way, similarities and differences in instructional processes can be identified, and factors involved in the construction of lessons can be explored (Everton, 1985; Green & Rasinski, 1985; Weade, 1985).

Microanalysis of individual lessons and the construction of descriptive models and representational maps are a first step, a step that seeks to make the invisible and ordinary aspects of everyday life in a classroom visible. During this analysis, the obtained descriptions and identified patterns are used to predict the types of actions that will occur at certain points or under certain conditions (e.g., get a turn by raising your hand and being designated as the responder). In the present study, testing of hypotheses occurred within the case under examination across phases of the lesson; however, cross-case comparisons are also possible (Erickson & Shultz, 1981; Erickson & Wilson, 1982; Green & Bloome, 1983; Heath, 1982).

The present analysis required a series of steps. Step 1 involved the development of detailed transcriptions including paralinguistic information (e.g., pitch, stress, intonation, rhythm, pauses) of the unfolding teacher-student-material interactions. The transcripts reflect a view of the classroom as a communicative environment with asymmetrical relationships between teacher and student. Events in the classroom are orchestrated by the teacher (teacher talk is capitalized at the margin while student talk is in lowercase and indented below the teacher talk). Other types of lesson or activity structures may need different forms of transcription (Bloome & Theodorou, in press; Cochran-Smith, 1984; Mishler, 1984; Ochs, 1979).

Table 2. Analytic Steps Used in Mapping Instructional Conversation

Step 1. Transcription
   a. *Typescript* is prepared from audio. Transcript lines are assigned, numbering from 1–*n* on each page.
   b. Transcript is segmented into *message units* through audio and video (when available) observation of co-verbal/prosodic cues.
Step 2. Map Construction
   a. Student talk/actions that interrupt or potentially interrupt rhythm and flow of the teacher's apparent instructional theme are designated as *potential divergences.*
   b. *Interaction units*, e.g., sequences of tied or cohesive message units are determined post hoc on the basis of prosodic cues and the social and conversational demands made and/or responded to by students.
   c. *Instructional sequence units*, e.g., segments of tied interaction units are determined post hoc on the basis of thematic cohesion.
   d. *Themes*, e.g., topic threads, are designated post hoc in hierarchial units to characterize an interaction unit, a series of interaction units, instructional sequence units, a lesson phase, etc.
Step 3. Analysis
   a. *Bases of inference* are recorded where necessary throughout the mapping process.
   b. *Questions and issues for triangulation* are recorded as they arise throughout the mapping process.

Step 2 involved the construction of detailed "maps" of lesson structure (cf. Green & Wallat, 1981b). These maps serve to facilitate the identification and examination of particular instructional variables: the establishment of norms and expectations for participation, topics of discussion, emerging and recurring themes, pedagogical strategies, among others. The maps also provide a representation of lesson structure in terms of hierarchical units. Units reflected on the maps include message units, interaction units, and instructional sequence units. *Message units* are minimal units of meaning and are determined by considering delivery (e.g., pitch, stress, intonation, relationship of item to other items, pauses, nonverbal behaviors) (see Fig. 1, lines 165, 166, 167, . . . 197). *Interaction units* (IU) are sequences of conversationally tied message units (see Fig. 1, column 2: units 167–171; 172–173; 174–176; 177–182; 183–185; 186–190; 191–194; 195–197). *Instructional sequence units* (ISU) are sequences of thematically tied interaction units (Fig. 1, column 2: 165–176; 177–182; 183–197). *Phase units* (PU) are pedagogically tied instructional sequence units (e.g., the introduction to task, question–response segment, story discussion segment). Lesson units are tied sequences of phase units. Lessons from this perspective are constructed during interaction and are a product of the activity between teacher and students. Maps are constructed by observing the *conversational work* of participants as they cooperate (or fail to cooperate) in "lesson" construction. Table 2 summarizes the steps to map construction and analysis.

Step 3 involves analysis of maps. Once the map is constructed, it is possible to explore the "frozen" actions and talk for recurrent patterns. Figure 1 presents a representative example of a map segment. This segment reflects communicative patterns in the beginning of the first phase of the lesson. Table 3 presents the conventions for map construction.

While the maps form the basis for the analysis, the broader record (the videotape, audiotape, narrative record) is used to contextualize information. In this way data reduction is minimalized while systematic searches are facilitated.

Patterns are identified by considering what is normal or ordinary and what is varied or formed an anomaly. For example, in Figure 2, samples of ordinary interactions in two different phases of the lesson are presented, phase 1 and phase 4. As shown in this figure, what was ordinary varied by phase. In other words, how one was to speak, about what, and in what way differed by phase. The difference was due to both content and social participation demand. As indicated in Table 1, phase 1 required that students give the past and past participle of a verb when called on. In contrast, in phase 4, students were given a sentence with either a verb used incorrectly or an incorrect verb. They were to correct the verb and then read the sentence aloud when called on. The two phases had a similar number of ISUs (20 in phase 1 and 18 in phase 4) and equivalent number of IUs (88 and 86, respectively). Therefore, the two phases were structurally similar; differences were due to the type of social and academic demand accomplished in these units.

In Figure 3, an example of unordinary talk in each phase is given. The unordinary talk in phase 1 was a result of an error on the part of the student. The teacher responded to the error and tried to explain why the student made the error.

(As will be explained in the findings section, the error was due in part to the structure of the task; that is, all but the final two items were irregular verbs.) The last two verbs were regular ones. In phase 4, the unordinary talk also related to unexpected action. The teacher provided information about the appropriate answer to an item that a larger number of student missed. By examining the contrasts between the ordinary and expected behaviors and instances which differ from the ordinary, the instructional intent, the rules for behavior, the academic expectations, and so forth, are made visible. In other words, at these points, a breach in expectations (Mehan, 1979) or frame clash occurs (Green & Harker, 1982). By observing what information is transmitted and how participants work with what occurs, the teacher expectations, theories, and goals can be extracted as can student thinking and performance. Once a pattern is identified, the maps are then reanalyzed to determine if each instance of the pattern is functionally equivalent and to determine the frequency of occurrence of the pattern within and across phases of the lesson.

For the present study, three aspects of lessons were considered: patterns of time distribution, academic themes and frames of reference constructed, and social demands for participation. The map provided the basis for retrospective analysis and exploration of the recurrent patterns of instruction and participation patterns in a grammar review lesson. While the map facilitated systematic exploration of the unfolding events, the audiotape served as a major source of information and as a check on the accuracy of the cues to interpretation about delivery of instruction (e.g., when "all right" served as praise, when it served as a place holder, and when it served as a frame to shift focus).

The use of audiotape rather than videotape required procedural adaptations in the discourse analysis system (Green & Wallat, 1981b). These changes were made where necessary as determined by the character of the observational record available for analysis and where necessitated by the question under study. These adaptations in procedure from the original procedures reflect a change in specific procedures and not a change in the theoretical framework or in the basic premises and approach to discourse analysis.

REPRESENTATIVE FINDINGS

The findings focus on analysis of the ways in which this teacher orchestrated both academic and procedural processes in a grammar lesson and the interrelationship of the two processes within the lesson. As already stated, the discussion serves a heuristic purpose—to make visible the often invisible factors involved in the management and orchestration of communication of social and academic content of the lesson. Two aspects of lesson orchestration will be considered: (a) general structural aspects of the lesson including timing, distribution of content, and general nature of communication; and (b) content demands and theme development in a grammar review lesson. In other words, the findings illustrate what can be learned about the teacher's contribution to lesson construction in terms of interaction, instructional sequencing, and the nature of demands signaled for academic and social participa-

Transcript line	Message Unit	Interactional Units within Instructional Sequence Units	Potential Divergences	Academic content–Thematic Development	Social Demands	Instructional Pattern	Theme
165	OKAY	OKAY			Shift focus to next item	Frame(signals new focus)	a
166	HOW ABOUT "CHOO—SE"?/	HOW ABOUT "CHOO—SE"?/		Irregular verb (*choose*)	Wait for teacher	Designate item / Holds teacher turn	b
167	LET'S SEE,	LET'S SEE			Response when designated	Designate responder	c
168	MIKE	MIKE				Check if student knows	
169	DID YOU GET	DID YOU GET				correct response (3 parts)	
170	Mike: um, choose, chose, chosen	"CHOOSE"? Mike: um, choose, chose,					
171	GO—OD	chosen GO—OD				Praise	d
172	NOW YOU HAVE TO BE CAREFUL OF SPELLING	NOW YOU HAVE TO BE CAREFUL OF SPELLING		spelling		Attend to spelling	g
173	Mike: I'm chosen	Mike: I'm chosen				Student responds	
174	HOW MANY O'S IN CHOSEN?	HOW MANY O'S IN CHOSEN?		spelling		Request spelling information	g
175	Sue: one	Sue: one				Correct Response	
176	ONE	ONE				Repeat student response	
177	OKAY, AH	OKAY, AH			Shift focus to item	Frame(signals new focus)	a
178	ELEVEN	ELEVEN				Designate item	b
179	DELANA?/	DELANA?/				Designate responder	c
180	SEE?/	SEE?/		irregular verb (*see*)		State item	
181	Delana: see, saw seen	Delana: see, saw seen			Respond when designated	Correct response (3 parts)	
182	OKAY	OKAY				Praise	d

Line					Action	Code
183	AND SWIM,	AND SWIM, TERESA/?!	irregular verb (swim)		Designate item	b
184	TERESA/?!	Teresa: swam, swum		Response when designated	Designate responder	c
185	Teresa: swam, swum	ALL RIGHT	Principle parts	Shift focus	Correct response (only 2 parts)	a
186	ALL RIGHT	IT HAS TO GO LIKE THAT			Frame(signal new focus)	e
187	IT HAS TO GO LIKE THAT	EVERYBODY			Give rationale	
188	EVERYBODY	"SWAM—" IS THE PAST			All attend	
189	"SWAM—" IS THE PAST	"SWUM—" IS THE PAST PARTICLE			State item 1 and tense	f
190	"SWUM—" IS THE PAST PARTICLE				State item 2 and tense	f
191	AND SINCE WE HAVE TO KNOW TO DO TENSES	AND SINCE WE HAVE TO KNOW TO DO TENSES			Give rationale	e
192	WHICH IS PAST	WHICH IS PAST			Attend to past tense	f
	AND WHICH IS PAST	AND WHICH IS PAST			Attend to past participle	f
193	PARTICIPLE	PARTICIPLE	Principle parts—tenses		Attend to order of tenses	
	IT'S IMPORTANT TO GET	IT'S IMPORTANT TO GET				
194	THEM IN THAT ORDER	THEM IN THAT ORDER				
195	[IF] WE JUST HAD TO NAME THE PARTS IT WOULDN'T MATTER	[IF] WE JUST HAD TO NAME THE PARTS IT WOULDN'T MATTER			Continue rationale (conditions)	e
196	BUT WE HAVE TO USE THESE LATER ON TO DO TENSES	BUT WE HAVE TO USE THESE LATER ON TO DO TENSES	Principle parts		Continue rationale(use later)	e
197	S IT DOES MATTER	S IT DOES MATTER			Continue rationale	e

Figure 1. Sample Map of Phase I of Test Review Lesson

17

Table 3. Description of Categories and Conventions Used in Mapping Instructional Conversations

Transcript line	Message unit	Potential divergence	IU	ISU	Theme
Designation of discrete message units by number in sequential order from beginning to end.	Discrete, elemental segments of talk designated through observation of co-verbal/prosodic cues.	Student talk that interrupts or potentially interrupts the rhythm and flow of the teacher's apparent instructional goal or a particular instructional theme.	A discrete sequence of tied or cohesive message units determined post hoc on the basis of prosodic cues and the conversational and social demands made and responded to by participants.	A discrete sequence of tied interaction units determined post hoc on the basis of thematic cohesion.	A main topic or topical thread that characterizes an instructional sequence unit. Subthemes and broader themes that span instructional sequence units can also be identified.
	Typing Conventions: a. Individual message units are arrayed in separate lines associated with a single transcript line number. b. TEACHER TALK IS REPRESENTED IN UPPERCASE LETTERS. c. Student talk is represented in lowercase letters. d. Student talk is indented and is preceded by ''s :'',		*Mapping Convention:* Boundaries between interaction units are marked by single horizontal lines spanning the column. Single vertical arrows are used to connect se-	*Mapping Conventions:* a. Message units are represented according to form as responses (R) or questions (Q). Lines are used to connect thematic ties between	*Mapping Conventions:* Topical themes are indicated within brackets that span the length of the instructional sequence unit. Academic tasks and themes are noted on

or "sX" where possible, where X indicates the first letter of the student's name, and "Ss" indicates a multiple or group response.

quentially ordered interaction units.

noncontiguous messages.

b. Boundaries between instructional sequence units are marked by double-barred and slashed vertical arrows.

c. Uppercase letters (R and Q) indicate teacher messages. A lowercase "r" indicates student responses.

d. RQ: Rhetorical question

r-q: Student response delivered as a direct question.

I: Inaudible/nonresponse.

A: Audible nonresponse (I don't know; I missed that one.)

the right-hand side of this column as they occur through the progression of the lesson.

Phase 1	Phase 4

Phase 1

FIRST

E——

S: . . . . (inaudible)

OKAY

SHE'S GIVEN THE OTHER TWO PARTS

THEY'RE THE SAME ALL THE WAY THROUGH

UH

WHAT ABOUT THE OTHER PARTS OF "RISE"

S——

S: rose and risen

OKAY

YOUR SPELLING COUNTS REMEMBER

Phase 4

WHAT ARE WE GOING TO USE

E——

S: . . . . . (inaudible)

KAY

GO LIE DOWN

IS THAT HARD FOR YOU?

DOES IT SOUND FUNNY TO YOU OR ANYTHING

S: uh–huh

IT'S BEGINNING TO SOUND BETTER

S: (inaudible or nonverbal response).

GOOD

THAT ME— THAT MEANS WE'RE MAKING PROGRESS

OKAY

WHAT ABOUT THREE

KIM

S: . . . and burst.

BURST

OKAY

HOW ABOUT BURST

HOW DO YOU FEEL ABOUT THAT?

Figure 2. Comparison samples of ordinary interactions: Phases 1 and 4

Phase 1	Phase 4

OKAY
NOW WHAT ABOUT "RAISE"
 	
M—
'D YOU GET "RAISE"
    S: raise and rose
 	
OKAY
M—
YOU'RE THINKIN' ABOUT "RISE"
I BET
RISE, ROSE, RISEN.
 	
I MAY HAVE MADE A
DID I MAKE A MISTAKE ON YOUR PAPER THERE
    S: inaudible or nonverbal response
OKAY
 	
HE TRIED IT
HE TRIED SOMETHING ELSE WHEN HE TOLD US
AND THAT DIDN'T WORK EITHER DID IT
WE'RE GOING TO HAVE TO HELP M—— WITH THIS VERB
 	
B—
    S: ri, raise, raised
OKAY
 	
WHAT ARE YOU SAYING ON THE END OF THAT
    S: e;
	OKAY
	NUMBER FOURTEEN
	DID YOU GET THAT ONE
	OH THAT WAS A HARD ONE
	I GUESS YOU TAKE VOLUNTEERS
	M—
	    S: he rose up and opened his eyes
	OKAY
	
	YOU KNOW
	REALLY
	LET'S THINK ABOUT THAT A MINUTE
	NOW I GAVE YOU CREDIT IF YOU CHANGED IT TO ROSE
	BECAUSE WE DIDN'T TALK ABOUT THIS AND
	IT'S REALLY PARTLY MY FAULT
	WHICH
	WHAT DOES "ROSE" MEAN
	    Ss: go up
	ALL RIGHT
	
	NOW LET'S PUT IT IN THE PAST TENSE
	NOT GO UP
	BUT WHAT
	    Ss: went up

Figure 3. Comparison samples of elaborate interactions: Phases 1 and 4

21

tion by using a sociolinguistic perspective. Embedded in this discussion will be a set of select issues related to this type of microanalysis of recorded events.

Lesson Structure and Participation Demands

The first set of findings focus on the nature of lessons as differentiated communicative contexts. In Table 1, the description of the general structure of the grammar lesson was presented. As discussed previously, the grammar lesson consisted of five separate but related (tied) phases. The common thread across all phases of the lesson was discussion and identification of irregular verbs during a review of a grammar test. Each phase of the lesson required students to demonstrate knowledge about verbs in different ways. In phase 1 students were required to give the past and past participle of a set of 18 verbs. The set of verbs consisted of 16 irregular verbs and 2 regular verbs. Students were called on to answer the items in order. Turns were distributed by the teacher.

In phase 2, students were required to identify the tense of a given verb when called on. Students were expected to volunteer answers since many students had missed items in this section. Teacher statements signaled the change in expectation for participation. In phase 3, students were required to complete a sentence in which the verb was missing. Students were called on by the teacher. In phase 4, students were required to identify the incorrect verb in a sentence and then correct the sentence and use an appropriate verb. More than one correct version of the sentence was possible. One student was designated as responder. Other students were then invited to offer alternative sentences by raising their hands and waiting to be given a turn to respond. In phase 5, students were required to listen as the teacher provided the correct response and then to ask questions if there was a problem. The teacher changed the structure of the final phase completely so that she could complete the review lesson. Rather than having students interact and respond, the teacher provided all of the answers quickly. Analysis of her comments showed that she felt that time was limited and that she needed to complete the task. In other words, she had to "get through the lesson." This aspect of lesson delivery Bloome has labeled "procedural display" (Bloome, Chapter 6, this volume).

The brief description demonstrates how content shifts within a lesson across phases and how these shifts in content are also related to shifts in participation demands. As the teacher proceeded through this review lesson, she shifted both the academic and social tasks. Lesson, therefore, was not a unitary phenomenon but a phenomenon with highly differentiated parts in which teacher demand for student participation and demonstration of knowledge varied across phases.

Social Demands and Lesson Structure. Comparison of demands for participation made visible the ways in which the teacher adapted a group lesson to attend to individual needs and to signal what was important to remember about difficult irregular verbs (e.g., *rise, choose*). Teacher comments indicated that she was focusing on reasons for individual errors. For example, in the examples of elaborative interactions (Fig. 3), the teacher provides possible reasons for student errors (e.g.,

You're thinking about "rise," I bet). In addition, the teacher took responsibility for some errors (see phase 4 example, Fig. 3). The teacher also tried to have the group help individuals and to personalize instruction within the group. These actions can be interpreted as attempts to consider students and to establish a positive "helping" environment.

This interpretation is strengthened by the way in which the teacher designated turns. The apparent ordered distribution of phase 1 is shifted to a "bid" approach in phase 2. Teacher comments showed that the change in turn distribution strategies in phase 2 was because many students had missed items in this section. Rather than call on students who might not have the correct answer, the teacher asked those who knew the answers to volunteer (bid for a turn). In this way, the correct information was provided, and students were not asked to demonstrate their lack of knowledge publicly. In all phases the teacher designated who could respond and the conditions for getting a turn. Stability existed, then, in the fact that students were expected to speak only when called on. The manner of response and the way in which a turn was obtained varied. In other words, the social dimensions of lesson structure were a major contributor to lesson organization, fluidity, and atmosphere. The prominence of social structure cues meant that what appropriate participation meant at any given time required "reading" the signals and cues that co-occurred with the content.

This example demonstrates one way in which patterns can be identified; once the patterns are identified, confirming and disconfirming information (within-case validation) can be obtained. Confirmation and disconfirmation procedures were limited in this study by the use of audiotape without additional narrative information, still photographs of physical organization, or recordings of nonverbal behaviors Exact specification of the turn distribution approach of the teacher was, therefore, not possible, since audiotapes rather than videotapes were used. The audiotape eliminated the possibility of retrieval of nonverbal information about physical organization, teacher and studdent actions, proxemics, and so forth.

The discussed interpretation, therefore, is limited. It is one reconstruction—not *the* reconstruction. In addition, it is further limited by the fact that this was a secondary analysis and the teacher and students could not be involved in validating the description. Secondary analysis, therefore, provides a description that can be used to highlight process; it is a heuristic tool. The model obtained, however, is *internally consistent*, and cues used to obtain the interpretation can be specified as can the systematic approach used to construct and retrieve information. The value of this analysis and the remainder of findings to be presented is that they provide a rich description of what was observed (heard) and therefore can be used as a base for comparison of other lessons for this teacher and her students and of other work. With this limitation acknowledged, other representative findings will be presented.

Content Coverage and Lesson Structure. Another way to consider the structure of the lesson is to consider the amount and type of content covered within and across lessons and the distribution of teacher–student(s) interactions. Content coverage in the grammar lesson was considered by phase and by ISU. An instructional sequence unit is defined by the major theme or topic (e.g., irregular verb *lay*). Each time the topic of discussion shifts, a new ISU is formed (e.g., when the topic shifts from the irregular verb *choose* in Figure 1 to the irregular verb *see*).

Analysis of Table 1 shows that the lesson varied not only in type of phase but in length of phase, number of instructional sequences (i.e., topics), and in number of interaction units (i.e., conversational exchanges with students). In other words, in each phase, different amounts of content (topics) were covered (e.g., ISUs of 20, 32, 22, 18, 16 for phases 1–5, respectively). However, these figures do not provide the complete picture. The existence of the difference does not explain t he nature of the difference, what contributed to the difference, or what effect the difference had on student participation and student learning. Therefore, a combination of qualitative and quantitative steps was needed. The qualitative analysis identified recurrent patterns, and difference in frequency of occurrence identified points at which the data could be reentered to explore the functional equivalence of units identified and factors that influence what occurred (see Green et al., 1986; and Marshall & Weinstein, in press, for elaboration of this issue).

To begin to explore content structure and content coverage, the relationships among such factors as time, content, and demands were considered. As already discussed, social structure differences (e.g., turn distribution) were related to content and task as well as to student performance. These differences are at a macro level. To explore patterns of content presentation and coverage, the dimension of time by topic and time by teacher–student interaction was considered. As indicated previously, on a general level, the total number of ISUs (20 and 18, respectively) and IUs (88 and 86, respectively) for phases 1 and 4 did not differ; however, the length of time for these phases differed (527.8 s for phase 1 and 618.1 s for phase 4). The quantitative difference in time suggested a point of contrast that deserved further exploration: What contributed to the time difference and what did these differences reflect?

Time difference between the two phases was partially due to the nature of the task. When the content of the ISUs and the social demands for participation were considered, the reason for the time difference became evident. The task in phase 1 is a more constrained task than the one in phase 4. In phase 1, students were asked to read or give a one- or two-word answer. In contrast, in phase 4, they were required to engage in a variety of steps: Read the sentence and provide the correct verb. The amount of time required to complete these tasks contributes to the majority of the time differential.

Consideration of time provided a means of reentering the data and asking questions about what was occurring. By plotting the distribution of ISUs by time (in seconds), patterns or norms for time related to content (what was ordinary) were identified as were variations in time. For example, in Figure 4, the time per ISU is presented for phases 1 and 4. In this figure, ISUs were aggregated and ISUs that were longer than the norm (the mode) could be identified. The ISUs that were elaborated in time were then considered. As indicated in Figure 4, in phase 1, the ordinary ISU was less than 10 s, while in phase 4, the ordinary ISU was 10–20 s. Factors contributing to these differences were then considered.

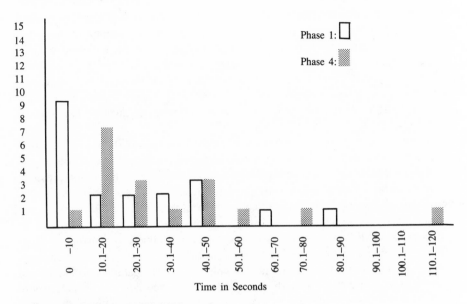

Figure 4. Number of ISUs in Seconds

   In Figures 2 and 3 presented earlier, samples of interactions in normal and elaborated ISUs were presented. In the normal (modal) ISU, the interaction patterns were
similar; they fit the expected pattern established by the teacher. An example of the
normal pattern in phase 1 can be found in Figure 1 (177–182). In the ordinary ISUs,
the teacher brought attention to the new item, designated the item, designated the
speaker, and provided feedback on accuracy. In those ISUs where an elaboration of
time occurred, the teacher changed the interaction pattern. As shown in Figure 1
(165–176; 183–197), elaborated time resulted from extension of information. In the
ISU on lines 165–176, the teacher began with a normal interaction pattern but then
proceeded to provide additional information. In this instructional sequence, she focused students on the way in which *chosen* was spelled. While the content of the
elaboration differed in the ISU on lines 183–197 (the focus was on tenses and principle parts), the ISU began with a variation of the normal interaction pattern. Exploration across elaborated ISUs led to the identification of two patterns of elaboration.
Elaboration generally occurred: (a) to clarify content or provide minilectures, and
(b) to present content information when student answers did not do as expected on a
written assignment (e.g., an error was made, a misunderstanding occurred, etc.).
   By focusing on timing in the lesson, what was ordinary and extraordinary was
explored. The fact that interactions differed in time, content, and function supports
the constructed nature of lessons. Analysis showed that the lesson was goal directed
but not scripted. One way to think about the lesson is as a series of slots. In this
lesson, the teacher used a structure for content presentation that followed the test
format item by item. While structured, the teacher could constrict or elaborate the
interactions within a slot; she could also create new slots. Students could also
influence what occurred. For example, in phase 4, students volunteered sentences,

even though the teacher tried to speed up the lesson because class time was running out and the lesson was not finished. The students were responding to the initial frame for the phase and did not shift when the teacher informally indicated the need to "get through the lesson." Each participant, therefore, made decisions at a series of evolving points within a lesson. While a slot may be predicted and may occur, what will happen in that slot is not fixed. Teachers and students, therefore, select from a repertoire of options, actions deemed appropriate at a given point in the lesson.

The changes in patterns of interaction demonstrate some of the features of communication that teachers and students need to monitor in order to participate appropriately and gain access to learning. Exploration of points of elaboration provided further confirmation of the sensitivity of the teacher to both student needs and difficulty of content. Elaboration often occurred at points where the teacher found students had had difficulty on the test or at points where student verbal responses were incorrect. Both teacher and students, therefore, influenced content coverage. Lessons, from this perspective are dynamic, differentiated communicative environments in which time and content interact with social participation expectations and frames of reference to form the rhythm of different phases of lessons and classroom life. Content coverage, defined in this way, is integrally tied to delivery of instruction and classroom communication.

Content Demands and Theme Development. In the previous discussion, content coverage was considered in terms of time. This section focuses on a close look at content as it evolves thematically within a phase. Attention will be given to the nature of the frame of reference constructed and the influence of such frames on student performance.

When the content of each phase was considered, several factors that influenced student performance and content delivery were uncovered. In Tables 4 and 5, the evolving themes of phase 1 and phase 4 of the grammar test review lesson are presented. Each phase will be considered in turn; hypotheses will be generated; and findings from phase 4 will be used to compare and validate findings identified in phase 1. In Table 4, the topic and content themes signaled are presented along with the length of ISUs and IUs. As indicated in this table, the predominant theme is irregular verbs. Sixteen of the 18 items in this section were irregular verbs. Regular verbs were also presented as a subtheme as were the spelling patterns of irregular verbs, meaning of the verbs, and the concept of principle parts. The subthemes of spelling, meaning, and principle parts recurred across phases. The theme of regular and irregular verbs also recurred across phases but with less frequency than other subthemes. The pattern that the teacher appeared to be using was one of cycling and recycling information in different ways. Certain themes were used to highlight potential problems so that students would avoid these problems in future lessons (e.g., the number of *o*'s used in spelling *chosen*—see Fig. 1). Exploration of lessons across the year showed that correct spelling and usage were recurrent themes. Verification of this pattern was found when the first day of school was considered. Teacher statements on the first day verified the observed pattern (correct usage and spelling were primary goals for the class). Students, therefore, could be expected to bring the goal of correct usage and spelling to the lesson under construction. When the content of each instructional sequence was considered in terms of the types of interactions that occurred between teacher and student(s), a problem for students and teacher was identified. In this phase of the lesson, 16 of the 18 verbs were irregular. The task structure and the structure of the materials set a frame of reference for students (e.g., Frederiksen, 1981; Green & Harker, 1982; Heap,

Table 4. Content and Theme Distribution by Time (Phase 1)

(ISU)	Topic	Content themes signaled			IU	Length of ISU Time
1	(a verb)[a]				2	8.2
2	rise	irregular verb	spelling		2	8.0
3	lie	irregular verb		meanings	9	70.2
4	be	irregular verb			principle parts	7	59.2
5	(procedural statement: Skip C, she wasn't here)				1	4.8
6	have, has	irregular verb			3	13.2
7	Using have, has in sentences	irregular verb			13	98.6
8	choose	irregular verb	spelling		3	13.1
9	see	irregular verb			1	5.0
10	swim	irregular verb		principle parts	4	24.0
11	drew	irregular verb			1	6.1
12	lay	irregular verb		meanings	7	25.0
13	give	irregular verb			1	4.5
14	bring	irregular verb			8	37.5
15	ring	irregular verb			1	7.1
16	Inaudible interaction				1	3.3
17	take	irregular verb			5	30.6
18	drown	regular verb			9	51.9
19	raise	regular verb			9	52.5
20	Questions on part 1. Concludes part 1				1	4.9

[a]Student's response was inaudible. The teacher signaled that the response was correct.

Table 5.

Table 5. Content and Theme Distribution by Time (Phase 4)

(ISU)	Topic	Content themes signaled			Length of ISU IU	Time
75	ain't	correct the incorrect verb form	meaning	"Sound" is a clue; think of an alternative "Sound" is a clue	9	119.2
76	lay	correct the incorrect verb ↓		"Sound" is a clue	4	22.8
77	busted	correct the incorrect verb ↓		"Feel" is a clue	4	17.0
78	lay	correct the incorrect verb ↓			4	30.2
79	lying	correct the incorrect verb	meaning	spelling	7	43.6
80	drown	correct the incorrect verb ↓		spelling	7	40.7
81	have	correct the incorrect verb ↓			3	13.5
82	lay	correct the incorrect verb	meaning	Don't change tense mid-sentence	10	74.2
83	ain't	correct the incorrect verb ↓			3	18.2
84	froze	correct the incorrect verb ↓			3	24.6
85	rose	correct the incorrect verb		Don't just add "ed" to irregular verbs	2	13.4
86	ain't	correct the incorrect verb ↓			3	17.5
87	may/can	correct the incorrect verb ↓	meaning		2	10.4
88	rose	correct the incorrect verb ↓		"Sound is not always a good clue	6	53.6
89	saw	correct the incorrect verb ↓			1	6.5
90	may/can	correct the incorrect verb ↓	meaning		9	41.9
91	has risen	correct the incorrect verb		Use "up" with "rose when you need	5	22.5
92	Questions?				4	14.8

1980) that suggested what was required was to complete each item with an "irregular verb." However, the last two items featured regular verbs. Teacher comments suggested that these two items caused trouble for students. The teacher indicated that some students spelled "drown" wrong and that some had given the past and past participle of *rise*.

By considering the frame of reference that was reflected in the task structure, a reason for the confusion that occurred on the last two items can be formulated. There is a history that explains the confusion. The tasks that preceded these items can be thought of as setting expectations for students for they required students to give an irregular verb. The shift to regular verbs was tacit on the test; that is, it was not signaled overtly and placement occurred at the end of the test phase and not throughout the phase. One plausible explanation, then, is that students had established a frame of reference that said "We're supposed to give irregular verbs.' This frame may have overridden the shift in task to regular verbs. In addition, the emphasis across time on spelling and meaning may also have contributed to the error. If the student assumed that the task was to give an irregular verb, then you don't spell an irregular verb by adding *-ed*. The errors in spelling in the last two items, therefore, were logical errors, errors negotiated by the task. In other words, these errors might not reflect lack of knowledge on the part of the students but rather a misreading of the expectations.

This interpretation was supported by the teacher's comments related to these items. In the case of *drown,* the teacher indicated several students had spelled "drowned" wrong. Just prior to a review of this item, the teacher said:

Okay, what about drown? That seems like a harmless little um verb to remember, but a lot of people missed it because they misspelled it.

If the frame that a student was using was one of irregular verbs, then simply adding an *-ed* would be wrong since irregular verbs do not follow a simple pattern of adding *-ed*. The students might have missed the item not because they were not aware of how to spell the past tense of a regular verb but because of the frame of reference for irregular verbs established for all preceding items.

While this interpretation is a hypothesis, analysis of what occurred in the subsequent item lends support to this interpretation. In this item, the teacher indicated that she felt the student had been thinking of the irregular verb *rise* rather than the regular verb *raise:*

OK, Mike, you're thinking about rise, I bet. Rise, rose, risen. I may have made a . . . did I make a mistake on your paper there?

The teacher appeared to be aware of the fact that the students were confused. She was not, however, aware of what caused the confusion. Her discomfort as well as the types of errors suggest that the error was negotiated and that the types of errors made were unexpected. The interpretation suggests that the structure of the task and/or the materials may have overridden the students' knowledge and led to an incorrect answer. In other words, errors on the part of students may be a result of the way in which the task was read or not read and not due to a lack of knowledge. In this example, what occurred was a frame clash, a clash in what the student expected given the earlier aspects of the task and the local frame for the given item. To test this observation further, it would have been necessary to interview the students. However, given the secondary analysis aspect of this study, this interpretation remains an hypothesis. This example suggests that researchers and teachers need to consider the influence of task structure and material structure on student performance. What appears to be needed is student input that will illuminate student thinking.

When the content structure of phase 4 was considered in depth (Table 5), the consistency of frame within and across phases of the lesson was evident. In this phase, the teacher expected students to correct a sentence in which the verb was written incorrectly. The teacher began by calling on a student to read his sentence and told the students that they could also read their sentences. The primary theme established can be paraphrased as: Correct the verb used incorrectly and then share what you have done. The teacher also included the two subthemes introduced previously: spelling and meaning. She introduced a third subtheme—use the way a word sounds as a clue to correctness—that is, use your internal linguistic sense to help you determine what is right. She also pointed out that irregular verbs were not constructed by simply adding -ed.

This discussion, while speculative to some degree, illustrates the probabilistic nature of lessons for both teachers and students. It also highlights some factors that can contribute to possible confusion and to student errors. The examples show that errors in participation and demonstration of knowledge may result from errors in task structure and communication.

CONCLUSION

The findings in this chapter illustrate what can be learned by close in-depth analysis of instruction within lessons. Analysis of lessons was guided by constructs from sociolinguists, ethnography of communication, discourse analysis, conversational analysis, and research on teaching-learning processes. Application of these constructs in a systematic approach showed that lessons are constructed by the action of teachers and students as they build on their own messages and messages of others to reach the curriculum goals of the lesson. Lessons, while structured and goal directed, are not scripts to be followed by rote. Rather, lessons are dynamic, probabilistic phenomena that are created, not followed.

Understanding classroom literacy instruction, whether explicitly emphasizing reading and writing development such as a basal lesson or implicitly emphasizing literate features of language such as through a grammar lesson, required understanding the interpersonal context. In classrooms, the interpersonal context is constructed through the verbal and nonverbal interaction of students and teachers, classroom materials (such as the difficulty of a given text, see Barr, Chap. 7, this volume), and the structure of the academic and participatory tasks intended and constructed through teacher-student interaction (cf., Bloome, Chap. 6, this volume; Doyle, 1983; Erickson, 1982). As part of the process of lesson construction, frames for engaging in the lesson and frames for engaging written text are developed. These frames guide participation in the lesson including how to interact with a curricular text such as a textbook or worksheet. Where frame clashes occur between teachers and students, as well as between teachers and students on one hand and curricular programs on the other, miscommunication and misevaluation are likely to occur at specific points in the lesson. That is, what may appear to be deficits in the intrapersonal processes students use during classroom reading and literacy activities may at times be more appropriately understood as a function of the interpersonal nature of reading and literacy activity. Part of what is needed in the study of classroom reading and literacy activity and development are ways to look at lesson construction over time so that "pictures" can be developed of the interpersonal context of reading and literacy activities within and across lessons, classes, teachers, grades, and home, school and work settings.

REFERENCES

Amidon, E. & Hough, J. (1967). *Interaction analysis: Theory, research and application*. Reading, MA: Addison Wesley.

Bloome, D. (1983). Reading as a social process. In B. Hutson (Ed.), *Advances in reading-language research* (Vol. 2). Greenwood, CT: JAI.

Bloome, D., & Green, J. (1982). The social contexts of reading: A multidisciplinary perspective. In B. A. Hutson (Ed.), *Advances in reading-language research* (Vol. 1). Greenwich, CT: JAI.

Bloome, D., & Green, J. (1984). Directions in the sociolinguistic study of reading. In D. Pearson, R. Barr, M. Kamil, & P. Mosenthal (Eds.), *Handbook of research in reading*. New York: Longmans.

Bloome, D., & Theodorou, E. (in press). Analyzing teacher-student and student-student discourse. In J. Green, J. & Harker (Eds.), *Multiple perspective analyses of classroom discourse*. Norwood, NJ: Ablex.

Cazden, C. (1986). Classroom discourse. In M. Wittrock (Ed.), *Handbook for research on teaching* (3d ed.), New York: Macmillan.

Cazden, C., John, V., & Hymes, D. (1972). *Functions of language in the classroom*. New York: Teachers College Press.

Cochran-Smith, M. (1984). *The making of a reader*. Norwood, NJ: Ablex.

Collins, J. (1983). *A linguistic perspective on minority education: Discourse analysis and early literacy*. Unpublished dissertation, University of California, Berkeley.

Cook-Gumperz, J. (1986). *The social construction of literacy*. New York: Cambridge University Press.

Cook-Gumperz, J., Gumperz, J., & Simons, H. (1981). *School-home ethnography project*. (Final Report to the National Institute of Education. Washington, DC: National Institute of Education.

Corsaro, W. (1981). Gaining access to the child's world. In J.L. Green & C. Wallat (Eds.), *Ethnography and language in educational settings*. Norwood, NJ: Ablex.

Corsaro, W. (1985). *Friendship and peer culture in the early years*. Norwood, NJ: Ablex.

Doyle, W. (1983). Academic work. *Review of Educational Research, 53*(2), 159–200.

Dunkin, M., & Biddle, B. (1974). *The study of teaching*. New York: Holt, Rinehart, & Winston. (Reprinted, 1984, by University Press, Baltimore.)

Edwards, A.D., & Furlong, V.J. (1978). *The Language of teaching*. London: Heinemann.

Erickson, F. (1982). Classroom discourse as improvisation: Relationships between academic task structure and social participation structure in lessons. In L.C Wilkinson (Ed.), *Communicating in the classroom*. New York: Academic Press.

Erickson, F., & Mohatt, G. (1982). Cultural organization of participation structures in two classrooms of Indian students. In G. Spindler (Ed.), *Doing the ethnography of schooling: Educational anthropology in action* (pp. 132–175). New York: Holt, Rinehart, & Winston.

Erickson, F., & Shultz, J. (1981). When is a context? Some issues and methods in the analysis of social competence. In J. Green & C. Wallat (Eds.), *Ethnography and language in educational settings*. Norwood, NJ: Ablex.

Erickson, F., & Wilson, J. (1982). *Sights and sounds of life in schools: A resource guide to film and videotape for research and education*. E. Lansing: Michigan State University.

Evertson, C. (1985, April). *Research, training and practice: the normative model and beyond*. Paper presented at the American Educational Research Association Meetings, Chicago.

Evertson, C. (1985). Training teachers in classroom management: An experiment in secondary school classrooms. *Journal of Educational Research*.

Evertson, C., & Green, J. (1985). Observation as inquiry and method. In M. Wittrock (Ed.), *Handbook of research on teaching* (3d ed.). New York: Macmillan.

Florio, S. (1978). *Learning how to go to school: An ethnography of interaction in kindergarten/first grade classroom* Unpublished dissertation, Harvard University, Cambridge.

Florio, S., & Shultz, J. (1979). Social competence at home and school. *Theory Into Practice, 18*, 234–243.

Frederiksen, C. (1981). Inference in preschool children's conversations—a cognitive perspective. In J.L. Green & C. Wallat (Eds.), *Ethnography and language in educational settings*. Norwood, NJ: Ablex.

Gage, N. (1977). *The scientific basis of the art of teaching*. New York: Teachers College Press.

Garnica, O. (1981). Social dominance and conversational interaction: The Omega child in the classroom. In J. Green & C. Wallat (Eds.), *Ethnography and language in educational settings*. Norwood, NJ: Ablex.

Gilmore, P., & Glatthorn, A. (1982). *Children in and out of school*. Washington, DC: Center for Applied Linguistics.

Goffman, E. (1981). *Forms of talk*. Philadelphia: University of Pennsylvania Press.

Green, J.L. (1983a). Exploring classroom discourse: Linguistic perspectives on teaching-learning processes. *Educational Psychologist, 18*(3) 180–199.

Green, J.L. (1983b). Research on teaching as a linguistic process: A state of the art. In E. Gordon (Ed.), *Review of research in education* (pp. 151–252). Washington, DC: American Educational Research Association.

Green, J.L., & Bloome, D. (1983). Ethnography and reading: Issues, directions and findings. In J. Niles (Ed.), *Thirty-second yearbook of the National Reading Conference*. Rochester, NY: National Reading Conference.

Green, J.L., & Harker, J.O. (1982). Gaining access to learning. In L. Wilkinson (Ed.), *Communicating in the classroom*. New York: Academic Press.

Green, J.L., & Harker, J.O. (1983). Reading to children: A sociolinguistic perspective. In J. Langer & M.T. Smith-Burke (Eds.), *Reader meets author: Bridging the gap*. Newark, NJ: International Reading Association.

Green, J.L., Harker, J.O., & Golden, J.M. (1986). Lesson construction: Differing views. In G. Noblit & W. Pink (Eds.), *Literacy in social context*. Norwood, NJ: Ablex.

Green, J.L., & Rasinski, T. (1985, April). *Teacher style and classroom management: Stability and variation across instructional events*. Paper presented at the American Educational Research Association Meeting, Chicago.

Green, J.L., & Wallat, C. (1981a). *Ethnography and language in educational settings*. Norwood, NJ: Ablex.

Green, J.L., & Wallat, C. (1981b). Mapping instructional conversations. In J.L. Green & C. Wallat (Eds.), *Ethnography and language in educational settings*. Norwood, NJ: Ablex.

Griffin, P. (1977). How and when does reading occur in the classroom, *Theory into Practice*, *16*(5), 376–383.

Gumperz, J. (1982). *Discourse strategies*. Cambridge: Cambridge University Press.

Gumperz, J., & Herasimchuk, E. (1973). The conversational analysis of social meaning: A study of classroom interaction. In R. Shuy (Ed.), *Sociolinguistics: Current trends and prospects*. Washington, DC: Georgetown University Press.

Hammersley, M., & Atkinson, P. (1983). *Ethnography: Principles in practice*. New York: Methuen.

Harker, J.O., & Green, J.L. (1985). When you get the right answer to the wrong question. In A. Jaggar & M.T. Smith-Burke (Eds.), *Observing the language learner*. Newark, DE: International Reading Association.

Heap, J. (1980). What counts as reading: Limits to certainty in assessment. *Curriculum Inquiry*, *10*(3), 265–292.

Heath, S.B. (1982). Ethnography in education: Defining the essentials. In P. Gilmore & A. Glatthorn (Eds.), *Children in and out of school*. Washington, DC: Center for Applied Linguistics.

Hymes, D. (1974). *Foundation in sociolinguistics*. Philadelphia: University of Pennsylvania Press.

Koehler, V. (1978). Classroom process research: Present and future. *Journal of classroom interaction*, *13*(2), 3–10.

Marshall, H.H., & Weinstein, R. (in press). Beyond quantitative analysis: Recontextualization of classroom factors contributing to the communication of teacher expectations. In J. Green, & J. Harker (Eds.), *Multiple perspective analyses of classroom discourse*. Norwood, NJ: Ablex.

McDermott, R.P. (1976). Achieving school failure. In H. Singer & R. Ruddell (Eds.), *Theoretical models and processes of reading*. Newark, DE: International Reading Association.

Medley, D., & Mitzel, H. (1963). Measuring classroom behavior by systematic observation. In N. Gage (Ed.), *Handbook of research on teaching* (1st ed.). Chicago: Rand McNally.

Mehan, H. (1979). *Learning lessons*. Cambridge, MA: Harvard University Press.

Mehan, H., Cazden, C., Coles, L., Fisher, S., & Maroules, N. (1976). *The social organization of classroom lessons*. La Jolla, CA: Center for Human Information Processing.

Merritt, M. (1982). Distributing and directing attention in primary classrooms. In L.C. Wilkinson (Ed.), *Communicating in the classroom*. New York: Academic Press.

Merritt, M., & Humphrey, F. (1981). *Service-like events during individual work time and their contributions to the nature of communication in primary classrooms* (Final Report NIE G-78-0082). Washington, DC: National Institute of Education.

Michaels, S. (1981). Sharing time: Children's narrative styles and differential acces to literacy. *Language in society*, *10*, 423–442.

Michaels, S. (1984). Listening and responding: Hearing the logic in children's classroom narratives. *Theory into Practice*, *23*(3), 218–260.

Michaels, S., & Cook-Gumperz, J. (1979). A study of sharing time with first grade students: Discourse narratives in the classroom. *Proceedings of the Berkeley Linguistic Society*, *5*, 87–103.

Mishler, E. (1984). *The discourse of medicine: Dialectics of medical interviews*. Norwood, NJ: Ablex.

Morine-Dershimer, G. (1985). *Talking, listening, and learning in elementary classrooms*. New York: Longman.

Morine-Dershimer, G., & Tenenberg, M. (1981). *Participant perspectives of classroom discourse* (Final Report NIE G-78-0161). Washington, DC: National Institute of Education.

Ochs, E. (1979). Transcription as theory. In E. Ochs & B. Scheffelin (Eds.), *Developmental pragmatics*. New York: Academic Press.

Philips, S.U. (1972). Participant structures and communicative competence: Warm Springs children in community and classroom. In C. Cazden, V. John, & D. Hymes (Eds.), *Functions of language in the classroom* (pp. 370–394). New York: Teachers College Press.

Philips, S.U. (1982), *The invisible culture: Communication in classroom and community on the Warm Springs Indian reservation*. New York: Longman.

Rosenshine, B., & Furst, N. (1973). The use of direct observation to study teaching. In R. Travers (Ed.), *Handbook of research on teaching* (2d ed., pp. 122–183). Chicago: Rand McNally.

Scollon, R., & Scollon, S. (1984). Cooking it up and boiling it down. In D. Tannen (Ed.), *Coherence in spoken and written discourse.* Norwood, NJ: Ablex. Shulman, L. (1985). Research programs for the study of teaching. In M. Wittrock (Ed.), Handbook of Research on Teaching (3d ed.).

Sinclair, J. McH., & Coulthard, R.M. (1975). *Towards an analysis of discourse: The English used by teachers and pupils.* London: Oxford University Press.

Spindler, G. (1982). *Doing the ethnography of schooling: Educational anthropology in action.* New York: Holt, Rinehart, & Winston.

Stubbs, M. (1983). *Discourse analysis: The sociolinguistic analysis of natural language.* Chicago: University of Chicago Press.

Tannen, D. (1979). What's in a frame? Surface evidence for underlying expectations. In R. Freedle (Ed.), *New directions in discourse processing.* Norwood, NJ: Ablex.

Wallat, C., & Green, J.L. (1979). Social rules and Communicative contexts in kindergarten. *Theory into Practice, 18*(4).

Wallat, C., & Green, J.L. (1982). Construction of social norms. In K. Borman (Ed.), *The social life of children in a changing society.* Norwood, NJ: Ablex.

Weade, R. (1985, April). *Lesson construction and instructional management: An explosion of social and academic content demand with lessons.* Paper presented at the American Educational Association Meetings, Chicago.

Wilkinson, L. (Ed.). (1982). *Communicating in the classroom.* New York: Academic Press.

2 The Development of Literacy: Access, Acquisition, and Instruction

Scott G. Paris and Karen K. Wixson
University of Michigan

The explosion of research on literacy during the past 15 years has yielded a remarkable number of insights about how people read, write, and communicate. The impetus for research was derived from many sources including advances in theories of communication, cognitive development, and instruction as well as political cries for educational reform. Consequently, the variety of research touches almost every aspect of literacy that one can imagine, and it has become increasingly difficult to integrate findings from diverse research orientations. During the conference on which this volume is based, we tried to relate various investigations to one another and to connect the findings from ethnographic studies with cognitive developmental research on reading, literacy, and schooling. Despite the enormity of the task, we believe that there are several significant links between traditional experimental psychological studies of literacy and field-based ethnographic studies of literacy in action.

We begin by calling attention to two related concepts, access and context, that help to reconcile diverse studies of literacy and that embed analyses of cognitive skills of literacy into larger social frameworks. Following the discussion of sociocultural influences we examine the knowledge, skills, and motivation that children have as they learn to read and write. We believe that the acquisition of literacy is influenced by personal access to appropriate knowledge and instruction as well as social access to situations that enable people to practice and develop literacy.

BECOMING LITERATE

Access to literacy denotes the conditions that foster active participation in literate activities—reading, writing, and communicating. The availability of schools, books, or writing materials are obvious examples of conditions that facilitate literacy, but availability of relevant institutions, agents, and tools is only the first step. Access to literacy can be influenced further by the quality of the instruction and the materials in these settings. Children who receive little instructional guidance, who are not corrected or praised for their performance, or who are given limited opportunities to read and write about restricted topics are being denied access to literacy despite their apparent participation. Whether subtle or overt, many factors operate in schools to constrain students' opportunities to develop literacy. Of course the self-motivated and continuous aspects of participation are also important. Children who are actively engaged in comprehending text or who use writing for creative as well as functional purposes are developing their skills and not just exercising them.

35

Access to literacy is a developmental phenomenon that can be enhanced by opportunities for learning with social guidance.

Becoming literate includes more than the cognitive skills of learning to read and write (Wagner, 1985). Opportunities to participate in literacy invite learning informally in many social situations other than schools and, thus, we regard access to literacy as a set of sociological conditions that enable transactions of learning and teaching to occur. The settings of interaction and even global contexts of social membership provide these conditions and thus provide a "visual field" in which to view the individual's learning and development (Brown, 1982). Our view is similar to a culturally sensitive theory of cognition that examines development within contexts of activity and regards socially assembled situations as the units of analyses (Laboratory of Comparative Human Cognition, 1983). These situations can be unwrapped and analyzed at different levels, but a contextualist approach begins with the situation rather than a decontextualized set of skills or outcomes. Ethnographic studies of literacy are valuable, because they reveal how factors at home and at school influence the processes of becoming literate. Observations of classrooms and the circumstances in which students confront, practice, and learn literacy provide direct evidence of the ways in which children use reading and writing in various situations.

We believe that theoretical interpretations as well as practical assessments of students' literacy are enriched by viewing the psychological acquisition of skills related to literacy within multiple layers of social and instructional contexts provided by schools, homes, and cultures. At each level factors operate to promote or constrain access to literacy, that is, access to resources, access to effective instruction, and access to participation. In the following section we identify some contextual factors that may constrain access to literacy, and, in turn, opportunities to acquire relevant skills. We hasten to add two caveats. First, we do not equate greater access to literacy with better acquisition. Access is a set of enabling conditions, and research must establish the connections that are necessary and sufficient to promote acquisition. Second, contexts always constrain opportunities, and we should be cautious in attributing malevolent motives to teachers, parents, or publishers who may provide limited opportunities for students to exercise literacy. Likewise, we should be cautious in calling for educational reform just because biases in access have been identified. Although ethnographic studies may reveal restricted opportunities, it remains to be answered empirically whether such biases influence students' literacy practice, enjoyment, or achievements.

CONTEXTS OF LITERACY

Children learn to read in a variety of settings. Most American children are exposed to books in the home prior to formal schooling, and many children participate in social groups devoted to "story time" or reading in their homes, nursery schools, or kindergartens. In school they usually learn to read in small groups with their classmates. In all of these settings children are exposed to print and the actions of reading and writing as functional social activities guided by knowledgeable adults. Informal literate activities removed from school often reflect the same characteristics wherever they occur—at home, in the marketplace, or in religious training. Schooling is not the only venue for literacy, and it is neither the first nor necessarily most enduring influence on people's acquisition of literacy. Becoming literate, in and out of school, occurs in social situations that shape purposes, conditions, constraints, audiences, standards, and motivation to engage reading and writing. These agendas cannot be ignored because they influence the acquisition and application of cognitive skills.

Cultural Agenda for Literacy

Experts cannot agree on a single definition of literacy because the attributes and standards are relative to the context in which literacy is observed. Wagner (1985) notes that some people view literacy as a global "cosmology" of skills, beliefs, knowledge, and functions that includes nearly any aspect of symbolic communication. An African boy chanting the Koran in a language he cannot understand, an old man clutching a bus ticket and schedule that he may not be able to read, and a student in a classroom stumbling to pronounce words in a primer are all participating in literate activities. Literacy is a social and cultural phenomenon that encompasses much more than school-oriented values and practices. Furthermore, as cultures change, so do definitions of literacy. For example, technological advances in recent years in American society have ushered in "computer literacy" as a new dimension.

Because of the contextual relativity of literacy, many scholars describe literate activities such as reading and writing from a functional point of view (Scribner & Cole, 1981; Paris, Lipson, & Wixson, 1983); that is, the uses served by print and how reading, writing, and literacy-related events fit into the total fabric of a cultural group. These sociocultural purposes of literacy partly determine both the value that is placed on literacy and those who have access to literacy within a particular culture. It is well known that literacy is given different levels of priority in various societies and that many cultures restrict access to literacy to certain portions of the population (Downing & Leong, 1982).

Schieffelin and Cochran-Smith's (1984) comparison of a group of educated, school-oriented parents and their preschool children from a Philadelphia suburb with a family in the traditionally nonliterate Kaluli society in Papua, New Guinea, provides an excellent example of how the forms and functions of literacy are determined by sociocultural factors. The children in the Philadelphia nursery school learn a broad kind of literacy as well as what is commonly referred to as functional literacy. For this social group, children's acquisition of these types of literacy is both desirable and assumed. In contrast, the Kaluli do not see their children's acquisition of literacy as particularly desirable. In fact, they discourage children's interest in books. For the Kaluli, the purposes of literacy are restricted to limited contexts and users; i.e., for adults who are interested in the Christian religion. Although the form of bookreading observed in the Philadelphia nursery school resembles the form of the book-looking activity of the Kaluli mother and her child, the functions and meanings of these literacy events are very different. Clearly, we cannot equate form, function, and meaning of literacy events across cultures, communities, or social groups.

The functions of literacy, the number of schools, and the degree of participation by citizens in a culture are overt indicators of access to literacy. For example, Clay (1976) found that in New Zealand the Western Samoans, an immigrant subculture, made better progress in the early stages of learning to read than the native Maori subculture. She attributed this to the Samoan children's early experiences of being read to and observing the high value their parents placed on reading and writing letters. The Maori children had no such early experiences with literacy. It is important to note that schooling is not necessarily a prerequisite for literacy. Scribner and Cole (1981) have shown that Vai people of Africa learn to read and write with their native script without formal instruction. Further, schooling is not a monolithic influence on access to literacy. The standards used in American schools have changed frequently, and there is no consensus on definitions of functional literacy or minimal competence (Chall, 1983). Thus, cultures determine access to literacy by establishing literacy tools, social functions of literacy, methods of instruction, and standards of competence.

In addition to overt indicators of access to literacy there are subtle influences too. Green and Bloome (1983) discussed how people can have similar or dissimilar "frames of reference" for the functions and activities of literacy. When students do not share with teachers the same expectations or rules for communication and participation in the classroom, students often devalue literacy or exempt themselves from instruction, thereby diminishing their opportunities to become literate. We realize that cultural context is a vague and global term, but it is important to recognize at the outset that the functions, values, and frames of reference in particular contexts influence who has access to literate activities and opportunities for learning.

The Influence of the Home Environment

Differences in home environments may contribute as much to children's academic achievement as school factors. According to Leichter (1984), conceptions about the ways in which home environments influence the child's experience with literacy can be grouped into three categories: physical environment, interpersonal interaction, and emotional and motivational climates. With regard to physical environment, one of the most frequently reported findings is that the availability of books is related positively to children's reading (Miller, 1969; Sheldon & Carrillo, 1952). Durkin (1966) observed that children who learn to read before entering school have many opportunities to examine books and read them with their parents. The availability of books, frequent library visits, and adults' involvement in children's beginning reading all predict children's early reading successes (Bing, 1963; Briggs & Elkind, 1977).

The influence of the interpersonal interactions within the home on the child's access to literacy is illustrated by a study in the homes of children from three literate communities in the southeastern United States (Heath, 1982). Although the results of this study should not be generalized to communities outside this region, they do indicate that patterns of language use and paths of language socialization differ strikingly for children in homes from these communities. In Maintown, a middle-class school-oriented community, literacy-related activities were part of a larger context of learning how to take meaning from the environment. In these homes, the focus was on labeling, explaining, and learning appropriate interactional patterns for displaying knowledge. Children learned how to use language in literacy events and were socialized into interactional sequences that were central features of class-room lessons. This is in contrast to homes in Roadville, a white working-class com-munity. Families in Roadville also focused on labeling and explanations, but they did not link these ways of taking meaning from books to other aspects of their envi-ronment. Consequently, children from these homes were well prepared for the lit-eral tasks of early reading instruction, but they had difficulty when reading assign-ments required for reasoning and affective responses.

The third group of homes under investigation was located in Tracktown, a black working-class community. The children in these homes were not taught labels or asked for explanations; rather they were asked to provide reasons and to express personal responses to events in their lives. As a consequence, these children were unprepared for the types of questions they encountered in beginning reading in-struction and were unfamiliar with the interaction patterns used in reading lessons.

The emotional and motivational climate of the home also has a significant impact on the child's access to literacy. Wigfield and Asher (1984) surmised that low ex-pectations for academic success and father absence, which are more frequent among lower-class families, contributed to poor academic achievement. Hess and Shipman (1965) found that middle- and lower-class black mothers both regarded education as important but viewed school as a place where they had little input or control.

Homes provide access to literacy materials as well as opportunities to engage print, and family members provide the opportunities and motivation for learning. The quality of the interactions within the home can vary considerably and thus pro-vide more or less access to the skills of becoming literate. For example, in a study of how mothers teach their children lowercase letters, Price (1984) observed that chil-dren who learned best were most encouraged to talk about the task. Joint problem solving with large amounts of verbal interaction seems to characterize effective parent–child instruction in many domains (Rogoff, 1985) and such guided participa-tion helps to shift the responsibility for learning from adult to child. Such episodes of socially guided participation are frequent in children's earliest exposures to liter-acy. Ninio (1983), for example, observed how mothers interacted with their 17–22-month-old infants as they "read" picture books together. Mothers were sen-sitive to their children's recognition of words, and upon subsequent appearances of the same word they tried to elicit labeling or pointing. If children did not know the word, mothers labeled it accordingly. Thus, the home environment plays a major role in children's acquisition of literacy.

The Instructional Context

Although there is a great deal of research on factors that limit students' access to literacy in the classroom, we shall focus here on only two, teachers' expectations and commercially produced materials for reading instruction. These two variables are important, because they are controlled to some extent by teachers and are therefore amenable to change. Obviously, many other characteristics of schools and students that are beyond teachers' control also exert powerful influences. In a later section we discuss instructional approaches that promote literacy skills.

It is well known that teachers' expectations influence their perceptions of how well students perform and their treatment of students in the classroom. Students who are expected to do well usually are asked more questions, receive more feedback and praise, and obtain more classroom privileges (Good & Brophy, 1977; Weinstein, 1976). These expectations are communicated by teachers to students who can clearly perceive the biases toward themselves. More damaging, though, is the finding that students' achievement tends to confirm teachers' expectations in such a way that perceived ability limits students' access to high-quality instruction (Paladry, 1969; Weinstein, 1984). Expectations may also reflect prejudices based on social class and race. Cooper, Baron, and Lowe (1975) observed that student teachers expected higher achievement, effort, and ability among middle-class students than among lower-class students. Wigfield and Asher (1984) reviewed evidence that suggested that lower-class and black students often felt alienated from school. These students may also have lower teacher expectations for success, poorer instructional interactions, and more anxiety about school than middle-class white students. Thus, teachers may unknowingly provide fewer opportunities, less challenge, and less satisfaction for literacy-related activities to those students most in need of participation and instruction.

Research has revealed that teachers provide little direct instruction about comprehension skills (Durkin, 1978–1979) and that teachers' manuals provide mostly questions and answers about passages rather than information about comprehension skills (Durkin, 1981). The lack of information about skills contained in commercial materials is alarming because it has been estimated that 90% of American school children use basal reading series and as much as half of their time devoted to reading instruction is spent completing workbook assignments (Osborn, Jones, & Stein, 1984). This estimate is even more disturbing given Osborn's (1984) observations that workbook tasks were often unrelated to other aspects of the basal reader, the directions to students were often unclear, important skills were often mentioned only once, and there was little systematic and cumulative review of the information learned.

But workbooks are not the only problem. Basal programs often contain a limited variety of stories and genre. Oftentimes the material is just plain dull. Beck, McKeown, McCaslin, and Burkes (1979) found that some commercial reading programs contained features that might hamper comprehension such as the use of indirect language, misleading pictures, inappropriate story divisions, and questions that focus on unimportant information. Armbruster and Anderson (1984) reached similar conclusions about the social studies and science texts that they reviewed. Pearson (1984) summed it up this way: "The texts are hokey and misleading, the teacher manual suggestions are scant, misleading, or unhelpful, and teachers do not seem to teach very much in the way of comprehension skills and strategies" (p. 7). Even if this grim indictment is only partially true, students in American classrooms are not provided with sufficient opportunities to confront text with challenging reading and writing assignments that foster skills for further literacy.

GAINING PERSONAL ACCESS TO LITERACY

In this section we examine characteristics of students that promote personal competence in literacy, specifically their knowledge, cognitive strategies, and attitudes. The psychological or interpersonal context of the acquisition of literacy by individuals is embedded in the layers of context already discussed. Although we review primarily research on reading, characteristics of successful readers are evident in other aspects of literacy as well.

Reading comprehension is an active process in which meaning is constructed as a result of an interaction among the reader's existing knowledge, the information suggested by the text, and the social interactions in the reading situation. Comprehension is dynamic, not static, and it varies as a function of *reader factors* such as background knowledge (Pearson, Hansen, & Gordon, 1979) and reading ability (Tierney, Bridge, & Cera, 1978–1979) that produce large differences among people in their interpretation of the same material. *Text factors* such as content (Kintsch, Kozminsky, Streby, McKoon, & Keenan, 1975) and structure (Meyer, 1975; Stein & Glenn, 1979) influence the familiarity of the information and the ease of constructing meaning. *Task factors* such as purpose (McConkie, Rayner, & Wilson, 1973) and types of questions (Wixson, 1983) and *setting factors* such as formal assessment versus informal classroom situations (Mosenthal & Na, 1980) can influence the amount of effort and ability required to comprehend text meaning.

Research has shown that effective comprehenders tailor their activities to the competing demands of reader, text, task, and setting factors (Brown, Armbruster, & Baker, 1984). A growing body of evidence indicates that the spontaneous use of flexible processing strategies is a characteristic that differentiates good from poor comprehenders (see Golinkoff, 1975–1976) but what remains unclear is how one learns to be an effective comprehender. Recently, several investigators have suggested that becoming an expert comprehender requires: (a) the acquisition of general knowledge about how text features, task goals, strategies, and learners' characteristics influence reading (Brown et al., 1984); (b) acquisition of cognitive control processes that help readers evaluate, plan, and apply this knowledge (Baker & Brown, 1984; Paris & Lindauer, 1982); and (c) positive attitudes toward reading. Such changes that accompany expertise in reading are evident in children's cognitive development in other domains as well, such as communication and self-directed learning (Paris & Cross, 1983). Part of our purpose in this section is to illustrate how knowledge, control, and attitudes influence children's intrapersonal access to literacy in a manner that complements the interpersonal conditions that promote participation in literacy activities. Both aspects are embedded in a developmental orientation in which instruction promotes social and psychological access to literacy.

Knowledge About Reading

Understanding a task to be learned or a skill to be measured is a critical part of learning. For example, a great deal of research on cognitive development has shown that children's learning is enhanced by knowledge about specific stimuli or domains (Chi, 1978), knowledge about person, task, and strategy variables (Flavell & Wellman, 1977), and knowledge about when you know, what you know, and what you need to know (Brown, 1978). These kinds of knowledge are generally referred to as *metacognition*, because they reflect children's expanding knowledge about their own cognitive states and abilities. Despite the lack of consensus regarding definition, measurement, taxonomy, or function of these types of metacognitive knowledge, most researchers would agree that metacognition encompasses what you know about a cognitive skill and how to use it; i.e., both *declarative* and *procedural* aspects of thinking (Resnick, 1983). However, Paris et al. (1983) have suggested that declarative and procedural knowledge alone are insufficient to ensure that children are able to become strategic readers. They propose that readers must also acquire *conditional* knowledge regarding *when* and *why* to apply the various actions which are part of their declarative and procedural knowledge. Conditional knowledge provides the motivational and pragmatic connections between thought and action (Paris & Cross, 1983).

There is ample research evidence to suggest a strong relation between knowledge about reading and reading skill. For example, Mason (1984) believes that there is a direct relation between what a child knows about reading before beginning to read and the acquisition of reading skill. She identifies three areas of knowledge that appear to be related to beginning reading: knowledge about the relation between speech and print; knowledge of the interrelatedness between letters and sounds; and knowledge of reading terms and the rules that govern the actions of reading such as reading from left to right and top to bottom.

One of the first studies to examine young children's knowledge about reading was conducted by Reid (1966) who interviewed 5-year-old beginning readers to examine their ideas about reading. She found that children lacked specific expectancies regarding reading and did not understand the purposes or uses of reading. In addition, none of the children had a clear sense of a ''word.'' Some identified entire sentences as words, some made random guesses, and some said that words, phrases, and sentences were all words (see also Downing, 1970). Clay (1972) found that 66% of 5-year-old school entrants in New Zealand did not know that the message was carried by the print rather than the pictures. After 6 months, nearly 90% of the children knew this, although some still confused the purposes and nature of reading after a year of schooling. More recently, Johns (1980) found that while all groups of first-grade readers possessed book-orientation and print-direction concepts, below-average readers were inferior to above-average readers in print-direction concepts, letter-word concepts, and advanced print concepts.

The research suggests that knowledge continues to be a factor in reading proficiency in older readers as well. Myers and Paris (1978) interviewed second- and sixth-grade students and found that younger children had less knowledge about texts, tasks, and strategies than older children. For example, older readers knew that skimming involves selecting the most informative words from a text, whereas younger readers believed that skimming was accomplished by reading the easier words. Thus, declarative, procedural, and conditional knowledge about reading continue to develop well beyond children's initial experiences with literacy.

Control Strategies

The importance of metacognitive knowledge about reading for the development of independent, flexible readers should not be underestimated. Children need to acquire knowledge regarding the what, how, when, and why of their own abilities as *readers*, the *strategies* that they have available for reading, the various demands of the *texts* they are likely to encounter, and the requirements of various reading *tasks* (Baker & Brown, 1984).

But knowledge alone does not ensure skilled reading or good comprehension. Children need to control their own reading and adjust their strategies according to task demands. Such control functions are referred to variously in the literature as selecting, adapting, monitoring, evaluating, checking, planning, and so forth (e.g., Brown, 1978; Paris & Lindauer, 1982; Ryan, 1981). Paris and Lindauer (1982) described three fundamental aspects of self-controlled reasoning: *evaluation* refers to the analysis of the goals and purposes of a task and an assessment of the range of abilities one has available and that are required to complete a task; *planning* refers to the deliberate selection and ordering of skills and strategies to fulfill task goals; and *regulation* refers to the continuous monitoring of progress toward a goal and to the redirection of effort when trouble is detected. As children learn to evaluate, plan, and regulate their own reading, they become better comprehenders and independent readers.

There is a growing body of literature that suggests that beginning and/or poor readers lack control over their reading. Among beginning readers, data regarding self-correction of oral reading errors provide a clear illustration of the relation between control processes in reading and skilled reading. In general, young or less skilled readers correct a smaller proportion of their oral reading errors than proficient readers do (Wixson, 1979). Furthermore, even when they do make corrections, their substitutions are rarely plausible (Beebe, 1980). In addition, proficient readers are more likely to correct errors that disrupt the sentence meaning than less skilled readers who correct disruptive and nondisruptive errors at the same rates (Weber, 1970).

Studies that document the relation between reading skill and the ability to adjust one's reading activities to the demands of the text and/or the task provide additional evidence of the relation between control processes and reading skill. For example, Owings, Petersen, Bransford, Morris, and Stein (1980) asked skilled and less skilled fifth-grade students to read and study logically structured and arbitrarily structured versions of stories. Only the better students adjusted their reading and studying activities according to the features of the text. Less skilled readers not only do not adjust their apportionment of study time to fit the text, but they also fail to adjust their study activities to meet the demands of the task (Paris & Myers, 1981).

Additional evidence of the relation between control processes and reading skill comes from studies that focus on comprehension monitoring. Reviews by Wagoner (1983), Baker and Brown (1984), and Brown et al. (1984) provide overwhelming evidence that students are surprisingly tolerant of ambiguities and inconsistencies in passages they read. Even under explicit directions to search for internal inconsistencies when reading, a substantial number of mistakes were undetected by fourth graders (Paris & Myers, 1981) and sixth graders (Markman & Gorin, 1981). Thus, it appears that both knowledge about reading and control over one's own reading activities are essential for skilled reading. Just as knowledge differences can limit one's ability to apply control processes (Brown, Bransford, Ferrara, & Campione, 1983), the ability to self-regulate one's cognitive activities defines one's success as a learner (Brown, 1980).

Attitudes Toward Reading

We have tried to encompass a broad range of cognitive skills in our categories of knowledge and control. The terms *conditional knowledge* and *metacognition* are also intended to include motivational aspects of when and why such cognitive skills should be applied. But a central factor affecting children's reading is their attitudes toward the task. Do they enjoy reading? Is it worth the extra effort to employ comprehension strategies? Is it worth the risk of failure to try hard to read? Good readers generally have positive attitudes toward reading (Alexander & Filler, 1976). Downing and Leong (1982) described the results of a survey conducted in Kent, England, that indicated that by age 11, 87% of good readers but only 37% of poor readers had positive attitudes toward reading. In fact, children's attitudes and satisfaction derived from reading are significant predictors of reading achievement for 11–12-year-old children who have already mastered basic reading skills (Oka & Paris, 1986).

A related finding is that high interest in reading material results in greater desire to read and in increased comprehension (Asher, 1980). Similar work by Shnayer (1969) indicated that interest enabled students to read beyond their measured reading ability. This research also indicated that low-achieving students were more affected by interest than high-achieving students, suggesting that interest is of particular importance for the less skilled student.

Attitudes and expectations become more negative with failure, and they can provoke less effort which in turn yields poor achievement and worsening motivation (Dweck & Bempechat, 1983). In a study of the attitudes of normal and disabled readers, Wallbrown, Vance, and Prichard (1979) observed that disabled readers expressed greater difficulty with reading, viewed reading groups and instructional materials more negatively, and were less likely to read for the pleasure of reading. Butkowsky and Willows (1980) characterized the behavior of poor readers in the fifth grade as "learned helplessness," because they had low expectancies for success, little persistence, and blamed their failures on low ability compared to average and good readers. Although these attitudes may be understandable for low-achieving children, they perpetuate cycles of poor attitudes, little effort expended, devaluation of literacy, and low achievement. Certainly, these attitudes diminish both access to and acquisition of literacy.

LITERACY, DEVELOPMENT, AND INSTRUCTION

We have reviewed evidence that shows that skilled readers acquire knowledge, control strategies, and positive attitudes for reading. These same factors are also important for composition (e.g., Scardamalia & Bereiter, 1983) and other aspects of literacy. It is important to note, though, that knowledge, control, and attitudes emerge from the contexts in which literacy is used. The functions and values of literacy-related activities are conveyed to children who begin to form their own aspirations and expectations for reading and writing. Literacy observed in the individual is thus a cumulative product of social forces that shape learning and development. That is why we have embedded acquisition in contextual issues of access to literacy. Now we would like to call attention to two points of convergence among contemporary theories of cognitive development and literacy learning because they have direct implications for instruction. We shall briefly describe "functionalism" and the "zone of proximal development."

Learning as a Stimulus for Development

Literacy serves practical purposes and people acquire literate skills as tools within their contextual niches. Evidence from cross-cultural researchers, anthropologists, and ethnographers remind us that literacy is not a set of decontextualized cognitive skills. Because literacy serves diverse social functions of recording information and expressing interpersonal communication, we can only attain a comprehensive picture of literacy by analyzing the range of functions served by literacy in particular settings (e.g., Scribner & Cole, 1981). Heidbreder (1933) summarized the old school of functionalism cogently, and the orientation seems to be heuristic yet today:

> functionalism was interested primarily in activities—in mental processes not merely as contents but as operations. Furthermore, it was interested in studying them in their natural setting and from the standpoint of their utility . . . It had about it, too, an air of common sense, unabashed by academic taboos. In examining mental processes, it asked the questions of the practical man: "What are they for?" "What difference do they make?" "How do they work?" Obviously such questions cannot be answered by studying mental processes in and by them-

selves . . . To answer that question, it is necessary to go beyond the process itself and consider the connections it makes: to investigate both its antecedents and its consequences, to discover what difference it makes to the organism, and to take into account its whole complex setting in the complex world in which it appears. (p. 202)

The "new functionalism" (if one continues to emerge) is built upon this contextual framework that examines pragmatic consequences of mental processes. Reading and writing simply do not serve the same purposes for all people, and our theoretical orientations can be enriched by investigating the functions of literacy in specific contexts. In these detailed investigations we need to focus on the social value of the goals and the personal significance of the activities as well as the utility and economy of becoming literate. The "costs" in terms of effort, instruction, and self-esteem are measured against potential gains and losses to individuals in their social groups. If our theories include analyses of these functional aspects of learning and motivation for literacy, we may achieve a better understanding of individuals' responses to literacy instruction and how literacy affects social and cognitive development.

Another construct that can help us to understand how learning and development interact in literacy is Vygotsky's (1978) notion of the "zone of proximal development," which he defined as "the distance between the actual developmental level as determined by independent problem solving and the level of potential development as determined through problem solving under adult guidance or in collaboration with more capable peers" (p. 86). According to this view, learning "awakens" internal developmental processes that are able to operate only when children are interacting with others. This view of learning and development emphasizes how external learning processes are converted into internal developmental processes through social interaction.

Vygotsky (1978) believed that high-order cognitive skills such as reading and writing are acquired gradually from social interactions. Other people help children to identify problems, to use strategies deliberately, and, with practice, to take more responsibility for applying the strategies independently and automatically. There is a transfer of responsibility in becoming literate (e.g., Pearson & Gallagher, 1983) that enables children to internalize the means and goals, or literacy tools and objectives, from other people (Paris, 1978; Wertsch, 1979). Therefore, it is important to determine the role of instruction in the development of literacy as cognitive skills become internalized, automatic, and generalized.

Instructional Methods that Promote Literacy

Recent research has revealed a startling lack of explicit classroom instruction on higher-order strategies for reading and writing. Neither teachers nor materials provide instruction that nurtures slow students and challenges high achievers. Although some alternative methods are beginning to appear, researchers have begun to forge a clearer notion of what constitutes effective instruction for literacy. Teachers should describe skills directly, what they are, how they operate, when to use them, and why they promote literacy. The content, genre, and difficulty of the materials should stimulate students. Classroom exercises (e.g., workbooks) should be closely related to the contents and skills taught by the teacher. Students can benefit from working together cooperatively as they read and write. Guided participation facilitates learning more than explanation, demonstration, or practice alone, because teachers assess and correct students' performance as they encourage them to think independently. Effective instruction is considerate of students' prior knowledge, attitudes, and social contexts within and outside the classroom. Instruction for better literacy combines reading, writing, speaking, and listening into related activities that stimulate students to reason and to communicate about important information.

The evidence for these claims is derived from recent studies designed to improve children's reading and studying. All the factors cannot be included in a single study, but the combined results of various investigations suggest that they can be implemented by effective teachers. Let us begin by examining some early training studies that fostered strategy use by students. Brown, Campione, and Day (1981) categorized these studies as *blind, informed,* and *self-control. Blind* studies tell students what to do, but the training does not include full explanations of the functions, significance, or operation of the skills being learned. In contrast, informed and self-control instruction teaches students to use skills independently. Generally, *informed* training provides learners with additional information regarding the activity they are being taught to use, and *self-control* training provides the learners with explicit instruction about how to monitor and regulate the activity. Thus, self-control training emphasizes both *knowledge,* which forms the basis for informed training, and *control.*

Although there have been few informed and self-control training studies in the area of reading comprehension, the results are encouraging. A series of studies suggest that informed and self-control training techniques are effective in promoting students' abilities to draw inferences (Gordon, 1980; Hansen, 1981; Hansen & Pearson, 1982) and to evaluate and monitor their own question answering behavior (Raphael & Pearson, 1982). Day (1980) used four different training approaches to teach strategies for the summarization of prose passages to average and remedial community college students: (a) a fairly traditional *self-management* procedure that encouraged students to check their work carefully; (b) explicit instruction in the use of *rules* for summarization; (c) *rules plus self-management;* and (d) explicit instruction in the integration of the rules and the *control* of the rules. For the better students, training in the rules alone was sufficient to bring about large improvements. However, for the less skilled students, training in the integration of the rules and self-control were both necessary for improvement.

Informed and self-control studies both include a good deal of discussion among teachers and students so that students regard the skills as sensible and useful. Increasing the quantity of direct instruction is an improvement over many current practices, but the *quality* of teacher talk is critical. Duffy, Roehler, Book, Meloth, and Vavrus (1984) found that effective teachers emphasized: (a) assistance rather than assessment during reading; (b) a metacognitive understanding of "how you know"; (c) conscious connections to previous and future learning; (d) the context in which new skills will be applied; (e) making invisible cognitive skills tangible; and (f) responding to student confusion with advice about how to think strategically. Three recent research projects, one in Illinois, one in Michigan, and one in Hawaii, have tried to build research findings into instructional programs that can be used by classroom teachers with their regular curricula.

In a series of studies, Palincsar and Brown (1984) employed what they have called a "complete" or "combined" training package aimed at improving the comprehension abilities of learning disabled junior high students. This combined training package included three levels of instruction: (a) training in specific *skills* of summarizing, questioning, predicting, and clarifying; (b) explicit instruction in monitoring the application of these skills (*self-control* training); and (c) information concerning the significance and utility of the skills (*informed* training). In both laboratory and classroom settings the students' abilities to answer comprehension questions as assessed on passages independent of the training materials improved significantly. The effect was durable up to 8 weeks, and transfer was found on novel tasks of summarizing, predicting questioning, and clarifying.

Paris and his colleagues (Paris, Cross, Lipson, 1984; Paris & Jacobs, 1984) conducted a longitudinal, experimental study designed to teach children in the third and fifth grades about reading strategies and their functional value for reading. Two classes at each grade level received 4 months of instruction about reading strategies that included 2 half-hour group lessons each week. The lessons revolved around concrete metaphors (e.g., "Be a reading detective," "Plan your reading trip") which served as the bases for bulletin board displays, class discussions, and worksheet activities. The emphasis was on informing students through practice and discussion of the significance and utility of various strategies for reading and, thus, the program was called Informed Strategies for Learning (ISL). A comparison of pre- and posttest scores indicated that children in the experimental classes scored significantly higher than children in the control classes on measures of metacognition, cloze, and error detection. In a subsequent study 50 teachers used ISL lesson plans and materials to teach their students in third and fifth grades about comprehension strategies. The data again revealed significant improvements in metacognition and comprehension strategies following informed training (Paris, Jacobs, Cross, Oka, DeBritto, & Saarnio, 1984).

Finally, the Kamahameha Early Education Project (KEEP) is a dynamic instructional program that reflects the benefits of student collaboration and instruction designed to fit students' "zones of proximal development." Teachers in KEEP use the Hawaiian tradition of talk stories to promote children's comprehension. The method involves asking children questions about their experiences and background knowledge of the topics before reading. Teachers then ask children questions about the text after reading that focus on the text information and how it is related to their own experiences. The group discussions are gradually reduced as children learn to internalize the questioning and relating of information prompted by the teacher. Besides teaching children to reason about textual information, the talk stories fit the cultural traditions of native Hawaiian children and are quite motivating.

A broad theory of literacy that is based on cognitive development, instructional contexts, opportunities for exercising literacy, and social dynamics of learning and instruction includes a "functional" orientation for the development of knowledge and control processes that will enable children to become independent, flexible learners. The following four implications of the new approaches differ substantially from traditional practices:

1. Comprehension should be taught as a functional, goal-directed activity that occurs naturally in the life of a child; that is, teachers should try to make the context and content of comprehension instruction relevant and useful to students.

2. Instruction should emphasize the development of *concepts* of reading that will enable children to successfully comprehend written material under a variety of conditions. Traditional basic skills should be means to goals of effective comprehension ability rather than ends in themselves, and they should complement a conceptual understanding of literacy.

3. Instruction should operate at a level slightly beyond a child's current independent ability. Learning occurs in situations where coaching and guided participation transfer responsibility gradually to students.

4. Instruction should utilize informed, self-control training procedures so that children learn how text features, task goals, reader strategies, and situational characteristics interact to influence comprehension. Our review indicates that these principles are all important for the development of literacy and that they can be incorporated into instructional curricula and settings.

IMPLICATIONS FOR RESEARCH ON LITERACY

The position we have sketched in this chapter emphasizes the personal construction of knowledge about literacy in particular settings. It is clearly a contextualist perspective that focuses on the functions of literacy. The approach is by necessity social, instructional, and developmental, because we regard the situations of literacy as the units of analyses. A fundamental research goal then is to unwrap the layers of context and multivariate factors that influence access to and acquisition of literacy. This approach is radical only to the extent that it links together traditional investigations of education, psychology, and anthropology by studying practical literacy skills in their ordinary contexts. But what types of questions are raised by this orientation, and how do they inform us about children's acquisition of literacy?

One implication of a contextual approach to literacy is to study the social interactions that invite participation and learning. We could examine how mothers provide books to infants, how children learn to recognize pictures and print, and how adults motivate children with games and interactions to read and write. Researchers could also examine the dialogues that teachers and parents use to transmit information to children about print. In addition to instructional episodes, we might examine the kinds of materials available in a child's environment—road signs, magazines, toys, computers, chalkboards—that provide frequent yet informal occasions to learn about reading and writing. Opportunities for speaking and listening as well as the impact of media can be studied for the information that they provide about literacy. Clearly, educational materials in schools and homes should be scrutinized for their content and enjoyment for children. Research that illuminates the quality and quantity of literacy activities available to people can establish conditions of access that may impede or foster learning.

A second area of research is the study of everyday strategies. How do children learn the alphabet, how to identify a main idea, or how to compose an outline? How do people compensate for illiteracy in everyday situations, and what strategies do underachieving students develop for coping with literacy demands in schools? Such questions cannot be studied apart from the influence of home, school, and culture, because the settings define the appropriateness of strategies—cognitive, motivational, or social ways of coping with print and literacy tasks. A functional, developmental approach is necessary in order to understand the effectiveness and efficiency of particular strategies.

A third research topic implied by our approach is an analysis of the learner's perception of literacy. What kinds of knowledge annd attitudes foster or hinder learning to read and write? How can we promote self-directed learning and enjoyment of literacy so that language is used creatively? A lack of knowledge or motivation can dramatically alter children's orientations to literacy and their continuing motivation to participate in literate activities. Thus, learner's perceptions and knowledge should be assessed directly and related to their skills and motivation.

There are additional implications for research that can be adduced from contemporary theories. As a general rule, they have in common a focus on contextual influences and individual differences. Researchers who use the new approaches do not study cognitive skills dissected from ordinary settings, motivational influences, developmental history, and instructional agents. They eschew accounts of strategies that are presumed to be uniformly applied by different people in different settings and, instead, analyze domain-specific knowledge and skills. Literacy in this view is a means to accomplish personal and social goals and is not an end in itself. In order to understand the richness of literacy and the diverse ways that people use print and language, we need to study sociological conditions that promote access to literacy in conjunction with knowledge and motivation that affect personal access to the acquisition of literacy skills. Because social and personal access are combined in ordinary social situations that require literacy, it seems natural to analyze the multiple layers of context that surround everyday occurrences of reading, writing, and instruction. This enlarged perspective may help us understand more fully how literacy, schooling, and development interact.

REFERENCES

Alexander, J.E., & Filler, R.C. (1976). *Attitudes and reading.* Newark, DE: International Reading Association.

Armbruster, B.B., & Anderson, T.H. (1984). Content area textbooks. In R.C. Anderson, J. Osborn, & R.J. Tierney (Eds.), *Learning to read in American schools: Basal readers and context texts.* Hillsdale, NJ: Erlbaum.

Asher, S.R. (1980). Topic interest and children's reading comprehension. In R.J. Spiro, B.C. Bruce, & W.F. Brewer (Eds.), *Theoretical issues in reading comprehension.* Hillsdale, NJ: Erlbaum.

Baker, L., & Brown, A.L. (1984). Metacognitive skills of reading. In P.D. Pearson, R. Barr, M. L. Kamil, & P. Mosenthal (Eds.), *Handbook of reading research.* New York: Longman.

Beck, I.L., McKeown, M.G., McCaslin, E.S., & Burkes, A.M. (1979). *Instructional dimensions that may affect reading comprehension: Examples from two commercial reading programs* (LRDC Publication 1979/20). Pittsburgh, PA: University of Pittsburgh.

Beebe, M.J. (1980). The effect of different types of substitution miscues on reading. *Reading Research Quarterly, 15,* 324–336.

Bing, E. (1963). Effect of childrearing practices on development of differential cognitive abilities. *Child Development, 34,* 631–648.

Briggs, C., & Elkind, D. (1977). Characteristics of early readers. *Perceptual and Motor Skills, 14,* 1231–1237.

Brown, A.L. (1978). Knowing when, where and how to remember: A problem of metacognition. In R. Glaser (Ed.), *Advances in instructional psychology.* Hillsdale, NJ: Erlbaum.

Brown, A.L. (1982). Learning and development: The problems of compatibility, access, and induction. *Human Development, 25,* 89–115.

Brown, A.L., Armbruster, B.B., & Baker, L. (1984). The role of metacognition in reading and studying. In J. Orasanu (Ed.), *A decade of reading research: Implications for practice.* Hillsdale, NJ: Erlbaum.

Brown, A.L., Bransford, J.D., Ferrara, R.A., & Campione, J.C. (1983). Learning, remembering, and understanding. In J.H. Flavell & E.M. Markman (Eds.), *Carmichael's manual of child psychology* (Vol. III). New York: Wiley.

Brown, A.L., Campione, J.C., & Day, J.D. (1981). Learning to learn: On training students to learn from texts. *Educational Researcher, 10,* 14–21.

Butkowsky, I.S., & Willows, D.M. (1980). Cognitive-motivational characteristics of children varying in reading ability: Evidence for learned helplessness in poor readers. *Journal of Educational Psychology, 72,* 408–422.

Chall, J.S. (1983). Literacy: Trends and explanations. *Educational Researcher, 12,* 3–8.

Chi, M.T.H. (1978). Knowledge structures and memory development. In R.S. Siegler (Ed.), *Children's thinking: What develops?* Hillsdale, NJ: Erlbaum.

Clay, M.M. (1972). *Reading: The patterning of complex behavior.* Auckland, New Zealand: Heineman Educational Books.

Clay, M.M. (1976). Early childhood and cultural diversity in New Zealand. *The Reading Teacher, 29,* 333–342.

Cooper, H.M., Baron, R.M., & Lowe, C.A. (1975). The importance of race and social class information in the formation of expectancies about academic performance. *Journal of Educational Psychology, 67,* 312–319.

Day, J.D. (1980). *Teaching summarization skills: A comparison of training methods.* Unpublished doctoral dissertation, University of Illinois.

Downing, J. (1970). Children's concepts of language in learning to read. *Educational Researcher, 12,* 106–112.

Downing, J., & Leong, C.K. (1982). *Psychology of reading.* New York: Macmillan.

Duffy, G.G., Roehler, L.R., Book, C., Meloth, M.S., & Vavrus, L.G. (1984). *Instructional character-*

istics which promote strategic awareness in reading. Paper presented at the annual meeting of the American Educational Research Association, New Orleans.

Durkin, D.R. (1966). *Children who read early.* New York: Teachers College Press.

Durkin, D. (1978–79). What classroom observations reveal about reading comprehension instruction. *Reading Research Quarterly, 14,* 481–533.

Durkin, D. (1981). Reading comprehension instruction in five basal reader series. *Reading Research Quarterly, 16,* 515–531.

Dweck, C.S., & Bempechat, J. (1983). Children's theories of intelligence: Consequences for learning. In S.G. Paris, G.M. Olson, & H.W. Stevenson (Eds.), *Learning and motivation in the classroom.* Hillsdale, NJ: Erlbaum.

Flavell, J.H., & Wellman, H.M. (1977). Metamemory. In R.V. Kail & J.W. Hagen (Eds.), *Perspecties on the development of memory and cognition.* Hillsdale, NJ: Erlbaum.

Golinkoff, R. (1975–1976). A comparison of reading comprehension processes in good and poor comprehenders. *Reading Research Quarterly, 11,* 623–659.

Good, T.L., & Brophy, J. (1977). *Educational psychology: A realistic approach.* New York: Holt, Rinehart, Winston.

Gordon, C.J. (1980). *The effects of instruction in metacomprehension and inferencing on children's comprehension skills.* Unpublished doctoral dissertation, University of Minnesota.

Green, J., & Bloome, D. (1983). Ethnography and reading: Issues, approaches, criteria, and findings. *Searches for meaning in reading/language processing and instruction* (32nd Yearbook of the National Reading Conference). *New York: National Reading Conference.*

Hansen, J. (1981). The effects of inference training and practice on young children's comprehension. *Reading Research Quarterly, 16,* 391–417.

Hansen, J., & Pearson, P.D. (1982). An instructional study: Improving the inferential comprehension of good and poor fourth grade readers. *Journal of Educational Psychology, 75,* 821–829.

Heath, S.B. (1982). What no bedtime story means: Narrative skills at home and school. *Language in Society, 11,* 49–76.

Heidbreder, E. (1933). *Seven psychologies.* New York: Appleton-Century-Crofts.

Hess, R.D., & Shipman, V.C. (1965). Early experiences and the socialization of cognitive modes in children. *Child Development, 36,* 369–386.

Johns, J.L. (1980). First graders' concepts about print. *Reading Research Quarterly, 15,* 539–549.

Kintsch, W., Kozminsky, E., Streby, W.J., McKoon, G., & Keenan, J.M. (1975). Comprehension and recall of text as a function of content variables. *Journal of Verbal Learning and Verbal Behavior, 14,* 196–214.

Laboratory of Comparative Human Cognition (1983). Culture and cognitive development. In W. Kessen (Ed.), *Handbook of child psychology: History, theory, and methods* (Vol. I). New York: Wiley.

Leichter, J.L. (1984). Families as environments for literacy. In H. Goelman, A. Oberg, & F. Smith (Eds.), *Awakening to literacy.* London: Heinemann.

Markman, E.M., & Gorin, L. (1981). Children's ability to adjust their standards for evaluating comprehension. *Journal of Educational Psychology, 83,* 320–325.

Mason, J.M. (1984). Prereading: A developmental perspective. In P.D. Pearson, R. Barr, M.L. Kamil, & P. Mosenthal (Eds.), *Handboook of research in reading.* New York: Longman.

McConkie, G.W., Rayner, K., & Wilson, S.J. (1973). Experimental manipulation of reading strategies. *Journal of Educational Psychology, 65,* 1–8.

Meyer, B.J.F. (1975). *The organization of prose and its effects on memory.* Amsterdam: North-Holland.

Miller, W.H. (1969). Home prereading experiences and first grade reading achievement. *The Reading Teacher, 22,* 641–645.

Mosenthal, P., & Na, T.J. (1980). Quality of children's recall under two classroom testing tasks: Towards a socio-psycholinguistic model of reading comprehension. *Reading Research Quarterly, 15,* 504–528.

Myers, M., & Paris, S.G. (1978). Children's metacognitive knowledge about reading. *Journal of Educational Psychology, 70,* 680–690.

Ninio, A. (1983). Joint book reading as a multiple vocabulary acquisition device. *Developmental Psychology, 17,* 445–451.

Oka, E.R. & Paris, S.G. (1986). Patterns of motivation and reading skills in underachieving children. In S.J. Ceci (Ed.), *Handbook of cognitive, social, and neuropsychological aspects of learning disabilities.* Hillsdale, NJ: Erlbaum.

Osborn, J. (1984). The purposes, uses, and contents of workbooks and some guidelines for publishers. In R.C. Anderson, J. Osborn, & R.J. Tierney (Eds.), *Learning to read in American schools: Basal readers and content texts.* Hillsdale, NJ: Erlbaum.

Osborn, J., Jones, B.F., & Stein, M. (1984). *The case for improving textbook programs: An issue of quality.* Paper prepared for the National Forum "Excellence in Our Schools: Making It Happen," San Francisco.

Owings, R.A., Peterson, G.A., Bransford, J.D., Morris, C.D., & Stein, B.S. (1980). Spontaneous monitoring and regulation of learning: A comparison of successful and less successful fifth graders. *Journal of Educational Psychology, 72,* 250–256.

Paladry, J.M. (1969). What teachers believe, what children achieve. *Elementary Schhool Journal, 69,* 370–374.

Palincsar, A.S., & Brown, A.L. (1984). Reciprocal teaching of comprehension fostering and monitoring activities. *Cognition and Instruction, 1,* 117–175.

Paris, S.G. (1978). Coordination of means and goals in the development of mnemonic skills. In P.A. Ornstein (Ed.), *Memory development in children.* Hillsdale, NJ: Erlbaum.

Paris, S.G., & Cross, D.R. (1983). Ordinary learning: Pragmatic connections among children's beliefs, motives, and actions. In J. Bisanz, G. Bisanz, & R. Kail (Eds.), *Learning in children.* New York: Springer-Verlag.

Paris, S.G., Cross, D.R., & Lipson, M.Y. (1984). Informed strategies for learning: A program to improve children's reading awareness and comprehension. *Journal of Educational Psychology, 76,* 1239–1252.

Paris, S.G., & Jacobs, J.E. (1984). The benefits of informed instruction for children's reading awareness and comprehension skills. *Child Development, 55,* 2083–2093.

Paris, S.G., Jacobs, J.E., Cross, D.R., Oka, E.R., DeBritto, A.M., & Saarnio, D. (1984). *Improving children's metacognition and reading comprehension with classroom instruction.* Paper presented at the annual meeting of the American Educational Research Association, New Orleans, LA.

Paris, S.G., & Lindauer, B.K. (1982). The development of cognitive skills during childhood. In B. Wolman (Ed.), *Handbook of developmental psychology.* Englewood Cliffs, NJ: Prentice-Hall.

Paris, S.G., Lipson, M.Y., & Wixson, K.K. (1983). Becoming a strategic reader. *Contemporary Educational Psychology, 8,* 293–316.

Paris, S.G., & Myers, M. (1981). Comprehension monitoring in good and poor readers. *Journal of Reading Behavior, 13,* 5–22.

Pearson, P.D. (1984). *Twenty years of research on reading comprehension.* Paper presented at the "Contexts of Literacy" Conference, Snowbird, UT.

Pearson, P.D., & Gallagher, M.C. (1983). The instruction of reading comprehension. *Contemporary Educationaal Psychology, 8,* 317–344.

Pearson, P.D., Hansen, J., & Gordon, C. (1979). The effect of background knowledge on young children's comprehension of explicit and implicit information. *Journal of Reading Behavior, 11,* 201–209.

Price, G.G. (1984). Mnemonic support and curriculum selection in teaching by mothers: A conjoint effect. *Child Development, 55,* 659–668.

Raphael, T.E., & Pearson, P.D. (1982). *The effects of metacognitive strategy awareness training on students' question answering behavior* (Tech. Report No. 238). Urbana: University of Illinois, Center for the Study of Reading.

Reid, J. (1966). Learning to think about reading. *Educational Research, 9,* 56–62.

Resnick, L.B. (1983). Toward a cognitive theory of instruction. In S. Paris, G. Olson, & H. Stevenson (Eds.), *Learning and motivation in the classroom.* Hillsdale, NJ: Erlbaum.

Rogoff, B. (1985). Social guidance of cognitive development. In E. Gollin (Ed.), *Colorado symposium on human socialization: Social context and human development.* New York: Academic Press.

Ryan, E.B. (1981). Identifying and remediating failures in reading comprehension: Toward an instructional approach for poor comprehenders. In T.G. Waller & G.E. MacKinnon (Eds.), *Advances in reading research.* New York: Academic Press.

Scardamalia, M., & Bereiter, C. (1983). Child as co-investigator: Helping children gain insight into their own mental processes. In S. Paris, G. Olson, & H. Stevenson (Eds.), *Learning and motivation in the classroom.* Hillsdale, NJ: Erlbaum.

Schieffelin, B.B., & Cochran-Smith, M. (1984). Learning to read culturally: Literacy before schooling. In H. Goelman, A.A. Oberg, & F. Smith (Eds.), *Awakening to literacy.* Exeter, NH: Heinemann Educational Books.

Scribner, S., & Cole M. (1981). *The psychology of literacy: A case study among the Vai.* Cambridge, MA: Harvard University Press.

Sheldon, W.D., & Carrillo, L. (1952). Relation of parents, home and certain developmental characteristics to children's reading ability. *Elementary School Journal, 52,* 262–270.

Shnayer, S.W. (1969). Relationships between reading interest and reading comprehension. In J.A. Figurel (Ed.), *Reading and realism,* Newark, DE: International Reading Association.

Stein, N.L., & Glenn, C.G. (1979). An analysis of story comprehension in elementary school children. In R.O. Freedle (Ed.), *New directions in discourse processing.* Norwood, NJ: Ablex.

Tierney, R.J., Bridge, C., & Cera, M.J. (1978–79). The discourse processing operations of children. *Reading Research Quarterly, 14,* 539–573.

Vygotsky, L.S. (1978). *Mind in society.* Cambridge, MA: Harvard University Press.

Wagner, D.A. (1985). When literacy isn't reading (and vice versa). In M.E. Wrolstad & D.F. Fisher (Eds.), *Toward a new understanding of literacy.* New York: Praeger.

Wagoner, S.A. (1983). Comprehension monitoring: What it is and what we know about it. *Reading Research Quarterly, 18,* 328–346.

Wallbrown, F.H., Vance, H.H., & Prichard, K.K. (1979). Discriminating between attitudes expressed by normal and disabled readers. *Psychology in the School, 16,* 472–477.

Weber, R.M. (1970). First graders' use of grammatical context in reading. In H. Levin & J.P. Williams (Eds.), *Basic studies on reading.* New York: Basic Books.

Weinstein, R.S. (1976). Reading group membership in first grade: Teacher behaviors and pupil experience over time. *Journal of Educational Psychology, 68,* 103–116.

Weinstein, R.S. (1984). *The teaching of reading and children's awareness of teacher expectations.* Paper presented at "The Contexts of Literacy" Conference, Snowbird, UT.

Wertsch, J.V. (1979). From social interaction to higher psychological processes: A clarification and application of Vygotsky's theory. *Human Development, 22,* 1–22.

Wigfield, A., & Asher, S.R. (1984). Home, school, and reading achievement: A social-motivational analysis. In P.D. Peaarson, R. Barr, M.L. Kamil, & P. Mosenthal (Eds.), *Handbook of reading research.* New York: Longman.

Wixson, K.K. (1979). Miscue analysis: A critical review. *Journal of Reading Behavior, 11,* 163–175.

Wixson, K.K. (1983). Postreading question-answer interactions and children's learning from text. *Journal of Educational Psychology, 30,* 413–423.

3 Illiteracy as Social Fault: Some Principles of Research and Some Results

David M. Smith

University of Pennsylvania

INTRODUCTION

Fifty-three-year-old Richard Rice is not just well off, he is a self-made millionaire. He had been a crackerjack salesman for a major insurance company and before that had been a successful Marine. While in Japan on military duty, he became so fluent in Japanese that he trained other Marines in the language and the culture.

I know about Mr. Rice, because the director of an adult literacy program had referred him to Katheryn Miller, a colleague of mine, as an "illiterate" she should interview. He had, in fact, taught himself to read after his business success.

Thomas Striker came to the same literacy center for help. He is a foreman in a local shop and is known as a devoted family man. Despite his successes, he was tired of having to depend on his wife to help him meet the literacy demands of his daily life. For example, if he knew that he was going to have to fill out a form, he would have his wife prepare a "cheat sheet" (his term) for him, which he would carry in his pocket. He would then copy the information in the correct places on the form.

Striker sought help in the literacy center when he became embarrassed because his daughter had discovered that he was not really reading the bedtime stories in her books.

Although the extent of Mr. Rice's business success may be unusual, in many ways neither he nor Mr. Striker are atypical of the "illiterates" seeking help in the two literacy centers that Miller investigated. While 5 of the 13 men whose stories she elicited were unemployed, few sought help because they needed the skills to function adequately in their jobs.

If functional illiteracy means not reading at a high enough skill level to function adequately in the workplace, then none of these men could be considered functionally illiterate. Most were successes in their work, comfortable in their communities, and participating in fulfilling personal relationships. Each was able to encode and to decode text at a level needed for written communication. Why then, given the serious stigma they risked in a public admission of their "illiteracy," would they come to a center for help?

The answer, I believe, lies in a meaning literacy holds for these men and many others that is frequently overlooked in much of the current thinking about illiteracy and its treatment. These stories demonstrate that illiteracy is not simply a skill deficiency with social implications, but that from the perspective of the illiterate may well constitute a serious social fault.[1] Consequently, while the directors of the literacy center may well have seen their tasks as that of skill remediation, the students saw the promise as one of redemption.

The recognition, that for people in the real world, the social fault imputed by a perception of illiteracy may be a more fundamental concern than is their lack of reading skill, presents both a pedagogical challenge (How best to deal with illiteracy?) and a research challenge (How best to understand it?). Although the latter question is the primary concern of this chapter, the approach to research outlined here recognizes that the two concerns are, in fact, inseparable. The way illiteracy is understood determines the way in which it will be treated.

The remainder of this chapter outlines what I have found to be a useful approach to research and is followed by brief comments on two sets of issues raised by the research: (a) the role of schooling in literacy development has received a great deal of attention in the literature but usually regarding its degree of success in skill development; and (b) the effects of gender on the social meaning and functions of literacy, while closely related to the first, have been little explored. In both cases, this chapter, recognizing that the meaning and functions of illiteracy will vary from context to context, aims more to stimulate ways of thinking than to present conclusions.

Our research has been guided by a set of underlying principles derived from the essential inductive, holistic, and participant–observation nature of ethnography. It takes the construct of culture as its heuristic. Taken together, these principles constitute a collaborative approach to social phenomena that seeks to explicate meanings to participants. This is in contradistinction to the goal of much current social research that either is satisfied to explain what works or that purports to uncover cognitive processes.

RESEARCH PRINCIPLES

1. Start with No Preconceived Notions About What's Happening and What This Means to Participants

The key notion here is not that we start without preconceptions (clearly an impossibility) but that we hold interpretation in abeyance. The goal of understanding social phenomena must be not simply to discover what is going on in a given situation *but how participants understand them;* not simply to predict behavior (or even to postdict it) but also to *assess the human costs of decisions.*

2. Let the Important Questions to Be Answered About Literacy, and the Answers, Emerge from the Context

If we approach a research site as merely the place to answer the questions we bring to it, we will severely limit the amount of information we glean and will

---

[1]It has been pointed out to me that both Sylvia Scribner and Denny Taylor (1983), in her book *Family Literacy,* have referred to illiteracy as social fault. While I have not been able to locate a reference for Scribner, I would like to acknowledge these earlier uses of the term.

scarcely advance the cause of understanding what activities mean to participants. If, for example, Miller had started her research by questioning the men about their reading and writing, she likely would have missed the importance of illiteracy to them which was little to do with facility in the skills of reading and writing. Her approach was to encourage each of the students in the program to tell their own life stories. In reflecting on these, she found herself confronted with a number of questions she otherwise would not likely have thought to ask.

3. Do not View Participants as Subjects but as Co-Learners with the Investigator, Each Using the Other to Reach Shared and Ever-Deepening Understandings

Since the primary instruments for researching social phenomena are the researchers themselves, it follows that a major research resource becomes the ability to form empathetic, sharing relationships. (It also follows that gaining new insights, definitionally, changes the researcher as well, a fact often discovered in the emotional reactions experienced by ethnographers.)

4. Take Seriously the Uniqueness of Each Setting and Set of Events

Meaning is created contextually. If a goal of research is to reach an understanding of what things mean to participants, its quest must necessarily reject a research ideology that only counts generalizable[2] knowledge as valid.

5. Take as of Primary Importance Relationships Rather than Relata

The target of research on social phenomena is not the individual nor other facets of a particular context looked at in isolation. While much research maintains that relationships are important, the use of extrinsic instruments, coupled with concern for generalizability and reliability, frequently demands operationalizations that omit relational data. For example, while functional illiteracy is often defined as lacking skills needed to function adequately in some context (a relational notion), this is frequently operationalized as reading at a certain grade level as reflected in a test score. While functional illiteracy could be a useful concept in the kind of research I am advocating, its definition would not only change from context to context but could change over time for the same individual. Witness, for example, the steel workers who were thrown out of work in western Pennsylvania recently. Many of them were functionally literate until it came time for them to seek jobs in the new high-tech sector of our economy, at which point they were found to be functionally illiterate. A grade-level criterion would be inadequate to reflect this.

6. Remember That People Inevitably Act to Make Sense of Their World as They Experience It

This, of course, is a basic assumption of anthropologically oriented research. Whenever we encounter people acting in surprising or "unpredictable" ways, it is our job to account for this in terms of their own context. These explanation will entail an understanding of the way the universe they are inhabiting is structured, the way they perceive it, and their place in it.

---

[2]I mean, of course, artifactual generalizations. That is, conclusions that meet an arbitrary set of criteria for being valid across contexts. The conclusions of ethnography are often profoundly generalizable in that they resonate with a wide range of human experiences.

7. Note That Patterns of Behavior Meet the Needs of the Social Group

While the particular needs of the group being met may turn out to be elusive, and in fact, may never be uncovered, adherence to this principle becomes a powerful discovery tool. Ogbu (1984) in his study, "Literacy in Subordinate Cultures," provided a striking demonstration of this. Noting the exceptionally high illiteracy rates among black youngsters, he assumed that the explanation could be found in some social need. He concluded that this was the presence of a de facto caste system.

8. Recall That Real Understanding Can Only Come Through Real Participant–Observation

Real participant–observation means minimally finding and filling an authentic status created by the group, establishing authentic relationships (also as defined by the group), and meeting all of the obligations of these relationships. It also implies a disciplined effort to maintain an observer stance.

9. Recognize That Only Participants in an Activity Can Solve Their Problems or Even Determine What They Are

That they may not solve them may be due to their inability to see that they have the answers or to their view of themselves as structurally powerless. This is not to suggest that outside information cannot be helpful. As will be noted, however, the problem must first become "owned" by participants.

10. Recognize That Change Takes Place When We Hear Another's "Story" Resonate with Our Own Experience, and We Feel Free to Take from It for our Own Particular Uses

Attending to this principle has the effect of shaping the form of our ultimate product. Research results that are ultimately usable do not have to be first digested and regurgitated by a researcher. Few real-life decisions are based on either statistical generalizations or other conclusions drawn by experts. As researchers, we see our task as that of recovering and presenting in authentic and credible form the individual stories we have gained access to.

Principle 9, "ultimately only participants to an activity have solutions to problems," is key to the argument adduced in this paper. At first blush this may not even appear to be a principle of research. This would be true, of course, from a research ideology that views research as being done for a research establishment in which ownership of the findings remains vested in the research end of the enterprise. However, as indicated earlier, if a goal of the research is to find solutions that both work *and whose perceived psychological costs are reasonable,* distinctions between problem understanding and resolution turn out to be specious.

The relevance of this to the study of literacy is crucial. Research on illiteracy usually starts with a clear notion of what the problem is—inability to read and write—and almost as often, with a solution. As a result, while certain kinds of knowledge may be amassed, understanding is little advanced. Research proceeding from these principles, on the other hand, seeks first to discover the meaning of literacy, or, as the case may be, of illiteracy to individuals. As indicated earlier, this may turn out to have little relationship to popular notions.

The utility and potential richness of this approach can perhaps be best illustrated by discussing two of the insights gleaned from our research.

ILLITERACY AS SOCIAL FAULT: TWO ISSUES

The Role of Formal Schooling

In our first West Philadelphia research project, one of our research team, Fiering (1981), discovered that a great deal of the writing that went on in the classroom did not count as writing by teachers. It turned out that teachers were aware of much of this "unrecognized" writing; it was simply not officially sanctioned in the classroom context. Some writing, however, especially that engaged in by lower-track students, was not known to exist by teachers who started with a belief that these students could not write.

Gilmore (1983, 1984), also on the research team, added further clarity to this situation in her treatment of what she called "sub-rosa literacy." She pointed out that not only did middle- and upper-level elementary school girls engage in sophisticated language and literacy-related activities that school people considered them incapable of, but that they carried out these displays in a way to directly, through powerful symbolism, challenge the school's assessment. In a related study Gilmore (in press) showed that preadolescent boys, through their captivating involvement in Dungeons and Dragons, exhibited literacy skills and a willingness to engage in demanding literacy activities that went far beyond what the schools thought they were capable of.

On the one hand, those of us with significant experience in schools did not find these results terribly surprising. They confirmed what has been known for a long time—that a major function of schools is the control of knowledge and that a primary mechanism for exercising this control is definition of what counts as knowledge. What Fiering and Gilmore observed in later elementary school can be seen as a continuation of the processes that Heath (1982) and others have documented for us: the development of pre- and early-school langauge and discourse patterns that serve to disadvantage some children and to reward those who are school oriented. In fact, so strong is the school's vested interest in controlling the acquisition of literacy skills that much of the "naturally" acquired skill in encoding and decoding that children bring with them to school is systematically overlooked.

On the other hand, however, I think that these findings may have deeper significance. Questions of what counts as reading and writing in school soon become the question, "Is this person literate or illiterate?" In other words, what may have been first thought of as the presence or absence of a skill becomes a question of personal identity.

Furthermore, given the inordinant importance schooling plays in the lives of virtually all Americans, this labeling by schools becomes a concern for parents, and, ultimately, a major factor in how individuals see themselves. This self-labeling may have little to do with the ability to encode or decode text and even less with the amount of literacy-related activity one engages in. In our West Philadelphia study, for example, one of the mothers who was hired as a member of the research team carefully documented the literacy activities of several boys, some of whom referred to themselves as nonreaders and some as readers. She found little difference in the reading material they collected or the reading and writing they actually did (Robinson, 1982). Nevertheless, such a self-perception can reflect, and affect, a child's school performance.

By adulthood this process can have the results referred to at the beginning of this chapter. Miller's (1985) study has revealed among the most striking examples I have encountered of literacy-related self-labeling that had little to do with the skills of reading and writing. The adults saw themselves as illiterate. Yet on careful analysis, we had to conclude that their de facto definition of literacy meant "a certified successful school experience." The success of the literacy programs in the area, as I suspect is the case througout the country, *was not that they provided remediation of skill deficiency but that they offered an officially sanctioned avenue for redemption.* The promise of redemption rested in the center's offer of certification.

Two anecdotes reveal rather poignantly the depth of the need to atone for school failure. Mr. Rice, the self-made millionaire, had a particularly painful school experience. He was born with a cleft palate. In school his inability to speak properly resulted in his being put back several times and ultimately in his placement in a special education program. Now that he is successful, his dream is, first through the offices of the Adult Literacy program, to get his high school equivalency certificate and then to donate one million dollars to the school as a scholarship fund to help youngsters like himself. (He jokingly refers to it as the "Plumb Dumb and Ignorant Award.") Thus, only in his dream will his rehabilitation be complete.

Another group member told of visiting the local library where he got out his class yearbook. He found the place where his senior class picture would have been had he been graduated; then he told himself how he would be able to see himself in the picture, when he successfully finished the literacy program.

These experiences clearly demonstrate not only that certifiable school success can become a definition of literacy but how deeply internalized school labeling can be. Before leaving this point, another aspect of the school's effects on literacy perceptions deserves comment: the notion that literacy skills, unlike speaking, for example, cannot merely be learned, they have to be taught.

When the stories of Miller's adult literacy students were perused and compared, we were struck by the amount of self-teaching they revealed and by the ingenious strategies individuals had developed to cope with their illiteracy. However, not one student would admit to having taught him- or herself to read or write. Mr. Rice had struggled through two books (the first taking well over a year) on making money—books he credited with much of his financial success. Furthermore, he had become fluent in Japanese and had learned to read it well enough that he could use a Japanese-English dictionary to figure out the meaning of English words. Tom Striker was so sure he could not read and write that he called his wife's notes "cheat sheets" and refused to recognize his use of them as legitimate literacy activities.

It would appear that school experiences not only determine what "counts as being literate" but what counts as "learning" as well. This is consistent with a number of our findings and leads to possible explanation for some of the apparent gender-correlated differences we observed in individual attitudes toward literacy and illiteracy. It is probable that they also have their roots in earlier school experiences.

Gender-Related Literacy Distinctions

The Miller study strongly suggested that, for at least some in our society, male and female conceptions of illiteracy and literacy differed significantly. Two findings lead us to this suggestion. First, when talking about the reasons for seeking help in the literacy program, none of the men (with one possible exception) gave as their primary motivation the importance of being literate to succeed in the workplace. Their motivation was more personal, and, as I have suggested, related to the need for official redemption from school failure.

The women, on the other hand, said they wanted to be able to compete in the workplace. One declared with some vehemence that "literacy is everything in this country. Without being able to read and write, you are nothing." This suggests the possibility that being illiterate for these men meant seeing themselves as personal failures, although they were public successes. For these women, being illiterate translated into public failure; they were unable to get good-paying jobs.

Second, in describing their coping strategies, virtually every man referred to the importance of a woman in his life—a wife or a girl friend—in meeting some of his literacy-related needs (e.g., the cheat sheets Tom Striker's wife prepared for him). Another man who had to prepare staff evaluation reports would have a secretary fill out some of the forms and would bring the rest home for his wife to do. In some cases, the man's supervisor knew of his illiteracy and at least tacitly agreed to the arrangements that had been created. In other cases, the problem was carefully concealed with the man and his wife or girl friend colluding to help him maintain his self-respect in public.

Some of this activity was a predictable outcome of the prevailing ethos of the social class represented by these students. All came from rural or small-town settings. The traditional pattern was for women to stay at home as homemakers, and incidentally, take care of most of the family's official literacy needs—letter writing, bill paying, tax preparation, etc. The man's existence was much more public. He left the house daily for the workplace and routinely engaged in social intercourse with strangers. He probably felt much more keenly the need for maintaining public face. At any rate, the result was a complementarity of roles that involved, among many other things, a division of literacy-related tasks.

This particular study did not yield the data that might answer a number of questions raised by these findings. For example, we have no way of knowing whether or not the women's literacy skills did in fact surpass those of their men. It is entirely possible that they had histories of failure similar to that of the men but, since the exercise of their skills took place in private, there was less pressure to not reveal their deficiencies. Hence, they were more willing to read to their kids or write letters and fill out forms, even though these activities, if examined by outsiders, would be filled with "errors."

On the other hand, it is equally plausible that these women were more literate than their men. In fact, given what we know about differential paths of socialization into literacy afforded by schools, this would not be at all surprising. That middle- and upper-school girls are considered to be more verbal than their male peers has long been taken as axiomatic. That girls are subject at this age to different kinds of peer and family pressures is also obvious. For example, in many segments of society, being labeled a "reader" rather than a doer is viewed as a stigma for boys.

A second colleague with whom I am working with, Wheeler, has been looking at the literacy socialization of fourth-grade boys. She became intrigued (and a little concerned) when her son, who had been an avid reader until his fourth grade, suddenly "stopped reading." On checking with other mothers, she found out that all of them had the same concern. Her investigation revealed that the real issue was not a change in the *amount* of reading so much as a change in the *types* and *meaning* of the reading. This turns out to be the time that boys begin to assert their independence from their mothers, get deeply involved in peer activities, and begin to emulate their fathers.

It was true that the boys no longer read the books their mothers had provided for them (except when they were home sick), but they were avid readers of the sports page and of adventure, science fiction, mysteries, and choose-your-own-ending stories. What mothers read as a decline in reading was more a decline in sharing with the mother. Furthermore, if the boys did check out books from the library, the books were often those their friends had read. (In fact, it was common practice for the boys to check the slips in the back of books to see who had been reading them.) In many cases, there was little evidence that the boys read the books; they were more interested in signaling their "in-ness" with their peers.

For these boys, the social function of being literate was already beginning to take precedence over reading itself. Again, Wheeler's data said nothing about what was happening to girls in this age group. Presumably, they were continuing to share their literacy activities with their mothers.

It should be added that all of the boys in Wheeler's study were considered to be at least adequate students in school. None of them seemed to be having the negative experiences related by the adults in Miller's research. Nevertheless, they revealed the beginnings of the divergent paths of male and female socialization that contributes to the different notions of literacy exhibited in adult life.[3]

While the point of this discussion is simple, when literacy or being literate is

---

[3]It is tempting to discuss a parallel situation, often noted: The greater the success of men, the less literacy demands they encounter. Successful men are almost always supported by a cadre of women employees, one of whose main roles, it turns out, is to take care of literacy tasks. The implicit message, quite different from the overt appeals to become literate, is that literacy skills are only necessary for those aspiring to the more onerous jobs.

viewed as a social phenomenon, male and female definitions and functions vary widely; the implications for teaching and motivating students are significant. It would appear that a primary motivation for literacy for males has to do with the maintenance of public face and in adults, redemption from failure. For females, the appeal is the acquisition of skills enabling them to fill secondary support roles. In neither case, contrary to conventional wisdom, is the acquisition of literacy skills necessarily empowering.

Moreover, we begin to see how the much-discussed "literacy drop-off syndrome" may be simply a consequence in common school pedagogy.[4] Typically, this consists in teachers presenting material to students—sometimes orally and sometimes in written form. Students are then expected to publicly demonstrate their grasp of the material, again either through recitation or some type of written task, before they can proceed. This display is what counts as learning.

However, this public display may begin to entail increasing social cost for boys given the changed importance of peers and their concomitant increasing concern for "public face." For girls, the process appears to be quite different. This is not to suggest that they are not concerned with peer opinion but the particular manifestations this takes are apparently less out of line with the demands of school pedagogy.

CONCLUSIONS

This chapter consisted of two parts. The first sketched a set of assumptions and methodological principles that I found useful in approaching literacy as a social fact. The second discussed several of the issues raised by this approach. This particular format was designed both to raise issues for reflections and possible future research attention and to provide an example of an approach that I think yields important insights.

The major substantive claims can be easily summed up:

- From a social perspective, definitions of literacy itself are problematic. They can range from "certification of a successful school experience" to "the possession of skills needed for a better job."
- In the asessment of literacy, schools and the school experience, both for adults and for children, are of paramount importance. Both school certification and being taught are important.
- Literacy and illiteracy take on different meanings for males and for females. In some cases, these constitute an unequal complementarity. At least part of the differences involve the different personal and public roles played by males and females.

---

[4]The "literacy drop-off" syndrome refers to the phenomenon frequently noted at about the fourth grade when the literacy learning process presumably takes a turn. Up to this time, children are said to be learning to read and write, developing coding and encoding skills. Now there is a shift toward comprehension or to using literacy skills. At this point, many minority students and boys, even though they may have made steady progress as measured by standard ability tests, begin to show a leveling off.

- Socialization into these different roles can be documented in middle and later school years. This can at least partially account for the fourth grade literacy drop-off phenomena among boys and minorities.
- Although gender differences result in different motivations for becoming certified literate, in neither case does the real motivation appear to be one of empowering, contrary to much popular opinion.

REFERENCES

Fiering, S. (1981) Unofficial writing. In D.H. Hymes (Principal Investigator), *Ethnographic monitoring of children's acquisition of reading/language arts skills in and out of the classroom* (Final Report to the National Institute of Education). Washington, DC: National Institute of Education.

Gilmore, P. (1983). Spelling Mississippi: Recontextualizing a literacy-related speech event. *Anthropology and Education Quarterly, 14,* (4).

Gilmore, P. (1984). Sub-rosa skills: Assessing children's language. *Language Arts.*

Gilmore, P. (1986). Sub-rosa literacy: Peers, play and Ownership in Literacy acquisition. In B.B. Schieffelin & P. Gilmore (Eds.), *The acquisition of literacy: Ethnographic perspectives.* Norwood, NJ: Ablex.

Heath, S. (1982). What no bedtime story means. *Language in Society, 11,* (2).

Miller, K. (1985). *Functional Literacy: Why and what difference.* Unpublished Masters Thesis, University of Pennsylvania, Graduate School of Education.

Ogbu, J. (1984). Literacy in subordinate cultures. *Literacy in historical perspective.* Washngton, DC: Library of Congress.

Robinson, A. (1982). Observations on the environment and lifestyles of a declared non-reader and two declared readers. In D.M. Smith (Principal Investigator), *Using literacy outside of school: An ethnographic investigation* (Final Report to The National Institute of Education). Washington, DC: National Institute of Education.

Taylor, D. (1983). *Family literacy: Young children learning to read and write.* Exeter, NH: Heinemann Educational Books.

PART TWO

ACCESS AND DEFINITIONS OF LITERACY AND SCHOOL

4 Using Cohesion Analysis to Understand Access to Knowledge

James Collins

Temple University

Two things are of paramount concern, I think, to anyone studying literacy, language, and schooling. The first is the fact of systematic failure of many students to meet officially determined notions of minimal levels of skill, a failure which reaches catastrophic proportions among working-class and minority students. The second is the paradox that although there do not appear to be consistent class-related differences in language ability, there are consistent class-related differences in literacy ability.

The first of these concerns has stimulated research in the United States and Europe which has shown that differential achievement has significant social structural causes. This research conceptualizes schools as institutions for the social transmission of knowledge which grant differential access to knowledge and thus reinforce and reproduce existing social inequalities in society (Bowles & Gintis, 1976; Bourdieu, 1977). If we grant that curricula represent a framing of knowledge for transmission (Bernstein 1975), then we must also grant that curricula are not equally available to all students. This much is suggested both by large-scale studies of educational achievement and small-scale studies of particular schools, classrooms, and educational activities (see studies in Karabel & Halsey, 1977).

There are many reasons for this state of affairs. Several seem important in the United States. For one, there is conceptual disarray concerning curriculum for general skills such as literacy as well as for particular educational objectives such as social science education. The result is that there is tremendous variation from one school or school district to the next in time devoted to one subject or skill versus another (Goodlad, 1983). For another, curricula are put into practice within the context of institutions permeated with an ideology that some students are better (more educable) than others and with a tradition of grouping students according to putative ability. One result is that even with the same formal curriculum, the actual "curriculum-in-use" will differ greatly depending on whether a given school serves upper- or lower-class students (Anyon, 1981). Within particular schools there will be high- and low-ranked tracks, the former stressing academic excellence and the latter making do with academic mediocrity and failure. Individual classrooms, at least in the early primary years, will have ability groups in which judgments of ability are frequently confounded with facts of social background in the creation of inflexible aptitude classifications.

The relevance of this for classroom studies is that modern urban classrooms must be seen as complex social arenas in which the communicative demands and interactional "ground rules" of particular learning activities are influenced by the sociocultural diverssity of students, by classroom-specific ability grouping, and by school-wide tracking policies. Access to literacy-related activities in classrooms is determined by knowledge of how to participate in those activities as well as by the interactional history of teachers with individual students and groups of students, a history influenced by ability classifications. If classroom research is to provide insight into the evolving relations between language use and literacy that ends either (a) in the progressive practice and command of literate discourse conventions or (b) the progressive alienation from and failure to become proficient in those same conventions, then it must be situated within a framework that attends both to the wider social processes by which classroom organization is affected and to the communicative/interactive bases of learning activities.

This brings us to the second concern—why there are consistent class-related differences in literacy ability but not in language ability. One might argue that there is no significant connection between the two skills. But reading, for example, is clearly a form of language use, and high correlations have been found between reading ability and language skills such as vocabulary, tests of grammatical knowledge, and metalinguistic awareness (see Snow, 1983, p. 166, and citations therein.) The question remains: If we find few social class differences in language ability, then why are there social class differences in literacy skills such as reading?

One approach which informs the research reported in this chapter seeks to identify some aspects of children's conversational strategies which seem to affect their acquisition of literacy skills, whether those of writing or reading. But it does so by locating such analysis in a framework which takes into account both the complex microenvironments of the typical classroom and the larger political forces which shape the school *qua* institution.

A major problem facing such research is how to conceptualize the relation between spoken and written language so as to determine whether there are major differences of linguistic form between spoken and written discourse, and further, what such formal differences might reflect about the essential differences of communicative situation in the two modes. This field has been of considerable interest to linguists for some time (e.g., Tannen, 1982). Early research concerning formal differences between spoken and written language was based on counts of lexical items and syntactic constructions. It argued that written language is more studied and complex, while spoken language is less studied, more simple, and direct. More recent research suggests that there are not hard and fast distinctions between spoken and written language. The communicative tasks of speakers and writers and the communicative events within which the spoken or written language occurs have more telling consequences for language form than does modality per se. So, for example, a technical discussion between two academics is likely to have more formal complexity than a casual letter exchanged between old friends; a formal petition compared with a casual chat will show the stereotyped relation between linguistic form (complex:simple) and modality (written:spoken).

The central reason that formal differences exist between the different modalities is that language users tailor their phrasing according to their estimates of their audience's ability to make particular inferences which depend on knowledge of both language and the real world (Green & Morgan, 1982). Since there are always situational constraints (audiences both real and imagined which must be taken into account), it is hard to find standards of comparison for spoken and written language. It is not the same, for example, as comparing the structure of two languages or even as comparing two literary genres. However, in the case of written versus spoken communication there are channel constraints, that is, conditions on communicative form which are derivable from the nature of the medium, conditions of which both writers and readers must become aware. If we consider for a moment what is involved in a speaker or writer estimating an audience's ability to make inferences, we regain an appreciation of the basic communicative differences in spoken and written language. For one, in written language there is little information about intonation. For another, there is no gestural or kinetic information. Last, there is no immediate feedback—no way of telling if the audience agrees or disagrees, follows the arguments, or has lost the point. Although this state of affairs is well known and frequently mentioned, especially by people concerned with writing, the linguistic and educational consequences are less well documented. But ethnographic evidence shows that linguistic problems, resulting from the different linguistic and discourse skills required in shifting from spoken to written modes, are frequently identified by the school system as problems of basic reasoning ability (Gumperz, Simons, & Cook-Gumperz, 1981).

Given these basic situational differences, what are important shared features of speaking and writing, whatever the communicative task? One shared feature is that in order to comprehend a discourse, a listener or reader must be able to perceive how one utterance or stretch of texts relates to what came before. Speakers and writers must somehow signal the relations, and when ways of signaling connections are not shared, the perception of a discourse as coherent and comprehensible usually breaks down. But little research comparing spoken and written language has focused on the ways in which connective ties between parts of a discourse are signaled. As we shall see, these issues are also germane to the study of reading.

In examining the form and communicative demands of spoken and written language, it is useful to distinguish, as Snow (1983) argued, between *strict literacy*— any activity or skill associated with the use of print—and *literatelike oral discourse*—speech characterized by explicitness of reference, a reliance on syntactic and lexical cues rather than intonational or gestural signals, and discourse-internal cohesiveness. These latter characteristics are all traits which make a message less dependent on the context of speaking (or participants' shared "historical context") for its interpretation. Snow argued that the ability to decontextualize print—to see it as part of a larger communicative system and not rely on immediate or recent historical context when "reading" or "writing"—was a skill that is developed late in literacy development, just as the ability to contextualize speech is a complex skill acquired late in language acquisition. Both are also skills acquired through collaborative exchanges between children and adults, whether shaping an oral discourse or learning the communicative conventions of written discourse as a reader or writer.

If we return now to our earlier discussion of curricula, a pertinent question would be this: Given the structure of the typical school day, for students of a given age, where do children encounter activities which allow them to practice literacy skills—the decontextualization of print media, whether as reader or writer, and the way of speaking associated with such decontextualization? We might phrase this differently: In what ways does curriculum-in-use determine the contexts in which students and teachers will meet for these pedagogical purposes, and further, in what ways do the specifics of classroom practice have longer time consequences for student achievement?

It was to answer these general questions that various of the following researches were undertaken. In describing this work I will very briefly summarize the early Berkeley research (Gumperz, Simons, & Cook-Gumperz 1981; Michaels, 1981; Collins, 1982, 1986; Michaels & Collins, 1984) and then focus on a more recent school and community investigation.

THE BERKELEY STUDIES

The Berkley studies were undertaken as part of a 2-year cooperative investigation of language use in a variety of school and nonschool settings. A major goal of this work was to examine whether sociocultural differences in discourse style influenced classroom activities and, if so, what the long-term implications for access to learning opportunities were.

Work by Sarah Michaels (1981) had shown ways in which mismatches in terms of general expectations about the structure of a narrative and in use of intonational formulas resulted in disharmonious student-teacher exchanges and lessened opportunity for some students to practice a decontextualized "literate style" of discourse during first-grade sharing time (also known as "show and tell") sessions.

The Narrative Study

In a later study Michaels and myself (Michaels & Collins, 1984) set up a naturalistic but controlled narrative elicitation procedure which allowed us to obtain oral narratives from black working-class students, who tended to have trouble during sharing time, as well as from white middle-class students, who tended to do well during sharing time. As part of the experiment we also collected both oral and written narratives from fourth-grade students from the same social backgrounds. We analyzed the oral and written narratives to see how speakers (and writers) established and maintained reference to major characters in their narratives.

We found that the black students used syntactic and intonational cues differently from their white counterparts. The former used a special prosodic cue—vowel elongation and rise-fall contours—to signal definiteness when reintroducing characters and, further, they were significantly less likely to use falling intonation contours at the ends of syntactic sentences. The white students, conversely, relied on a syntactic option—relative clauses—to maintain identity of reference (that is, to show that two mentions of a character were "the same") and, further, they were significantly more likely to use falling contours at the ends of syntactic sentences. Both groups of narrators delivered fluent, coherent, and stylistically complex discourses; both styles were communicatively effective, but they made different interpretive demands on an audience. Whereas the narratives of white, middle-class students required only general knowledge of English lexica and syntax, those of the black students required in addition knowledge of a particular prosodic cue—vowel elongation and rise-fall contour—used to signal "definite."

The eduational significance of these discourse differences is that in learning the strategies of discursive prose these latter students (and others like them) will have to learn a new convention for signaling cohesive ties between successive mentions of a character—or risk being labeled "incoherent" or "hard to follow." As Michaels's study showed, this use of prosody to maintain thematic connections also had direct implications for classroom interaction during the sharing time sessions.

The Classroom Study

This narrative study and Michaels' findings suggested that it might be profitable to explore links between the differences in strategies used for signaling thematic cohesion in narratives and the question of how language use affects access to other learning opportunities. I undertook such a study as part of the same ethnographic project but focusing on the issue of access to classroom reading instruction (for fuller dicussion, see Collins, 1986). The study examined the interaction of teaching techniques and communicative styles in first-grade reading groups in an integrated classroom. The high-ranked reading group was composed of white students from middle-class backgrounds and the low-ranked group of black students from working-class backgrounds. The primary research question was to discover the extent to which the learning opportunities that students encountered were influenced by two variables: (a) the ability groups into which students were placed; and (b) communicative background, as gauged by sociocultural background and analysis of oral narratives. The groups were audiotaped during reading lessons with the same teacher at different points during the year.

Analysis showed that different instruction strategies were used with the two groups. The difference consisted of an emphasis on decoding skills—for example, learning phono-grapheme correspondences and vocabulary words in isolation—versus an emphasis on comprehension skills—for example, drawing inferences from the text and learning the conventions of expressive intonation. The distinct emphases were obvious in the earliest days of the year and continued throughout the year, regardless of the difficulty of the text being read. Such differences are reported by many studies of reading instruction in urban schools, especially in those cases where ability-grouping works to segregate socioculturally diverse classroom populations (Allington, 1980; Gumperz & Herasimchuk, 1972; McDermott, 1976). Table 1 presents the percentage of time spent in phono-grapheme and vocabulary drill versus the amount of time spent reading aloud and discussing connected text. It is based on a sample of 16 lessons taken from the beginning, middle, and end of the school year.

In addition to the survey summarized in Table 1, four lessons were selected in

Table 1. Percentage of Time Spent on Decoding and Comprehension

Group	Decoding (%)	Comprehension (%)
High	17	70
Low	47	37

which the same teacher worked with high-ranked and low-ranked students reading from texts of similar complexity. Detailed analysis of these lessons—of the prosodic characteristics of students' reading and of the nature and timing of teacher's questions and students' responses—revealed several things. First, students in the two groups used different intonational strategies when reading aloud. Although both read in a staccato fashion, the staccato quality was more emphatic with low-ranked readers; high-ranked readers were more likely to use falling intonation contours at the ends of sentences. Second, the teacher responded to the two reading styles differently, treating what was objectively the same behavior—a mispronunciation or a hesitation—in different ways. She would give low-ranked readers phono-grapheme and vocabulary cues, but she would provide high-ranked readers with syntactic and semantic cues and with models of how a sentence or longer passage sounded.

The differing strategies seemed to result in part from interactional history: that is, the teacher's early and consistent emphasis on decoding drill contributed to a staccato word-by-word reading style among low-ranked readers. There was evidence, however, drawn from the analysis of oral narratives, that the use of prosody in reading was related to other aspects of oral discourse. In particular, high-ranked readers tended to place tonal nuclei at the ends of clauses, near tone group boundaries. Low-ranked readers, on the other hand, tended to place tonal nuclei in the middle of clauses, away from boundaries (cf. Collins & Michaels, 1986; Michaels & Kadar, 1981, for further discussion of this narrative style).

Both ways of organizing narrative discourse are communicatively effective, but they sound different. The high group talked in such a way that sentence boundaries were more easily discerned by the casual adult listener. Additionally, their habit of placing tonal nuclei clause-finally translated more easily into the use of falling intonation on sentence-final words when reading aloud. It sounded proficient, even when the reading performance was broken and halting, because it was easier to hear the sentence boundaries. Conversely, the low-ranked readers' habit of placing nuclei in mid-clause translated less easily into the use of falling intonation on sentence-final words when reading aloud. It sounded less proficient, because it was difficult to hear the sentence boundaries in the text being read aloud.

Whatever the causes, the differences in instructional emphasis and student reading style began early and continued throughout the year. Low-ranked readers thus received little practice in applying their knowledge of spoken language to the task of reading. And, as much experimental research has shown, a key trait distinguishing good from poor readers is that good readers expect a text to be meaningful. They expect it to somehow fit with what they already know about the workings of their language and of the world. Poor readers, on the other hand, lack such expectations (cf. Canney & Winograd, 1979, for a review).

THE CHICAGO STUDY

In acquiring and mastering the skills of literacy, young students must gain access to situations which allow them to learn and practice a variety of interpretive skills under the guidance of an adult. How the language used by students and teachers influences the learning opportunities to which children gain access was the concern of the two studies just summarized. In the remainder of this chapter I will discuss a study which tried to build upon this to develop a fuller account of the relations between language use, instructional strategies, and ability grouping. In this latter study we will be dealing with similar issues but in a different situation. The research was undertaken in order to refine communicative, social background, and pedagogical variables and to test hypotheses about the importance of discourse style and ability grouping on classroom interaction.

In designing the following study, I tried to achieve classroom ecological validity, a working sense of extraclassroom school processes that might impinge on the classroom, some control of classroom-independent measures of discourse skills, and a sense of the wider community from which the students were drawn. The study was accordingly longitudinal. It combined weekly classroom observation and audiotaping of reading lessons over a 4-month period, parent and community interviewing, and use of traditional tests and a narrative experiment to assess reading and discourse skills.

The field research was conducted at a public school in Chicago that served an inner-city minority neighborhood on the city's southside. In order to have comparative material which would also permit intensive conversational analysis, two classrooms were selected, a second-grade class and a third-grade class. There were different teaching styles and student characteristics, but reading levels were approximately the same and turn-allocation procedures were identical for both high-ability and low-ability groups in both classes.[1] Lessons were observed and audiotaped on a weekly basis, the tapes serving as the basis for later analysis. In addition to audiotapes, notes were kept in a journal for each observed lesson. They indicated such things as the physical layout of the reading group vis-á-vis the re-

---

[1]The second-grade classroom was "high track" and relatively homogeneous in terms of ability and family background: the class reading mean was above grade level; the low-ability and high-ability groups' means were relatively high and close together; the family income and education levels were relatively high and close together. The third-grade class was "low track" and relatively heterogeneous: the class reading mean was below grade level; the low-ability and high-ability groups were far apart on reading scores; parental income and educational measures were dissimilar. But the classrooms were reading at about the same level: The high-ability groups in both rooms were reading from the same level-eight text in Xerox Ginn 700 series; and the low-ability groups were reading from adjacent-level texts (second grade at level six; third grade at level five). See Collins (1983) for more discussion.

mainder of the classroom, the procedure used in assigning reading turns, disruptions caused to the groups by other class members, and observable indications of attention or inattention on the part of teachers or students.

In order to obtain various independent measures of students' reading and discourse skills, subject scores on the reading section of the Iowa Test of Basic Skill were analyzed as was skill at establishing and maintaining reference in a narrative experiment.

The research setting differed from the Berkeley study in a number of ways. In this earlier study the school was integrated and ability grouping followed the ethnic and class divisions of the student population: High-ranked readers were from white middle-class backgrounds; low-ranked readers were from black working-class backgrounds. The study focused on one classroom and found that important differences in instructional style correlated with differences in discourse style. In the Chicago study the school was in an inner-city minority community. All students were black and from working-class or lower-middle-class backgrounds. There were correlations between social class and ability ranking, but not the striking differences seen in the Berkeley study, where race and class were compounded. The study looked at two classrooms whose students were drawn from slightly different backgrounds; the second-grade classroom had a more homogeneous mix of slightly more affluent students; the third-grade classroom had a more heterogeneous mix of relatively affluent and poor students. The teachers in the study shared an instructional focus on comprehension but differed in other aspects of their teaching style. Because of these differences, there was a shift in research emphasis from the effects of sociocultural differences in discourse style to the effects of ability grouping on classroom interaction.

Previous Approaches to the Study of Classroom Discourse

Two of the best-known early attempts to analyze classroom communication are those of Flanders (1970) and Bellack, Kleibard, Hyman, and Smith (1966). In both the goal was to analyze instructional conversation in terms of frequency of interaction categories. The categories were defined in terms of affective variables (Flanders) or a model of language games (Bellack et al.). Although both frameworks were used extensively in the 1960s and 1970s, neither has achieved its primary goal: characterizing effective versus ineffective teaching styles (Barr & Dreeben, 1975; Doyle, 1977; Rosenshine, 1971). More pertinent to this discussion, neither approach actually concerned itself with the organization of *conversation* (Green, 1977; Griffin & Humphry, 1977; Sinclair & Coulthard, 1975). Because both approaches concentrated on small discourse units—the equivalent of question-answer pairs—neither developed a conception of discourse beyond what was essentially a two-part stimulus-response model.

More recent work, developing out of the ethnomethodological study of conversation and the microethnographic study of classroom lessons, has provided a general account of classroom communication. This research shows that classroom discourse is characterized by (a) power and knowledge asymmetries; (b) a basic tripartite interaction sequence; and (c) a larger organization into lesson phases. These traits distinguish it from other types of naturally occurring conversation.

As Sacks, Schlegoff, and Jefferson (1974) have shown, the sine qua non of conversation is turn-taking: in conversation speaker-change occurs, at least once. This requires some conventional procedure for allocating turns at speaking. Although the articulation of verbal and nonverbal signals in turn allocation in so-called normal conversation is extremely complex (cf. Duncan, 1972; Sacks et al., 1974), turn allocation has a basic equality. As long as their contributions are timely and relevant, participants can "bid" for the right to speak.

Conversation in classrooms, however, is not symmetrical. Typically there is one teacher who assigns turns at speaking and a host of students who must know whether, when, and how to bid for a turn at speaking. This asymmetry reflects differences in the social power of actors. Teachers know more than students and are expected to control students' activities (McHoul, 1978). This power and knowledge differential underlies another fundamental distinguishing characteristic of classroom discourse, the tripartite "elicitation sequence" (Mehan, 1979).

The sequence consists of three sequential acts: initiation, reply, and evaluation. An example can be seen below.

1. T: Johnny, tell me something about the bunny.
2. C: It can run and hop.
3. T: Very good, it can run and hop.

In line one the teacher selects a respondee and elicits information (initiation); in line two the student replies; in line three the teacher positively evaluates the response.

In lessons these tripartite exchange structures are organized into topically related sequences. These can vary in length and complexity, depending on instructional plan and the exigencies of students' responses. The topically related sequences are concentrated in the instructional phrase of the three lesson phases—the introduction, instructional phase, and conclusion—which together comprise the lesson, the largest level of instructional discourse.

The power relations and hierarchical framework I have just described—teacher control of turn allocation, a tripartite cycle of elicitation-reply-evaluation; and three phases comprising a lesson—have been reported in classroom studies in the United States (Au, 1980; Johnson, 1979; Mehan, 1979; Griffin & Humphry, 1978; Philips, 1972), Britain (Barnes, 1976; Sinclair & Coulthard, 1975), Australia (Malcolmn, 1977), France (Anderson-Levitt, 1981), French schools on Tibuai (Levin, 1977), and Western-influenced schools in the Philippines (Campbell, 1981) and Papua New Guinea (Miller-Souviney, 1981). It is thus a transnational, institution-specific organization of discourse.

But by its very generality such a model gives only the abstract form of instructional conversation. In order to understand how participants assess the pedagogical and interactional demands of a particular message, one must investigate how activities are contextualized. Contextualization is related to coherence because knowledge of context is part of the knowledge used in coherence judgments. In contextualizing discourse, speakers use linguistic cues, background knowledge, and extralinguistic context to assess the social activity in which they are involved and the communicative intentions of others (Gumperz, 1982a). In classrooms there are formulaic utterances (''Let's get out our English books'') which are contextualized cues signaling the start of a given activity. Further, within a given activity there are signals for various phases. Consider, for example, the group reading lesson.

At a statement from the teacher such as ''All right, I want to meet with the group in *Feelings*'' (name of a basal text), part of the class separates into a special activity group. The remaining students continue at their independent activity, with very little talking. There may be a few minutes of introductory talk by the teacher, connecting the current lesson to a preceding lesson or apprising students of special projects. The teacher usually then pauses, says ''OK'' or ''All right,'' and faces a particular student, whom she calls on to read. This act initiates the group reading; henceforth, turns at reading are assigned by the teacher, frequently wordlessly, and a series of questions are asked of individuals and the group after each turn at reading aloud. Topically related sequences are usually bound by a formulaic ''OK,'' ''All right,'' and a pause. In determining the boundaries of lesson phases and of topically related sequences, students must attend to formulaic utterances as well as prosody. The teacher's questions frequently presuppose both the text and preceding talk (as attested by remarks such as ''Karl, we're not on that page yet''). In assessing the referential antecedents and illocutionary intent of a given utterance, students must be aware of several stages of contextualization processes (Green, 1977), one setting off their current activity from the larger classroom, another determining position within the series of turns at reading aloud and answering questions that each lesson devolves into, another being the immediate antecedent and apparent purpose of the utterance. As will be shown, turn violations and lack of shared interpretation of topic are two salient features distinguishing interaction during low-ranked lessons from interaction during high-ranked lessons.

Bearing in mind the foregoing account of classroom discourse and the importance of conventions for establishing what activity and phase of an activity is relevant at a given time, let us now turn to the analysis of classroom materials. I will focus first on the instructional variable of teaching style, discussing differences and similarities between the two teachers in the study, and then examine the question of how ability grouping influences interaction during reading lessons. Later, the question of possible differences in discourse strategies is discussed together with standardized measures of reading skills.

Teaching Styles: Differences and Similarities
The teachers' instructional styles differed in several ways that have been shown to influence student reading achievement, especially when the novice learners are speakers of Black English Vernacular (BEV). The teachers differed in their response to and ability to use dialect during instructional exchanges. They also differed in their use of what Durkin (1979) has called comprehension preparing versus comprehension assessing questions. Finally, they differed in the average amount of time spent in low-ability versus high-ability lessons.

Dialect Attitudes and Code Switching The instructor in the second-grade classroom was an experienced black teacher who was quite adept at code switching. Although she typically spoke a rather elegant version of Standard English and used vocabulary one might consider complex for 7-year-olds, she also switched registers into dialect when discussing texts with students. A few examples should suffice to give the reader a sense of the stylistic shifts.

The following conversational segment shows register shifting. It occurs during a discussion of the meaning of *horrified* and *terrified*. After several definitions have been offered, a student suggested a synonym:

1. C1:   Shocked
2. T: OK.
3. C2:   "Shocked" is— . . . "shocked" is real scared?
4. T: Yes, we sometimes become terrified. You can't
5.   um . . . you abandon your faculties . . .
6.   you can't get yourself together . . . you're in shock.

Note the shift from ornate phrasing "abandon your faculties" to colloquial "get yourself together," a Black English Vernacular idiom.

As might be expected of a teacher who is willing to shift language varieties, this teacher did not correct BEV pronunciation, unless it appeared to affect reading. But the teacher did spend considerable time distinguishing phono-grapheme correspondences that might be difficult for young speakers of BEV. After a reader had confused *scowled* and *scold,* and another had pronounced scold as "sco'd" (with characteristic -*l*- deletion), the teacher spent considerable time contrasting the vowels in the two words and their meaning.

The teacher in the third-grade classroom, who was a young white woman, was officially opposed to BEV. Her opinion, shared by many prominent black educators (cf. Hentoff, 1982; Labov, 1982), was that BEV was an educational and social hindrance that should be corrected when possible. This sentiment was expressed to me during an afterclass discussion and put into practice in corrections in the following example. This example shows BEV consonant metathesis in the form *aks* for *ask.* The student is reading and the teacher corrects:

1. C: " . . . for goodness sake why? aksd Olive—"
2. T: *asked*
3. C: *aksd* _____ Olive Owl."

We should note that the student does not seem to understand the correction. That the teacher's utterance is a correction is a judgment on my part, based on what the teacher said about dialect, on other corrections made, and on the salience of *aks* as a marker of BEV. We should note that this is not a case where the student has failed to recognize or has misperceived a word in the text. Instead, this is a common word being read in the vernacular. The student responds to the teacher's utterance by correcting her stress, that is, by mimicking the teachers' stress pattern. That the student does not understand the full pragmatic import of the teacher's utterance (glossable as something like: "Do not say *aksd,* say *asked*; that is, permute the *s* and the *k*") is perfectly understandable and fully consistent with other dialect studies showing that young dialect speakers systematically turn features of Standard English into Black English Vernacular in translation and mimicry tasks (Labov, 1972). The third-grade teacher, of course, never shifted to Black English Vernacular when instructing.

Question Strategy: Preparing Versus Assessing   The second-grade instructor used a different questioning strategy than did the third-grade teacher. She used a comprehensive preparing strategy. First, at the beginning of each lesson, she taught a subset of the official lesson plan's recommended vocabulary. Second, before each student's turn at reading aloud, she elicited information about the passage to be read, which students were to silently read and discover. This sometimes involved precise directions for what to look for.

1. T: Now I want you to read the last part of this page
2.   with your eyes . . . I want you to tell me . . . at this
3.   time . . . how does Timothy's father feel?

As Durkin (1979) argued, such comprehension preparation is extremely rare in classroom instruction, though it seems one of the most effective strategies for encouraging meaning-directed approaches to text processing. We should note that it also causes double reading, once silently and once aloud.

The third-grade teacher provided less stage setting. She covered vocabulary as it arose during the reading—not before the beginning of each lesson, as prescribed by the curriculum guide. In questioning she used a comprehension assessing strategy, asking questions after students had read aloud. This strategy, while providing the instructor with information about how well the students understood the lesson, would not provide students with an anticipatory overview of what was to be read nor would it cause double reading.

Time Spent in Lesson   The second-grade teacher spent slightly more time in the low-group lessons. This is unusual. The mean lesson time is given in Table 2.

The differences are not significant, of course; what is striking is the evenhandedness of treatment. It is more common for less time to be spent in low-group lessons (Eder, 1981; McDermott, 1978; Rist, 1970). The third-grade teacher followed the common pattern. She spent less average time in low-group lessons.

This teacher was frank about the reasons for the difference. She had to teach and control a large and diverse group of children. Working with the high group required

Table 2.   Average Minutes per Lesson by Groups

Group	Low	High
Class two[a]	21[c]	20
Class three[b]	24	33

[a]Sample of 12 lessons.
[b]Sample of 14 lessons.
[c]Figures rounded to nearest minute.

less effort and provided more enjoyment, while teaching the low group required extra effort. Such a decision is not atypical, as the studies cited earlier indicate. It is, in fact, reinforced by job evaluation procedures. Teachers know that their performance is evaluated on the basis of students' achievement scores and, by implication, that their time is most efficiently spent working with high-ranked, fast-learning students (see Anyon, 1981; Leacock, 1969; and Schwarz, 1981, for more discussion of the reasoning and practice).

While these style differences certainly contribute to the differential achievement discussed later, their importance should not be exaggerated; or, more precisely, their malleability should not be overestimated. The ability to shift subtly between two distinct language varieties is a sociolinguistic skill that cannot be easily taught. As I have argued, the less time spent in low-group lessons in the third-grade classroom is the normal practice, more the result of administrative policy, time pressure, and personnel evaluation procedure than any individual proclivity to favor certain kinds of students (Eder 1986). While the difference in questioning strategies does seem to confer an advantage on the second-grade teacher, additional research with more careful controls over socioeconomic background and skill diversity would be necessary to better assess the importance of this aspect of instructional procedure. Teaching styles are part of a larger whole. School-wide tracking decision, district-wide funding policies, and the sociocultural background of students are all aspects of the complex social arena that is the modern urban classroom. To modify teaching styles without considering the other forces that impinge on the classroom would be a superficial reform at best.

Similarities in Teaching   Despite the differences described earlier, there were important similarities in the instructional styles of the two teachers and in the way the organization of instruction differed when ability group lessons were contrasted.

Both teachers used what can be characterized as a comprehension-oriented teaching style. Their emphasis was on word definition and supraword text meaning rather than on decoding drill (phono-grapheme correspondences and simple word identification). This was the approach prescribed in the basal reading series. Although one teacher followed the basal instruction plan more closely and discussed vocabulary before the lesson, both discussed special vocabulary items as they occurred in the text.

In the second-grade and third-grade classroom, turn-taking was organized in an identical round-robin fashion for both high and low groups. Both teachers bounded each turn at reading with a set of questions concerned with text comprehension.

However, there was a clear sign of lessened instructional complexity when the high-ranked and low-ranked lessons were compared. In each classroom, framing remarks occurred at the introduction of the lesson and consisted of information from the teacher providing a brief synopsis of what the lesson was about. When introductory framing remarks were omitted, it was from the lessons of low-ranked readers. The reasons for lessening instructional complexity probably lie in the realm of ability group effects on learning contexts, to which we now turn.

Grouping Effects in Classroom Discussions

An important part of the organization of most early primary classrooms is the ability group. As I have argued elsewhere (Collins, 1983), ability grouping may be seen as one part of the school's response to skill diversity. The ostensible justification for ability grouping is that it permits instruction to be tailored to student aptitude and that, being flexible, it can be adjusted to the given student population and to changes in that population. In practice it represents a very inflexible classifying procedure, permitting little movement into or out of groups once ability status has been assigned. Recent reviews by Eder (1983) and Rosenbaum (1980) discuss the lack of fit between individual aptitude and ability grouping. They report that variance in measurable aptitude accounts for less than one fifth of the variance in ability group assignment. Variables such as socioeconomic background and classroom size are more important in determining placement. Typically, teachers and administrators believe in the necessity and effectiveness of ability grouping, despite accumulating evidence to the contrary. In short, ability grouping represents a powerful and rigid classifying procedure which restricts mobility, because groups are not added, deleted, or changed, despite initial or subsequent heterogeneity of student aptitude. Although initial grouping may be based on measurement and teacher evaluation, it is an enduring classification that is insensitive to individual ability differences that may develop in children as they mature, and it creates learning styles that children have trouble escaping from.

Students who are perceived as less prepared or less attentive in early primary grades are grouped together as of low ability. These decisions are made when children are 5 and 6 years old, an age when "ability" is very difficult to determine. Once ranked, low-ability students are given different instruction from their high-ranked counterparts. The difference is due in part to teacher expectations but also to the organization of activity. Microethnographic studies of reading groups have shown that in low-ranked lessons there is more apparent inattention and distraction (both from inside and outside the groups), with the result that less time is spent actually reading, even when equal time is allocated to lessons in the two groups. Thus, students most likely to have difficulty learning are assigned to groups where the social context is much less conducive to learning. There are clear and well-known effects on achievement.

The picture I have drawn so far is one in which an ideology regarding the classification of aptitude results in a social organization of classroom activity such that learning contexts differ radically for students classified in different ways. In particular, in low-ranked groups there seems to be less sustained attention to actual reading. Attention in groups is a social accomplishment; it is signaled through verbal and nonverbal cues and maintained through sanctions. The giving and receiving of sustained attention requires that participants in a communicative encounter be involved—that is, that they share some sense of the purpose of the communicative encounter and that they pay one another sufficient heed for the exchange of relevant information (Goffman, 1972; Gumperz, 1982a). However, as Goffman (1963) has pointed out, having to manage attention during an interaction is itself a form of inattention. It is a departure from the central purpose of an encounter so as to create or maintain the necessary conditions for an encounter. In educational activities, time spent managing attention is time not spent teaching or learning.

Measures: Turn Disruption, Uptake, and Coherence   In what follows, I will try to tease out some of the ways differential attention affects verbal communication in classroom lessons by examining the relations between turn disruption, local conversational uptake, and global patterns of referential coherence. The data for the analysis are taken from reading lessons in the second-grade and third-grade classrooms described earlier.

In each classroom, the lessons consisted of an introduction in which the teacher would link the current lesson to preceding lessons and perhaps discuss vocabulary. This was followed by the instructional phase consisting of a variable number of *reading turns,* in which one student read aloud, and *question turns,* in which all students in a group were asked questions about a passage which had just been read. Question turns consisted of a variable number of questions, usually comprising several topically related sequences. Questions were treated as part of elicitation-reply-evaluation sequences. The lesson ended with a concluding phase, consisting of instructions for seatwork or an announcement of the next story to be read.

When a sample of 26 lessons was examined, it turned out that less average time was spent in low-ranked lessons (see Table 2). More important, it appeared that low-ranked readers had less access to comprehension practice (i.e., drill and instruction aimed at sentential and intersentential meaning). It is to be distinguished from decoding practice which is drill and instruction aimed at identification of phono-grapheme correspondences and word recognition.

Differing access to comprehension practice is significant because comprehension lies at the heart of the current literacy crisis. Although decoding and comprehension skills are both essential for competent reading, the former are taught more effectively to all students, regardless of social background (Rosenshine, 1971). Additionally, it is precisely when text comprehension becomes an important part of standardized achievement testing—that is, from the third grade onward—that working-class and minority students begin to fall behind their middle-class counterparts (Ogbu, 1978). In short, it is in the realm of comprehension that social class effects on literacy skills (not language skills) become manifest. I would like to suggest, tentatively, that it is by focusing on episodes of apparent comprehension practice that we can draw the most plausible connections between the nature of communication in the classroom and what is known about the text-comprehension strategies of the skilled reader.

In order to get a better idea why there was less comprehension practice during low-ranked reading, eight lessons were analyzed in detail. As noted earlier, I focused on turn disruption, local uptake, and global referential coherence.

The first, *turn disruption,* was defined in terms of the incidence of turn violations and management acts. The model of reading assumed by this measure was that of the normative order of classroom lessons with the teacher assigning turns. In the instructional phase of reading lessons only one student reads aloud at a time. The teacher may correct errors, but the other students follow silently in their books. *Turn violations* consisted primarily of "calling out" answers. This occurs when one or more students correct the oral reading performance of another student by calling out the answer when the oral reader makes a mistake or hesitates. It has negative effects because it eliminates the opportunity for self-correction, which is an essential aspect of learning to read. In a recent comparative survey, Allington (1983) reported that allowing more calling out during low-ranked lessons was a common and damaging practice in most classrooms. Turn violation also consisted of unsolicited reading aloud, that is, when one student reads aloud during another student's reading turn. It has the negative effect of distracting both other students and the teacher.

Management acts were defined as verbal attempts by the teacher to keep or recall student attention or ward off external distractions. Management acts lessen attention because they distract the instructor from monitoring oral reading and probing comprehensive, and further, distract the students from the text being read or the question on the floor. Microethnographic studies of classrooms have shown that there is a higher incidence of managing behavior in low-ranked lessons (Eder, 1981). McDermott (1978) reported that one-third less time was spent actually reading in low-ranked lessons.

The second measure, *uptake,* was defined in terms of overt, zero-anaphoric, or paraphrastic incorporation of a student's answers into a subsequent question (examples of each type of incorporation are discussed later). There are two preconditions for uptake. First, the student's answer has to make an original contribution rather than simply paraphrase what the teacher has said. Second, that original contribution must be incorporated into the subsequent *question* and not be merely acknowledged by the teacher. What this measure attempts to get at is the local linkage of topically related sequences. In terms of the "elicitation cycle" already discussed, we are looking at the referential and illocutionary ties between a reply and a subsequent elicitation. As I use it, the notion of uptake is restricted to two consecutive speaker turns. It is thus focused on a contextually restricted class of what might be called initiations of dialogue—the beginning of a dialogue about the student's understanding of a text—rather than mere isolated questions intended to assess but not necessarily stimulate understanding. Recent studies in the process-product paradigm of educational psychology have shown that teacher uptake of student's answers is a complex but important variable in classroom interaction, one which correlates positively with reaching achievement (Green, 1977; Piestrup, 1973).

The third measure, referential *coherence,* was defined in terms of processes interfering with the establishment and maintenance of reference to topics during question turns. (Question turns, as noted previously, followed a turn at reading aloud and consisted of a series of questions about the text directed to all members of the group.) Special attention was paid to instances of potentially ambiguous shifts in reference. These occurred when topics were introduced or brought into focus with pronouns that could have more than one antecedent, given available discourse information. As will be discussed, examination of such potentially ambiguous shifts provides insight into the sorts of discourse knowledge participants in a conversation seem to draw upon when interpreting a stretch of talk.

Findings Let us now look at the findings on all three measures. A total of 8 lessons were analyzed out of 26 observed: one lesson from the beginning and end of the study period for the low groups and high groups from the second- and third-grade classrooms. This gave a corpus of approximately 3½ hours of conversation and reading. In the tables, numbers of instance, N, are listed in the left columns; mean averages, expressed in events per minute, are in the right columns. The rows key the groups, for class two (second grade) and class three (third grade).

A comparison of high groups with low groups for indices of *turn disruption*, showed that in the high lessons turn violations occurred 0.45 times per min, while in the low lessons they occurred 1.44 times per min—that is, three times as frequently. Comparing groups for management acts, in the high lessons there were 0.29 per min, while in low lessons there were 0.67 per min—that is, they were more than twice as frequent. These differences, summarized in Table 3, are significant even without tests for intervariable effects.

The findings on turn violations indicated that low-ranked students had less of an opportunity to engage in self-monitoring and self-correction, and further, that some form of inattention or disruption occurred twice as frequently during their reading. In short, the act of reading was granted less dignity.

The measure of local *uptake* was whether questions incorporated any part of an immediately preceding answer. This is a simple formal measure of teacher uptake and indicates where there is at least referential continuity between a response and a subsequent question. As is shown in Table 4, in the high lessons 49% of all questions incorporated an immediately preceding answer, while in the low lessons only 39% did so.

Although I have not performed statistical tests for significance on this measure, the different amount of uptake seems important. Greater uptake of student responses is pedagogically beneficial, because it involves teacher-guided expansion of student

Table 3. Measures of Turn Disruption

Group	Turn violations		Management acts	
	N/min	Per min.	N/min	Per min.
Class two				
High	16/39	.41	11/39	.28
Low	61/43	1.42	19/43	.44
Class three				
High	32/67	.48	20/67	.30
Low	70/48	1.46	42/48	.88
Total				
High	48/106	.45	31/106	.29
Low	131/91	1.44	61/91	.67

Table 4. Measures of Uptake

Group	Uptake/No uptake	% Uptake
Class two		
High	51/99	52
Low	55/127	42
Class three		
High	129/249	48
Low	66/177	37
Total		
High	171/248	49
Low	121/304	39

contributions. It shows a fine-tuned adaptation of instruction to student performance.

Uptake included three related types of engagement: (a) actual overt incorporation of some portion of a preceding utterance; (b) elliptical incorporation, where the subsequent question unavoidably presupposed the preceding answer; and (c) paraphrase, where a word or phrase in a subsequent question provided a close restatement of a preceding answer. All three types are illustrated in the following two conversational segments.

The first conversational segment concerns a passage in which street lights have been mentioned. I think it is clear that uptake, marked with a plus in parentheses, provokes an elaboration of the discussion and draws out the students' knowledge of the passage and the topic.

Incorporation of answer into question (+):

1.	T:	All right, what are they looking for?
2.	C:	Signals.
3.	T:	What signals? (+)
4.	C1:	Red.
5.	C2:	Red light and green.
6.	C3:	Three signals.
7.	T:	All right, traffic signals.
8.		Where do you find those? (+)
9.	C:	On the street.
10.	T:	All right, where on the street? (+)
11.	C1:	Corners.
12.	C2:	Uh, corners.
13.	T:	The corner of the street . . .
14.		At the corner of what kind of streets? (+)

All of the uptakes involve overt incorporation, but the phrase "traffic signals" in line 7 is an example of paraphrase. The subsequent question overtly incorporates the paraphrase "Where do you find those?" (those = traffic signals = red light and green, etc.)

The next conversational segment is taken from a discussion which occurs after reading a passage from *Puss in Boots*. The passage concerns a cat's plans to advance the social position of his master by following a king.

Incorporation of answer into question (+):

1. T: What was the plan?
2. C: To make Jack play like he was the Duke of Willowonder.
3. T: Yes? (+)
4. C: To jump and then run into the river, but leave your clothes.
5. T: And pretend that he was doing what? (+)

The second question, line 3, is simply "Yes?" It is an example of *elliptical* incorporation. Because it fully presupposes the preceding answer, it is like a "Why?" or "What else?" question in isolation; it signals, "Continue with what you are saying, I'm listening and curious." The student responds in line 4 by reading a passage from the book, with slight modifications. The original text is "(I want you) to run and jump in the river, but leave your clothes under a stone." The teacher responds to the reading with a question in line 5, which incorporates an overt pronominal reference to the "your" of the preceding answer (i.e., 'he') and which requests a further specification of the protagonist's activities.

I would like to contrast the preceding with two cases of nonuptake. The following conversational segments show an acknowledgment of answers but no attempt to elaborate on the student's responses. Nonuptake is indicated by a minus in parentheses. In the examples the instructors seem to be covering a preset list of topics. The discussion in the first conversational segment concerns a passage based on a variant of the Chicken Little story, in which a chicken and several animals are going to inform a king that the sky is falling.

Nonincorporation of answer into question (−):

1. T: Why do you think they want to tell the king?
2. C: So they could get out of their city.
3. T: Okay, so maybe they can leave.
4. Do you think they think the king should know? (−)
5. C1: Yes.
6. C2: 'Cause he needta know too.
7. C3: 'Cause he the owner of the city.
8. T: All right, so they think that he should know.
9. that the sky is falling.
10. All right, what does this fox tell them? (−)

Even though the students have given causal explanations in lines 6 "'Cause he needta know too," and 7, " 'Cause he the owner of the city," the teacher merely acknowledges the positive nature of the response and then continues with a new topic.

In the next conversational segment, the discussion concerns a story about a rural Mexican family going to the market.

Nonincorporation of answer into question (−):

1. T: OK, when we think of village, what do we think of?
2. Of village, we had the word once before.
3. C: A little town.
4. T: A small town, yes.

5.   And, uh . . . the son's name is what? ($-$)
6. C: Raymon.
7. T: Raymon. And Raymon is going with his father and mother . . .
8.   to the village market to sell their pottery.
9.   Um, who had the reins? ($-$)

In this example we again see a perfunctory pattern of answers being acknowledged and then followed by questions which introduce different topics. In sequence the students are asked to define "village," the name of "the son," and finally, in line 9, "Who had the reins?" (of the burro in the story).

The analysis of referential *coherence* revealed that the typical way of establishing and maintaining question topics was for the topic to be introduced with a lexical noun phrase (NP) or name and subsequently referred to with a pronoun or zero-anaphor during a series of elicitation-reply-evaluation cycles. Topic shifts were accomplished by introducing the new topic with a lexical NP or name. This is a common pattern in English and most languages. New topics are established with relatively nonpresupposing lexical nouns and thereafter referred to by means of anaphoric devices such as pronouns and ellipsis.

There is a departure from this pattern in the lessons, however. Sometimes shifts in topic perspective occurred which are not accomplished with lexical NPS, but rather with potentially ambiguous pronouns. Such shifts are interesting for several reasons. For one, they threw into relief the kinds of contextual and semantic knowledge the participants use to infer antecedents in a discourse. For another, conflicting inferences occur far more frequently in the low-ranked lessons, forming a complement to the heightened turn violation and lessened uptake previously discussed. Finally, in recounting and commenting upon the events contained in a text, students are practicing a variety of inferential strategies for determining antecedents in a discourse. It seems plausible that these are similar in kind to the strategies which skilled readers employ in comprehending text (see also Gibson & Levin, 1975; Trabasso, 1981; and Webber, 1980).

The use of text knowledge, prior discourse, and semantic information to infer antecedents can be seen in the following example. As an aid to the reader, the text which the discussion concerns is included.

Successful resolution of ambiguous pronominal reference:

Text: *The city mouse wanted to see the country mouse. "I know what I can do,"* he said. *"I'm going to the country. I will surprise country mouse."*

1. T: All right, so what does the city mouse$_i$ want to do?
2. CC: See the—— go to the country.
3. T: Go to the country and visit who?
4. CC: The country—the country mouse$_j$.
5. T: The country mouse$_j$.
6.   All right, does the country mouse$_j$ expect him$_i$?
7. CC: No.
8. T: No he$_j$ doesn't, he$_i$'s going to what?
9. CC: Surprise.
10. T: Surprise him$_j$, he$_i$'s gonna surprise him$_j$.

In line 8 there is a sudden shift in the reference of the pronouns: the first "he" refers to the country mouse, who does not expect the visitor; the second "he" refers to the city mouse, who is going to surprise his rural counterpart. Since the second "he" is said without emphatic stress which might indicate a shift in reference, a decision based solely on lexical pronoun features could select either mouse. This being so, it strikes me as potentially unclear just which mouse is intended by the second "he." In following the sudden, unmarked shift concerning who is in focus as the agent, the students had to apply their knowledge of the passage which had been read as well as their knowledge of what aspects of the passage had been discussed thus far in order to predict—as they successfully do—the likely antecedent of "he" in "He's going to what?"

But this sort of reference maintenance occasionally breaks down. That is, situations occur in which contradictory interpretations are assigned to a pronoun with the result that two or more topics are simultaneously on the floor. These situations occur much more frenquently during low-ranked reading lessons. One result is that discussion time is given over to "repairing" reference, that is, to establishing just what is being talked about at a particular moment in the lesson.

The following conversational segment is taken from the same lesson as the discussion of the "city mouse." The discussion concerns the story of the city and country mouse, but occurs later, after the country mouse has invited the city visitor to dine with him.

Referential misfire:

Text: *City mouse wanted to eat. But he did not like the food. "You are not eating," said country mouse. "Why don't you eat with me?" "I can't," said city mouse. "I don't like this food. Why do you eat it, country mouse?"*

1.	T:	Who's not eating the corn?
2.	CC:	The city mouse$_i$!
3.	T:	why not?
4.	C1:	He$_i$ don't like it.
5.	CC:	He$_i$ don't like it.
6.	T:	He$_i$ doesn't *like* it.
7.		But does the country mouse$_j$ like it?
8.	CC:	Yeh!
9.	T:	Yes he$_j$ does——
10.	C1:	——He$_i$ like eat *insects.*
11.	T:	——he$_i$ likes that————
12.	C1:	——He$_i$ like eat insects.
13.	T:	Who?
14.	C1:	Uh . . .
15.	T:	Which one?
16.	C1:	The gray one$_i$.
17.	T:	Well, which one is he, the gray one?

Lines 4–13 are most important. A student, C1, refers to the city mouse as "he" in line 4 ("He don't like it"). The teacher then talks about the country mouse in lines 7 and 9: "But does the country mouse like it? . . . Yes he does." In lines 10–13 we

see the temporary breakdown which ensues as the teacher tries to establish just which mouse is being referred to by "he." It is clear from the pictures in the book (the city mouse is gray, the country mouse, brown) and from what the student later says that the student intends the city mouse when he says "he" and "the gray one."

Although such referential 'misfires' are not pervasive, they do occur regularly in low-ranked lessons, usually one or two per lesson. When they occur, question topics are typically abandoned or returned to only after a lengthy discussion aimed at clarifying who said or did what to whom. Although these examples show probing by the teacher, answers which were referentially ambiguous were also likely to be ignored, whether correct or incorrect. Situations where contradictory inferences are drawn probably contribute to increased turn disruption and lessened uptake. But such reasoning should not proceed in an overly deterministic fashion.

Discussion   In thinking about causes for these findings, the various measures should be seen as different parts of a mutually reinforcing cycle. Heightened turn disruption results in lessened uptake and referential coherence; these, in turn, lead to further turn disruption. All three measures are aspects of a synergistic process resulting in reduced communicative involvement.

The components of turn disruption are complex in themselves. "Calling out" may start as help—students providing the correct answer when someone hesitates or miscues. But it very quickly becomes a divisive form of rivalry, annoying each reader in turn, yet tolerated by the instructor. It prevents self-monitoring and self-correction and reinforces a fragmented oral reading style. By lessening the respect paid a turn at reading and the intelligibility of reading and discussion during and after a turn, calling out lessens involvement in reading. This, in turn, provokes management acts as teachers attempt to maintain attention by reprimanding inattention. The reprimands further disrupt the process of reading and discussion, contributing, albeit in a limited way, to lessened uptake.

If we ask why differential uptake occurs, several potential answers suggest themselves. One is that turn disruption directly reduces the possibility of uptake. If we focus on the difference between high-group and low-group management acts ($N = 30$), we find that 11 of those 30 acts occurred during a question turn, when students had been asked a question and had responded with an answer which was correct but provoked no elaboration. Assuming that a distraction during an initiation-reply-evaluation cycle will lessen the likelihood of uptake, then the intersection of the two categories of events provides an explanation for part (approx. 10%) of the lessened uptake in the low-ranked lessons. But this is only a partial explanation.

An additional hypothesis is that differential uptake simply reflects either (a) the teacher's expectations about students and the pedagogical agenda thus employed, or (b) the inappropriateness of the students' responses. Both sides of this hypothesis are difficult to prove. If subsequent analysis were able to isolate a number of identical question and response patterns which showed uptake with one group of students and lack of uptake with another, that would provide direct evidence of expectation effects or a site for contrastive analysis of the appropriateness of student responses. It would still leave unanswered the question of what it is about the general communicative environment which maintains and reinforces the teachers' apparent predilections for differing uptake.

In the case of decreased referential coherence, the question is how contradictory, yet equally plausible interpretations of topics get established in the rapid give and take of classroom discussion. It may be that low-ranked readers do not have as coherent a model of the text as their high-ranked counterparts, with the result that their anaphoric inferences are less constrained, more open-ended. It would be very difficult to establish such differences outside of controlled experimental conditions. There is little evidence from the lesson transcripts, however, that such is the case. Low-group readers seem no more prone to make "wild" interpretive leaps than high-group readers. It may also be that the oral discourse style of low-ranked readers places an additional interpretive burden on the teacher. These readers sometimes used a fragment of reported speech when introducing a new topic, as if compensating for the shift in reference by clearly indexing the speech of the character. This way of introducing characters may require additional inferential work by the teacher to determine what is the intended topic. It was to test this possibility that the following narrative experiment was devised. Last, in many of the referential misfires timing is important. In several cases, some sort of distraction occurred just prior to the misfire.

CLASSROOM INDEPENDENT MEASURES

The Narrative Study

As a complement to the analysis of classroom interaction, a narrative experiment was conducted with the members of the high and low groups in the two classrooms. The goal of the experiment was to provide evidence for whether or not subjects' classroom-independent discourse skills could be said to have a bearing on the referential coherence found in classroom reading lessons.

Recall that one aspect of the lessened communicative coherence of low-ranked lessons was the higher incidence of referential misfires. Referential misfires occur when the teacher and student assign different interpretations to an utterance containing a pronoun, with the result that there are two or more topics simultaneously on the floor.

A plausible hypothesis, which I wished to test, was that the misfires were due to discourse skills and habits of low-group members, that is, that these students spoke in a less explicit fashion than their high-group counterparts, with the result that there were more overt misunderstandings during their lessons. The question could be posed in the following fashion: Was there evidence from verbal performance outside the reading group context that some of the children were more likely than others to presuppose nonshared background in establishing and maintaining reference in discourse?

In order to have data bearing on that question, narratives were collected from 21 members of the second- and third-grade reading groups, working in pairs in a relaxed setting but with a controlled topic. The students' skill in establishing and maintaining reference was analyzed in terms of a narrative-context variable—whether first mention or subsequent mention of a character—and a nounphrase variable—whether a lexical noun, a third person pronoun, or a zero-anaphor was used. In the analysis I focused on whether appropriately (in)definite noun phrases were used to establish a character in the narrative and later to maintain reference to the character.

There was considerable individual variation on both measures—appropriate definiteness in establishing and maintaining reference—as would be expected from a subject population of their age. But there was highly significant agreement between measures (using a Spearman's rank-order correlation test and .02 significance), suggesting that a genuine discourse skill was being tapped. There were no group effects, however: the mean scores of the low and high group on both measures were nearly identical (.19 low vs. .18 high for inappropriate establishment of reference; .049 low vs. .043 high for inappropriate maintenance of reference).

These findings strongly suggested that it was not some type of classroom-independent discourse skill—or lack of skill—that caused the referential misfires in the lessons of one group rather than the other. There was no discernible tendency for members of one ability group to introduce topics in an inappropriately definite or inexplicit fashion. Nor was there a tendency for reference to topics to be maintained in an inexplicit fashion. Whatever the causes of the referential misfires during the low-ranked lessons, they must have their sources in the interactional organization of classroom verbal exchanges and the task-specific characteristics of those exchanges. For they do not appear linked to the children's typical ways of establishing and maintaining reference in narratives.

At this point it may be pertinent to review why one would think that there might be some connection between reading problems and ability to produce a referentially coherent narrative. It is important to recall that we are not talking about reading problems per se—i.e., problems recognizing phono-grapheme correspondences or words or even drawing inferences from the text—but rather about interactional stalls which occur during discussion aimed at text comprehension. A central feature of the referential misfires is the introduction or reintroduction of topics in an inexplicit or ambiguous fashion—with the consequence that shared interpretation of discourse falters. In short, the very basis of the problem that occurs only in low-ranked reading lessons—divergent interpretations of ambiguous pronouns—is found randomly distributed in the narratives of speakers from both groups.

Standardized Measures and Grouping

When we turn to standardized achievement measures, there were clear differences in the test scores of the different groups and classrooms for the beginning and end of the research period. To put it briefly: those in the high groups entered with higher aggregate scores and showed more improvement over the year. The improvement is not surprising given the picture we have of how lessons transpired in the different groups.

More interesting in this regard are the differences between the two classrooms. Although there was no explicit policy of tracking at the research school, it was common knowledge that some classes were "better" (i.e., more academically advanced) than others.[2] Classroom two was one of the better classes of the second grade; classroom three was not one of the better classes of the third grade. Classroom two was more homogeneous regarding socioeconomic background and reading skills; its students came from relatively more educated and prosperous working-class backgrounds and had higher mean reading test scores. Classroom three, conversely, was composed of a more heterogeneous group with regard to socioeconomic status and reading skills; its students came from relatively less educated, less prosperous, working-class backgrounds and had lower mean test scores. In classroom two both the low and high group improved, although the high group improved more. In classroom three only the high group, which came from a much more prosperous background than the class norm, improved over the year, while the low group, which came from a poor background, declined drastically in its relative class position.

The reasons for the relative differences in the achievements of high and low groups in the two classes are probably a mixture of sociocultural, institutional, and pedagogical factors. As previously discussed, the mean income for classroom two was high vis-á-vis the school norms. Both the low- and high-ability groups were from higher than usual S.E.S. backgrounds. They would be expected to achieve by their parents, their teachers, and the school administration. Classroom two was a high-track classroom with some of the best students entering the second-grade class at Mayberry. The teacher was scrupulously fair, spending slightly more time with low-ability readers and using a successful comprehension-probing questioning strategy during the question turns. These differences reveal another aspect of the issue of social class and educational grouping but at the level of classroom tracks rather than intraclassroom groups: The relatively privileged go into the best classrooms, where they can hope to improve rather than merely hold their rank (or, as happened to low-group members in classroom three, sink lower on the academic scale).

CONCLUSION

In all of the foregoing studies, the ways in which speakers signal and listeners infer coherence in a discourse have been used to examine the communicative bases of learning activities and access to those activities. This provided evidence as to whether or not children's communicative background has obvious consequences for communication in classroom settings. That in the Berkeley studies we found positive evidence and in the Chicago studies, negative evidence, should not be surprising. Models for classroom communication, and for narrative and conversational dis-

---

[2]The lack of explicit policy on tracking is pervasive in American schools, as Rosenbaum (1980) discusses. Given that educational grouping is basically antidemocratic, it is often quietly practiced as an institutional response to diversity, with little or no overt statement on the policy.

course in general, are still formulated in an inexplicit fashion, and much remains to be done specifying how syntactic, semantic, and pragmatic factors contribute to successful, comprehensible communication. That community-specific conventions were found for the structuring of narratives and the use of prosodic cues in conversational and narrative discourse should not surprise. It agrees with a growing literature showing that conventional ways of combining prosody with syntactic and lexical forms are frequently specific to ethnic and social groups (see Vanderslice & Pearson, 1967; Goulet & Morales-Goulet 1974; Gumperz, 1982b).

That a careful analysis of linguistic skills of textual cohesion (how to appropriately introduce reference to a topic) showed considerable individual variation but no group effects indicates that we should question loose talk about "inexplicit" ways of speaking as to its factual basis. It suggests, positively, but with a narrower focus, that there may not be social class differences on this type of task. It is important, however, to see what type of task was posed. The narrative was essentially a monologue in which it was clearly explained that the listener did not have prior knowledge of the story. This is several steps removed from a classroom discussion of a text being read as a group. Future research might gain additional insight by setting up a group discussion of peers and analyzing how topics are introduced and maintained in group discussion as well as in individual narratives.[3]

Whatever the ultimate causes of increased turn violations and lessened uptake and coherence during the classroom lessons, it seems clear that the different ability groups encounter strikingly different contexts for learning. It is a sad irony that students perceived as having low aptitude are grouped together so that, as a group, they are less involved in the task of reading. Their experience is in reading sessions that are stigmatized, because for slow learners, and characterized by high levels of distraction and lessened instructional engagement and topical coherence. Understandably, these students are less motivated and have less opportunity to become involved in reading as a communicative experience.

The next question is what to do about this grouping practice. Many people can see that the practice is supported by a false and inflexible ideology regarding ability and that it reinforces existing ineualities of access to learning opportunities. Several decades of research into the effects of abililty grouping have shown two interesting correlations: a weak correlation between high-ability placement and increased achievement and a much stronger correlation between middle-ability or low-ability placement and decreased achievement. That is, there are weak benefits for those placed high, and strong disadvantages for the rest. Given that the practice is implicated in reinforcing class and ethnic prejudice under the guise of ability discrimination and that it fails on its own criterion of efficiency in skills improvement, the use of ability grouping is highly questionable and should be eliminated (see Goodlad,

---

[3]Some of the early work by Bernstein (1975) and collaborators took this approach; a critical review of these early findings is reported by Edwards (1976).

1983, for a similar proposal, and Oakes, 1983, for a review of emerging constitutional issues).[4]

In the Berkeley and Chicago studies we examined some ways in which communicative styles, pedagogical variables, and educational grouping practices influence whether children appreciate reading as a communicative experience or view it as a pointless set of formal procedures for "making sounds." These different early expectations about what reading entails have important consequences over time. The large literature on children's conceptions of reading reports a simple but persistent dichotomy: For poor readers, from early primary through secondary school, the final purpose and hallmark of proficiency is fluent and rapid reading aloud, with little concern evinced for possible meaning; for good readers, however, the goal of reading is the extraction of meaningful content (see Canney & Winograd, 1979, for review of literature). However, these general expectations about the purpose(s) of reading apparently have specific consequences. As we have already discussed, it is from the third grade onward—the point when comprehension becomes increasingly important on standardized tests—that minority and working-class students progressively decline in achievement.

This decline was dramatically evident at the Chicago school. The neighborhood served by the school was a stable, albeit poor, community. There were generally good relations between parents and the school, and education was valued as a means of social mobility. But there was a sad disparity between this optimism and the average achievement at the school (a nationwide occurrence, see Hentoff, 1977). For average reading achievement, rates closely followed the national rates for low-income minorities. Students read at grade level in the second grade; they declined precipitously during the third grade; by the time they were in the sixth and seventh grade they were 2–2 ½ years behind grade level.

It seems the low-ranked readers of classroom three are typical: They initiate a decline replicated, on a larger scale, throughout the upper primary grades. It is difficult to determine what becomes of the high achievers. They may join the pool of underachievers, or they may go to other schools. As I have discussed elsewhere (Collins, 1983), it was the parents of high-ranked students who knew of alternative schools and were seeking to transfer their children to those other schools. The relative social privilege that favored a child's placement in a high-ability group also favored the chance of the child being moved to a better endowed, less problem-ridden school for upper primary and secondary education.

In the foregoing chapter, I have tried to show how analysis of conversation and narrative discourse can improve our study of the communicative bases of learning

---

[4]As Guthrie (Chap. 13, this volume) points out, care must be taken in the organizational structures which replace abillity grouping. If the conditions which call for elimination of ability grouping are regenerated within new organizational structures, then as Guthrie states, students' needs will not be served. The elimination of ability groups should not be viewed as a surface-level change but as a means to realize equitable access for all students to literacy comprehension instruction.

activities and of differential access to those activities. By identifying subcultural differences in discourse style which influence classroom interaction and by devising analyses which allow us to separate group-specific discourse conventions from individual differences in discourse skill, we can begin to specify how communicative style and sociocultural background interact with pedagogical variables and institutional grouping practices to produce different contexts for learning. In the Berkeley and Chicago classroom studies, I have attempted to do more than document the effects of teacher expectations. In the latter study, in particular, I proposed a few exploratory measures for assessing the overall coherence of communication within learning microenvironments. The measures were discussed within the framework of a very general taxonomic model of classroom discourse, but the primary concern was to get at the preconditions for attentive, sustained involvement in the collaborative process of learning to read. These preconditions seem to include an orderly way of assigning turns, the right to a turn and to time for self-monitoring, a certain amount of teacher responsiveness to student contributions, and participants' ability to establish and maintain a shared sense of topic. Taken together, these preconditions indicate the complexity of the communicative events involved in acquiring the skills of literacy. Properly analyzed, they can enrich our understanding of the social, linguistic, and cognitive variables which play a role in those communicative events. In the classroom and narrative studies the focus has been on discourse cohesion: what participants in a communicative event must know in order to relate what is being said or written to preceding discourse, both at the level of reference (what is literally said) and illocution (what is intended). Cohesion analysis, when not a preoccupation with reified technique but rather a general research orientation, can be extremely valuable, because cohesion is one of the most sensitive ways of showing what social differences are as well as their long-term consequences in institutional settings.

REFERENCES

Allington, R. (1980). Teacher interruption behaviors during primary-grade oral reading. *Journal of Education Psychology. 72*, 371–377.

Allington, R. (1983). The reading instruction provided readers of differing abilities. *Elementary School Journal, 83*, 548–559.

Anderson-Levitt, K. (1981). *What counts as success in first-grade in France.* Ph.D. dissertation, Stanford University, Stanford, CA.

Anyon, J. (1981). Social class and school knowledge. *Curriculum Inquiry, 11*, 4–42.

Au, K. (1980). Participation structures in teaching. *Anthropology and Education Quarterly, 11*, 91–115.

Barnes, D. (1976). *From communication to curriculum.* London: Penguin.

Barr, R., & Dreeben, R. (1975). Instruction in classrooms. In L. Shulman (Ed.), *Review of research in education* (vol. 5). Itasca, IL: Peacock.

Bellack, A., Kleibard, A., Hyman, H., & Smith, L. (1966). *The language of the classroom.* New York: Teachers College Press.

Bernstein, B. (1975). *Class, codes and control.* New York: Schocken.

Bowles, S., & Gintis, H. (1976). *Schooling in capitalist America.* New York: Basic Books.

Bourdieu, P. (1977). Cultural reproduction and social reproduction. In J. Karabel & A. H. Halsey (Eds.), *Power and ideology in education*. New York and London: Oxford University Press.

Campbell, D. (1980). *'Going for the answers' with questions in a Philippines elementary mathematics classroom*. Ph.D. dissertation, Stanford University, Stanford, CA.

Canney, G., & Winograd, P. (1979). *Schemata for reading and reading comprehension performance* (Technical Report No. 120). Champaign: Center for the Study of Reading, University of Illinois.

Collins, J. (1982). Discourse style, classroom interaction and differential treatment. *Journal of Reading Behavior, 14*, 429–37.

Collins, J. (1983). *A linguistic perspective on minority education: discourse analysis and early literacy*. Ph.D. dissertation, University of California, Berkeley.

Collins, J. (1986). Differential treatment in reading instruction. In J. Cook-Gumperz (Ed.), *The social construction of literacy,*. New York and London: Cambridge University Press.

Collins, J., & Michaels, S. (1986). Discourse and the acquisition of literacy. In J. Cook-Gumperz (Ed.) *The social construction of literacy*. New York and London: Cambridge University Press.

Doyle, W. (1977). Paradigms for research in teacher effectiveness. In F. Kerlinger (Ed.), *Review of research in education* (Vol. 7), Itasca, IL: Peacock.

Duncan, S. (1972). Some signals and rules for taking speaking turns in conversations. *Journal of Personality and Social Psychology, 23*, 283–292.

Durkin, D. (1979). What classroom observations reveal about reading comprehension instruction. *Reading Research Quarterly, 14*, 481–533.

Eder, D. (1981). Ability grouping as a self-fulfilling prophecy: A micro-analysis of teacher-student interaction. *Sociology of Education, 54*, 151–162.

Eder, D. (1983). Family background and ability group assignment. In R. Hauser, D. Mechanic, & A. Haller (Eds.), *Social structure and personality*. New York: Academic Press.

Eder, D. (1986). Organizational constraints on individual mobility: ability group formation and maintenance. In J. Cook-Gumperz (Ed.), *The social construction of literacy*. New York and London: Cambridge University Press.

Edwards, A. (1976). *Language in culture and class*. New York and London: Heinneman.

Flanders, N. (1970). *Analyzing teacher behavior*. Reading, MA: Addison-Wesley.

Gibson, E., & Levin, H. (1975). *The psychology of reading*. Cambridge, MA: MIT Press.

Goffman, E. (1963). *Behavior in public places*. New York: Free Press.

Goffman, E. (1972). The neglected situation. In P. Giglioli (Ed.), *Language and social context*. London: Penguin.

Goodland, J. (1983). *A study of schooling*. New York: McGraw-Hill.

Goulet, R., & Morales-Goulet, R. (1974). *Making it in the United States*. Quezon City, Philippines: Phoenix Press.

Green, J. (1977). *Pedagogical style differences as related to comprehension performance: Grade one through three*. Ph.D. dissertation, University of California, Berkeley.

Green, G., & Morgan, J. (1982). Writing ability as a function of the appreciation of differences between oral and written communication. In C. Frederickson & J. Dominic (Eds.), *Writing* (Vol. 2), Hillsdale, NJ: Erlbaum.

Griffin, P., & Humphry, F. (1978). Task and talk. In R. Shuy & P. Griffin (Eds.), *The study of children's functional language and education in the early years* (Final Report to the Carnegie Foundation of New York). Arlington, VA: Center for Applied Linguistics.

Gumperz, J. (1982a). *Discourse strategies*. New York and London: Cambridge University Press.

Gumperz, J. (Ed.)(1982b). *Language and social identity*. New York and London: Cambridge University Press.

Gumperz, J., & Herasimchuk, E. (1972). Conversational analysis of socia l meaning: a study of classroom interaction. In R. Shuy (Ed.), *Sociolinguistics: Current trends and prospects*. Washington, DC: Georgetown University Press.

Gumperz, J., Simons, H., & Cook-Gumperz, J. (1981). *Final report on school home ethnography project*. Washington, DC: National Institute of Education.

Hentoff, N. (1977). *Does anybody give a damn?* New York: Knopf.

Hentoff, N. (1982, August 23). Profiles: The integrationist (profile of Kenneth Clark). *The New Yorker.*

Johnson, M. (1979). *Discussion dynamics: An analysis of classroom teaching.* Rowley, MA: Newbury.

Karabel, J., & Halsey, A.H. (1977). *Power and ideology in education.* New York and London: Oxford University Press.

Labov, W. (1972). Is BEV a separate system? In *Language in the inner city.* Philadelphia: University of Pennsylvania Press.

Labov, W. (1982). Objectivity and commitment in linguistic science: The case of the Black English trial in Ann Arbor. *Language in Society, 11,* 165–199.

Leacock, E. (1969). *Teaching and learning in city schools: A comparative study.* New York: Basic Books.

Levin, P. (1977). *Students and teachers: A cultural analysis of Polynesian classroom interaction.* Ph.D. dissertation, University of California, San Diego.

McDermott, R. (1976). *Kids make sense: An ethnographic account of the interactional management of success and failure in one first-grade classroom.* Ph.D. dissertation, Stanford University, Stanford, CA.

McDermott, R. (1978). Relating and learning: An analysis of two classroom reading groups. In R. Shuy (Ed.), *Linguistics and reading.* Rowley, MA: Newbury.

McHoul, I. (1978). The organization of turns at formal talk in the classroom. *Language in Society, 7,* 183–213.

Malcolm, I. (1977). Interaction in the aboriginal classroom: A socio-linguistic model. In J. Maling-Keepes (Ed.), *The study of classroom processes and practices.* Perth: Australia Institute of Technology.

Mehan, H. (1979). *Learning lessons.* Cambridge, MA: Harvard University Press.

Michaels, S. (1981). "Sharing time"; An oral preparation for literacy. *Language in Society, 10,* 423–442.

Michaels, S., & Kedar, L. (1981, December). *Prosody in children's narrative discourse and differential access to literacy.* Paper presented at the Annual Meetings of the American Anthropological Association, Los Angeles.

Michaels, S., & Collins, J. (1984). Discourse style and acquisition of literacy. In D. Tannen (Ed.), *Coherence in spoken and written language.* Norwood, NJ: Ablex.

Miller-Souviney, B. (1981). Teaching community school math: A comparison of five sites. In *Indigenous mathematics project series working paper* (No. 18). Papua New Guinea: Department of Education.

Oakes. J. (1983). Tracking and ability grouping in American schools: some constitutional questions. *Teachers College Record, 84,* 801–819.

Ogbu, J. (1978). *Minority education and caste: The American system in cross-cultural perspective.* New York: Academic Press.

Piestrup, A. (1973). *Black Dialect interference and the accommodation of reading instruction in first grade.* Berkeley: Language-Behavior Research Laboratory, University of California.

Philips, S. (1972). Participant structures and communicative competence: Warm Springs children in community and classroom. In C. Cazden, V. John, & D. Hymes (Ed.), *Functions of language in the classroom.* New York: Teachers College Press.

Rist, R. (1970). Student social class and teacher expectations: The self-fulfilling prophecy in ghetto education. *Harvard Educational Review, 39,* 411–450.

Rosenbaum, J. (1980). The social implications of educational grouping. In D. Berliner (Ed.), *Review of research in education* (Vol. 8), Washington, DC: American Educational Research Association.

Rosenshine, B. (1971). *Teaching behaviors and student achievement.* Windsor, Berkshire: National Foundation for Educational Research in England and Wales.

Sacks, H., Schlegoff, E., & Jefferson, G. (1974). A simplest systematics for the organization of turn-taking for conversation. *Language, 50,* 696–735.

Schwartz, F. (1981). Supporting or subverting learning: Peer group patterns in four tracked schools. *Anthropology and Education Quarterly, 14,* 99–121.

Sinclair, J., & Coulthard, R. (1975). *Towards an analysis of discourse*. New York and London: Oxford University Press.

Snow, C. (1983). Literacy and language: Relationships during the preschool years. *Harvard Educational Review, 53*, 165–89.

Tannen, D. (1982). Oral and written strategies in spoken and written narratives. *Language, 58*, 1–21.

Trabasso, T. (1981). On making inferences during reading and their assessment. In J. Guthrie (Ed.), *Comprehension and teaching*. Newark, DE: International Reading Association.

Vanderslice, R., & Pierson, L. (1967). Prosodic features of Hawaiian English. *Quarterly Journal of Speech, 53*, 156–66.

Webber, B. (1980). Syntax beyond the sentence: Anaphora. In R. Spiro, B. Bruce, & W. Brewer (Eds.), *Theoretical issues in reading comprehension*. Hillsdale, NJ: Erlbaum.

5 Sulking, Stepping, and Tracking: The Effects of Attitude Assessment on Access to Literacy*

Perry Gilmore

University of Alaska, Fairbanks

The research discussed in this chapter demonstrates some ways in which a group of urban black elementary school students were allowed differential access to literacy based on teacher assessments of their "attitude" (i.e., social interactions which communicated their alignment with the prevailing ethos of the school). Though teachers believed themselves to be making their selections of students based on the capacity for handling certain attitudinal learning and literacy skills, analysis of the data shows that they were, in fact, using a very different and unconscious set of social criteria based largely on communicative style to form their evaluations. Although all the children observed over the 3-year period displayed extensive literacy and language skills in peer and nonschool contexts, only some were admitted to the special academic programs and higher-track classes which maximized opportunities for literacy success. Despite the presence and demonstration of literacy competence, many of these children were never seen as possessing such skills, because performances of their competencies were contextualized and embedded in attitudinal displays that were considered inappropriate. Thus, the issue seemed not to be the *acquisition of literacy*— implying a growing set of reading and writing skills; instead it appeared to be an exchange of appropriate attitudes for what can more accurately be described as an *admission to literacy*, a gatekeeping enterprise.

The 3-year study was conducted in a predominantly low-income black urban community and elementary school. A central focus in the initial phase of the research was to identify school-and community-perceived problems concerning literacy achievement. The problems seen as important by the participants and voiced within the setting then guided the direction of the study.

The major concerns expressed by the administrators, faculty, and parents were much less focused on reading and writing skills per se than might have been expected. Community members' most frequently articulated concerns about literacy achievement were focused on *social* rather than cognitive dimensions of behavior.

---

*The research reported here was supported by two grants from the National Institute of Education, to Dell H. Hymes, principal investigator (1979–81) and David Martin Smith, Principal investigator (1981–82), University of Pennsylvania. This paper has benefited from critical comments on an earlier draft offered by David M. Smith, Erving Goffman, Ray McDermott, Bambi Schieffelin, and Susan Florio-Ruane.

LITERACY ACHIEVEMENT: A QUESTION OF ATTITUDE

The major literacy achievement problem identified and voiced repeatedly by teachers, parents, administrators, and even the children in the community was "attitude." A "good attitude" seemed to be the central and significant factor for students' general academic success and literacy achievement in school. This concern with attitude is by no means unique nor restricted to this particular study site. The reader's own experience probably suggests that this concern is a significant issue in most school and work situations. However, in this particular setting, talk about attitude was dramatically more prominent than talk about intelligence or reading and writing ability. In fact, it was made clear to staff and parents as well as students that in cases of tracking and/or selection for honors or special academic preference, attitude outweighed academic achievement or IQ test performance.

The specific dimensions and features and actual meanings of "attitude," can dramatically differ from one setting to another. To document them in this particular setting was one of the goals of the investigation. The approach taken here was concerned with *how* attitudes were *communicated, understood,* and *interpreted.* The functions and uses of the concept as it was constructed in this particular context were considered.

By observing actions and reactions to behaviors related to attitude and by noting the language used to describe or evaluate these behaviors, a profile of the constructed meanings of attitude was developed. A picture began to emerge of what linguistic and social behaviors "counted" as attitude and of how these behaviors were affected (both in performance and interpretation) by the different contexts in which they occurred. The process of identifying a domain of the concept of attitude required the discovery and description of the related "folk" categories used by the participants.

For example, a student with a "good attitude" was described as "completing homework," "being punctual," "having involved parents," or "having good work habits." The descriptions were extensive and quite varied in terms of the dimension of behavior they encompassed.

Further, in talking to many of the staff and in the initial phases of general observation in the school and community, it became apparent that attitude was delicately woven into a broader context of what might be labeled "propriety." Proper standards of what was socially acceptable in conduct or speech appeared to be a consistent concern in both the community and the school. On my initial visits to the school, the neatness and the well-mannered, orderly behavior of the children in halls and classrooms were regularly pointed out and emphasized by administrators and staff. The school took pride in being "well run," and the parents voiced their approval of this image. The school had an excellent reputation among the majority of the community members.

At times in talking about students, other descriptions were offered that seemed related to the use of "good" and "bad" attitude. The label "street kid" or "child of the streets'' seemed to be used to describe students who were not neatly groomed, did not have "involved parents," had little supervision at home, were often absent or late, or did not complete homework. These street kids were often the same children who were characterized as having "an attitude" or a "slight attitude." (In these cases the use of the term "attitude" alone conveys the notion of a negative or bad attitude.) On the other hand, labels like "cultured," "ladylike," "nice kid," and "respectful," which seem to imply politeness and propriety, were used synonomously with "good attitude."

A good attitude appeared to be central to inclusion in special high-track classes, referred to as an Academics Plus Program. The Academics Plus Program was described by staff as a rigorous "back to basics" curriculum in which academic a chievement and excellence was the primary goal.

To qualify, a student not only had to be working at a certain grade level, but also had to display a "cooperative attitude." The program was, in effect, a tracking procedure for attitude as well as academic achievement. Teachers sometimes talked about the process as one of "weeding out bad attitudes." A student working at a relatively low grade level might be admitted to the program, if his or her behavior indicated a desire to work and be cooperative. In such a case, a "good attitude" outweighed limited academic achievement. In other reported instances, a bright child who might be achieving academically but whose behavior was characteristic of a "bad attitude" would not be admitted. In such a case, "attitude" again outweighed academic achievement.

The staff often expressed pride and identification when talking about the school and its students, especially the Academics Plus students, referring to "our kids" in a proud and affectionate tone. One teacher, attempting to illustrate the exceptional attitude and reputation of the students, asked, "Have you seen our sixth-grade Academic Plus students? They're cultured. They're not street kids. Have you seen the way they carry themselves?" The reference to the way that students "carried themselves" suggested demeanor and propriety. In this particular urban black low-income community and school, where upward mobility and success in middle-class society were expressed goals, attitude rather than reading ability or intelligence was the means for assigning stable, stratified social ranks among students.

SULKING AND STEPPING: ENACTING AN ATTITUDE

Less than a third of the population in each intermediate grade level (3–6) was selected for the special academic program. It was clear to the staff, the children, and the parents that although the participation in the Academics Plus Program did not guarantee literacy success and general academic achievement, it certainly maximized the chances for it. It created an elite. It stratified the students. It made mothers cry with their children when they were rejected. And the key factor for admission was something everyone called a "good attitude."

In the case of assessing attitude, few hesitated to question their ability to judge it.

Yet try to grasp it for study, to understand its dimensions, and it became peculiarly abstruse. We were much more capable of saying whether you had it or not than of saying what it was you had. Yet, based on attitude, some children were admitted to classrooms where literacy skills were made more available to them and other children were not.

In order to unravel the meaning of attitude in this school community, the study focused on discrete linguistic and social behaviors. Two key behavioral events were observed which provided fertile ground for careful analysis of the enactment of attitude. Correspondences and contrasts in the way people *talked* about attitude and the way people actually *behaved* with regard to attitude were detailed.

Both behavioral events stood out prominently in the data, almost inviting further attention and analysis. In much the same way, they stood out as behaviors that were readily noticed, controversial and problematic for the teachers at school. Both key behaviors were counted as inappropriate—representative of bad or deteriorating attitudes. Both were performances that stood out and received attention from the staff.

The first key behavioral event was a characteristic response in face-to-face clashes of will between student and teacher. These were conventional displays of emotion that appeared regularly in my field notes and were prominent and noticeable in the classroom interactions. These displays of *stylized sulking* were usually nonverbal and often highly choreographed performances which seemed to, in the teacher's words, convey "rebellion," "anger," and a stance of "uncooperativeness." The displays were themselves discrete pieces of behavior which conveyed information. They were dramatic portrayals of an attitude. They were postures that told a story, to the teacher and to onlooking peers. They were face-saving dances. And they were black. They were regularly interpreted as part of black communicative repertoire and style. Students who frequently used the displays were also students who were identified as having bad attitudes.

The second key behavioral event that will be analyzed is the performance of a distinctive genre of street rhymes which seems to have grown out of the tradition of drills and cheers. The genre was locally referred to as "steps" (or "doin' steps"), and it involved chorally chanted rhymes punctuated with footsteps and handclaps which set up a background of rhythm. It was performed by groups of girls, and, consistent with tradition in children's folklore, it was full of taboo breaking and sexual innuendo in both the verbal and nonverbal modes of its performance. The dances were striking, the chants full of verbal virtuosity. They turned passersby into audiences. They were polished. They were "nasty." They were seen as defiant. They were seen as black. They were seen as representing "deteriorating attitudes." And they were banned from the school.

The two behavioral events, stylized sulking and doin' steps, provided "windows" through which underlying cultural themes could be examined. Both communicative events detailed concrete and specific aspects of behavior that could be analyzed as to their relatedness to attitude. Both events were seen as part of black communicative style, and both were interpreted as conveying "bad attitudes."

Yet the two performances were a dramatic contrast to one another in almost every other way. Though both were communicative events, the nature of their performances differed on all levels, including participants, settings, key, mode, audience, channel, etc. One was silent, the other verbal. One was an individual performance done by both sexes; the other was performed in all-girl groups. One was performed largely in formal school contexts where an adult authority was in control. The other was performed in informal peer contexts—on the playground and at home in driveways, on steps, and the like.

Due to the rather striking nature of the contrast of these behaviors, an extensive examination of each of them promised to offer a complementary view of the question of propriety and the enactment of attitude. Because they differed in so many of the elements of communicative performance, their juxtaposition could provide a fuller range of behavior through which to examine and better understand "attitude." By exploring the pragmatics of silence and talk through these examples, the socially constructed meanings of language and literacy in the setting could be detailed.

Appropriate displays of attitude seemed to determine access to contexts where opportunity for literacy acquisition was maximized. Attitude was seen as "bad," if it conveyed alignment with the black community rather than the white middle-class community. Portrayals of attitude in this context were declarations (conscious or unconscious) of alignment that inevitably determined whether or not access to literacy would be possible.

It was no surprise that students who were viewed as having good attitudes were also viewed as being good kids. The label became a part of the constitution and indicative of one's worth. Yet when we examined the behaviors subsumed under the "attitude," we discovered that they consisted largely of a set of linguistic, paralinguistic, and kinesic communicative adornments which were associated with a particular ethnic style and socioeconomic class rather than a set of character traits reflective of the nature of individuals.

In the following two sections a detailed analysis of each of the key behavioral events will be presented. Stylized sulking and doin' steps will be considered in terms of the immediate shape of their performances, their functions and uses, the metaphoric nature they suggested and the social meanings they held for the participants. The final section of this chapter will discuss the data as they relate to attitude assessment in general and the effects on literacy achievement in particular.

STYLIZED SULKING

Although recent years have witnessed a steadily growing body of ethnographic data concerning classrooms, the realm of emotions has largely been ignored. The sociolinguistic emphasis in classroom research has been primarily focused on verbal aspects of communciative (Hymes, 1962) or interactional (Mehan et al., 1976) competence (see, e.g., Cazden, John, & Hymes, 1972; McDermott, 1976; Mehan, 1979; Gilmore & Glatthorn, 1982; Spindler, 1982; Edwards & Furlong, 1978;

Bellack, Kliebard, Hyman, & Smith, 1966). This body of ethnographic literature illustrates that beyond academic competence there is a need for students to demonstrate interactional competence in social settings in order to do well in school. These studies have primarily demonstated that not only the academic knowledge must be present but that the student must also know when and how to display that knowledge according to socially acceptable rules of classroom interaction.

Though this sociolinguistic research has certainly enriched the study of schooling and expanded our awareness of important dimensions of the interactions surrounding learning events in school, it has somehow failed to address some of the most essential aspects of classroom life.

Urban classrooms are often scenes of clashes of will. Many of the most crucial social interactions in school settings are highly charged with emotion and regularly interpreted with regard to attitude. The ways in which these confrontations are interpreted and treated by teachers and students will strongly affect the nature of the attitudes conveyed as well as any learning which takes place in classrooms.

Attitude Displays: Portrayals and Masquerades

All situations carry with them a sense of what feelings are appropriate to have. Hochschild (1979) addressed this issue when she discussed "emotion work," which she described as "the act of evoking or shaping as well as suppressing feeling in oneself" (p. 552). Hochschild suggested that there were "feeling rules" which were learned and used as baselines in social exchanges. Classrooms provided an excellent setting in which to capture the pedogagy involved in "emotion work" and the teaching and learning discourse that surrounded "feeling rules." In classrooms such rules were frequently articulated.

Consider the emotion work embedded in this brief classroom interaction taken from my field notes:

> There is a loud chatting and calling out, and several students are out of their seats while the teacher is trying to explain how to do the assignment. The teacher suddenly shouts in a loud and angry voice, "Sit down, sit up . . . (more softly), and don't look surprised or hurt 'cause we've gone over this before."

The teacher first showed anger, shouting at the class to "sit down" and "sit up" (i.e., get in your seats and sit tall at attention). When several students portrayed looks of "hurt" or "surprise," she told them it was not acceptable to feel or, more accurately, to look as if they felt that way. In this particular instance the teacher might have been mediating her expression of emotion by telling the class that it wasn't a serious enough situation by which to be hurt. The teacher reminded them that they knew the rules they were breaking (e.g., calling out, walking around the room while she was talking to them as a class, side-chatting loudly). This reminder was conveyed in the phrase, "We've gone over this before." Therefore she was able to justify her own angry response while instructing the class about the appropriate emotional response she expected them to *have* and, even more significant, to *show*.

Thus, a three-part lesson was being learned by the students: (a) there was an appropriate set of feelings to have in a given context; (b) there were conventional ways (e.g., postures, facial expresions, and the like) that were used to express one's feelings to the other participants in the setting; and (c) if you were *not* actually feeling the appropriate feelings in a given situation, you could and were in fact expected to, enact the conventionally accepted bodily and facial configurations that corresponded with the given emotion. *Emotional masquerading,* knowing when and how to disguise inappropriate feelings, is an essential aspect of classroom survival.

Silence and nonverbal behavior are particularly important in classroom interactions, because much of student emotional communications must take place without talk. The traditional classrooms I observed support the generalization that most of the talk is by teacher (Anderson, 1978) and that "children's time is spent overwhelmingly in listening and reading" (Cazden, 1979b). "Silent communication" was frequent between students and teachers. My classroom observations specifically focused on interactional silences; that is, the features and boundaries of silence in face-to-face interactions other than pauses for thought. (This excluded, for example, the silence which may have occurred while doing independent assigned seatwork such as reading or writing exercises.)

Silence Displays

In the following two examples from my field notes each student replied to the teacher's question with silence. In one case the silence was acceptable, in the other it was not (see Table 1).

These two examples suggest that it was not merely whether the silence was or was not appropriate, but the way in which the silent performance was adorned with

Table 1.   Examples of Silences

Speaker	Utterance	Gestural adornment
Example 1 (Acceptable silence)		
Teacher:	What were you doing?	
Student 1:	(silence)	Looks up at teacher with slightly bowed head, eyebrows turned up with slightly quizzical look, shrugs shoulders, raising arms with elbows bent and palms up.
Teachers:	OK. But don't do it again.	
Example 2 (Unacceptable silence)		
Teacher:	What were you doing?	
Student 2:	(silence)	Chin up, lower lip pushed forward, eyebrows in a tight scowl, downward side glance to teacher, left hand on hip which is thrust slightly forward.
Teacher:	Answer me.	
Student 2:	(silence)	same
Teacher:	I asked you a question . . . Answer me . . . I said answer me!	Walks toward student

bodily configuration and gestures. In the first example the gestural adornment was interpreted by the teacher and by the student's peers who were also part of the audience as a public confession as well as a public apology. The teacher was allowed to remain in authority and the social structure was not disrupted. In the second example, however, the nonverbal postures and facial expressions were interpreted quite differently. This assorted package of bodily signals was seen as defiant, a public challenge to the teacher's authority. The child was sent to the principal's office a few minutes later.

Ritual displays have been described as behaviors which provide a "readily readable expression of (an individual's) . . . situation, specifically his intent" as well as "evidence of the actor's alignment in the situation" (Goffman, 1976, p. 69). It seems reasonable then to review the behaviors described under the label "gestural adornments" in Table 1 as *silence displays*. These silent responses are, in fact, conventionalized acts which are choreographed predictably and perfunctorily in portraying alignments and attitudes. The reader can, no doubt, make an accurate guess as to which of the two students would be designated as having a "bad attitude."

The student communicative silences that were most visible occurred in teacher-student confrontations such as those shown in Table 1. Usually these encounters were ones in which the student was being reprimanded and often took place in front of other class members. In these cases I observed two kinds of student silence displays, *submissive subordinate* and *nonsubmissive subordinate*. The first, submissive subordinate, was only observed with interactions with the teacher or other adult authority, never with peers. This display was marked with body gestures such as a bowed head, quizzical expression around the eyes, a smile, even a giggle, if the offense was not too serious, a serious but relaxed facial expression, etc. (recall example 1 in Table 1). The following example describes such a display.

> Johnny plays with his hat. The teacher interrupts the lesson and tells him to stop playing with his hat. Johnny looks down, bowing his head briefly, then looks up at the teacher, his eyes raise first, then his head follows. His eyebrows curl questioningly, and he smiles a rather tentative but affectionate smile. The teacher continues speaking, and as she verbally threatens that he might stay after school, the smile disappears quickly from his face during her utterance.

By contrast, the nonsubmissive subordinate display of silence, which I have labeled *stylized sulking*, carries with it a very different bodily configuration (recall example 2 in Table 1). The protocol in Table 2 illustrates the difference.

The example in Table 2 demonstrated some of the power and control that could be exercised by a student with a silent display of emotions. It appears to be an effective face-saving device for one who must be subordinate. The bodily configuration was easily noted, as the teacher's detailed comments illustrate, but very difficult to modify in a face-to-face encounter.

The performance of this display was often highly stylized and differed for boys and girls. Girls would frequently pose with their chins up, closing their eyelids for elongated periods and casting downward side glances, and often markedly turning

Table 2. Example of A Student's Silent Display of Emotions

Speaker	Utterances, Gestures, and Actions
	(Ann has been kept after school along with several others. Each student is being called to the teacher's desk individually to discuss what they did wrong that day. Ann is called to the teacher's desk as Willa, Ann's friend, is dismissed. Andrea stands at the desk with her chin up, her face tight and fixed, her eyelids closed for elongated periods, and her gaze shifts mostly downward to a side glance, only briefly and rarely looking to the teacher. Ann taps her foot as she stands silent and distant.)
Teacher:	When you stop tapping your toe and looking like that, I'll talk to you.
	(Ann is silent. Her mouth is set tightly, and her lids are lowered and taut—"mean eyes". She continued to tap her foot.)
	(The teacher asks her why she's here, and with no change in affect Ann answers cryptically that she was "yellin' in the hall.")
Teacher:	You're angry?
Ann:	Yeah.
Teacher:	(inaud.) . . . let people know you're angry without being nasty, tapping your toe, calling people names . . .
	(Ann, unchanged, remains silent.)
Teacher:	You're tapping your finger, too. I can see you're still angry . . . come on (almost pleading tone)
	(Teacher makes several other attempts (including a reminder that she's keeping her friend Willa waiting—and Willa is sick), but Ann remains silent and retains her body configuration with no sign of leak. Teacher asks if she would like to sit down and think about it. Ann says "Yeah" and leaves the teacher's desk.)
	(Ann gets a drink, chats with her friend, Willa, while teacher talks to John.)
	(After a few minutes, Ann walks past the teacher's desk to get a handout they were to take home.)
Teacher:	(smiling) Oh, you lost it already.
Ann:	(smiles) Yes.
	(Teacher hands Ann the folder containing the handout.)
	(Ann and Willa are chatting. Ann is smiling. Both girls stand near the teacher's desk, and all talk and laugh, kidding with Ben, Gary, and John about "boyfriends.")
Teacher:	(to Ann) Your whole body and face are different now . . .
	(Teacher continues to comment on her affect change and asks again what was going on before. Now Ann goes into a fluent narrative about her argument with Sam. The teacher responds, saying, "But that doesn't tell me about all this other stuff . . . tapping your toe . . .")
	(They continue to talk briefly; then the teacher asks if Ann will try to behave tomorrow. Ann mumbles "Yeah", and the teacher smiles, saying, "Can you say it differently?" Ann smiles and says, "Yes, Miss Davis," as she turns to leave.)

their heads sideward as well as upward. Girls also would rest their chins on their hand with elbow support on their desks. Striking or getting into the pose was usually with an abrupt movement that would sometimes be marked with a sound like the elbow striking the desk or a verbal marker like "humpf." Since silence displays could easily go unnoticed, it was necessary to draw some attention to the silence, and with the girls it seemed to be primarily with a flourish of getting into the pose.

Boys usually displayed somewhat differently. Their "stylized sulking" was usually characterized by head downward, arms crossed at the chest, legs spread wide and, usually the desk pushed away. Often they would mark the silence by knocking over a chair or pushing loudly on their desk, ensuring that others heard and saw the performance. Another noticeable characteristic of the boys' performance was that they sat down, deeply slumped in their chairs. This was a clear violation of the constant reminder in classrooms to "sit up" and "sit tall." Teachers would often talk about "working on" sitting up, feet under the desk, lining up, et al. The silence displays went against all the body idiom rules of the classroom. Even when less extreme postures were taken, however, the facial expression remained an easily read portrait of emotion.

How did students use the sulk? What functions did it seem to perform? One of the major results of the silent display was that it clearly got attention. Although teachers referred to it differently as "pouting," "fretting," "acting spoiled," "rebellious," "acting nasty," or "having a temper tantrum," all noticed it and usually responded. Often the student benefited.

Students often got in trouble in classrooms for fighting with each other. I had observed several silent devices for avoiding confrontation. If a student had been in an argument with another student, for example, getting into a sulk that attracted the teacher's attention would often result in the teacher moving the student's desk or sending the child out of the room. Sulking among peers was generally short-lived. In these cases of elongated peer–peer sulking, the audience appeared to be the adult in control.

Stylized Sulking: Its Meaning and Treatment in Context

The behavioral event of stylized sulking was a characteristic response in face-to-face clashes of will between student and teacher. Students who frequently used the displays were also students who were often identified as having "bad attitudes," and as a result, were tracked out of academic programs.

Stylized sulking as a school-related problem seems age-related. Though these displays were not performed exclusively by students in the intermediate grades (4–6), they were significantly more prominent in these grades. Sulking was primarily performed in a silent channel and an angry key. It seems, in fact, a last holding place to express defiance. For those students who did cross the line, the predictable verbal accompaniment transformed the crime from one of "bad attitude" to one of insolence and insubordination. These latter labels usually were associated with treatments more extreme than low-track classes (e.g., suspension, psychological guidance, etc.).

Stylized sulking was usually performed to an authority figure. The individual sulker was subordinate in status to the receiver of the display. Though the display, which was often used as a face-saving device, is certainly meant to be seen by on-looking peers, the primary audience was the adult in control. Sulking generally appeared in settings where an authority figure was in control and usually in direct conflict with the performer. Classrooms, hallways, and lunchrooms were predictable settings for this kind of display. Further, the behavior appeared more in classes which had not "weeded out bad attitudes." In settings where propriety had been selected for (Academics Plus classes), few, if any, sulking events were observed (even for the few students who had been observed sulking in the heterogeneous classes the year before). Certain agreed-upon expectations of attitude and behavior in the Academics Plus classes changed the classroom context in a way that made sulking no longer adaptive. The demeanor was no longer appropriate for the teacher or the peer group in the setting. Though the act of sulking itself was rarely, if ever, mentioned and was almost never consciously a part of the assessment of a student's attitude, students who sulked repeatedly had negative characteristics attributed to them as a result. Stylized sulking was not consciously, but nonetheless quite effectively, selected out in the process of identifying "good attitudes."

Another concern focuses on how stylized sulking was treated in this community. As mentioned earlier, though the entire student population observed was black, the faculty was half black and half whites. The data suggest that there were in general commonly held views about these displays that were different for most blacks and white. (The data consisted of views directly expressed about stylized sulking, observations of the ways in which black and white teachers behaved in response to these displays and, finally, comments made by the faculty and parents about the differences they themselves were conscious of concerning the way white teachers and black teachers generally responded). In general it was felt that white teachers tended to be more "lenient" and "permissive" where this type of communication was concerned. A black teacher was more likely to discipline a dramatic sulking display, send the child to the office, call the parent, or in some way immediately chastize the student. Black parents often scolded or threatened to hit children for such displays. In church and community contexts, an "attitude" was quickly conveyed in such displays, and children were told to leave or modify their behavior. A white teacher, on the other hand, might more likely ask a child to verbalize his or her feelings as well as directly refer to the feelings the display seemed to communicate (e.g., I can see you're feeling angry). In general, whites were seen as less likely to discipline these "temper tantrums." Acceptance of the behavior tended to escalate student use of it, creating classrooms which were viewed as having bad attitudes.

Stylized sulking seemed to be seen as a "cultural" variation of expression and communication. Sulking in the highly stylized way it was performed by many of the students was viewed by both black and white teachers as part of a stereotypic communicative style of blacks. Much the way Jewish or Italian gestural style might be characterized, so, too, this behavior might easily be interpreted as a black gestural performance.

Black parents and teachers suggested that white teachers might be more tolerant of such behaviors because they were "intimidated by black children and their parents." White teachers tended to talk about student "hostility" and the need to be more verbal about feelings. Controversies over the use of nonstandard varieties of English and recent concern with bilingual and multicultural education provided a background of growing sensitivity to and awareness of cultural variation in communication which might help explain white teachers' acceptance of sulking. By allowing such behaviors, white teachers might believe they were expressing acceptance of cultural diversity: "It's part of their culture."

Black teachers and parents frequently expressed concern that this permisiveness and lenience were signs of "low standards" or of "not caring about" these black kids and whether they learned the necessary skills, attitudinal and academic which were seen as prerequisites to success. White teachers, too, expressed similar concerns about "low standards," often after looking to stricter black teachers for appropriate models for reaction.

Humor, teasing, and affection were instructionally effective strategies used by both black and white teachers in reponse to sulking displays. These behaviors tended to minimize the intensity of the confrontation and the tone of insubordination on the part of the student.

In observations of language acquisition in poor white working-class families, Peggy Miller (personal communication, May 10, 1981) found that mothers would tell their babies (under 2 years old) to make "mean eyes" as part of a communicative routine. In the black community in which this study was conducted, expressed norms of appropriate interaction demeanor included "looking ready to fight" (Davis, 1981), and "not taking shit" (May, 1981).

The stylized sulking could be interpreted as one behavioral element of a "tough" demeanor; yet how sulking behavior was interpreted appeared to be highly dependent on contextualization cues. One child's sulk was read as "anger and hostility," while another, appearing to display the same or very similar physical characteristics, was merely "being dramatic" or "needing attention." Very similar behaviors were interpreted in very different ways. In one case the behavior could be glossed as style and in another case "bad attitude."

It appeared that student sulking could be interpreted positively or negatively depending on when and how the display was performed in a particular context. Certain children could signal the message "this is play" (Bateson, 1972a), but for the most part it was a behavior that carried the image of incorrect deference and demeanor and was usually interpreted as indicative of a "bad attitude."

Goffman (1976) has commented that "the human use of displays is complicated by the human capacity for reframing behavior (p. 71). Rituals become ritualized and transformations can be transformed. Performances become styled and coded in distinguishable ways as a result of cultural influences. Comedians typically draw on these styles and use these displays in parenthesized fashion as a resource for humor. Most popular for young audiences is actor Gary Coleman's quotable line and memorable posturing of "stylized sulking" on the TV situation comedy "Different

Strokes." When he says to his big brother, "What chu talkin' about, Willis?" his eyes are narrowed and his demeanor is clearly tough and black. But the display is contextualized in such a way that it is a parody of being tough and black. It is rekeyed in such a way that it becomes lighthearted and funny. Moods as well as ethnic and class styles are being played with.

Geertz (1973) described what he called a stratified hierarchy of meaningful structures as he detailed the subtle yet distinct differences between twitches, winks, fake winks, parodies of winks, and rehearsals of parodies of winks. In much the same way this example of stylized sulking can be "unpacked." It can be performed by design for comic effect as well as threatening effect.

In addition to expressing emotion, displays provide evidence of an actor's alignment. Sulking displays therefore must also be considered this way. In general, sulking displays function as face-saving devices which maintain dignity through individual autonomy when confronted by an authority in control. The display indicates the actor's refusal to be aligned with the authority figure. The stylized sulking characteristic of black communicative repertoire seems to be interpreted as a statement of alignment with the student's own ethnicity and socioeconomic class.

STEPS

I first noticed steps early in the spring of my first year of fieldwork. Girls would almost burst out of the hall at recess onto the playground, form lines, and begin "doin' steps," chorally chanted rhymes similar to, yet distinct from, drills and cheers. The chanted talk was punctuated by a steady alternating rhythm of footstepping and handclapping. The steppers lined up and performed in chorus as well as individually down the line. There were numerous rhymes, and each rhyme had its own choreography and rhythm. Entire recess periods would be spent "doin' steps," and it was often difficult for students to stop when they went back to their classrooms. Girls would chant or "step" in the room and be told to "stop" or "settle down." The steps were not unique to this school, and, in fact, one could see the same performances in parks, driveways, and on front steps all over the city throughout the fair-weather months.

Within the community, challenges and competitions were held in which different neighborhood blocks would peform the rhymes for judging. Groups had names like "Stars" or "Bad Girls" and often had captains who were in charge. In some cases groups had uniforms, paid for by church or community groups.

In the spring the staff and administration turned attention to this group activity. The dances were labeled as "lewd," "fresh," "inappropriate for school," "disrespectful," and simply "too sexual." One morning the principal banned the dances in the school over the public address system, saying, "Nice girls don't do that."

The genre was viewed as representing "deteriorating attitudes." It broke norms of propriety which were of central importance in the school ethos.

When studying children's peer-group culture all over the world, not only the "playful whimsical and artful aspects" emerge but also the "aggressive, obscene, scatological, antiauthoritarian, and inversive elements" (see Bauman, 1982). Peer culture folklore is often representative of counterculture values. Goody (1968) noted this "gap between the public literate tradition of school and the very different and indeed often directly contradictory private oral traditions of the pupil's family and peer group" (p. 59).

Although steps demonstrated a wide variety of language competencies in their verbal performances, none of them "counted" as verbal skill in school contexts. Each performance indicated an alignment with peer-group culture. Each was considered inappropriate and was associated with bad or deteriorating attitudes.

The group of girls I observed sometimes participated in competitions. Although several different neighborhood block groups were represented, none had uniforms, but some said they were getting them soon. At school the girls in one class would practice together to compete with another class at school. The performances would occur spontaneously wherever an appropriate setting was available. When the playground performances were no longer permitted after the ban, many of the girls could be found doing steps in the school bathrooms.

Stepping and Spelling Mississippi

One of the stepping street rhymes, "Mississippi," seemed to be not only related to matters of propriety and attitude in general but to literacy in particular. "Mississippi" was performed in a variety of ways, each version having its own choreography and rhythm to accompany and accent the verbal alternations. Each version had as its core the spelling of the word *Mississippi*. These variations included description of the metaphorical references to the letters and ongoing narratives which played with the letters as beginnings of utterances.

Thus, the performance of "Mississippi" was an intersection of visual and verbal codes by using the body dramatically as an iconic sign for the letters. The most prominent, noticeable, and controversial use of bodily representation of the letters was the formation of the letter *s*, or "crooked letter." The transformation of the body into the letter *s* was demonstrated in a limbolike dancing movement with one arm forming a crook at the shoulder. It was not uncommon to find an elementary school teacher asking students to make their bodies shape a letter or to treat letters as representatives of familiar objects or person as part of reading instruction. Yet although the steppers successfully performed such bodily letter representation, it was interpreted negatively; the iconic sign was dressed with too sexual a body idiom for school and (often) family contexts.

It appeared that few observers actually associated the dance movement with the words or letters. The performances were not studied but only casually observed, if observed at all, by most of the staff. The range of teacher responses to the dance movements in "Mississippi" included "You have to be an adult to know it was suggestive," "It's like an orgasm," "It's like nothing I've never seen before; it could be a nice kid, then all of a sudden it just comes over her," "It's like an epileptic fit," "It's bad," or "Nasty."

Mississippi: A Display of Literacy-Related Competencies

In informal interviews and discussions, teachers regularly commented that their students lacked necessary language and literacy skills. They were concerned that students had deficiencies in word analysis skills such as rhyming, syllabification, and identifying initial and medial blends. They said their students lacked comprehension skills such as being able to identify main ideas, develop narrative themes, recognize semantic differences in homonyms, and so on. Finally, they were concerned that their students lacked the good citizenship skills that were necessary for school instruction in language arts and literacy—listening to or cooperating with one another, getting organized, or working in groups. These teacher concerns provided a background for considering the following description of one of the most popular steps.

Several versions are presented in Table 3. These examples of oral group performance provide strong evidence that both the citizenship skills and the language skills identified by teachers as deficiencies for this population were demonstrated regularly in peer-group contexts.

Each girl took a turn for an individual performance, stepping out of the line with an expression such as "Give me room." Each was expected to have her own style within the conventions and boundaries of the performance, using embellishments and markers of individuality. The degree of oral composing varied, but performers who were creative were recognized for their virtuosity and often became captains, organizing and instructing the others.

While teachers and parents had heard and seen the steps performed often enough to notice and ban them, most had never really listened enough to be aware of the general content. Instead, they were aware of isolated words (e.g., example 4 of Table 3) or dance movements (e.g., the performance of the "crooked letter") that were considered too sexual or improper. Although stepping performances were public and prominent, the melodic prosody of the chants made the words and meaning almost unintelligible. Once the "sirens" lured a listener in, the taboo words could be heard with an assaulting clarity.

Mississippi: Its Meaning and Treatment in Context

An interesting aspect of this speech event was the way it was treated. As with stylized sulking, the data suggest that there were general commonly held views about this event that were slightly different for most blacks and whites. In general, as with sulking, it was felt that white teachers tended to be more "lenient" and "permissive" concerning the Mississippi dances. Black teachers in general were less likely to permit performances of the dances and stopped them immediately. White teachers tended to be more ambiguous about the behavior and less likely to stop it when it first appeared in the spring.

Stepping, like stylized sulking, was viewed as a "cultural" variation of expression and communication. "Doin' steps" was something that black girls do. The musical chants and movements were referred to by several white and black teachers as "ethnic type dances" reminiscent of "African music" and "Caribbean music."

Teachers were concerned about associated racial statements and were responsive

Table 3. Mississippi

Oral performance	Description
1. *M I SS I SS I PP I*	A straight spelling, reciting, each letter in rhythmic, patterned clusters, the most concrete form of the rhyme.
2. *M I* crooked letter, crooked letter, *I* crooked letter crooked letter *I*, hump back hump back, *I*.	A spelling that includes a description or metaphorical reference to the physical features of some of the letters. In this version, "crooked letter" refers to *S* and "hump back" to *P*. The children sometimes refer to the entire genre of steps as "Kookelater" (crooked letter) dances". The children perform the *S* in a limbolike dance movement with one arm forming a crook at the shoulder.

3.   *M* for the money
    I if ya give it to me
    S sock it (to me)
    S sock it (to me)
    I if I buy it from ya
    S sock it
    S sock it
    I if I take it from ya
    P pump it
    P pump it
    I : : : :
	This version is often followed by version 2 with a smooth transition. The spelling uses the letters of *Mississippi* to produce the first word of each line in an ongoing narrative.

4.   Hey (name), yo
    You wanted on the phone
    Who is it? Your nigger. I bet he
    wants my lips, my tits, my butt, my
    smut. My crooked letter, crooked letter, *I*
	A controversial narrative that is only punctuated with parts of the spelling. The play with the narrative rather than the orthography dominates the verbal content. The "crooked letter" by its position in a series of "wants" take on an ambiguous sexual meaning, especially as the letter is being adorned in dance.

5.   Hey, Deedee, yo
    Spell Mississippi
    Spell Mississippi right now
    You take my hands up high
    You take my feet down low
    I cross my legs with that gigolo
    If you don't like that
    Throw it in the trash
    And then I'm bustin out
    With that Jordache
    Look in the sky
    With that Calvin Klein
    I'm gonna lay in the dirt
    With that Sergiert (Sergio Valente)
    I'm gonna bust a balloon
    With that Sassoon
    Gonna be ready
    With that Teddy
    I'm gonna be on the rail
    With that Vanderbail
    With the is-*M* is-*I*
    Crooked letter crooked letter *I*
	This version of *Mississippi* was performed by fewer individuals and was viewed as an accomplished recitation by peers. That jeans theme made it a favored version of the narrative performance.

to them. One white teacher told me that she had been too lenient about the Mississippi dances. She came to this conclusion when she overheard a black teacher's comment about another white teacher's tolerance of the dance until his *own* white daughter learned it.

As with sulking, black teachers and parents frequently expressed concern that the permissiveness and lenience toward the peformance of steps indicated "low standards" for the students. Some parents and support staff who were influential in having it banned expressed concern for the children's safety, suggesting suspicious men had been seen "cruising" the area while the girls danced in the playground. One youngster said she agreed with the ban because her mother had told her about a girl who did the dance and was raped afterward. In this primarily low-income neighborhood, concern with crime was familiar to the children. Thus, many who opposed the dances seemed to be concerned more with the girls' potential vulnerability rather than their "bad attitudes."

Those who spoke earliest and most strongly against the dances were usually black faculty and parents who were active religiously (Muslim and Christian) and more middle-income economically. Influential parents in this community who were strongly active in the Home and School Association were often (though not always) representative of the higher income families in the community. The community itself was aspiringly upwardly mobile and concerned with styles of life that were often described by community members as "decent" (Anderson, 1981). This was consistent with school's focus on "attitude." The dances were thought of as indecent and reflective of bad attitudes all too easily.

However, just blocks away and in many parts of the city, the same dance performances met with a very different interpretation. There they were viewed as representative of black culture but were treated very differently. For example, one city school known for its arts program held a spring festival where performances of Mississippi and other steps were (in modified version) applauded by large parent audiences. In addition, the International House on a city university campus was the setting for an all-day festival organized by the directors of a drama, drum, and dance ensemble—Matunda ya Africa (Fruit of Africa). The festival was a city-wide competition for steps, drills, and cheers. The schedule of events from the Jump for Joy Festival indicated a striking contrast to the school with the ban—a very positive and proud emphasis on the black heritage of the lyrics and dances. It is interesting to note, however, that although the Jump for Joy Festival was held only a few miles away, none of the parents or the children from the study site attended.

There was not, however *complete* uniformity of opposition to the dances in the study site community. Some community members, both parents and staff, thought the school had overreacted. They thought the kids were entertaining and skillful. They also thought they were "just being kids."

This particular community could be characterized as being extremely responsive to the expressed norms of the school. Many parents who had initially permitted the dances enforced the ban at home, after the school banned them. One student who had been a stepping captain the year before told me that she didn't do steps anymore because her mother wanted her to get into the Academics Plus Program.

Another way of handling the choice was suggested by a parent in a neighboring community who stopped her daughter from doing steps which were nasty and taught her traditional African folk dances instead (Schieffelin, personal communication, June 10, 1981). These dance genres carried with them a hierarchy of status and were seen as statements of alignment with social class. The dances (steps and folk dances) themselves might not be *structurally* very different, but the *messages* they conveyed about social and economic class were vastly different.

Differences in how doin' steps is interpreted can be seen by looking across black communities. For example, in one community was located the previously mentioned Fruit of Africa's School for Understanding. Its presence and influence might account for some of the difference in how that community responded. The school, known for its arts program, used steps as an aesthetic educational resource. The "arts school" community was similar to, if not higher and more middle class socioeconomically than the study site community. However, in the study site community the goals of back to basics and propriety were strongly influential in contributing to its response to steps. In brief, although there were similarities across communities (e.g., black, urban) there was a wide range of response to steps; nasty, black culture, aesthetic peer culture. In those communities where the dance was viewed as black culture or as aesthetic peer culture, it was also viewed as an educational resource.

Mississippi Conveys Social Messages

The performance of "Mississippi" can be examined as an instructional routine. In many ways the routine sounded like what one might expect in a school classroom. Directions were called to an individual to spell a word—*Mississippi*. Yet there were several aspects of the instruction that seem to break with expected norms of speech and politeness and with predictable co-occurrence rules of classrooms.

First, instead of a single teacher's voice, the entire group of steppers chanted the request in loud chorus. This was the reverse of the stereotypic model of an individual teacher's request followed by an entire class's choral response. The request itself had marked characteristics that countered expectations of what a classroom teacher would say.

> Hey, (Wendy). Spell Mississippi.
> Spell Mississippi right now!

The request sounded like a challenge or a dare. Consider some of the linguistic markers that run counter to expectations of co-occurrence rules. The use of the word "hey" is informal, usually considered inappropriate for school, and had a slightly threatening quality—as if one was being "called out" rather than "called on." Further, there was an impatient tone to the demand as a result of the quick repetition "Spell Mississippi" and the conclusion "right now." It has been pointed out that teachers tended to use politeness forms frequently to modify the power and control they have. These forms softened acts of instruction that might be interpreted as face-threatening to students (see Cazden, 1979b). The teacher request in "Mississippi" seems to do exactly the opposite. Politeness forms were absent and the face-threatening nature was intensified, even though the tone was an angry one.

The stepper who was called on to perform the spelling task usually uttered a quick phrase like "gimme room" or "no sweat" as she jumped forward to begin her routine. These utterances indicated the stepper's willingness to take on the dare and the stepper's confidence that the performance was fully within the range of her competencies. Thus the instructional routine set up an aggressive and suspicious teacher command and a student stepper who took on the challenge with a sexual swagger and obvious confidence about her spelling prowess.

A spelling exercise, ordinarily practiced in the classroom, was transformed through linguistic play and dance with a marked shift ownership. By reframing the instructional exchange, the literacy-related behaviors were recontextualized—taken from the school's mode of literacy instruction and made a part of the children's own world. Interpretive frames were created that signal to onlookers that this particular performance of literacy-related behaviors did not belong to or count for school.

The syncopation of this spelling lesson allowed children, as subordinates, to mock school instruction. In much the same way, skits and jokes can present concrete formulations of an abstract cultural symbol, the images conveyed in the "Mississippi" performance can be seen as containing interpretations of the children's symbolic constructions of their own social portraits of the dynamics of schooling.

Thus the message conveyed by these students through the performance of "Mississippi" can seem quite a poignant one. It was not merely defiant. It was not merely black. It can easily be seen as face-saving, a way of maintaining dignity through collective autonomy when confronted with the school's undermining doubt in their ability. At the end of "Mississippi" the entire group does the spelling performance in a striking flourish, declaring for all to see their excellence as literate spellers, dancers, and as kids.

CONCLUSION: LITERACY—IT'S AN ATTITUDE

In a recent ad in the *New York Times* there is a picture of a striking blonde dressed in casual elegance and posed in a relaxed and sophisticated posture. The ad, for JH Collectibles, reads:

JH. It's an attitude.

Indeed, it is an easy portrayal to read. The total composite of stance, facial expression, dress, and overt cues of ethnic physical origins, conveys a message of alignment with upper-class social status. In just this way teachers read student portrayals of attitude, alignment, and readiness for literacy.

This chapter was concerned with identifying the domain of the concept of attitude in a particular community. The focus on attitude was stimulated by the significance it held for the participants in the setting. Attitude was the key element for student success in the school. It was the identifying ingredient for stratifying classes and tracking students. A "good attitude" was a prerequisite for admittance to the "success" track of this particular school. When discussing the program with a group of new incoming parents, the principal made it clear that if parents made sure the kids came with a "good attitude," the school would do everything in its power to assure their success in reading and writing skills and their chances of getting into "better" schools (magnet and academic schools in the city). This exchange was clear to all participants. It was a trade of appropriate attitudes for literacy. Literacy was a commodity in the school's domain, and the school made decisions as to when it would be parceled out.

"Attitude" had different meanings to different individuals and in different contexts. Yet if the exchange was to be understood in terms of its social significance as well as its behavioral manifestations, both attitude and literacy had to be understood in terms of not only the way they were talked about but also in terms of the way they functioned.

Two key events, *stylized sulking* and *doin' steps*, were selected for specific attention for several reasons. They were both prominent and controversial and they were both behaviors that consciously or unconsciously were associated with assessments of attitude. Teachers regularly evaluated attitude, yet it was difficult to identify just what went into those judgments. The articulated characteristics were an assorted set of attributes which ranged from getting homework done and having involved parents to being respectful and ladylike. Some categories focused on "work habits" while others suggested a concern with signs of appropriate deference and demeanor. All the categories indicated some signals of alignment, if not allegiance, to the school, its ethos, and its agenda.

The silent display of stylized sulking and the speech event "Mississippi" were seen as representative of bad or deteriorating attitudes and were squelched by tracking, which effectively phased out the former behavior, and school banning, which prohibited the latter behavior. As demonstrated earlier, both behaviors were interpreted as part of black gestural and communicative style.

Beyond the issue of school and community response to "attitude," expressive forms such as stylized sulking or steps can be viewed as signs of sociocultural processes occurring within certain sets of institutionally structured situations. The expressive forms used by the student can be seen as a message of individual (in the case of stylized sulking) or collective (in the case of "Mississippi") autonomy in the face of authority. Further, expressive forms point to a major contradiction between what students were capable of in terms of literacy behaviors and what was expected concerning their ability. The expressive forms discussed are face-saving devices which allow for pride and ownership in circumstances where opportunities for such prizes are scarce.

The fact that a prominent behavioral event which was significant regarding the assessment of attitudes was associated with a display of black culture raises another important issue. Is there a trade of blackness for literacy success in the study site? The answer is a complicated one.

The particular community in which the study was conducted was recently black (in the last 15 years); formerly it had been largely Jewish and Irish. A general theme in the neighborhood was one of upward mobility. Moreover, the community was widely supportive of and responsive to the school as an institutional leader.

The theme of black pride was very strongly dominant in the school community, though in classrooms, in church, and at home students would be reprimanded for using nonstandard vernacular or stylized sulking displays. Many teachers and parents had taken trips to Africa, taught black history, and participated in various African cultural activities. Several families in the community were from Africa (10 children in all). Teachers focused curriculum projects on black history and black pride themes. In regular assembly programs student choruses sang out in clear and vibrant tones "To be young, gifted, and black, that's where it's at."

These examples are offered in order to demonstrate that, indeed, the school and the community were not consciously attempting to squelch blackness or pride in being black. The examples indicate that black pride and black history were prominent themes in the school and community.

The examples of sulking and stepping seemed more to be associated with a certain set of black communicative displays that had typically been a class marker for failure in our society. Like nonstandard vernacular, these "street" behaviors tended to close rather than open doors for black children who were trying to be upwardly mobile in our society. No matter how legitimate a linguistic or behavioral analysis of such behavior is, the key factor of legitimacy is how these behaviors are interpreted in the social world in which they are performed. For the children in the study site most parents and teachers agreed: The cost was too high. Symbols of black "street" behavior such as stepping and stylized sulking were seen as ethnic, class, and socioeconomic markers which interfered with success and might, as the discussion has shown, even limit access to socially valued commodies such as literacy.

Since fear about the focus on good attitudes made community members especially sensitive to any markers associated with black vernacular "street" culture, little latitude was allowed for any displays concerning sex (particularly for girls) or aggression (particularly for boys). For example, sexual ambiguity in stepping dances was interpreted quickly as an indicator of the performer's sexual experience. Disgruntled looks and postures (e.g., stylized sulking) were read as threats of violence and potential aggression.

Yet preadolescent peer culture (across cultures and subcultures) has been widely documented to be full of sexual, aggressive, and antiauthoritative elements. In other communities and cultures, these behaviors are seen as natural and developmental rather than as representative of bad attitudes. Though more inversive aspects of peer culture behavior may not be encouraged, more tolerance is often extended for their playful expression.

In the case of assessing attitudes in the study site, in Bateson's (1972) terms, the "nip" became the "bite" rather than denoting it. The sign was read as the act rather than a suggestion of it. Attitude and not literacy became the primary instructional focus. Although a good attitude was viewed as a means to an end (i.e., literacy achievement), the focus was so intense and exclusive that instructional interaction simply got stuck there.

Though the parents and faculty in the study site continued to strive for the academic success of these students, test scores remained low and a fear of stereotypic ghetto failure dominated the atmosphere. Any behaviors that signaled potential failure were squelched quickly. In particular, assessments of behavioral displays associated with black vernacular culture were perceived as indicators of bad attitudes. As a result, students with "an attitude" were placed in lower-track classes and were, in turn, seen as skill deficient. Their performance errors (which might have been interpreted as careless mistakes in more affluent and middle-class classes where the predicted scenario was one of success) were regularly viewed as skill deficiencies. Once students were tracked in lower classes, teachers assumed that they *could not*, rather than *would not*, do the work. The former implied a skill deficiency, the later, an issue of social control. The assessment here tended to measure the degree of student acceptance or resistance to the school's values rather than student language or literacy abilities. By confusing the two areas we make little progress in ameliorating the circumstances of either one.

REFERENCES

Anderson, E.S. (1978). *Learning to speak with style: A study of sociolinguistic skills of children.* Unpublished dissertation, Stanford Univeristy.

Bateson, G. (1972a). A theory of play and fantasy. In *Steps to an ecology of mind.* New York: Ballantine.

Bateson, G. (1972b). Social planning and the concept of duetero-learning. In *Steps to an ecology of mind.* New York: Ballantine.

Bauman, R. (1982). Ethnography of children's folklore. In P. Gilmore & A. Glatthorn (Eds.), *Children in and out of school.* Washngton, DC: Center for Applied Linguistics.

Bellack, A., Kliebard, H., Hyman, R. T., & Smith, F. L. (1966). *The language of the classroom.* New York: Teacher College Press.

Cazden, C. (1979). Language in educational variation in the teacher-talk register. In *Language in public life,* Washington DC: 30th Annual Georgetown University Round Table.

Cazden, C., John, V., & Hymes, D. (Eds.). (1972). *Functions of language in the classroom.* New York: Teachers College Press.

Davis, A. (1981). Harriet Tubman School: Community perspectives. In D. Hymes (Principal Investigator), *The ethnographic monitoring of children's language arts skills* (Final Report to National Institute of Education). Washington, DC: National Institute of Education.

Edwards, A., & Furlong, V. (1978). *The language of teaching.* London: Heineman.

Geertz, C. (1973). *The interpretation of cultures.* New York: Basic Books.

Gilmore, P., and Glatthorn, A. (Eds.) (1982). *Children in and out of school.* Washington, DC: Center for Applied Linguistics.

Goffman, E. (1976). Gender advertisements. *Studies in the Anthropology of Visual Communication, 3,* (2).

Goody, J. (1968). *Literacy in traditional societies.* Cambridge: Cambridge University Press.

Hochschild, A., (1979). Emotion work, feeling rules and social structure. *American Journal of Sociology, 85* (3), 551–575.

Hymes, D. H. (1962). The ethnography of speaking. In T. Gladwin & W. C. Sturtevant (Eds.), *Anthropology and human behavior.* Washington, DC: Anthropological Society of Washington.

May, L. (1981). Spaulding School: Attention and styles of interaction. In D. Hymes (Principal Investigator), *The ethnogaphic monitoring of children's language arts skills* (Final Report to National Institute of Education) Washington, DC: National Institute of Education.

McDermott, R. P. (1976). *Kids make sense: An ethnographic account of the interactional management of success and failure in one first grade classroom.* Doctoral Dissertation, Stanford University, Stanford, CA.

Mehan, H. (1979). *Learning lessons: The social organization of classroom behavior.* Cambridge, MA: Harvard University Press.

Mehan, H., Cazden, C., Coles, L., Fisher, S., & Maroules, N. (1976). *The social organization of classroom lessons.* San Diego: Center for Human Information Processing, University of California.

Spindler, G. (Ed.). (1982). *Doing the ethnography of schooling.* New York: Holt, Rinehart & Winston.

PART THREE

LITERACY AND INSTRUCTION

6 Reading as a Social Process in a Middle School Classroom

David Bloome

University of Michigan

The primary purpose of this chapter is to explore the nature of reading as a social process in urban, middle school classrooms. Of special concern is how reading as a social and cultural process mediates students' interaction with and interpretation of printed text.

A second purpose is to document part of the experience of students in urban, middle school classrooms. Documentation is important for at least two reasons. First, too frequently the history of nonmajority groups within society's institutions is lost or distorted. Second, given the contemporary concern and political rhetoric with education, it is important to have grounded descriptions of what actually occurs in classrooms so that political debate and policy-making can be properly informed.

The chapter is organized into three sections. In the first, recent research concerned with building a theory of reading as a social process is briefly discussed (see Bloome & Green, 1982b, 1984, for extended discussions of related research). The research is primarily based in anthropology, sociolinguistics, the sociology of education, and the ethnography of communication. In the second section, findings from an ethnographic study of reading in an eighth-grade classroom is presented. The findings are part of a series of studies on reading and writing as social processes in urban, middle school classrooms (see also Bloome, 1983a, 1983b, 1984a, 1984b; Bloome & Argumedo, 1983; Bloome & Golden, 1982; Bloome & Green, 1982a). Finally, in the third section, the implications of the findings for building a theory of reading as a social process are discussed.

Underlying the discussion in this chapter is a view of reading and literacy development as the process of becoming a member of a community based on written language (see Robinson, Chap. 14, this volume). A community may be broadly defined (such as a profession or ethnic group) or narrowly defined (such as a family or classroom). Regardless, the community sets standards and determines appropriate ways of constituting written language events, i.e., ways of interacting with and interpreting text. Almost by definition, then, reading is a social process—a means to participate in and establish a community or social group. In this chapter, I am especially concerned with the social relationships among those people actually participating in a reading event. That is, the emphasis is on the face-to-face interaction of people engaged in a reading event, how they establish social relationships among themselves including means for interacting with the interpreting written language. Less emphasized are those literary and psychological issues studies concerned with the social relationships between author and reader (for a discussion of these issues, see Golden, Chap. 8, this volume; Robinson, Chap. 14, this volume; Bruce, 1981).

RESEARCH ON READING AS A SOCIAL PROCESS

Recent research concerned with reading as a social process can, for heuristic purposes, be divided into three groups. A first group of studies views reading as a cognitive-linguistic process embedded in a social-communicative context. The social-communicative context influences the nature of reading as a cognitive-linguistic process. A second group of studies is primarily concerned with the social uses of reading. Reading and writing are viewed as manifestations and reflections of the culture in which the children's day-to-day activities are embedded. Reading and writing, like sewing, working on cars, playing baseball, dating, and going to church, are viewed as manifestations of a culture. The description of reading and writing is the further description of people's culture. Among the questions asked by these studies are: What are the roles of reading in society? How, where, and when do people read? For what purposes? What counts as reading? How does what counts as reading differ across situations? How are reading activities interpersonally organized? The third group of studies is primarily concerned with literacy as a sociocognitive process. Both learning to read and reading itself are viewed as part of a society's enculturation process. Through reading, children not only learn culturally appropriate information, activities, values, and interpersonal relationships, they also learn culturally appropriate ways of thinking about the world, ways of problem solving, and other cognitive processes. Among the questions asked by these studies are: How does literacy learning influence how one views the world? How does literacy learning influence thought, problem solving, and other cognitive processes.

Reading as Embedded in a Social/Communicative Context

In order to participate in classroom reading events, students need to gain access to those events. Gaining access requires more than being present (although as McDermott, 1976, has shown, being present is itself a social accomplishment). Gaining access to classroom reading events involves gaining opportunities to interact with text or language in ways appropriate to school-based reading development.

On one hand, gaining access is a matter of communicative competence. Students need to know how to gain the floor, hold the floor, demonstrate group membership, and engage in communicative behavior appropriate to the situation. However, gaining access can also be a matter of cross-cultural interaction between school culture and students' home culture. For example, Michaels (1981) has described how access to literacy learning situations can be denied because of students' culturally based narrative styles. However, the issue is not only whether or not students gain access to literacy learning opportunities, it is also the kinds of literacy learning opportunities students receive (Paris & Wixson, chap. 2, this volume). Collins (1981) has described how the distribution of literacy learning tasks may be related to students' culturally based prosodic style during oral reading. That is, the distribution of different kinds of literacy learning tasks rather than being based on developmental needs may be based on the manifestation of students' home culture within the classroom.

In addition to gaining access, students need to appropriately display their reading behavior. For example, students who have read and understood a text but do not raise their hands in response to a teacher's question may not be viewed as having read the text. Cross-cultural differences between students and teachers may result (a) in some students not appropriately displaying reading knowledge (e.g., Gumperz & Tannen, 1979), and (b) in teachers misevaluating student reading knowlege (e.g., Gumperz & Tannen, 1979; Scollon & Scollon, 1982). For example, if a student answers a set of comprehension questions in terms of his/her own experience and background knowledge, the student may get answers that disagree with the answers designated as correct by the textbook or teacher (e.g., Bloome, 1983b). Yet, in terms of the student's background knowledge and experience the answers may be sensible. There is a potential in such situations for the student to be misevaluated. Part of what many students need to learn in school is not to answer questions in terms of their own background knowledge and experience but rather in terms of the text and the background knowledge and experience assumed by the text (Bloome, 1982; Scollon & Scollon, 1982).

The Social Uses of Literacy

What counts as reading and writing may vary across situations. The expectations for what reading and writing will look like, the social meanings of reading and writing, and the purposes for which people read and write vary across situations. For example, reading prayers in a church looks different and is done for a different purpose than reading an insurance contract at Sears.

Researchers have explored the range and social meanings of literacy activities across communities (e.g., Heath, 1982, 1983; Scheiffelin & Cochran-Smith, 1984; Scollon & Scollon, 1984; Reder & Green, in press), within a community (e.g., Anderson & Stokes, 1984; Jacob, 1984; Taylor, 1983; Taylor & Dorsey-Gaines, 1982); across classroom and home cultures (e.g., Bloome & Green, 1982a; Bloome, 1984a; Cook-Gumperz, Gumperz, & Simons, 1981; Heath, 1982; Gilmore, 1981; Hymes, 1981; Philips, 1983); and within classrooms (e.g., Au, 1980; Griffin, 1977; Bloome, 1982). The findings of these studies have suggested five constructs that are important for building a theory of reading as a social process.

1. The interpersonal organizations and meanings that people have for reading and writing activities are consistent with and extensions of the cultural organizations and meanings of narrative events and other communicative, interpersonal events within their community.
2. The social meaning of reading evolves from how reading affects interpersonal relationships.

3. Across settings (e.g., across communities, institutions, school and nonschool settings, classrooms), there is a great deal of variety in the nature of literacy activities. However, the evaluation of literacy behavior—that is, the determination of what counts as reading or writing—tends to be both ethnocentric and situation specific. For example, in classrooms reading is typically viewed as what happens during reading groups with the basal readers. However, during school, students may engage in many other activities that involve the use of written language. But because these literacy events are not part of the formally recognized literacy curriculum they may not be counted by the teacher or the students as 'reading.'

4. The social status given to reading ability and to engagement in reading activities depends (a) on the nature and organization of the reading activity, and (b) on the people assigning status. For example, Gilmore (1981; Chap. 5, this volume) described how the peer literacy activities of a group of urban, black, adolescent women were often overlooked as literacy activities by teachers and were viewed as low- and even negative-status activities. However, among the adolescent women, proficiency in the peer literacy activities was accorded high status.

5. Literacy learning and practice, as promulgated through classroom instruction, are neither based upon nor necessarily related to, in general, the reading and writing activities that actually occur outside of school at home or at work (Heath, 1983; Hendrix, 1981; Kirsch & Guthrie, 1983). Yet, it is primarily through the evaluation of school reading and writing that students gain academic status that may be translated into job and career opportunities. The connection between school literacy practice and jobs may have more to do with students acquiring social status (Smith, Chap. 3, this volume) and the dominant culture's ways of organizing talk and information (which is not to state that any one way of organizing talk or information is either more efficient or productive than another). That is, students learn—or perhaps, more accurately put, are taught—how and where to "fit" into the dominant culture which, in general, controls job and career opportunities (cf. Heath, 1983).

Reading as a Sociocognitive Process

To describe reading as a sociocognitive process suggests that reading involves both social and cognitive processes. However, as used here, the description of reading as a sociocognitive process means not only do social and cognitive factors affect reading behavior, but that reading itself is simultaneously a process of socialization, enculturation, and cognition. In brief, learning to read involves the learning of culturally bound ways of thinking (including problem solving, inferencing, and conceptualizing), which is, in part, a consequence of and a influence on the socialization of interpersonal relationships. In other words, as used here, the term *sociocognitive* refers not to a combination of separate social and cognitive processes but rather to a unitary set of processes whose nature is simultaneously social and cognitive.

It is difficult to discuss the cognitive effects of literacy learning without discussing schooling. After all, most literacy learners attend or have attended schools. Further, in schools students spend a great deal of time learning specific ways to interact with written language. Thus, schooling is viewed as not only fostering cognitive development but as fostering certain kinds of cognitive development and processes (Goody & Watt, 1968; Olson, 1977; Vygotsky, 1962).

Scribner and Cole (1977, 1981) were able to explore literacy learning and practice outside of schooling among the Vai in Liberia. Their findings suggested that the effects of literacy learning and practice on the acquisition of cognitive processes depended on the kinds of literacy activities in which people engage and the kinds of cognitive processes inherent in those literacy practices. When the range of functions and complexity of literacy activities is limited, then the cognitive skills fostered by literacy activity will also be limited.

Building on the research of Scribner and Cole (1977, 1981), questions can be asked about the cumulative effect of the kinds of literacy practices fostered by schools. If different literacy practices tend to foster different cognitive skills, then literacy curricula can be viewed as part of the means for transmitting culturally bound ways of thinking about the world and engaging the world. As such, reading and writing events become culturally bound ways of mediating reality.

READING AS A SOCIAL PROCESS IN AN EIGHTH-GRADE CLASSROOM

During the 1981–1982 school year and following summer, an ethnographic study of adolescent reading was conducted both in and out of school. The research setting was an urban middle school (grades 6–8) that served a predominately black, working-class community.

Data collection and analysis followed a type-case analysis framework. First, a general ethnographic study of classrooms, school and community was conducted (cf. Spradley, 1980). Second, based on the general ethnographic study, specific classroom events—especially recurrent gatekeeping events involving reading—were identified and videotaped. The microanalysis of the videotapes was based on recent work in the analysis of classroom face-to-face interaction, especially recent work within sociolinguistic ethnography (cf. Green & Wallat, 1981; Cook-Gumperz et al., 1981; Erickson & Shultz, 1981). Microanalysis provided a means for extracting models of social, interpersonal behavior within recurrent reading events. These models provided insights into the nature of reading—as it naturally occurred—within and across classrooms and across instructional and noninstructional settings.

Three sets of related findings have previously been reported: (a) classroom reading as text reproduction (Bloome, 1983a, 1984a), (b) classroom reading as procedural display (Bloome & Argumedo, 1983), and (c) differences in reading across instructional and noninstructional settings (Bloome, 1984a; Bloome & Green, 1982a). These findings are briefly reviewed in the next section and provide a starting place for further findings and discussion.

Text Reproduction, Procedural Display, and Reading Across Instructional and Noninstructional Settings

In the classrooms studied, reading events were typified by text reproduction. Text reproduction manifested itself in many ways including the oral rendition of printed directions and printed text, the copying of assignments written on the blackboard, the copying of reading exercises from a textbook, and the repetition of phrases and texts designated as correct by the teacher. The occurrence and dominance of text reproduction was not an explicit goal of instruction in either classroom. Rather, text reproduction was, in general, invisible and only revealed through the microanalysis of direct reading instruction events. In part, text reproduction was tied to the kinds of tasks students were asked to perform, in part to teacher-student interaction, and in part to student responses to classroom assignments independent of teachers and/or task demands.

Text reproduction also manifested itself as a kind of classroom language. For example, if during reading instruction a student knew the answer to a teacher question, it was, in general, not appropriate to respond in one's own way of speaking. Responses, in general, needed to be put into a "book-language" form. That is, responses had to be elaborated and decontextualized. An obvious case in which book language was demanded of students was when teachers asked students to put their correct answer in the form of a "complete sentence."

A number of institutional constraints in the school fostered text reproduction. First, a limited supply of textbooks meant that students did not have their own texts to take home. It was often necessary throughout their K–12 experience to copy text in order to use it later. Second, the reading programs mandated for use in K–8 required copying, the repetition of phrases and written text, and extended amounts of oral rendition without subsequent reference to the meaning of the text. Further, given that skill work was completed separate from meaningful reading, there was neither purpose nor incentive for either students or teacher to engage in anything more than text reproduction. Fourth, the experience of many students in grades K–5 (and, perhaps, even earlier than kindergarten) often focused on copying as writing and oral rendition as reading (Bloome, 1984). Thus, the middle school students might expect—even demand—that tasks presented to them be interpreted in terms of text reproduction (see also Doyle, 1983).

Text reproduction was, in part, related to procedural display, that is, the display by teacher and students to each other of a set of academic and/or interactional procedures that themselves counted as the accomplishment of a lesson. Procedural display might not necessarily be related to the acquisition of academic content or to learning cognitive strategies. Simply put, procedural display occurred when teachers and students were primarily concerned with displaying to each other that they were "getting the lesson done"; whatever academic learning occurred was, at best, secondary or accidental. Procedural display can be compared to a group of actors who have memorized their parts and who enact the play for each other's benefit without necessarily knowing what happens in the play or what it means.

Procedural display was a dominant feature of direct reading instruction in the classrooms studied despite what appeared to be important differences in classroom climate and academic content. For example, in a sixth-grade classroom studied, reading skills were emphasized with little student discussion. There were few opportunities for personal expression. In an eighth-grade classroom in the same school, the explicit focus was on literature and literary analysis (e.g., plot, characterization, theme) with explicit instructional emphases on student discussion and the expression of personal reaction to literature. However, given that procedural display and text reproduction were dominant features of both classrooms, questions can be raised as to whether explicit differences between the classrooms were actually substantive differences.

Both outside of and in classrooms, students engaged in noninstructional reading and writing activities. In classrooms, noninstructional literacy activities consisted of covertly reading a book (e.g., a comic book, magazine, or paperback book) and writing, reading, and passing notes. While both instructional and noninstructional literacy events involved the public display of procedures, noninstructional literacy events were characterized by the expression of personal feelings and relationships and by group text production. Moreover, while instructional literacy behavior was associated with social status (e.g., whether one was in the top or bottom group), noninstructional literacy behavior was not.

Neither text reproduction, procedural display, nor the differences described between instructional and noninstructional activities are psychological constructs or descriptions. They are not descriptions of learning processes. Rather, they are descriptions of social and communicative processes. They are partial answers to the question ''What is happening within a specific set of literacy events among people? And between people and texts?''

Overview of the Lesson
The following lesson involved patterns of teacher-student-text interaction that were recurrent across analogous lessons in the eighth-grade class as well as across analogous lessons in other classes within the school. The lesson focused on a short story called ''The Saint.'' Previously, parts of the story had been read aloud during class time. Students had also been given class time to read the story silently, and they had been assigned to read the story for homework. In preparation for discussion, students had been assigned the task of identifying words that they did not know in the story.

The lesson began with vocabulary. The teacher asked students which words they did not know. Students provided words. Using the dictionary and teacher explanation, vocabulary words were reviewed.

Following the vocabulary segment, the teacher lead a discussion on characterization focusing on one of the main protagonists. The discussion of characterization overlapped the vocabulary segment since many of the vocabulary words were descriptors of the protagonist.

Finally, the teacher assigned an essay. Students were to write on one of two questions. Each question was directly related to the day's discussion of vocabulary and character.

In the sections that follow, a detailed description is provided of the target students who were the focus of the videotape analysis, of the story, of the teacher-student discussion, and of what the students wrote.

The Students

A group of eight students was the focus of intensive ethnographic study, and in particular, emphasis was placed upon the male students. The group was chosen primarily for logistical reasons—the angle of the camera, placement of electrical outlets, windows, desks, permission slips received from every member of the group, etc. The teacher considered the group academically higher than other groups in the classroom (although there were individuals outside of the group who were considered academically equal to the group). Ethnographic interviews were conducted only with the male students. Thus, there is less background data on the female students.

The Four Female Students.   Tina and Fran always sat together at one end of the group. They frequently passed notes back and forth. They tended to remove themselves from peer activities not initiated within the group and/or having to do with the rest of the class. They rarely volunteered to answer teacher questions or to pass out books, etc.

Linda sometimes sat with Tina and Fran and sometimes sat with Betty at the other end of the table. Like Tina and Fran, Linda rarely volunteered to answer teacher requests. Unlike Tina and Fran, Linda would participate in peer events (e.g., note passing) that were initiated by students outside the group. Linda was also more likely to talk with the male students. Tina and Fran limited their interaction with male students to Mark and Louis (which might have more to do with the fact that Mark and Louis were the class leaders rather than simply the fact that Tina and Fran always sat next to Mark and Louis).

Betty always sat at the opposite end of the group from Fran and Tina. Occasionally, Betty would sit outside of the group. Like Linda, Betty participated in peer events whether initiated inside or outside the group. Betty and Linda would readily interact with any of the male students in the group as well as with students outside of the group.

All four female students were considered by the teacher as ''among the better students in the class.'' They always had notebooks, paper, pencils, pens, etc. When the teacher made seatwork assignments, the four would be among the first to actually begin the seatwork (this was especially true of Tina and Fran.)

The Four Male Students.   Mark was recognized as the leader of the class. He was good looking, tall, well built, athletic, gregarious, and desired by nearly every female student in the eighth grade. He was liked by both teachers and students. Teachers could count on Mark to comply with their requests, if not the first time, then certainly the second time. Yet, Mark was not a teacher's pet; he would talk during class, pass notes, fool around, etc. However, he seemed to be able to "fool around" within acceptable guidelines, knowing when to stop and when to be serious about school work. Except on rare occasions, Mark had a notebook, paper, and a pencil.

Though not as athletic, tall, nor as good looking, Louis was also viewed as a class leader. He played sports earnestly—if not excellently. He was viewed as the male class intellectual. Unlike Mark, Louis would respond to teacher questions. Furthermore, when the teacher wanted a correct answer, Louis was likely to be asked. Like Mark, Louis usually had a notebook and paper. Unlike Mark, Louis would have several pencils which he would lend to other students.

Bob came to the class about midyear. He spent the first several weeks quietly reading a book about Martin Luther King, Jr., during lunch and when there was time for peer interaction. Because of his reading, he was viewed by students as "smart," although when asked about his reading he stated that he needed something to do until he got to know the other students. Bob usually had a notebook, but frequently he needed a pencil or needed to sharpen a pencil. Unlike Mark or Louis, Bob was not viewed as a class leader. He was more an observer of peer events than a participant. Most important to note about Bob was his religious background. His family belonged to a fundamentalist Baptist sect. They spent nearly every evening and all day Sunday either in church or doing church-related activity. When not involved in church activity, Bob usually had responsibilities around his house (e.g., taking care of siblings). Of the eight students in the group, Bob and Ray were bussed to school from a predominately black, lower working-class neighborhood. Other students came from nearby neighborhoods that had larger lots, bigger houses, and more trees, and they were generally considered to be middle class or upper working class.

Ray had been held back a year. His parents predicted that he would not finish high school, although Ray stated that he was determined to finish high school no matter how many years it took. Ray viewed himself as "slower" than other students, but he also insisted that, given enough time, he "could get it." Like Bob, Ray was not viewed as a class leader. However, he played sports and was viewed as one of the insiders. Ray primarily interacted with Louis, Linda, Betty, and Bob, though he would freely interact with other students in the class. Ray usually had paper and pencil for class work.

Though the eight students formed a group, on a day-to-day basis the group usually consisted of at least one other student; that is, one of the eight would usually be absent, Betty would decide to sit with other friends, or one of the eight would come to class late. When there was an opening in the group, another student would typically occupy that seat. Sometimes the newcomer would be a close friend of one of the eight, or else it might be a student wanting to get friendly with one of the female students; it might also be a student wanting to become part of the group. The teacher usually overlooked isolated changes in the seating plan until there was a disruption. At times, the teacher tried to reform a student by assigning that child with the group. With the exception of friends who were invited to sit with the group, others who sat with the group were ignored and isolated.

What the Students Read

For the lesson, students read "The Saint" by V.S. Pritchett. Students began the story with a brief introduction by the teacher, and this was followed by whole-class round-robin reading. When the class eventually became disorderly, the round-robin reading was ended and students were told to read silently in class and to finish the story at home.

The story was about a 17-year-old boy and his loss of religion. He belonged to a religious sect that taught that misery, pain, discomfort, and lack of money were illusions, since God would not allow his children to suffer. Suffering was the result of "letting in error" or sin. The boy's family was visited by Timberlake, one of the sect's hierarchy from out of town. At first, the boy's doubts regarding the sect's dogma were alleviated by Timberlake's visit. The boy was extremely impressed by Timberlake's demeanor. However, after a boating accident in which Timberlake fell in the river and made a fool of himself trying to ignore the cold and discomfort, the boy realized that his doubts about the sect's dogma were well-founded.

The content of the story could be viewed as closely related to the students, especially Bob. About half of the students regularly attended church on Sundays, and almost all had had religious training. Most participated in church social activities (e.g., church basketball leagues, barbeques). During the spring, summer, and fall, the neighborhoods that served the school were regularly solicited by Jehovah Witnesses and other sects. There was a big billboard two blocks from the school proclaiming "Believe in the Lord and Thou will be saved." In brief, students frequently came into contact with a broad range of church-related activities.

Teacher-Student Discussion

Teacher-student interaction provided a framework for interpreting and interacting with text. As mentioned earlier, previous microethnographic analysis of teacher-student-text interaction in the eighth-grade class (as well as in other classes) suggested that text reproduction and procedural display were part of the framework for student-text interaction. The following description suggested that, in conjunction with procedural display and text reproduction, the framework for interaction with text provided through teacher-student interaction could be characterized as cataloging. *Cataloging* is the listing of parts that count as the whole (which is not to say that all of the parts of the whole are listed but rather that what parts are listed do count as the whole). Cataloging differs from analysis. *Analysis* is a process of segmenting a whole into parts in order to gain insight into the nature of the whole. With cataloging, the goal is the display of a list. The whole disappears, or rather, the whole becomes the list. As is true of any catalog—e.g., the Sears catalog, a telephone book—the listing does not necessarily reflect nor is related to the nature of the whole from which it comes. A telephone book provides no information about the nature of the society or social organization of the people listed. Similarly, a catalog of vocabulary words provides little information about the nature of the story or what that story might mean to students. Yet, in the following lesson, it was the catalog of vocabulary words that provided the basis upon which students responded to the text.

The teacher-student discussion began with vocabulary. The teacher had asked students to finish reading the story at home and to make a list of vocabulary words. As shown in the transcript, either no one had made a list or no one was willing to admit to making a list.

01	T	WHO'S DONE THAT [MADE A VOCABULARY LIST] PLEASE
02		WHO HAS A LIST OF WORDS THAT THEY NEED HELP WITH
03		YOU MEAN I CAN THROW ANY ONE OF THOSE WORDS OUT AND YOU'LL KNOW THE MEANING
04		AND YOU'LL JUMP RIGHT UP AND YEAH THAT'S IT
05	Ss	Yup . . . uh huh
06	T	OK
07	Ss	no . . . no
08	T	AH
09	Ss	I know . . no . . yup
10	T	ROBERT
11	R	I wasn't here yesterday
12	T	ALL RIGHT
13		RHONDA
14		(UNDECIPHERABLE COMMENT)
15	R	(undecipherable comment)
16	Ss	(loud background talking)

Students began talking with each other. One student interrupted, stating that someone from the previous class had left a book on the desk. The interruption and the disruptive talking provided an opportunity for students to scan through the text and find vocabulary words. In addition, the disruption provided an excuse for both the teacher and students since they were unable to continue, because no student could (or, perhaps, would) appropriately fill the slot created by the teacher.

The importance of noting that no one had apparently prepared a vocabulary list is that it seemed to make no difference. The lesson continued as if students had had the lists. Students raised their hands and identified vocabulary words based on scanning the pages for unfamiliar words. On one hand, this could be explained as procedural display, completing a lesson merely for the sake of completing it. It could also be explained as a refusal by the teacher to acknowledge that students did not complete the assignment. Publicly acknowledging that the students had not completed the lesson might have forced the teacher to become punitive, resulting in friction between teacher and students. More positively, continuing with the lesson could be seen as an effort to teach vocabulary and vocabulary skills. At the same time, continuing with the lesson provided one way to discuss the story and provided students with knowledge about the story.

Rodney helped to continue the lesson by raising his hand and offering a vocabulary word for discussion. Once a word was offered, the teacher established an instructional pattern: (a) the word was located in the text; (b) someone was assigned to look up the word in the dictionary; (c) the portion of the text containing the vocabulary word was read while the dictionary was being searched; (d) the dictionary definition was read and related to the use of the word in the story; and (e) the teacher elaborated on the definition, relating the vocabulary word to student experience.

However, the surface-level description of the instructional pattern does not fully describe what occurred. As mentioned earlier, text reproduction is a part of the teacher-student-text interaction. For example, consider the following transcript segment in which the teacher read from the book in order to provide a semantic context for one of the vocabulary words.

42	T	SINCE THAT HE SAID
43		HAS
44		HE HAD A PINK SQUARE HEAD
45		AND VERY SMALL EARS AND ONE OF THOSE TORPID ENAM-ELED SMILES WHICH WERE
46		SAID BY ENEMIES TO BE TO COMMON IN OUR SECT
47		OK
48		THINK ABOUT TEETH
49		WHAT ARE THEY MADE OF
50	S	enamel
51	T	OK
52	s	ivory
53	ss	ivory
54	ss	(background talking)
55	s	rhonda your mother

Reading the text surrounding the vocabulary words (enamel and torpid) did not provide any insights into the meaning of the vocabulary words. The text, for the students, was impenetrable, especially since the teacher read the text in a "flat" prosodic style. (As shown later in the teacher-student discussion of Mr. Timberlake's character, what the students remembered was "small ears.") What reading the text seemed to do was to establish the dominance of text reproduction as a definition of problem solving and of interacting with text.

Also feeding into the dominance of text reproduction as a definition of problem solving and interaction with text was the time taken and effort made to locate the vocabulary words in the text.

26	T	ALL RIGHT RODNEY AGAIN
27	r	torpid on page 29
28	T	ALL RIGHT ON PAGE 29 WOULD YOU COUNT
29		PUT US IN THE RIGHT PLACE WHAT PARAGRAPH
30	r	last one
31		at the bottom of the page
32	T	LAST PARAGRAPH
33	r	it's the second sentence from the bottom
34	T	SECOND SENTENCE
35		ENAMELED SMILE
36	r	and torpid
37	T	ALL RIGHT

Students spent a great deal of time attempting to find the right page, paragraph, and line. Many students were still trying to locate the right spot after the text had been read by the teacher. That is, it was not clear from the teacher-student interaction whether the teacher wanted the class to find the right spot. She made the location public, and, at other times when asked by a student, repeated the location. However, the teacher read the text before most of the students had had a chance to find the right spot (e.g., lines 42–46) and then moved on away from the text (e.g., lines 47–55).

Text reproduction also manifested itself in the rendition of dictionary definitions. Students read aloud the dictionary definition. The vocabulary and syntactic structures of the dictionary definitions made them nearly impenetrable for students. The hesitating and broken prosodic manner in which the definitions were read by students made the text even more impenetrable.

```
56  T    ALL RIGHT
57       MICHAEL HAS FOUND THE WORD IN THE DICTIONARY
58       RODNEY
59       HE WILL GIVE US THE DEFINITION IT GIVES
60       AND THEN HE'LL FIND WHICH ONE FITS YOUR SENTENCE
61       OK
62  M    number one
63       tempora temporary loss of
64       number one
65       number one
66       has lost most of power
67       power of
68       convention or failure
69       in functioning in functioning
70       oration
71       number 2
72       lacking in energy or vigor
73       vigor
74  T    OK
```

Even though the dictionary definition had been read (lines 62–73) and the vocabulary words had twice been placed in the context of the surrounding text, students were unable to determine what the words meant. They did not respond to the teacher's request for a definition. Instead, students began a disruption (line 85):

```
83       OK NOW HOW WAS THE WORD TORPID USED
84       HOW WAS THE WORD TORPID USED
85  ss   (background talking)
```

The teacher responded to the disruption by extending the slot she created for the students. That is, she provided additional opportunity for students to respond and gave them additional information that they could use to respond (lines 86–93):

```
86   T      ALL RIGHT
87          SHOW
88          HOW HE SMILED
89          HI HOW YOU DOING
90          THAT KIND OF THING
91          OR DID IT COME JUST NORMAL
92          A JUST KIND OF A
93          (Teacher models an expressionless smile)
94   ss     (undecipherable comments and background talking)
95   T      ALL RIGHT A LACK OF WHAT
96          LACK OF WHAT
97   s      lack of expression
```

The students, or rather at least one student, responded to the teacher's dramatization of a torpid smile and her prompting of student response (lines 93–97). However, the teacher was unable to build in the student response (lines 98–102), and finally, the teacher filled in the slot she created by once again telling students what the word meant by dramatizing it (lines 103–112).

```
98   T      LACK OF FEELING
99          LACK OF EXPRESSION
100         LACK OF
101         LACK OF FEELING
102         ALL RIGHT AND
            (extended pause)
103  T      SO A TORPID SMILE
104         LATICIA
105         WOULD BE A SMILE THAT DIDN'T HAVE MUCH FEELING
106         ONE THAT WE MIGHT OF AUTOMATICALLY WITHOUT THINKING
               OR WITHOUT GIVING IT A LOT OF UMPH
107         A LOT OF VIGOR
108         ALL RIGHT
109         IT WAS JUST THERE
110         HI HOW ARE YOU
111         YOU KNOW THAT ISN'T ONE THAT HAS A LOT OF ENERGY OR A
               LOT OF FEELING BEHIND IT
112         ONE THAT YOU'RE NOT SURE OF
```

The interaction between the teacher and the students can be characterized as procedural display. The teacher was attempting to get the procedures of the lesson publicly displayed. However, the students were either unable or unwilling to display their part of the interactional procedure of the lesson. That they were probably more unable than unwilling to help in the procedural display is shown in the next transcript segment. The teacher attempted to solicit on-task student response by creating slots that could be answered without necessarily knowing the content. That is, the only knowledge needed was that of conversational routines. One did not need to know the meaning of torpid in order to correctly answer the question in line 113.

```
113   IF    SOMEONE HAD A TORPID SMILE WOULD YOU SAY THEY WERE A
             GENUINE PERSON
114   Ss    no
```

However, the teacher made a conversational error. She created an expectation that
students could appropriately respond to questions on the basis of conversational routines. When she asked "is genuine real?" (line 115), she crossed student expectations created in the previous question-answer interaction. Students expected to be
able to answer the question appropriately by responding to only the form and prosody of the teacher's question—not the content. The teacher acknowledged that she
violated conversational expectations (lines 117–120) and reestablished the expectation that student responses to questions could be based on conversational knowledge
only (lines 121–127):

```
115   T     IS GENUINE REAL
116   Ss    no
117   T     AH
118         OK
119         MAYBE I MISUSED THE WORD
120         OH I DON'T MEAN THAT THIS DID
121         BUT WOULD BE A PERSON THAT YOU WOULD FEEL THAT
122         HIS FEELINGS COULD ALWAYS BE TRUSTED
123         THAT HE'S GIVE YOU HIS OR HER GENUINE FEELINGS
124         THEIR REAL FEELINGS
125   Ss    no
126   T     NO
127         SO IN THAT WAY THAT WOULDN'T BE GENUINE
```

Finally, the class moved on to another word, and the pattern of text reproduction
and procedural display reoccurred.

Although the vocabulary segment helped establish a cataloging framework for
interacting and interpreting text, cataloging was easier to see both in the teacher-
student discussion of the story itself annd through comparison with other lessons.

In discussing "The Saint" the teacher chose "character" as the explicit frame
and set the task:

```
202         ON THE BOARD ARE THREE THINGS THAT HAVE TO DO WITH
            MR. TIMBERLAKE
203         APPEARANCE PERSONALITY AND INFLUENCE ON THE BOY
204         NOW
205         THE AUTHOR TELLS YOU WHAT MR. TIMBERLAKE LOOKS
            LIKE
206         HE
207         HE GIVES SOME VERY DESCRIPTIVE
208         DESCRIPTION OF MR. TIMBERLAKE
209         HE EVEN TELLS US A BIT ABOUT HIS PERSONALITY
210         BUT WHEN YOU COME TO THE INFLUENCE ON THE BOY
```

137

211		EVERYBODY HAS TO READ BETWEEN THE LINES
212		BECAUSE THE AUTHOR DOESN'T TELL YOU WHAT INFLU-ENCE HE HAS ON THE BOY
213		BUT HE KIND OF GIVES YOU A HINT TOWARD IT
214		THIS IS THE KIND OF INFLUENCE HE HAD
215		ALL RIGHT LET'S START WITH THE APPEARANCE
216		AHH
217		LET'S FIND WHAT MR. TIMBERLAKE LOOKS LIKE
218		ALL RIGHT IN YOUR BOOK YOU MAY
219		I DON'T KNOW
220		SOMEONE HAVE AN IDEA
221		SOMEONE REMEMBER FROM WHAT THEY READ

The teacher outlined the broader communicative task framework, providing an overview of the teacher-student tasks to come (describing appearance, personality and influence; lines 201–214). Implicitly, teacher-student discussion of appearance involved cataloging based primarily on the previous vocabulary discussion. That is, students used the previous vocabulary discussion as the primary source of information for responding to teacher questions.

222	T	RODNEY
223		YOU HAD ONE HE HAD A TORPID WHAT [Lines 223–226 are based on lines 42–114 during the vocabulary segment]
224	r	a smile
225	T	ALL RIGHT
226		HE HAD A TORPID ENAMELED SMILE
227		ALL RIGHT, WHAT ELSE DID HE HAVE
228		ANYTHING ELSE
229		YES
230	r	small ears ["Small ears" comes from the teacher's oral rendition of the text during the vocabulary segment.]
231	T	SMALL EARS
232		LAWRENCE SAID THAT
233	s	enameled smile
234	T	GOT THAT
235		YOU ARE JUST REINFORCING THAT I UNDERSTAND THAT
236		HE HAD A SMALL ["Small head" and student's reading in line 238 derived from lines 44–45 during the vocabulary segment.]
237		WHAT ELSE DID HE HAVE
238	s	a head as small as a (undepipherable)

The prompts that the teacher used to solicit student response were directly taken from the vocabulary discussion. Students completed the teacher's sentence, and the class built a catalog about Timberlake's appearance. But the catalog was a vacuous list. Students were providing items for the sake of creating a list, but the items themselves, either individually or as a group, had no significance. The items were merely repetitions of the previous discussion (including repetitions of the text read during the previous discussion) or descriptions read directly from the text without interpretation. For example, consider the following interaction.

138

253		MARK
254	m	i don't know the word
255		it says his eyes sparkled
256	T	SHH
257		ALL RIGHT HIS EYES WHAT
258	m	his eyes sparkled with (undecipherable)
259	T	VERY GOOD
260		ANYONE ELSE FIND SOMETING ELSE ABOUT HIS APPEARANCE

A descriptor about Timberlake's appearance needed to be said and listed. Mark did not understand the description he read, and the teacher's response suggested that he did not need to understand it, merely list it. Interestingly, Mark was reading a description of another character, not Timberlake. Similar interactions occurred through the discussion of character.

The teacher might assume that in publicly cataloging items about Timberlake's appearance, students were doing more than merely cataloging. However, from the student perspective, what seemed to count was merely having an item about appearance to display that had not already been listed. For example, consider the following interaction which seems similar to the street game of one-upmanship.

240	T	RUTH HAS FOUND ONE THAT YOU MIGHT NOT HAVE THOUGHT OF
241	r	(undecipherable)
242	s1	I just said that
243	s2	I said that
244	T	IT DOESN'T MATTER WHO FOUND IT FIRST OR LAST
245		WE JUST WANT IT
		(background talking and laughing)
246	ss	shhh
247	s	hey I found one

The listing or cataloging of items is a communicative framework for interacting and interpreting text. As a framework it is imposed through teacher-student-text interaction. That is, teacher-student interaction mediates how students interpret what they are about and what it means.

Cataloging is a school phenomenon (as well as, perhaps, a phenomenon of other situations) that can also mediate other nonreading experience that students have. It may be part of the ways of thinking about experience fostered through school culture—or, at least, school culture as manifested in some low-track, urban middle school classrooms. (Given the hypothesis-generating nature of the study, it was not possible to specify the extent to which cataloguing exists across classrooms. Preliminary review of videotapes from three other urban, middle school classrooms—both low-track and heterogeneously grouped—shows the recurrence of cataloging across the classrooms). For example, cataloging becomes a framework for mediating the students' experience of a field trip they took to Chuck E. Cheese's pizza restaurant and video game parlor.

The field trip is described in detail for two purposes. First, it provided a comparative perspective for understanding cataloging. And second, it raised another issue about the classroom or school frame that mediates student experience and student interaction and interpretation of text. The second issue was the passivity or alienating nature of the mediating classroom frame.

The trip to Chuck E. Cheese's had been suggested by a student. The teacher told the student that if the students could find out all the information needed, make the appropriate arrangements, and set rules and organization for the trip, then the class could go on the trip. There was general agreement among the students to do so. Rachel, who suggested the trip, took leadership in making the agreements, but the discussion of the arrangements involved nearly the whole class. These discussions took place during lunch (which was eaten in the classroom). The arrangements made by the students included how much each student would pay, how many pizzas were needed, how many game tokens each student would receive, when the trip would take place, how long the trip would be, and who would share each pizza. Students also collected permission slips and money for the field trip. In order to make the trip financially feasible, another class had to be invited. The second class was told what arrangements they needed to make (e.g., figuring out who would share each pizza).

On the bus ride to Chuck E. Cheese's, antagonism was expressed toward the second class. According to the teacher, the antagonism was based on the tracking of students. The second class was recognized as a higher section, and their higher academic status was resented.

At Chuck E. Cheese's students followed the organization they set. Students moved through Chuck E. Cheese's in groups, waiting for or playing a video game. Several students would cluster at a video game to watch another student perform.

Several students seemed to be experts at specific video games. For example, Ray used only two tokens and played Pac-Man for nearly two hours. When he went to eat his pizza, he left his game to Neil, who kept the game going until Ray returned. Students shared strategies for being successful with the video games and traded stories about people they knew who were really good at the video games. A few of the girls, for example, Linda and Theodora, did not spend much time at the video games but played skee-ball and collected tickets that could be used for prizes. The collection of tickets was both an individual and group enterprise. That is, although each person collected his/her own tickets, the group shared tickets to enable individuals to get desired prizes.

The trip to Chuck E. Cheese's showed students as doers, capable of organization. As opposed to most school situations where the school prescribes and students follow, students prescribed the activity.

After returning from the field trip, students sat in their usual classroom seats. Class discussion focused on improvements they would make at Chuck E. Cheese's. Student responses were primarily lists of the additional video games they would like. Students were interested in listing improvements and additional video games. Students tried to "top" each other's list.

Like the discussion of "The Saint," the class discussion of going to Chuck E. Cheese's primarily involved cataloging. Also like the discussion of "The Saint," the purpose of cataloging was the display of the catalog. Unlike the discussion of "The Saint," students were eager to participate in discussing Chuck E. Cheese's. They volunteered for rather than avoided turns. However, a distinction must be made betwen enthusiastic or interested participation and participation related to student experience. Although interesting to students, the classroom tasks and discussion about the field trip had little to do with the actual experience of students at Chuck E. Cheese's. The only complaining done by students on the field trip concerned the second class, not getting sausage on their pizza when they had ordered it, and other students (typically, complaints by the female students about the male students who either gave too little attention or the wrong kind of attention). There was no discussion of needed improvements. Further, the class discussion moved students away from how active they had been in "doing" the event. That is, they had organized the event, they had created the social context and organization, and while at Chuck E. Cheese, they had taken control. The discussion tasks were outside of the experiences they had had at Chuck E. Cheese and frame the event as if the students had merely been passive consumers and/or followers.

Similarly with "The Saint," the discussion framed students as passive respondents to text that was unrelated to their experiences (with few trivial exceptions such as the teacher's dramatization of vocabulary words). As mentioned earlier, almost all of the students were or had been intensely involved with religious enterprises (e.g., Sunday school), and a handful belonged to religious sects that were similar to the religious sect described in "The Saint." In neither the discussion of the trip to Chuck E. Cheese's nor "The Saint" were the mediating frames established through teacher-student interaction grounded in student experience.

What Students Wrote

Part of the lesson on "The Saint" and part of the field-trip "lesson" involved writing essay responses to teacher questions. Student writing is discussed here as a dimension of student reading. That is, the writing was one reflection of student reading. The following writing samples are not presented in order to discuss student writing ability per se but only as it affected or reflected student reading.

The two topics/questions the teacher wrote on the blackboard about "The Saint" were:

1. What the boy thought of Mr. Timberlake before and after the boating incident.
2. Tell what influence Mr. T. had on the boy's loss of religion.

The following samples of student writing come from the eight previously described students. Tina's essay is omitted because she declined to allow it to be reproduced. However, the content and nature of her essay was consistent with the general comments made about the essays. (In the samples, an asterisk (*) refers to a cross-out.)

(1)

Betty XXXXX
Section XX
May 11, 1982

What The Boy Thought of
Mr. Timberlake's * befor
********* He fight like
it was not his fight at first
But after That he Taught
it was his

(2)

Fran XXXXXX

The man had made no
influence on the boy he had
just gave up and the man
did have infeucence at him again
he wanted to have the clothes and
money and afther values.

(3)

Ray
Minnis
Sec. 14
May 11–1982

(Ray turned in a blank paper with just the
heading shown above.)

(4)

Your thoughts:

Mark XXXXXX
Sec XX
May 11, 1982

(1) What the boy thought of Mr.T. before
and after the boating incident.

(2) Tell what influence Mr. T. had
on the boy's loss of Religion.

(5)

Louis XXXXX
Sec. XX
May 11, 1982

Reading

By the way Mr. Timberlake handled himself, the boy's
doubts were edivible of him. The boy was impressed because
Timberlake was a retired merchant captain.

After

(6)

Linda XXXXX
May 11, 1982

Your Thoughts

1.) What the boy thought of Mr. T. before
and after the boating *** incident. He
thought he was really religious.

2.) Tell what influence Mr. T. had on
the boy's loss of religion. His behavior
and the way he acted towards him.

(7)

Bob XXXXXXX
5–11–82
Sec XX

1. The boy thought of Mr. T. ar an important
man like a Movie star our something.
After Mr. T had fallen in the boy felt
imbaviert surprized and scarded
he had faith in the man and was surprized
by the wau th Man acted. startled
with amazement

As samples of writing, these essays reveal problems with grammar, mechanics,
cohesion, clarity of references, organization, etc. Several students did little more
than copy the essay questions (e.g., 4, 6), if even that (e.g., 3). Those students who
did respond made short, one or two sentence responses (e.g., 1, 2, 5, 6, 7, 8) that
were unelaborated and almost telegraphic.

There are several possible explanations for the writing products the students
produced—e.g., lack of student ability and/or knowledge, failure of the academic
task or other instructional factors, student engagement in procedural display and/or
mock participation. However, the essays were also one source of data about student
reading. After all, the students were to base their responses on what they had read
and the classroom discussion of what they had read.

Much of the content of student responses was based on the class discussion. For
example, Linda's comments were taken directly from the teacher's comments made
during the discussion of Timberlake's personality and during the discussion of the
essay questions. Fran's response was a reiteration of teacher comments and an item
from the "catalog" discussion of Mr. Timberlake's appearance. In discussing the
essay question, the teacher had said to notice: "the way the boy acted," "the way
Mr. Timberlake handled himself," "Did Mr. Timberlake have an influence on the
boy or did he have no influence on the boy?" The teacher's phrases, meant only as
aides for students, became student written responses. In part, the reiteration could
be viewed as a manifestation of text reproduction. Throughout earlier grades and

when studying grammar, students copied directly from the text. The spelling tests and assignments that the students had throughout middle school (grades 6–8) called for students to write down every word dictated by the teacher. While it is not suggested that there was a direct connection between how grammar and spelling tasks were acted out and text reproduction within essay writing, there is a potential that the cumulative effect of student participation in text reproduction-type activities provided a frame for students to respond to reading tasks.

Some student written responses were unrelated to both the task and the story. For example, the content of Betty's essay, although seemingly related to the task, had nothing to do with the story. There was no fight in the story.

The content of Louis's essay and Bob's essay contained items not found in previous class discussion. Louis noted that the boy had been impressed because Mr. Timberlake had been a merchant captain. Despite the fact that the story said nothing about a merchant captain (Timberlake had been in insurance before going into religion), Louis showed that he understood the task. That is, he responded with an opinion supported by "fact." Bob's written response was the only one not to involve text reproduction. He described the boy's impression of Timberlake in his own words ("like a movie star") and made an appropriate before-and-after comparison.

With the exception of Bob (and to some extent Louis), student responses were vacuous. Either there was no response or the response seemed primarily based on text reproduction. Further, the text reproduced by students was not always appropriate to the task, suggesting that either students did not understand the task or they interpreted the task in other ways. Specifically, they interpreted the task in terms of the previous class discussion. That is, they pulled items out of the catalog created in the class discussion that might not have had anything to do with the task.

The effect of classroom discussion can be seen in comparing what the students wrote about an experience with what they wrote about something they had read. After returning from the field trip to Chuck E. Cheese's (pizza restaurant and video arcade), there was a class discussion about Chuck E. Cheese's. As mentioned earlier, the discussion concerned improvements that students would have liked to make to Chuck E. Cheese's. After the discussion, the teacher assigned an essay on one of two questions:

1. If you were the designer of Chuck E. Cheese, what new things would you add?
2. Explain how going to Chuck E. Cheese's is educational.

The student's essays were longer than the ones written on "The Saint." But, similar to the essays written on "The Saint,' the content of the essays reflected the content of the class discussion. (The essays on Chuck E. Cheese contained a longer list of content items from class discussion than the essays on "The Saint" did, which partially explains the greater length of the Chuck E. Cheese essays). For example, each listed in Mark's essay came from the class discussion.

Mark XXXX
Sec. 14
May 13, 1982

2. If I were the designer of (C.E.C.) I would
add some more games like ms. Pac-
Man popeye pacman and pooltable.
Then I would have different Kinds of
food beside Pizza. I would Have
French Fries, and some sandwiches. That
Hippie That sings Needs a man to sing.
To

Like the class discussion, student essays were primarily lists. Those few students who attempted to answer the second question—about why the field trip was educational—wrote shorter essays and reiterated comments made by the teacher when she presented the task. For example, consider Louis' essay. He began with the "educational" question, gave up, and attempted the "designer" question.

Louis XXXXXXX
Section 14 Grade 8

Not only Chuck E. Cheese is fun and entertaining,
it is educational. They show *** us the uses of comput
ers and entertainment mixed together.

If I was the designer of Chuck E. Cheese

The construction of the classroom frame for mediating experience—whether the experience was interacting with a text or going to a field trip—involved an interesting contribution from student-student interaction. As mentioned earlier, during class discussion students played one-upmanship or "Can you top this?" In so doing they helped create lists, though the items on the list were not always related to the task (e.g., listing qualities about Timberlake that were not in the book). Also interesting is that the catalog frame provided a means for students to play "street games." The relationship between the classroom catalog frame and student-student interaction is almost always implied and not overt. For example, when students tried to list increasingly exaggerated improvements for Chuck E. Cheese it was less a result of creatively doing an academic task than a student-student game of "Can you top this?" When interactional games such as "Can you top this?" become explicit (e.g., when students incorporate direct insults into their responses), they are negatively sanctioned by the teacher. In Ray's essay on Chuck E. Cheese, the relationship between student-student interaction and the mediating classroom framework is made explicit.

145

Ray
XXXXXXX
Section 14
5/13/82

1. If I was the
designer of C.E.C.
I would make my
game room more
bigger and I would
add more games I
also have the little
pupetts come around
and talk to the people
and I wouldn't let
Bob come in because
he likes to tear up
**** your game like
Ms. Pac Man and
supper Cobra.

IMPLICATIONS

These detailed descriptions about the nature of reading events in a low-track, urban middle school classroom yielded four theoretical constructs. The theoretical constructs involved the nature of the frame concertedly constructed by teacher and students for interacting with the interpreting text. Specifically, the frame involved (a) text reproduction, (b) procedural display, (c) cataloging, and (d) a passive, "alienated" stance toward extended text. In part, the frame was constructed through teacher-student interaction; and, in part, the frame was constructed by the tasks (both explicit and implied) presented to students.

In many ways, the frame was functional for both teacher and students, because it provided a means for getting through and displaying accomplishment of the lesson. The frame also allowed teacher and students to appropriately operate within institutional constraints. That is, school requires progress to be made—or, at least, displayed—on the prescribed curriculum. The frame allowed for display of curriculum coverage although that coverage might be to an extent "hollow."

Review of videotapes within the corpus of data collected on reading events in the other middle school classrooms participating in the study confirmed the validity of the theoretical constructs. That is, text reproduction, cataloging, procedural display, and a passive stance toward extended text were recurrent patterns across the classrooms. Even when classrooms differed in their overt pedagogical approach to the teaching of reading (e.g., isolated skills mastery approach vs. a broader, comprehension-based approach), the identified patterns reoccurred across classrooms (for further discussion see Bloome, 1983a, 1984a).

The findings raise additional questions. First, questions need to be asked about the extent of the recurrence of the findings across schools and classroom situations.

In particular, questions need to be asked about the recurrence of the findings across schools within an urban setting, across urban and suburban schools, across magnet versus nonmagnet schools, across schools with predominately Anglo populations versus predominately black populations, and across grade levels.

Questions also need to be asked about the extent to which ways of interacting with text acquired in the classroom influence ways of interacting with text outside of the classroom. Part of the difficulty in exploring the influence of classroom-acquired frames is that literacy tasks and situations outside of the classroom may not be analogous to tasks inside the classroom.

In addition, the findings also raise questions about the nature of reading development. Specifically, to what extent can reading be viewed as a decontextualized process, extractable from the face-to-face contexts in which reading development occurs? The findings reported in this chapter suggest that reading development may not necessarily be extractable from the face-to-face contexts of its occurrence. That is, reading deveelopment should be viewed not only as a question of magnitude but also, and perhaps more importantly, as a question of direction and substance. Questions need to be asked about the directions and substance of reading development and their ties to the cumulative social and communicative agendas within which reading events occur. To respond to these questions, new conceptions of reading are necessary which are both comlementary to current cognitively based definitions of reading and definitions of reading as a social process.

REFERENCES

Anderson, A., & Stokes, S. (1984). Social and institutional influences on the development and practice of literacy. In H. Goelman, A. Oberg, & F. Smith (Eds.), *Awakening to literacy*. Exeter, NH: Heinemann Educational Books.

Au, K. (1980). Participation structures in a reading lesson with Haawaiian children. *Anthropology and Education Quarterly, 11,* 91–115.

Bloome, D. (1982). *School culture and the future of literacy*. Paper presented at Future of Literacy Conference, Baltimore (ERIC #ED231 899).

Bloome, D. (1983a). Classroom reading instruction: A socio-communicative analysis of time on task. In J. Niles (Ed.), *32nd yearbook of the National Reading Conference*. Rochester, NY: National Reading Conference.

Bloome, D. (1983b). Reading as a social process. In B. Hutson (Ed.), *Advances in reading/language research* (Vol. 2). Greenwich, CT: JAI Press.

Bloome, D. (1984a). A socio-communicative perspective of formal and informal classroom reading events. In J. Niles (Ed.), *33rd yearbook of the National Reading Conference*. Rochester, NY: National Reading Conference.

Bloome, D. (1984b). *Gaining access to and control of reading and writing resources: K–8* (Final report submitted to National Council of Teachers of English Research Foundation). Urbana, IL: National Council of Teachers of English.

Bloome, D., & Argumedo, B. (1983). Procedural display and classroom instruction at the middle school level: Another look at academic engaged time. In T. Erb (Ed.), *Middle school research: Selected studies*. Columbus, OH: National Middle School Association.

Bloome, D., & Goldman, C. (1982). Literacy learning, classroom processes, and race: A microanalytic study of two desegregated classrooms. *Journal of Black Studies. 13,* (2), 207–226.

Bloome, D., & Green, J. (1982a). *Capturing social contexts of reading for urban junior high school youth in home, school and community settings* (Final report to the National Institute of Education). Washington, DC: United States Department of Education.

Bloome, D., & Green, J. (1982b). The social contexts of reading: A multidisciplinary perspective. In B. Hutson (Ed.), *Advances in reading/language research* (Vol. 1). Greenwich, CT: JAI Press.

Bloome, D., & Green, J. (1984). Directions in the sociolinguistic study of reading. In P. Pearson, R. Barr, M. Kamil, & P. Mosenthal (Eds.), *Handbook of research on reading*. New York: Longman.

Bruce, B. (1981). A social interaction model of Reading. *Discourse Processes. 4*, 273–311.

Collins, J. (1981). Differential treatment in reading instruction. In J. Cook-Gumperz, J. Gumperz, & H. Simons (Eds.), *School-home ethnography project* (Final report to the National Institute of Education). Washington, DC: United States Department of Education.

Cook-Gumperz, J., Gumperz, J., & Simons, H. (1981). *School-home ethnography project* (Final report to the National Institute of Education). Washington, DC: United States Department of Education.

Doyle, W. (1983). Academic work. *Review of Educational Research. 53* (2), 159–199.

Erickson, F., & Shultz, J. (1981). When is a context? Some issues and methods in the analysis of social competence. In J. Green & C. Wallat (Eds.), *Ethnography and language in educational settings*. Norwood, NJ: Ablex.

Gilmore, P. (1981). Shortridge school and community: Attitudes and admission to literacy. In D. Hymes (project director), *Ethnographic monitoring of children's acquisition of reading/langauge arts skills in and out of the classroom* (Final report to the National Institute of Education). Washngton, DC: United States Department of Education.

Goody, J., & Watt, I. (1968). The consequences of literacy. In J. Goody (Ed.), *Literacy in traditional societies*. London: Cambridge University Press.

Green, J., & Wallat, C. (1981). Mapping instructional conversations. In J. Green & C. Wallat (Eds.), *Ethnography and language in educational settings*. Norwood, NJ: Ablex.

Griffin, P. (1977). How and when does reading occur in the classroom? *Theory Into Practice. 16*, (5), 376–383.

Gumperz, J., & Tannen, D. (1979). Individual and social differences in language use. In C. Filmore et al., (Eds.), *Individual differences in language ability and language behavior*. New York: Academic Press.

Heath, S. (1982). Questioning at home and at school: A comparitive study. In G. Spindler (Ed.), *The ethnography of schooling*. New York: Holt, Rinehart & Winston.

Hendrix, R. (1981). The status and politics of writing instruction. In M. Whiteman (Ed.), *Variation in writing: Functional and linguistic-cultural differences*. Hillsdale, NJ: Erlbaum.

Hymes, D. (project director). (1981). *Ethnographic monitoring of children's acquisition of reading/language arts skills in and out of the classroom* (Final report to the National Institute of Education). Washington, DC: United States Department of Education.

Jacob, E. (1984). Learning literacy through play: Puerto Rican kindergarten children. In H. Goelman, A. Oberg, & F. Smith (Eds.), *Awakening to literacy*. Exeter, NH: Heinemann Educational Books.

Kirsch, I., & Guthrie, J. (1983). *Reading competencies and practices: Reading practices of adults in one high technology company* (Technical Report #6). Newark, DE: International Reading Association.

McDermott, R. (1976). *Kids make sense: An ethnographic account of the interactional management of success and failure in one first-grade classroom*. Doctoral dissertation, Stanford University, Stanford, CA.

Michaels, S. (1981). "Sharing time": Children's narrative styles and differential access to literacy. *Language in Society, 10* (3), 423–442.

Olson, D. (1977). The languages of instruction: On the literate bias of schooling. In R. Anderson, R. Spiro, & W. Montague (Eds.), *Schooling and the acquisition of knowledge*. Hillsdale, NJ: Erlbaum.

Philips, S. (1983). *The invisible culture: Communication in classroom and community on the Warm Springs Indian Reservation*. New York: Longman.

Reder, S., & Green, K. (in press). Contrasting patterns of literacy in an Alaska fishing village. *International Journal of Sociology of Language.*

Schieffelin, B., & Cochran-Smith, M. (1984). Learning to read culturally: Literacy before schooling. In H. Goelman, A. Oberg, & F. Smith, (Eds.), *Awakening to literacy.* Exeter, NH: Heinemann Educational Books.

Scollon, R., & Scollon, S. (1984). Cooking it up and boiling it down. In D. Tannen (Ed.), *Coherence in spoken and written discourse.* Norwood, NJ: Ablex.

Scribner, S., & Cole, M. (1981). *The psychology of literacy.* Cambridge MA: Harvard University Press.

Scribner, S., & Cole, M. (1978). Literacy without schooling: Testing for intellectual effects. *Harvard Educational Review. 48* (4), 448–461.

Spradley, J. (1980). *Participant observation.* Holt, Rinehart & Winston.

Taylor, D. (1983). *Family literacy: Young children learning to read and write.* Exeter, NH: Heinemann Educational Books.

Taylor, D., & Dorsey-Gaines, C. (1982). *The cultural context of family literacy.* Paper presented at The National Reading Conference, Clearwater, FL.

Vygotsky, L. (1962). *Thought and language.* Cambridge, MA: MIT Press.

7 Classroom Interaction and Curricular Content*

Rebecca Barr

National College of Education and University of Chicago

In some classes students learn a little and in others they learn a lot. How can we understand this difference? Though responses to this question have varied, a long tradition of research on teaching suggests that the answer can be found in the interaction between teachers and students during instruction. For example, the theoretical work of Lewin, Lippitt, and White (1939), Anderson (1939), and Flanders (1970) treated teaching as classroom leadership and focused on direct and indirect forms of leadership manifest during instruction. This dichotomy in leadership style has been pursued recently by such researchers as Bennett (1976) and Rosenshine (1979) as well as by countless others over the last 40 years. Alternatively, Smith and Meux (1962) and Bellack, Kliebard, Hyman , and Smith (1966) have examined the logical structure of classroom discourse. Current researchers have elaborated the study of classroom discourse by applying methodological concepts and theoretical perspectives from sociolinguistics and ethnography (see Bloome and Green, 1984).

Undergirding the enterprise is the premise that the essence of instruction can be captured through detailed study of instructional interaction. While granting that interaction is an important part of instruction, other conditions as well as interaction must be studied if one is to understand the effectiveness of instruction. To clarify this point through analogy, classroom instructionm may be compared to a symphony performance. Conductors have different leadership styles and performances differ in quality and nuance, but in spite of these differences, orchestras will be recognized as performing the same work when they play the same musical score. The score is an integral part of the interaction, both defining and limiting what can occur. It is only when the demands of the score exceed the competence of the musicians that either the performance must be abandoned or something less than an acceptable rendition occurs.

In a similar fashion, curricular materials influence the interaction that occurs in many subject areas, but particularly during reading instruction. However, this influence has been ignored in most studies of instruction. Indeed, there has been a

---

*Darlene McCampell, the teacher whose work I studied, was most hospitable in welcoming me into her class, respectful of my methods for documenting her instruction and its effectiveness, supportive in helping me obtain needed evidence, and generous in the time she provided for our conversations about her goals and reasons for developing class activities. I am also indebted to the students enrolled in the course who permitted me to observe their class, shared their work with me, and patiently answered my questions.

I wish to thank Judith Green, Darlene McCampell, and James Mosenthal for their helpful comments on earlier drafts of this chapter.

conscious effort among some researchers to view instructional interaction in "content-free" terms (see, e.g. Anderson, Evertson, & Brophy, 1979; Fisher, Filby, Marliave, Cahen,Dishaw, Moore, and Berliner, 1978).

The purpose of this chapter is to consider alternative ways in which curricular materials have a bearing on classroom interaction. In the first section of the chapter, I consider the nature of the linkages between curricular content and instruction in theoretical terms. In this endeavor, I draw heavily on previous work undertaken with Robert Dreeben (Barr & Dreeben, 1983) that treats curricular materials as one of the central components of instruction. In the second section, I explore the influence of curricular materials on instruction empirically. The case of a high school English course which I observed each day for a school year is considered within the theoretical framework previously developed.

THE INFLUENCE OF CURRICULAR MATERIALS ON INSTRUCTION

One contribution of the formulative work which I have just completed with Robert Dreeben is to provide a view of instructional context that is based within the broader organization of schools. In this view "context" includes (but goes beyond) the treatment of interactional work as the context for individual learning and beyond the treatment of classroom climate and other class conditions as the context of instruction. The formulation develops a view of schools as hierarchically organized with the productive activities of one level constituting the context for the activities occurring at adjacent organization levels.

At the classroom level, teachers do not create instruction from scratch. The conditions of the class—its students and their competencies, the curricular materials, and instructional time—represent the opportunities and limitations within which teachers work. In public schools, these conditions are typically established by decisions occuring at the school and district levels of organization. By contrast, in private schools, some of these conditions are established by the teachers themselves. For example, it is not unusual for teachers to select the curricular materials they use or even to develop a course for a specific group of students. But however the conditions are established, it is up to teachers to organize students and interact with them so that their experiences with curricular materials and other resources result in the achievement of learning goals.

At the opening of the school year, teachers are first occupied with arranging their classes for instruction. An initially undifferentiated aggregate of students gets transformed into instructible units, and the instruction of these groups gets under way. Teachers engage students in learning activities designed at times to include everyone together in the class, at other times for small groups under close supervision, and sometimes individuals working independently. The prevailing classroom conditions are realities that in combination pose problems for teachers and constrain the variety of satisfactory solutions to them that must be worked out on a continuing basis.

In this chapter, I argue that an extremely important condition influencing the organization and nature of instructional interaction is the curricular material used by the teacher. It is, in effect, the "musical score" that shapes the development of the content of instruction. The case study to be later discussed demonstrates four distinguishable ways in which curricular materials have a bearing on instructional interaction and learning: (a) as an organizing rubic; (b) as an influence on class interaction; (c) as an integral component of instructional interaction; and (d) as a direct influence on learning.

Curricular Materials as an Organizing Rubric

In much the same way that conductors follow a musical score, teachers are influenced by the curricular materials they use. To be sure, teachers using the same materials will vary in the time they allocate to various sections of the materials, in the concepts they emphasize, and in their interpretation of the material being read. But while this is true, the general organizing function of curricular materials should not be overlooked. Indeed, recent research on teaching shows that teachers closely adhere to the content and sequence of their textbooks (Shavelson, 1983; Shannon, 1983).

But how should we think about the general influence that curricular materials have on instruction? Typically, interaction among teachers and students relates directly to curricular activities undertaken to achieve specific goals. That is, interaction in classrooms is not an undifferentiated process whose elements can be lumped together in order to examine its properties. Rather, interaction typically occurs to accomplish a number of distinguishable activities. For example, a reading lesson may consist of activities such as reading and discussing a story, writing about a character in the story, and developing vocabulary concepts associated with a story. These activities presume common knowledge that is based on the story content.

In this analysis, I argue that curricular materials in the form of stories or topics provide substantive linkages among a variety of instructional activities. And it is in this sense that curricular materials serve as a general organizing rubic for thinking about how activities that continue over a period of time are interconnected. The curricular "units of organization" serve to give conceptual coherence to a variety of component activities that span a number of days or even weeks. Further, the units of organization occuring during the course of a school year may also be interconnected and build on one another. When viewed from this perspective, curricular materials provide the means for conceptualizing the ways in which instructional activities are interconnected and relate to the general goals of instruction.

Material Difficulty as an Influence on Instruction

A major problem that teachers face in the design of instruction is that of matching their curricular materials and their teaching support to the needs of their students. Teachers solve this problem in several ways. They may elect to reorganize their students into subgroups so that the materials and the pace of their presentation will be appropriate for the learning rate of students. Alternatively, they may choose to instruct their class as a unit, providing special teaching support for those students for whom the materials are inappropriate. Or they may individualize instruction so that assigned materials are directly appropriate to student capabilities; this solution, however, provides limited opportunities for teaching support. For example, in our examination of first-grade reading instruction, we found that teachers subdivided the class into ability groups and geared the difficulty of the reading task to the aptitude of the reading group by varying the amount of material covered in the basal materials. High-ability groups typically covered three to five times as much material as lower-ability groups (Barr & Dreeben, 1983).

A different variation in the problem of instructional design exists in intermediate-grade subject-matter reading. Usually, the instructional group is the whole class, and frequently the materials are extremely difficult for all but the most able students in the class. The instructional problem posed for the teacher is how to achieve agreed-upon curricular goals by making the content in the curricular materials accessible to most class members. Typically, both time and materials represent fixed resources, at least in the short run. Instructional group composition is usually not altered. Thus, the mismatch between student capabilities and curricular material content must be alleviated through various teaching strategies. Teachers often combine textual oral reading with a detailed explanation of key concepts and terms in order to present curricular ideas, because the students cannot read the materials silently with sufficient comprehension for themselves.

In the extreme case, when serious mismatches exist, the workable ways in which teachers design instruction are extremely limited. The fixed nature of the resourses along with teacher and/or administrative commitment to their use results in such a wide gap between student knowledge and the knowledge presented by the curricular content that the most ingenious teacher strategies are unable to bridge the gap for most class members. Smith and Geoffrey (1968, pp. 187–189) described such a situation in their case study of a split-grade class. By contrast, when there is an appropriate match between instructional material difficulty and group competencies, teachers have the opportunity to design instruction in alternative ways, some ways more effective than others.

Curricular Content as a Component of Interaction

The content of curricular materials typically becomes a integral aspect of instruction, directly, as it is read aloud by teachers or students, and indirectly, as it is discussed and elaborated upon by teachers and students. Jointly, teacher and student comments and the content of curricular materials form the *content of instruction*. If the goal of instruction is to develop literal comprehension of a story, the content of instruction will closely approximate the content of the curricular materials. By contrast, if the goal of instruction is to develop interpretive skills, teacher and student extensions from the literal content will constitute the content of instruction. A good match permits such flexibility. However, less flexibility is possible to the extent that discrepancy exists between student knowledge and that presumed by the text, and, consequently, much of the instructional content will consist of teacher clarification of concepts contained in materials.

Content as a Condition of Learning

Finally, the content of instruction, whatever its source, constrains but does not completely limit what is learned by individual students. Some students may understand little of the content; others will master the content presented; and still others will elaborate further and learn beyond the content covered during instruction.

Instructional activities become the productive conditions that interact with individual talents to influence learning. In particular, the content relevant to objectives transmitted through reading materials and class discussion creates the opportunity for learning. These opportunities differ from class to class. The extent to which individual students are able to use the opportunities provided reflects their priorities and talents.

Summary

This formulation of class instruction identifies curricular materials as one of several important conditions that influences the viability and nature of instructional interaction, contributing to its content and thereby influencing learning. The creative activity through which teachers combine the conditions of the class into instruction is parallel in some respects to the creative work of students who combine instructional content with their background knowledge in order to derive new understandings. We now turn to a detailed examination of the role of curricular material in a high school Engish class in order to exemplify its influence on interaction and learning.

CASE STUDY OF A HIGH SCHOOL ENGLISH CLASS

The class described here was offered to juniors and seniors in an urban private school. The composition of the class was influenced in two ways by school-level decisions. (a) no more than 15 students were allowed to enroll in each section of the class; and (b) students with a history of reading and writing problems were encouraged to enroll. Standardized reading test results showed that students typically came from the lowest third of the school population; but when compared to a national sample, most scores fell between the 50th and 70th percentiles.

The class was selected for detailed study because of its reputed effectiveness. This effectiveness was determined in a variety of ways: student reports, examination of informal reading responses and writing samples, and more objective test evidence. Students claimed that through their course experience they learned strategies for going beyond a story to its deeper meaning and for writing expository themes. Test results involving an informal reading inventory revealed that students made significant gains in interpretive reading comprehension during the autumn quarter of the course ($t = 3.14$; $p < .01$).

The objectives for the course were twofold: to develop interpretive reading comprehennsion and skill in expository writing. In addition, the course included a component on vocabulary development and one on grammar. The class met four times per week from 11:40 a.m. to 12:30 p.m. Each day began with a short vocabulary review; other activities varied from day to day.

Unlike most instructional situations, the curricular materials for the course were not prescribed but rather had been compiled by the teacher over a period of several years. Thus, materials were not a condition established by decisions made at higher levels in the school or district; rather they represented a class condition established by the teacher. Accordingly, we would expect them to be appropriate to the goals of the teacher and the capabilities of the students. Just as student characteristics varied little from year to year, the curriculum changed only slightly from year to year. Four short stories were read during the autumn quarter, a short story and a novel during the winter quarter, and two more difficult short stories and a Shakespearean play during the spring. In any case, however, subsequent analyses showed that once the curricular materials were established, they constrained and supported instruction, interacting in definable ways with teacher and student comments to form the content of instruction.

The teacher was receptive to having her class observed. She did, however, place one restriction on the observation: no audio- or videotape recording during total class instruction. Thus, written notes were made concerning the time when major types of activity and interaction occurred. Teacher questions were recorded as accurately as possible to permit later examination. Extended explanations and student responses were recorded in summary form. The methodology limited the extent to which detailed analysis could be made of the interactional content and the form of instruction. At the same time, documentation of all class sessions that occurred during the school year presented an unusual opportunity for examining the role of curricular materials in instruction.

Further, observation was not the only source of information. Student written drafts and final compositions and their course evaluations were examined. The observer met frequently with the teacher to confirm impressions and interpretation of the evidence and to clarify teacher objectives and plans.

Curricular Materials and Units of Instruction

Evidence was collected from more than 100 class periods. The first problem was to organize the evidence in a way that permitted the observation of recurring patterns. Typically, in studies of the interaction between teacher and students, evidence is obtained from one or several lessons. Units of discourse or types of behavior are identified and classified, but often the sense of how these activities fit together and are organized within a lesson context is lost (e.g., see studies reported by Rosenhine & Stevens, 1984). Recently, some researchers have begun to describe the interconnections occurring among types of activity units within lessons (e.g., see Mehan, 1979). Almost never, however, are component activities and lessons placed within the larger context of instructional sequences that are designed to meet the goals of the teacher. To the extent that lessons differ in form and focus from day to day and to the extent that they are interdependent, it is important to understand their interconnections and how they constitute some larger instructional unit. Randomly selecting lessons for intensive study without specifying how these units fit into larger instructional units may lead to unfortunate sampling bias. More important, it fails to establish how a particular lessons may plausibly contribute to the learning objectives of a teacher and to actual learning.

The question of instructional effectiveness cannot be addressed, unless one knows the goals and means used by the teacher to achieve them. It is important to establish how lessons of varying types contribute to the achievement of a learning goal. A lesson of one type may be appropriate at one time during the sequence but inappropriate at a later time. For example, in the case of reading instruction with the objective to develop interpretive reading skills, if class discussion focuses only on the story line, the lesson may be judged inappropriate and be shown to be ineffective. However, focus on interpretive skills before students understand what the story is about may be equally ineffective.

But let us return to the problem at hand. In the case of the English class that was observed, what were the larger instructional units of which lessons were a part? Simply to graph time allocations to different instructional activities on a daily basis for the period of a quarter or the school year failed to come to terms with the question. Similarly, abstracting and sequencing types of lessons such as those focused on reading (or writing) or those involving class discussion failed to show the relationship between these lesson types and other activities used to achieve instructional goals; they, too, failed to address the question of larger units.

A curricular material-based solution was examined in this study. The short story was used as the unit of organization, and different sorts of reading and writing activities occurring within alternative social arrangements that pertained to a particular short story were graphed on a time line. The time line provided information about both the duration of activities in minutes and the date on which activities occurred. Figure 1 presents the evidence derived from 45 class sessions that occurred during the autumn quarter when four different short stories were read. Reading activities are indicated by "R" in the figure, and writing activities, by "W". Class instruction to achieve the development of interpretive reading comprehension occurred through a variety of reading and writing tasks that were organized as total class, small group, and independent work activities. For example, the first short story was initially read as independent work during a reading test. Then a writing assignment pertaining to the story was made, followed by an instructional session that focused on interpretive reading comprehension. Students then participated in evaluating each other's writing. The treatment of the first story ended with a second instruction session on story interpretation, followed by teacher reaction to the written assignments.

The time line shown in Figure 1 reveals several characteristics that may enhance the effectiveness of instruction. First, to focus only on reading instruction is to tell half the story. As shown in Figure 1, after the first reading of Hanley's (1961) "The Butterfly" and before class discussion of the story, students were given a writing assignment:

> Your assignment for Monday is to write a single paragraph about Brother Timothy or Cassidy. It should begin with a topic sentence. A topic sentence is an

opinion that can be supported. The topic sentence should be followed by three quotations that prove the topic sentence, and you should explain for each how the quote proves your topic.

Not only were students learning how to write expository prose, the writing assignment required use of the interpretive comprehension strategies that the teacher encouraged during reading instruction—that of going from evidence to a conclusion about a character. Later, the writing assignments required students to begin with a topic or source of conflict that seemed to be important in the story (innocence or guilt, training or teaching, justice or mercy) and to develop a thesis based on the story. Students were taught how to break the thesis into parts that could be supported by evidence contained in the story and to develop each part in a paragraph.

The power of the writing component came from its forcing students to objectify their interpretive conclusions and to support their conclusions in a systematic way with evidence. Further, the motivational power of the writing assignments was clear. Once an assignment was given, students appeared to be more involved in the reading instruction that followed.

In addition, the teacher encouraged internalization of the interpretive strategies in two ways. First, each subsequent story served as the occasion for using and further refining the interpretive reading approaches. Evaluations written by students indicated that the repeated application of a strategy was of central importance in its development. Second, the social organization of instruction facilitated independent use of the strategies. As shown in Figure 1, while interpretive strategies were first modeled during total class instruction, they were subsequently used by small groups of students working together and then independently during homework.

Although with a single case study it is impossible to demonstrate that these aspects of instruction were prime contributors to the effectiveness of the course, observer and participant reaction were consistent in identifying these as important components. The point to be made here is that whether or not their effectiveness can be demonstrated, it is important that such characteristics be represented in descriptions of instruction. Too many analytic schemes are sensitive neither to patterns in questioning that occur across instructional sessions nor to related tasks that may reinforce learning. But to ignore such conditions may have the consequence of attributing to limited aspects of instructional interaction and content more than they have the power to influence. Particularly, when it comes to intervention into practice, it is important that the instructional components that actually occur in exemplary cases be documented.

In sum, the solution of specifying larger instructional units in relation to the curricular materials has several advantages. It permits relationships that exist between various types of activities occurring within alternative social contexts to be seen. It is obvious that intensive reading work typically precedes writing activities, but also that writing co-occurs with reading. It displays the larger instructional context from which lessons selected for intensive study are abstracted and shows whether particular lessons occurred early or late within the development of story comprehension.

THE BUTTERFLY (Hanley)

Date	Codes
9/19	R / 1W
	W / TC
9/22	R / TC / SD*
	W / 1W
9/25	R / TC / SD*
9/26	W / TC

FIRST CONFESSION (O'Connor)

Date	Codes
9/27	R / TC / SD* ; R / TC / SD*
9/29	R / SG ; R / TC / SD
10/2	WR / 1WSG ; R / TC / SD*
10/3	W / 1W ; R / SG ; R / TC / SD*
10/4	R / TC / SD ; W / 1W
10/6	W / TC ; W / TC
10/9	W / TC
10/10	W / TC
10/11	W / TC ; R / TC / SD ; W / 1W
10/13	W / 1W-C
10/16	R / TC / SD
10/17	W / 1W ; W / 1W-C

THE NIGHTINGALES SING (Parsons)

Date	Codes
10/17	R / TC ; R / TC / SD* ; R / 1W ; W / 1W
10/18	R / TC / SD* ; R / TC / SD
10/20	W / 1W ; R / TC / SD ; W / C ; R / TC / SD
10/23	W / 1W ; R / TC / SD ; W / 1W ; R / TC / SD
10/24	W / 1W ; R / TC / SD ; W / 1W ; WR / C TC / SD*
10/25	R / TC / SD ; W / 1W

Figure 1. Reading and Writing Activities Accompanying Stories During the Autumn Quarter

R TC SD	R TC SD	W TC	R 1W	W TC	W TC	R TC SD	R TC SD*	R TC SD	W TC
	10/27		10/30	10/31		11/1		11/3	

W TC	W 1W	W 1W-C	W 1W-C	W 1W	W TC
11/6	11/7	11/8	11/10	11/13	11/14

OPEN WINTER (Davis)

R TC SD	R 1W TC SD	R TC SD	R SG GR	R TC GR	R TC GR	R TC GR	R SG GR	R SG	R TC GR	R TC GR
11/17	11/20	11/21		11/27	11/27	11/28		11/29

W TC	R TC GR	W 1W-C	W TC	R TC GR	W 1W-C	W 1W
12/1	12/4	12/5	12/6	12/8

R = reading; W = writing; TC = total class; SG = small group; 1W = independent work; SD = story discussion; C = individual conferences with teacher; GR = group reports; * = SD selected for analysis; 1/4 inch = 10 minutes.

Most important, it provides a bridge for relating detailed examination of class interaction back to the content and goals of instruction. As was argued earlier, teaching
effectiveness must be assessed in terms of the goals of instruction.

Influence of Material Difficulty on Instruction

The content of curricular materials may also directly influence the nature of instruction. As discussed earlier, if materials are difficult for students, the nature of instruction may focus specifically on concepts presented in the materials to make them
accessible. By contrast, if a good match exists between student knowledge and the
materials, instructional interaction is less constrained and may take alternative
forms. In this section, I examine the difficulty of curricular materials in relation to
the questioning interaction that occurred during reading instruction.

In order to provide some feel for the nature of instructional interaction during the
reading lessons,, Table 1 contains the transcript from the class discussion of the first
story, "The Butterfly" (Hanley, 1961). As can be seen, the interaction during reading instruction was recitational in nature with two main patterns: (a) a teacher question followed by a series of student responses and sometimes a teacher comment;
and (b) a teacher question followed by a student response and sometimes a teacher
comment. Typically, the first format was used when the teacher was gathering evidence about a character or his beliefs, and the second, when students were encouraged to draw conclusions on the basis of the evidence. The teacher's questions encouraged students to form a full understanding of the main characters and to identify
the conflict that was "built in." While she first approached the conflict by having
students focus on the characteristics of the two characters and the problem that their
differences may cause, when this was unsuccessful, she urged students to think
about the beliefs of both characters and how their different beliefs constituted an
inherent conflict.

The nature of the discourse shown in Table 1 was designed to foster the development of interpretive comprehension. But can this sort of interaction occur
irrespective of class conditions? In particular, how does the nature of the reading
material influence the development of interpretive comprehension? Within this case
study is a natural contrast. During the spring quarter, the teacher had the students
read a relatively difficult short story and a Shakespearean play. How did the nature
of class discourse change when students were dealing with easy short stories versus
more difficult selections?

In order to examine instructional interaction in relation to reading material
difficulty, it was necessary to characterize the difficulty of the material and to classify aspects of class discourse. The Fry Readability Formula (Fry, 1968) was used to
assess the difficulty of the short stories. Using a readability formula to characterize
the difficulty of material had obvious limitations; nevertheless, alternative means of
assessing content difficulty (cloze readability and the judgment of experts) were
consistent with the readability formula ratings. As shown in Table 2, while the first
three stories were judged to be at the fifth- and sixth-grade levels, the Faulkner short
story was at least of ninth-grade difficulty. Because of its extremely long sentences,

Table 1. Class Discussion of "The Butterfly"

Discussion: Friday (9/22: 12:05 – 12:30)	Blackboard

1. Now, let's look at the story. How do you read a story? It is important to learn how to approach a story. One way is to read aloud. You might want to underline words and phrases associated with Brother Timothy (BT) and Cassidy (C) as I read. (Students follow as teacher reads first paragraph aloud.)

T: What are some of the words that you associate with BT?

Brother Timothy

S: Nervous.

nervous   chaos of thought

S: Wild.

wild   bewildered

S: Angry

angry   aimless

S: Rage, His blood mounted.

rage (blood mounted)

S: Chaos of thought.

S: Bewildered

S: Aimless.

T: Obviously there is a pattern there, not joy. A pattern is building. (Students follow as teacher reads second paragraph aloud.)

T: What are some words you associate with C?

Cassidy

S: Serenity.

serenity

S: No conscience.

no conscience

S: Content.

content

S: Infernal silence.

infernal silence

T: Do all of these describe C?

S: Some are how BT sees C—"no conscience" and "infernal silence."

T: What does BT mean by "conscience?"

S: Guilt.

T: What is the conflict built into the story?

S: Psychosis.

T: Don't go beyond the story. What are some of the things that comprise BT's religion?

Brother Timothy believes in:

S: Religion with a capital "R."

religion
going to Mass

S: Going to Mass.

suffering shows devotion

S: He believes that suffering shows devotion.

church
authority

S: Church.

obedience to authority

Table 1. (*continued*)

Discussion: Friday (9/22: 12:05 – 12:30)	Blackboard

S: Authority.

S: Obedience to authority.

T: What are things that C believes in?

Cassidy believes in:

S: Being outdoors.

    outdoors

S: Freedom.

    freedom

    nature

S: Nature.

    being peaceful

S: Being peaceful.

    happy

    spontaneity

S: Being happy.

    exploration

S: Spontaneity.

S: Exploration.

T: What problem do you have built in? Given these two lists, why does BT care so much that C goes to Mass?

S: Maybe he's jealous, can't comprehend.

S: C broke a rule that BT believes in.

T: But why would that make him so angry? (Bell rings; students begin to gather together their things.) Be ready to turn in your paragraph at the beginning of the period on Monday.

Monday (9/25: 12:11 – 12:16)

T: Back to the "Butterfly." Who does the author want us to feel sympathy for?

S: Cassidy.

T: Does everyone agree? What does he do to make us like C?

S: He represents hope; he's innocent.

T: What else? What actions?

S: The way he played with the caterpillar.

T: He cares; he's curious. How does he interact?

S: He's gentle, caring.

T: BT torments, squashes it, kills it. What else?

S: The way he punishes C.

T: If he had really done something of moral significance, then it might be appropriate. But C is in the sunlight. Anything else? Sometimes in reading a story, that's a good question to begin with: "Who does the author favor?"

it fell below the norms presented on the Fry table. A readability formula was inappropiate for assessing the difficulty of the Shakespearean play, because it was insensitive to some characteristics of language (e.g., archaism) that made the reading difficult. In any case, *The Merchant of Venice* was a demanding play for most high school students.

Reading instruction was recitational in nature, consisting mainly of teacher questions and student responses. Thus, further study was made of the nature of teacher questions. Lessons were selected from the beginning, middle, and final stages of reading instruction accompanying the five selections. The lessons selected for the first three stories are identified by an asterisk in Figure 1. Questions and summary notes concerning the answers that followed were treated as units and were examined in relation to the content of the story being discussed.

Two main types of units were identified: those pertaining directly to the text to assure accurate understanding of the story line and those designed to lead students beyond text-based information toward greater understanding of characters and theme. The first type was further subdivided into questions and answers about the meaning of words and phrases and those concerning sentence and passage comprehension. Study of the interpretive questions and answers revealed three main types: (a) those concerned with gathering evidence in order to understand characters and their motives; (b) those concerned with drawing conclusions based on the evidence; (c) and those which were metainterpretive in nature in that they focused either on what the author was trying to achieve or on what the reader's understanding of, or view toward, a topic was. Table 3 includes examples of teacher questions that occurred within each of the five categories. With the exception of some questions in the last category, all questions posed by the teacher related directly or indirectly to the text.

As can be seen from Table 2, the preponderance of questions concerning the first three stories were interpretive in nature. By contrast, many more of the questions asked about "Barn Burning" and most concerning *The Merchant of Venice* were text based. It might be expected that the trend during the course of the school year would show an increase in interpretive questions as students mastered the strategies that they were being taught. This expectation assumes consistency in the difficulty of the instructional materials during the course of the year. But, to the contrary, the results showed an increase in text-based questions. Since the only condition that had changed other than the competence of students was the difficulty of the materials, it is highly plausible that material difficulty was responsible for the increase in text-based questions.

If we accept the validity of this conclusion, how should the results be interpreted? Will it always be the case that teachers using easy materials develop interpretive reading strategies, while those with difficult materials focus on relaying the essential content of the material? The relationship between materials and instructional interaction is probably not linear in form; rather, easy materials represent a less extreme constraint so that teachers who choose to focus on text-based comprehension may do so, while those who wish to develop beyond-text interpretive skill may do that. By contrast, very difficult materials may determine the instruction of

Table 2. Numbered Text-Based and Beyond-Text Questions Asked During Discussions of Three Easy and Two Difficult Selections

Story (Author)	Readability	Lesson	Time (min)	Text-based comprehension		Beyond-text interpretation		Meta-interpretive
				Vocabulary	Passage	Evidence	Conclusion	
"The Butterfly" (James Hanley)	G.E. 5	2	25	0	0	4	12	3
		3	6	0	0	0	0	12
"First Confession" (Frank O'Connor)	G.E. 6	1	8	1	0	1	4	1
		2	23	0	0	4	9	6
		4	12	0	0	0	5	0
		4	5	0	0	0	3	0
"Nightingales Sing" (Eliz. Parsons)	G.E. 5	2	10	1	6	0	7	1
		2	9	0	0	2	1	1
		6	23	0	0	0	6	3
		9	31	0	0	3	9	1
"Barn Burning" (Wm. Faulkner)	G.E. + 9	2	38	6	13	0	8	7
		3	47	2	9	5	4	9
		6	26	3	8	0	7	2
		8	48	0	5	5	11	3
The Merchant of Venice (Wm. Shakespeare)	College	1	25	0	13	0	1	1
		4	48	2	27	0	6	6
		8	39	1	17	1	3	1
		11	46	0	4	0	5	3

Table 3. Examples of Question Types

Text-based comprehension: Vocabulary
Does anyone know what the word "fastidious" means?
What is a "privy"?
What's a "cur"?
What is "justice"?

Text-based comprehension: Passage
Give a short summary of the story. What are the actions?
In a factual way what does it have to do with the story?
(Reads passage) What does that mean?
What is the first thing Harris does?

Beyond-text interpretation: Evidence
What are some of the words you associate with Brother Timothy?
Sweetness and light on the surface, underneath turning a knife.
What's the evidence?
How does this indifference show?
What are some of the things Scarty knew about courthouses?

Beyond-text interpretation: Conclusion
What does Brother Timothy mean by "conscience"?
Let me hear your conclusions about Nora?
How would you label the two worlds?
What does that say about the boy, about his quality?

Beyond-text metainterpretive
Who does the author favor?
What are some of your associations with it?
Whom do you think you're going to like?
What would you feel like (on the way to the hospital)?

all teachers, because the literal meaning is not accessible to students, and therefore teachers must find a way to present the content of the material before they can proceed to interpretive questions.

For this particular case, the analysis suggested that curricular materials might influence the level of instruction, that is, how text-based or interpretive its focus is. Because of the difference in the interaction that occurred in the autumn and spring quarters, it is likely that the learning was also of a different order: learning how to interpret during the autumn and how to do close textual reading along with higher-level interpretation in the spring. The teacher's selection of very easy short stories for the content of instruction during the fall quarter minimized the problems of text-based comprehension and permitted her and the class to focus almost exclusively on the development of strategies for interpretation.

Curricular Content as an Integral Part of Instruction

I have been arguing that in order to understand the nature of instructional interaction, it is also necessary to know something about the nature of class conditions, in particular, the difficulty of instructional materials. I have presented some evidence suggesting that the difficulty of materials may influence the level of instruction (text-based vs. interpretive). But in addition, printed text becomes an integral part of the instruction that occurs in many classes. That is, instructional interaction consists of a three-way interaction between text, teacher, and students. The analysis of question-answer units in relation to text content illustrates one way of connecting teacher-student interaction with textual content (see also Harker, in press).

The examination of question-answer units revealed a marked difference between the instruction during the autumn and spring quarters. What does not become obvious from a detailed study of questions considered one at a time is that the teacher, during autumn quarter instruction, was establishing generic question types that formed strategies for going beyond the text-based meaning of a story. These questions are summarized in Table 4. In some form, they reoccurred in each subsequent story considered. And as was discussed earlier, the teacher encouraged internalization of the strategies through application and refinement while reading subsequent stories.

Table 4. Generic Questions Posed During the Autumn Quarter

What evidence characterizes a character or his beliefs, and what conclusions do you draw from the evidence?
What conflict is built into the story?
Whom does the author favor?
What key terms are repeated in the story, and what are your associations with those terms?

Influence of Content on Learning

Our initial question was "How can we understand the difference between classes in which students learn a lot and those in which they learn a little?" The way in which content relates to learning outcomes is directly influenced by the objectives of the teacher. In beginning reading instruction and in subject matter instruction, the materials read may be a major contributor to the content covered and may be a good predictor of what is learned (Barr & Dreeben, 1983). In other reading instruction, the goal may be the development of reading strategies. For example, in this case study, what was to be learned was not simply the content of the short stories read, but in addition, a method for going beyond the story line to the deeper meaning of the story. Accordingly, in order to assess learning appropriately, measures must reflect the content of instruction and not simply the content of the materials read.

The informal reading inventory which assessed the degree of transfer of interpretive strategies to a new story provided evidence that was sensitive to the objectives and content of instruction. By contrast, simple retention of story information and interpretation would not have been as sensitive to the learning goals of the course during the autumn quarter, although a relationship might exist between knowledge and interpretation of story content (ongoing application of the strategy) and strategy development (transfer to a new story).

SUMMARY AND CONCLUSIONS

In this chapter I have argued that it is important to consider such class conditions as curricular materials in documenting instructional interaction. Four ways in which content bears on instruction were considered. First, as an organizing rubic, the short story provided a most useful means for portraying instructional events occurring in reading and writing and their interconnections. Second, as a constraint on class interaction, evidence was presented which suggested that the level of class discussion (text-based vs. interpretive) was responsive to the relative difficulty of the curricular materials. Third, as an integral part of class interaction, question-answer recitational units were classified in relation to story content in order to determine the extent to which the interaction focused on the story line versus beyond-text interpretation. Finally, as a predictor of learning, the content of instruction had direct implication for what might be learned during instruction.

While I believe that it is extremely important to consider ways in which curricular content interacts with instructional interaction and learning, it is also important to examine instructional cases—particularly, exemplary cases—in their own terms. Two components which might enhance the effectiveness of instruction were identified: (a) the development of an interpretive strategy over a series of stories, and (b) the integration of writing with reading activities to reinforce the development of interpretive reading strategies. Although no claims are being made that these characteristics are the ones that account for the effectiveness of the course, it is not implausible that the development of interpretive reading skills are enhanced by such conditions. The point being made here is that such conditions must be documented, if we are to begin to understand their influence. Such documentation involves looking at instruction over a longer time period than is usually the case and examining activities other than reading instruction.

REFERENCES

Anderson, H.H. (1939). The measurement of domination and of socially integrative behavior in teachers' contacts with children. *Child Development, 10*, 73-89.

Anderson, L.M., Evertson, C.M., & Brophy, J. (1979). An experimental study of effective reading in first-grade reading groups. *Elementary School Journal, 79*, 193-233.

Barr, R., & Dreeben, R. (1983). *How schools work.* Chicago: University of Chicago Press.

Bellack, A.A., Kliebard, H.N., Hyman, R.T., & Smith, F.L. (1966). *The language of the classroom.* New York: Teachers College Press.

Bennett, N. (1976). *Teaching styles and pupil progress.* London: Open Books.

Bloome, D., & Green, J. (1984). Directions in the sociolinguistic study of reading. In P.D. Pearson, R. Barr, M. Kamil, & P. Mosenthal (Eds.), *Handbook of research in reading.* New York: Longman.

Faulkner, W. (1958). Barn burning. In R.P. Warren & A. Erskin (Eds.), *Short story masterpieces.* New York: Dell.

Fisher, C.W., Filby, N.N., Marliave, R., Cahen, L.S., Dishaw, M.M., Moore, J.E., & Berliner, D.C. (1978). *Beginning teacher evaluation study* (Technical Report, V-1). San Francisco: Far West Laboratoy.

Flanders, N.A. (1970). *Analyzing teaching behavior.* Reading, MA: Addison-Wesley.

Fry, E.B. (1968). A readability formula that saves time. *Journal of Reading, 11,* 513-516.

Hanley, j. (1961). The butterfly.In R. Goodman (Ed.), *75 short masterpieces.* New York: Bantam.

Harker, J. (in press). The relationship between the evolving oral discourse and the discourse of a story. In j. Green & J. Harker (Eds.), *Multiple perspective analysis of classroom discourse.* Norwood, NJ: Ablex.

Lewin, K., Lippitt, R., & White, R.K. (1939). Patterns of aggressive behavior in experimentaly created social climates. *Journal of Social Psychology, 10,* 271-279.

Mehan, H. (1979). Learning lessons: Social organization in the classroom. Cambridge, MA: Harvard University Press.

O'Connor, F. (1958). First confession. In R.P. Warren & A. Erskine (Eds.), *Short story masterpieces.* New York: Dell.

Parsons, E. (1958). The nightingales sing. In R.P. Warren & A. Ersking (Eds.), *Short story masterpieces.* New York: Dell.

Rosenshine, B. (1979). Content, time, and direct instruction. In P. Peterson & H. Walberg (Eds.), *Research on teaching; Concepts, findings and implications.* Berkeley, CA: McCutchan.

Rosenshine, B., & Stevens, R. (1984). Classroom instruction in reading. In P.D. Pearson, R. Barr, M. Kamil, & P. Mosenthal (Eds.), *Handbook of reasearch in reading,* New York: Longman.

Shakespeare, W. (1965). *The merchant of venice. (K. Myrick, Ed.), New York: New American Classic.*

Shannon, P. (1983). The use of commercial reading materials in American elementary schools. *Reading Research Quarterly, 19*(1), 68-85.

Shavelson, R.J. (1983). Review of research on teachers' pedagogical judgements, plans and decisions. *Elementary School Journal, 83*(4), 392-413

Smith, B.O., & Meux, M.O. (1962). *A study of the logic of teaching.* Urbana: University of Illinois Press.

Smith, L.M., & Geoffrey, W. (1968). *The complexities of an urban classroom.* New York: Holt, Rinehart & Winston.

8 An Exploration of Reader–Text Interaction In A Small Group Discussion

Joanne M. Golden

University of Delaware

Recent work in the area of literary criticism, notably reader-response criticism, offers important insights into how individuals interact with literary texts. The contributions of reader-response criticism to exploration of the reading process complement studies investigating psychological processes in reading.

Within reader-response criticism, the role of the reader in the aesthetic experience is placed in a central position. Scholars address different aspects of the reader's role such as inquiries into the nature of feelings, individual response(s), interpretation(s), and interaction(s) between reader and text (Suleiman & Crosman, 1980). By addressing different aspects of the reader's role and responses theoretical frameworks are developed for understanding reader–text interaction.

Reader-response criticism involves a broad range of perspectives including perspectives from phenomenology, rhetorical theory, semiotics, structuralism, hermeneutics, and psychonalytical theory, While each of these perspectives brings something different to the exploration of reader–text interaction, each emphasizes the central role of the reader. The effect of reader-response criticism has been, in part, to generate a "new awareness of the audience [The reader] as an entity indissociable from the notion of artistic texts" (Suleiman & Crosman, 1980, p. 4). It is noteworthy that Louise Rosenblatt (1968) emphasized the importance of the reader as early as 1938 in her transactional theory of reading.

Reader-response scholars are primarily interested in the "reader in the text" as opposed to actual readers. This reader is constructed by the literary critic, who identifies textual features in literary works which potentially evoke reader operations. The literary text itself functions as a critical part of the inquiry, because actual text cues that potentially generate reader roles are identified. Thus the reader in these studies is a construct rather than an actual reader.

In this chapter, a theoretical framework for viewing reader–text interaction developed from phenomenological and semiotic perspectives is first presented. Second, the theoretical framework is illustrated through an analysis of reader–text interaction in a small group discussion. Throughout both the discussion of the theoretical framework and the analysis of reader–text interaction, ways in which constructs from reader-response criticism and psychological studies of reading complement each other will be highlighted.

A THEORETICAL FRAMEWORK FOR READER–TEXT INTERACTION

The theoretical framework presented here does not entail a comprehensive view of reader–text interaction but rather selects certain constructs which provide promising insights for understanding the *aesthetic* experience involved in process of reading literary texts. The view was developed from two key perspectives on reader-response—phenomenology and semiotics.

The purpose of this discussion is to identify those constructs which seem to be potentially useful for exploring reader–text interaction in a social context with "real readers." The basic view of the perspective that will be developed is rooted in he supposition that the meaning and structure of an aesthetic text are created out of the interaction between text and reader. The reader constructs the global, unified work guided by cues in the text base as well as by his or her intertextual and world experience frames.

In order to consider the nature of the interaction between a reader and a literary text, it is useful to begin with the text itself, since the text evokes the reader's ideational activity. The text can be viewed from a semiotic perspective as a linear arrangement of lexemes which form an expression plane (Eco, 1979). This linear text exists prior to the interpretive process operating as a potential sign which generates multiple interpretations. The move from a potential to an actual sign is achieved during the interpretive process when the aesthetic work is realized. Without the reader, then, the literary text remains a string of ordered, though unconnected, units of information. As one moves from the linear text or potential sign outward to the reader or interpreter of the sign, the interdependence of text and reader is illuminated.

The reader is quided by the cues in the text during the construction of the aesthetic sign. Some of the cognitive operations involved in reading occur, for example, when the reader fills in the blanks of the text and in a sense provides the unwritten part of the text (Iser, 1978). The reader contributes information that is not explicitly stated in the text. One example noted by Iser (1974) that illustrates this operation is in Fielding's *Joseph Andrews* where there was a gap between what the text said and what it meant. That is, the ironic style of the text created a conflict between "the familiar repertoire" in the novel and the divergences from that repertoire that the reader observed. When gaps between reader and text exist as in this illustration and are bridged, communication arises (Iser, 1978). The blanks in the text thus evoke the reader's imaginative activity.

In constructing the aesthetic work from the linear text, the reader also engages in pattern building. As the reader seeks to discover patterns, he/she formulates expectations about the text which undergo modification, expansion, or negation. This process of projecting expectations is one way in which the reader actively participates in constructing meaning. The nature of the text might be such that expectations are in a continual state of modification rather than fulfillment so that reader and text are equally balanced in the interaction. Iser (1974) contended that in didactic texts, the the reader's expectations are channeled in one direction and confirmed throughout the reading. A similar pattern is evident in highly formulaic stories such as modern romances and detective stories. Ideally, an aesthetic experience emerges during interaction with texts that can never be fully realized; that is, texts in which expectations are never completely fulfilled (Iser, 1974).

As the reader fills in the blank spaces of the text and formulates expectations about what is to come, he/she is also involved in the activity of combining textual perspectives and units of information in order to build a whole pattern of the text. Eco (1979) described this as the development of the expression plane into the content plane through a series of interpretive operations. When the reader meets the text and its codes, various kinds of interpretations occur, including those related to the discursive structure (lexical items), the narrative structure (plot, story), and actantial structures (functional roles of characters). Other interpretive processes are evident when the reader links the literary world to the world he/she knows, makes forecasts or predictions about the text based on intertextual frames, etc. These interpretive operations described by Eco (1979) do not suggest a hierarchy of cognitive operations but rather a range of operations the reader engages in as the expression plane is transformed into the content plane.

However, Riffaterre (1978), in his exploration of the semiotics of poetry, proposed two levels of discourse brought into play by the reader. At the mimetic level, meaning is conveyed through a "string of successive information units" while at the significance level, the text is "one semantic unit" (p. 3). This functional transfer from a lower level of text (mimesis) into a higher level of discourse (significance) involving the integration of signs was discussed by Riffaterre as a "manifestation of semiosis" (p. 4).

The notion of combining information into textual patterns was also addressed by Hrushovski (in press) in his theory of integrational semantics. Briefly, in his theory, the reader builds the patterns of the text by constructing meaning, speech, and position (who is saying and doing what, when, and where). The reader also constructs text references and the organized text. The reader is guided in these constructions by cues in the internal text, other texts, and the real world. Because of the linearity of text, all information about a character, for example, is not concentrated in one space. Instead, the reader gathers information about characters from a variety of sources such as the narrator, the dialogues among characters, and the actions of characters. The reader moves back and forth along the linear text, combining these textual perspectives into a pattern of characterization. Characters' views are one of four textual patterns or perspectives the reader constructs. Others are the narrator's view, the plot, and the fictional reader (Iser, 1978). A gestalt of the aesthetic work is achieved when these four perspectives are interrelated during the reading process.

The framework developed thus far has emphasized that the interaction between the reader and the text transforms the linear text into an aesthetic work. Through exploration of the interaction, we can gain insights into both the nature of the literary text and the role of the reader.

Two constructs which are central to the framework being developed here are (a) how the reader formulates expectations about the literary text, and (b) how the reader combines information into literary textual patterns. These constructs are discussed in more detail.

Formulating Expectation About Text

The literary text has been described as a string of lexemes arranged in a linear fashion which are aimed in the direction of things to come (Iser, 1974). This characteristic of text figures into the reading process in an important way. From a phenomenological perspective, the reader is described as driven by the need to discover consistency and patterns in a linear text. This need becomes evident during the interpretive activity when the reader projects expectations upon the text. These expectations are subsequently modified, confirmed, or abandoned as the reader moves back and forth along the text continuum. The guidelines for formulating these expectations as well as the strategies for engaging in the activity are represented in the text (Iser, 1978; Stierle, 1980).

The process involves a trial-and-error procedure which is motivated by a feedback system embedded in the text (Iser, 1974, 1978). What has been read is transformed into a background against which expectations are tested; therefore, reading is a dialectic between expectations and retrospection. The reader must continually restructure past syntheses (Iser, 1978).

Iser (1974) termed the process of making, modifying, abandoning, and restructuring expectations and syntheses "illusion building" and "illusion breaking." Illusions occur when consistent reading is manifested (Iser, 1974). In other words, illusion occurs when expectations are consistently confirmed. This is illustrated by contrasting different kinds of texts. A more powerful work of literature, for example, is characterized by its ability to create a tenuous relationship between the reader's expectations about characters, themes, events, and so forth, and new evidence in the text which calls for the reader to adjust these expectations. This activity is essential, if the interaction between text and reader is to evoke a new world or vision. In some literary texts (e.g., highly formulaic texts), the illusions or expectations formulated by the reader remain fairly constant throughout the interaction with text and no new world vision is created (Iser, 1974). In other words, the text cues have channeled the reader into a particular way of reading. Thus, in one sense, the reader might find almost a one-to-one correspondence with his/her expectations about the text and what occurs in the text. Perhaps the appeal of this kind of literature for some readers lies in the comfort and ease of reading texts which do not challenge their illusions.

The predictability of the text structures reflected in formulaic texts thwarts the creation of an aesthetic work, since an expected world is confirmed rather than a new world created. If, on the other hand, the reader's subjective expectations override the text, another kind of problem may arise. The reader, for example, who formulates expectations based upon idiosyncratic experience, negates the text that the author has created. The reader's view of the world in this case is superimposed upon the text rather than created out of an interaction with the text to create a new vision. While readers must draw upon their subjectivity as well as text cues to formulate expectations, the subjective perception paradoxically must be negated, if they are to experience a new reality through fiction (Iser, 1978). Through this negation, the familiar is denied so that readers can transcend the literal meaning into the multiple meanings, thereby entering the phase of significance.

Building Text Patterns

Readers have been described as seeking patterns in the text which involves linking the sequential images in the text. In essence, the reader connects a series of fixed elements in the text, filling in the gaps in the story when its flow is broken (Iser, 1974). The reader discovers relationships among the shifting perspectives of the text which include the narrator's view, the plot, the characters' views, and the fictional reader (Iser, 1980). The text, then, is a continuum representing information which may be strewn throughout it; therefore, the reader must combine these dispersed units into a larger pattern (Hrushovski, 1976, in press). Essentially, the reader is building the patterns of text, a process requiring sensitivity to the internal structure of given text, other texts, and the real world (Hrushovski, in press).

This process, occurring during the interaction between text and reader, entails the development of the expression plane (linear text) into a content plane through a series of interpretive acts involving intensional and extensional approaches (Eco, 1979). On the intensional level, the reader interprets discursive, narrative, actantial, and ideological structures, while on the extensional level, the reader contributes inferences, world structures, and so forth. The reader in this model plays a critical role in building text structures and in constructing meaning. The text structures were described by Hrushovski (in press) in terms of three constructs: speech and position; meaning and reference; and the organized text. Both Hrushovski's theory of integrational semantics and Eco's model of the role of the reader focused on illustrating the nature of the aesthetic work that is constructed by the reader through explicating the processes involved in reading literary texts.

There are two key notions which emerge from this view of the interactive process. First, the text is viewed as a continuum on which units of information are arranged. These units represent the basis for building various constructs in the aesthetic work such as plot, narrator, and character. The information for each construct is not concentrated in one place along the continuum. Thus the reader moves along the text plane selecting and connecting units of information in order to construct certain aspects of the content plane. The information is represented in a variety of ways. In a recent analysis of F. Scott Fitzgerald's short stories, the characters were constructed by combining several sources of information originating from the narrator's assertions, the characters dialogue, and the characters' actions (Golden, 1983). These sources were strewn throughout the text, requiring the reader to link them together to construct a character. The second notion that is notable in the process is the reader's discovery of the interrelationships among the various perspectives. Literary texts are comprised of certain perspectives such as plot and characterization, and to achieve a realization of the aesthetic work, these perspectives must be connected into a larger whole. In this sense the reader's operations are essential to the "concretization" of the aesthetic work (Ingarden, 1973). Without the reader, the text remains a linear sequence of images rather than an aesthetic work.

The process of identifying and combining information necessary for building literary constructs is not just a matter of the reader being guided by cues within a text. The reader certainly brings knowledge of world structures, personal experiences, and literary structures to the construction of the literary text. In fact, the nature of certain literary texts requires this kind of information for more complete interpretation. Consider an existential novel such as Sartre's *Nausea*, whose reading may be enhanced through an understanding of the underlying philosophy. Historical context of the reader and knowledge of how the real world operates may also be important. An eighteenth-century reader might have read Richardson's *Clarissa* differently from a twentieth-century reader. Thus the construction of the literary work requires the reader to focus on intratextual, intertextual, and extratextual cue systems in order to create the aesthetic work. The combining of information units into literary patterns, then, requires attention to both textual and contextual information.

A STUDY of READER–TEXT INTERACTION

The concept of the "reader in the text" provides important insights into the nature of textual cues that evoke reader response and the kinds of reader operations that are required to construct the aesthetic work. This perspective on reader–text interaction, as previously noted, is derived from the literary critic's construction of a "general reader." An important question suggested by these studies concerns whether the parallels exist between processes associated with this general reader and processes observed in real readers. The need to explore the similarities between the general reader and actual readers led to the development of the present study, which explores two literary constructs linked with reader–text interaction.

More specifically, the purpose of this investigation is to explore the nature of reader–text interaction during a small group discussion of eighth graders and their teacher. The study addresses four major questions: What are the cues in a short story which may potentially evoke readers' expectations about events (plot)? What is the nature of expectations that readers actually formulate about events? What are the cues in a short story which may potentially influence readers' construction of character? And what is the nature of the characters that readers actually construct?

DESCRIPTION of the STUDY

The Educational Setting

The setting of the study was an alternative school for students K–8 on the East coast. The school's philosophy was based on the belief that students should accept responsibility for their own education. Students and teachers collaborated to develop the curriculum in terms of what was learned and how it was learned. Learning through talk and direct experience was a major aspect of the learning process.

The Participants

The participants in the study were 9 eighth-grade students, 7 males and 2 females. The eighth-grade class was comprised of these 9 students and 1 other student who did not participate in the study. This student was involved in individual instruction for learning disabilities. The students had been a part of the school for at least two years, and half had been in the school since kindergarten.

Scores on the Gates-MacGinitie Reading Test for the vocabulary section revealed students' scores from the 76th percentile to the 99th percentile with a median in the 92nd percentile. These scores also indicated that students were above grade level in vocabulary. Scores on the comprehension section of the test ranged from 59th percentile to the 97th percentile with a median in the 91st percentile. All scores reflected that readers were reading above grade level.

The Literary Texts

A short story by Jim Kjelgaard (1975), "Blood on the Ice," was selected from a literature anthology designed for use with eighth-grade students. Several criteria were used in the selection process: (a) students indicated that they had not previously read the story; (b) the story could be read in a period of about 15 to 20 minutes; (c) the story was determined by the researcher to have interest value for eighth-grade readers; and (d) the story reflected effective use of literary elements (e.g., point of view, setting, style, characterization, plot).

Procedures

Two comparable groups of students were formed by the English teacher (4 students in one group and 5 in the other) on the basis of social interaction styles, general language abilities, and reading levels. Students were asked to read the short story during the first part of the 45-minute session. Following the reading, one group met with the teacher to discuss the story. The teacher and students were advised that the purpose was to discuss the story in order to make sense out of it. The teacher was encouraged to structure the discussion in a way that felt comfortable to her and that encouraged student talk. The discussion was videotaped. The small group discussion was designed to contribute to the ongoing English curriculum. Teachers and students were accustomed to reading a range of literary works and discussing their responses.

The discussion focused on in this chapter was a part of a larger study in which the students participated in a range of literary experiences, including think-aloud journals, interviews, and whole-class discussions. The study reported here, then, is a report of the first phase of a study that explored the nature of reader–text interaction.

Procedures for Data Analysis

In approaching the exploration of reader–text interaction in this study, two literary constructs were identified for analysis: (a) expectations about events (plot); and (b) patterns of characters. These constructs are particularly salient in adventure stories, where the characters are primarily revealed in terms of plot and the reader can expect to encounter surprises and turns in the plot (Donelson & Nilsen, 1980).

Adventure stories focusing on survival center on conflicts between characters and nature and on conflicts between characters (Donelson & Nilsen, 1980). In "Blood on the Ice," characters were in conflict with nature as they struggled to find food on the frozen, arctic ice pack. This conflict gave rise to a second conflict, when characters identified other characters as potential sources for food. A literary text of this kind, then, seemed likely to evoke reader responses about the nature of the characters and thoughts about who would survive.

The analysis of data involved two phases. In the first phase, the investigator functioned as a literary critic who read the text in order to identify text cues which might potentially evoke reader responses about events and characters. In this process, the critic began with an analysis of text features and moved outward to the analysis of reader operations that were required to construct the aesthetic work. Thus the critic constructed a virtual reader from the text. This approach to the reading of "Blood on the Ice" resulted in a confirmation of the expectations about salient features in a survival story, that is, a number of cues which could potentially evoke expectations about events and the nature of the characters were evident.

The second phase of the analysis involved the small group discussion. The analysis of discussion moved from the reader back to the text; that is, the focus was on how actual readers identified text cues during a particular kind of reading event. The participants' statements revolved around the articulation of the processes they engaged in during reading or a retrospective look at the reading event. Statements also focused on the viewpoints of the readers regarding the kinds of textual patterns they constructed in the adventure story.

Prior to exploring how students formulated expectations about events and how students constructed characters, statements in the discussions were coded to determine explicit references to particular literary elements: characters, events, evaluation, author's techniques, and personal experiences. Statements referring to characters related either to their specific traits or to the participant's attitude toward the character (based on his or her perceptions of traits). Statements referring to events reflected interpretation of events or expectations of events. Evaluation concerned general comments regarding the quality of the story, while author's techniques related specifically to style and point of view. Personal experiences included references to knowledge and experiences in the real world. The statements were coded independently by two raters and an interrater reliability check of .78 was obtained. The frequency distribution of the statements in each of the five categories is represented in Table 1 in which it is evident that the majority of statements referred to characterization. Events also were emphasized. Specific references to expectations

Table 1. Frequency of Statements About Literary Elements

	Character	Events	General evaluation	Author's techniques	Personal experiences
Students' statements	40	32	2	10	11
Teacher's statements	17	8	1	7	7
Total statements	57	40	3	17	18

about events comprised 18 of the statements. It is noteworthy that both the students and the teacher focused on the literary elements of events and characters.

The approach for analyzing reader–text interaction yielded different, yet convergent, perspectives on a reading event. The investigator in the role of literary critic identified textual cues that potentially evoke reader responses of formulating expectations and constructing characters. The participants, both students and teacher, in the small group discussion, articulated their expectations and views of the characters. The importance of these literary constructs, then, was confirmed from several different sources. This process of bringing together several data sources in order to validate information is one kind of triangulation strategy used to validate and verify results in qualitative analysis (Patton, 1980). It essentially involves the cross-checking of information, in part, by comparing the perspectives of people from different points of view. In this case, there was a convergence of perceptions on the construction of a text by both the investigator and the participants; thus, data on various forms of the interaction were explored. Data triangulation enables theoretical constructs to be tested in more than one way (Denzin, 1978). It is important to note that there was not always perfect consistency across data sources; participants, for example, discussed other elements which reflect different aspects of reader–text interaction. These differences are important to address at some point in subsequent studies. Since the intent of this study was to explore two literary constructs, the consistency of data sources regarding these constructs was of particular importance.

THE FORMULATION of EXPECTATIONS ABOUT EVENTS

The first part of this section focuses on an exploration of the nature of literary text cues in a short story that may potentially evoke readers' expectations about the events in the story. The second part addresses how actual readers articulate their expectations about events during a small group discussion.

Text Cues Signaling Events

In the short story, "Blood on the Ice," a polar bear, an arctic fox, and an Eskimo are struggling for survival on an ice pack. In discussing this text, cues which evoked expectations about events, particularly outcome, were identified, and the paragraph in which they occurred was noted following each excerpt. It was evident through the forward movement of the story that at least one character would not survive. The reader saw the world, first, from the bear's perspective, and second, from the fox's. Both characters were initially depicted as "partners in hunger," since the bear killed and the fox waited his turn to feed on the remains. The fox therefore staked his survival on the bear. (The numbers in parentheses following each excerpt indicate the paragraph placement in the story.)

> Bears always make kills, and eventually this one would do so. So long as the bear walked before him, the fox knew that he would eat. (11) [reproduction granted by permission of Blassingame, McCauley & Wood]

The bear is presented as a probable survivor because of his strength:

> Strength was a mighty factor, one that had never been defeated before. It could not be conquered this time, because it was all powerful. (14)

The reader, then, could begin to build a view that the bear, because of his strength, was unrivaled in the wilderness and therefore likely to win the struggle. A second view could be formulated: As long as the bear killed, the fox would survive. This expectation was challenged when the bear could no longer find seals to kill; the bear then becomes aware of the fox as something more than a vague form that followed him and left its scent on the carrion:

> But the foxes were fashioned of flesh and warmed with blood. The bear's nose told him that, and the new awareness of the little white fox was slowly instilled into his brain. (20)

This new awareness suddenly challenged the reader's expectation that the historical relationship between the fox and the bear had now shifted from "partners in hunger" to one which the fox emerged as a potential food source for the bear. Readers' expectations might shift at this point to anticipate the death of the fox, though this expectation was soon negated when the bear attempted to kill the fox:

> When he (the bear) lunged, both front paws slapped down on the fox's accustomed place. (21) But the fox was not there . . . . a split second before the bear's flashing paws had cracked down upon the ice, he had rolled sideways. (22)

This information that the fox was agile with "razor-keen" senses introduced another question about who would surive. The reader now weighed the evidence of a starving bear and a fox alone in the wilderness with no apparent food sources. Expectations about outcomes depended, in part, at this juncture on whether or not strength or keeness and agility were better attributes for surviving. A change in the text occurred when the point of view shifted from that of the polar bear and the fox. A man was rather abruptly introduced into this wilderness which created dissonance for the reader on a dual level. First, the world of the fox and bear had been constructed by the reader, who was now at the point of wondering about the outcome of these two characters, when the perspective and viewpoint suddenly shifted:

> At a shuffling lope, he (the bear) started into the darkness. (25) A mile and a half to the north, Agtuk, the Eskimo, was walking across the ice pack. (26)

Dissonance for the reader arose because the belief that the bear and fox were alone is now disturbed. Earlier the reader read:

> But except for themselves there was no tangible life here in the vast frozen reaches. (13)

The reader wondered where the Eskimo came from and felt that he was indeed out of place. Shortly after Agtuk was introduced, the reader learned that "no man had ever been where he was going" (27) on the arctic ice pack. This technique of introducing the Eskimo at this point in the story served to emphasize that man was alien in this land of polar bears and arctic foxes. The reader than took in information presented from the man's perspective in order to formulate a new hypothesis regarding the survivor. Since Agtuk's partner had died after provisions ran out and also because Agtuk was out of his element, it was possible to formulate an expectation that, pitted against the strength of the bear, Agtuk would be defeated. This expectation was soon challenged, however, when a flashback revealed that Agtuk had a .38 Magnum which was so powerful that it had shattered the back of the seal. The gun, then provided a new piece of information that challenged the expectation that the bear would survive. The reader then shifted perceptions according to this information and formulated yet another expectation: the Eskimo would be a formidable enemy. This assumption, however, was somewhat shaken by a subsequent line in the text that was confusing for the reader.

> Agtuk grinned. (33) The aurora borealis flickered across the ice pack, lighting it up like a pale moon. Agtuk staggered, and sank down. (34)

Had Agtuk grinned *following* the flash of light, the reader might have conjectured that the grin resulted from Agtuk's spotting the bear or some other animal in the lighted expanse. At the very beginning of the text the ice pack had been described as having "no sun, or light except when the aurora borealis flashed its weird radiance" (2). The reader, then, might not be certain whether Agtuk's collapse was due to a clever ruse to lure the bear or to his exhaustion from exposure and hunger. Several paragraphs later the text reveals:

> Certainly, when the aurora flickered and revealed a bear 20 feet away, no one could condemn a man, or call him a weakling, because he fell on the ice and lured the bear to where it could be shot. (38)

Even if the reader had concluded that Agtuk's collapse was a lure, the outcome is uncertain until the end:

> He (the bear) opened his great jaws. (35) Then there was a sudden roaring smash . . . the bear stiffened . . . collapsed on the ice. (36)

Until the actual account of the bear stiffening, the reader cannot know for certain that the sudden roaring smash was not the bear's flashing paws "that had cracked down on the ice" (22).

This constant shifting of expectations that the reader engaged in reflects the process of expectation building and breaking that was brought about by the textual cues previously described. It was possible to formulate a variety of predictions about what would occur, but these predictions were constantly negated by new information. The reader's uncertainty could not fully be resolved until the end of the story. The very nature of a suspenseful story may be attributed to the fact that the reader remains in a state of uncertainty as cues rapidly shift causing a process of formulating and reformulating expectations; therefore, security for the reliability of one hypothesis over another is difficult to achieve when reading this story.

It is interesting to note that the eighth-grade readers and their teacher in the discussion group brought to the surface some of the processes they engaged in while formulating their expectations about events. Readers, as a whole, seemed to share the feeling of uncertainty about outcome, yet differed about interpretation of text cues that evoked their ideational activities. Curiously, certain points in the text were signaled as salient by several readers in guiding their formulation of the expectations. In the following section, the readers' discussion is used to illustrate how "real readers" construct expectations about text and how group as well as text affect this construction.

Readers' Responses About Events

In the previous discussion, some text cues in "Blood on the Ice" that potentially gave rise to reader expectations about events were identified. An analysis of the small group discussion revealed the question of outcome as a central topic. Both student and teacher-initiated sequences of talk addressed expectations about which character would survive. The topic surfaced at several points in the discussion illustrating different aspects of the process. This focus on expectations might suggest the power of this text to evoke this kind of exploration by readers.

One observation emerging from the data is that students formulate expectations about outcome, and these expectations are not necessarily uniform across students, as evidenced in the following exchange initiated by a student:

> Paul: I wanted the polar bear to kill the guy.
> Amy: Yeah, I thought the bear was going to kill the guy.
> Mike: So did I.
> Paul: I didn't. I knew when he picked up that Magnum that that was the end of the polar bear.
> Mike: Yeah, but I thought the guy, I thought, I don't know what I thought.

Amy and mike indicated their expectation that the bear would win, though they did not pull in support for this view. In contrast, Paul indicated that he was certain the man would win because of the Magnum. This prompted Mike's uncertainty about his position as he shifted from his original stance influenced by Paul's point; yet he had difficulty in articulating his thoughts.

The text reference to the gun (introduced by Paul) was picked up by Neal, who described his confusion about whether Agtuk really kept the gun:

> Neal: When he said, you know, he was thinking about the gun and how it belonged to this other guy, he said that he put it back in the holster. I thought he meant he put it back in the holster. I thought he meant he put it back in the other guy's holster, not his.
> Paul: No, he said he took the holster from him.
> Neal: I know, but I'm just saying I didn't remember that, so when he shot it, I thought, where'd the gun come from? Oh yeah, he must've put it back into his holster.
> Paul: Also, the part where it said—you must have forgotten the part—where it said he was walking, but he kept walking because the man who owns that kind of gun has to be brave or something.
> Neal: Yeah, I know, but he said he thought, you know, it belonged to the other guy, so then he put it back in the holster.

There are several points that this dialogue suggests. First, Neal recounted the thinking he engaged in with reference to a certain point in the text that he misread. This traced the source of the confusion to that point and followed it through to the end when it created a disruption in his reading. The outcome involved the shooting of the bear, and Neal wondered where the gun came from. Because of this reading, Neal could not formulate the same expectation about outcome that Paul did. Paul responded to Neal by correcting him about what really happened, citing textual support to verify that the man had picked up the gun. Paul was therefore directing his comments toward getting the text cue straight rather than on listening to Neal's explanation of how he figured out his own mistake. Neal asserted his own recognition of the text cue by responding to Paul's comments with ''I know. . .''

The significance of the gun for these readers became apparent in another segment of the discussion which grew out of talk about characters. This time the teacher initiated a question which related to expectations about what might have happened to the characters after the story ended. This focus shifed from a look backward at expectations already formulated during reading toward speculations about the eventual fate of the characters. To respond to this, readers might still draw upon text cues for their speculations, as illustrated in the following interaction:

Teacher:	What's going to happen? Did you have any feeling about what was going to happen to the fox then in the end? After the story?
Paul:	He follows the guy.
Teacher:	But he's eating, the guy's walking off. Do you think he'll follow?
Neal:	Yeah.
Amy:	Yeah.
Neal:	But at a safer distance.
Mike:	Yeah.
Teacher:	But if he's staked his survival on the polar bear?
Amy:	He followed the polar bear.
Neal:	No, the man will probably after a long time, shoot the fox and eat the fox after a while.
Mike:	True, plus the fox is trying to follow the guy and trying to steal the food the guy cut off the bear. A race for survival kind of story.
Teacher:	Yeah, right. The issue of survival—who's going to make it? I didn't have a clue until the end who was going to make it, did you?
Amy:	No.
Mike:	Well, you had that hint when the guy was sitting there talking about the guy, and you knew the guy was armed, but you also knew that he was weak. He was the weakest of the three out there besides the fox.
Teacher:	Do you think the man was the weakest of the three?
Mike:	Yeah, like the man would have no chance against the bear.

Two students who expressed some confusion about outcome earlier in the discussion became more certain in their expectations about what might eventually happen to the fox. Neal predicted that the man would eventually kill the fox. Mike was able to articulate his thoughts more clearly at this point in the discussion. He signaled the presence of the gun, as Paul had earlier, yet also noted the weakness of the man. This is, perhaps, suggestive of the fact that the text generates alternatives and expectations which may be challenged by other evidence. It is noteworthy, however, that the teacher ended the line of speculation about the future of the fox in her response to Mike about the issue of survival. In the middle of that same segment, she switched the focus back to expectations about outcomes within the story. This shift tied off the previous speculation and refocused the discussion on the outcome. The second segment, also led by a question about clues to the outcome, was parallel thematically to the first segment discussed in this analysis. Mike picked up on the questions revealing the dilemma of whether or not the man had the advantage. Amy's "no" in response to the teacher's question was in contradiction to her earlier response where she thought the bear would win. With the caution of avoiding over interpretation of Amy's responses, it is still possible to suggest that as she often took the role of agreeing with ideas put forth by other members, these possibilities might be ones she had entertained herself. She was certainly more tentative about articulating and perhaps formulating her own.

In one final segment of the story which pertains to formulating expectations, the observations noted previously about the tenuous nature of readers' expectations and textual information were evident. It was stated that this type of survival story creates an uncertainty about outcome right up until the point of resolution. The earlier analysis of text cues suggested how this uncertainty might arise due to shifting expectations. In this case the reader did not find the outcome easily stated in the text:

> Mike: At first when they said—when suddenly they started talking about—like it stopped. I was thinking, the guy—suddenly it was talking about the guy's thought and then suddenly it just stopped. I didn't realize it was the bear that got shot. I thought it was just like the guy was just sitting there thinking, I'm going to die. The bear—and suddenly the guy shot the bear. First you think the guy is dead, and then suddenly the bear's got his brains blown out.

The text cues identified previously helped to clarify Mike's confusion. When Agtuk collapsed, his point of view abruptly ended and the reader had to shift to an objective point of view describing the encounter between the man and the bear. Until the bear collapsed on the ice, the reader could not be absolutely certain about outcome. Thus the suspense and shifting expectations were carried right to the climax of the story. This commentary by Mike revealed that expectations were formulated and reformulated, sparked by cues throughout the text. The subsequent talk initiated by the teacher following Mike's observation illustrated this further. A question raised before surfaced again through the teacher. This repetition takes on new meaning, if we look at where it occurred in the discussion (and the text).

Talk generated by Mike had focused the group on the climax of the story, and the teacher stimulated another set of responses:

> Teacher: Did you have any clue about who was going to make it at the end?
> Neal: No, not really. Actually, I thought the polar bear caused the guy to collapse—well, so much for that guy and the polar bear.
> (discussion on whom readers want to win)

Amy: I thought maybe the fox would make it, because he kept following him and getting food.
Teacher: Yeah, right. He staked his survival on the polar bear—the polar bear's dead.
Mike: He eats the polar bear and then goes and follows the guy. Whichever one proves more the strongest, then that's the best way to go.
Neal: The only way to go.

Neal signaled the same segment in the text that caused Mike's puzzlement, though the specific point they referred to differed. Neal expected the man to be in danger because he collapsed. Both readers had missed the subtle point of the ice pack lighting up and Agtuk grinning, clues that the collapse might be related to a plan to lure the bear. The discussion switched back after Neal's reference to an earlier topic involving speculation about the fox's fate. The same conclusion of the fox following the survivor was stated a second time.

It is notable that the topic of formulating expectations about outcome is a major thread in this discussion. It was recycled at several points, grew out of talk on other issues, and was generated by different participants. What came through in this discussion was that expectations were formulated, modified, and abandoned during the reading process as well as during the interpretive activity following reading. Readers described their thinking, clarified it, brought in textual support, and reshaped it in response to others' talk about the text and their processes. The tentativeness about articulating these expectations was evident in the talk. The discussion served as a forum for evoking metacognitive responses about reading, linking readers to text cues, and providing opportunity for talk to shape interpretation.

THE CONSTRUCTION OF CHARACTERS

In this section, the literary text is analyzed in terms of potential cues that may contribute to the reader's construction of the characters. Following this discussion is an exploration of how readers articulate their construction of characters in a small group discussion. Again, the nature of the literary text invites this kind of focus, because three characters in their struggle to survive are at the center of the conflict, and their individual traits are an important feature of the aesthetic work created by the reader.

Text Cues and the Construction of Characters

For the purpose of exploring units of information that were relevant to characterization in "Blood on the Ice," it was useful to consider three text features(a) the information that was represented; (b) the point where the information occurred along the linear text; and (c) the filter through which the information was revealed. These features reflected aspects of the text which potentially influenced the reader's ideational activity of discovering appropriate information and connecting dispersed bits of information into the construct of a character. The reader's interpretation of characters and the stance taken toward them might be influenced by the filter through which the character was unveiled as well as by the reader's own view of the world. In this section, these three features will be examined in terms of Kjelgaard's story.

The text conveyed many references to the three characters, with the greatest number apportioned to the polar bear, who was the protagonist. To illustrate how the reader constructed a character guided by information provided in the text, the polar bear will serve as the focal point. Information pertaining to the bear came in a variety of forms including commentary on his traits, his situation, and his past. His traits, for example, were revealed through various descriptive passages which were placed throughout the text.

> The dull eyes of the polar bear could hardly discern only what was beneath his black nose. (1)

> So perfect was his camouflage, that he had seemed another ice hummock, a pile of snow. (4)

This and other information relevant to the characteristics of the polar bear was revealed in a similar fashion along the text continuum.

Not only were the bear's traits depicted but also the dilemma of the bear, who was caught in a situation of fighting for his survival. This was another source of information used to build the construct of this character. The following passages exemplified the problem that the bear was facing.

> In the following five days the bear had killed only one seal, and two days afterward he had backtracked 40 miles to eat the frozen skin. (6)

> Had his belly been full, no wind could have disturbed him. But his belly was empty. (10)

The reader, then, had at least two kinds of information to draw upon as she constructed the character of the polar bear—his traits and his dilemma. This information related primarily to the bear as he existed in his present situation.

Another kind of information which contributed to the profile of the main character was his life prior to the present situation. That is, a flashback unraveled details about the bear's life as a young cub, and the approaches he was accustomed to employing for survival which is suggested in the following:

> Born in an ice-sheathed cave 20 miles inland, he had drunk coldness and savagery with the milk that flowed from his mother's dugs. (16)

> Ever since, as a yearling cub, he had broken away from his mother, he had been followed by foxes. (18)

> He had never eaten—save for his mother's milk—anything except seals, and until he had grown as hungry as he was now it had never occurred to him that anything else was good to eat. (20)

These passages, then, provided more information about the nature of the bear. In the last passage, there was a shift from the development of the bear's attitude and survival instincts to present crisis where, desperate with hunger, he focused on the fox in a different way. This information revealing his former life was used to contrast how the bear had lived with his current need to adapt to new ways to combat hunger. The reader thus could identify different kinds of information about the character, interweaving these as he moved through the text.

Interspersed with the strands mentioned previously were aspects of the character that emerged through interplay with other characters. The characters of the polar bear and the fox were revealed as they related to each other:

> He had no strength, but turned that of the bear to his own devices. Bears always made kills, and eventually this one would do so. So long as the bear walked before him, the fox knew that he would eat. (11)

> Like an inquisitive kitten he (the fox) watches his mighty host. He knew that the bear would have killed and eaten him. But that inspired neither fear or resentment because the fox understood such actions. (22)

These and other passages confirmed and extended the construct the reader shaped as she gathered and linked information units throughout the text.

The kind of information about characters, then, was important for the reader to identify in order for the aesthetic work to evolve. The arrangement of the information along the text continuum was also a notable feature. Since the text was linear in nature, all of the bits of information regarding a particular character were not concentrated in one part of the text. Not only was information distributed throughout the text, but it was also interspersed with information relevant to other constructs such as the narrator's description of the setting and the unveiling of another character. The reader, in a sense, was engaged in a process of developing single constructs and interweaving these with other constructs which were being simultaneously built. Evidence for the notion that text information about a character was dispersed along the continuum is evident in the excerpts previously identified. Each reflected information about the polar bear and was distributed across 10 paragraphs (1, 4, 6, 10, 11, 15, 16, 18, 20, and 22). Since this reflected only the samples selected for illustrative purposes, the amount and distribution of information in a text about one character was formidable. Whether real readers assemble all information for a composite picture of a given character is a question for further studies, though this will be addressed on one level in the following section.

The third text feature relevant to characterization that will be briefly addressed is that of the filter through which the information is presented. To frame this concept more fully, support from rhetorical theory is important. The text represents a series of assertions about the characters and the imaginative world (Pratt, 1977). These assertions are made from several perspectives, and each perspective creates its own influence on the construction of character. The narrator, for example, presents one perspective and the characters' viewpoints represent other perspectives. Point of view was a critical aspect of the story because it was one filter through which the information was interpreted. In the first line of the story, the polar bear's perspective was initiated and remained the predominant one for the first 25 paragraphs of the story. The bear's view of the world was essentially laid out for the reader, who saw how the bear perceived and reacted to the present as well as how he, sensed the past. The only interruption in the bear's viewpoint was when the two other characters emerged.

The fox's viewpoint was a shifting one as the narrator moved back and forth between the two characters. The fox's viewpoint was however, influenced entirely by his perception of the bear and his relationship to the bear. Thus when the viewpoint shifted, two purposes were served. First, the character was revealed on one level, and, second, the character he perceived was revealed. The story remained the bear's story since he perceived a range of things while the fox was limited primarily to his relationship with the bear. The effect of this arrangement of text perspectives might influence how the reader aligns himself with the characters. It would seem likely that the bear would command the greatest empathy because he was the protagonist—the story began and ended with him.

The power of shifting viewpoints became very apparent when the Eskimo was first introduced in paragraph 26. He clearly had invaded the story, disrupting its flow. The reader questioned whether he belonged in the story about a bear and a fox on an arctic ice pack. Soon after his entry in the text, the reader learned from the Eskimo's perspective that he was the first man to be in that area. In 9 paragraphs Agtuk's perspective was presented. The wandering viewpoints of man and bear were connected when the bear was killed, and the final paragraph focused on the fox:

> He (the fox) had known that he would eat if he followed the bear far enough. (39)

One of the filters for revealing information, then, is point of view. This feature influences both the kind of information that is presented as well as the stance the reader takes toward the characters.

Another filter for information is the narrator's interpretive voice which appears among the characters' viewpoints.

> No one could condemn a man, or call him weakling, because he fell on the ice and lured the bear to where it could be shot. (38)

> As living things, the continuance of the spark that actuated them depended on their ability to find, and kill, and eat, other living things. (13)

This voice influenced the reader in shaping how she would interpret the events as was particularly evident in the second excerpt.

Related to the narrator's interpretive voice is the lens through which objective events are witnessed. Interpretation by a narrator was not as apparent in these instances where actions were described:

> Without breaking the bear whirled about and cast himself backwards. (21)

While other ways of filtering information exist, these viewpoints illustrate the potential influences on the reader's interpretation of a character. As Iser (1978) suggested, wandering viewpoints must be identified and connected by the reader in order to construct text perspectives such as characters.

In the next section, four eighth-grade readers' discussion with their teacher about characterization in the story will be explored.

Reader's Responses on Characterization

The observation made in the previous section highlighted some textual features that potentially influenced the reading process. The reader constructed the characters by connecting dispersed units of information along the text continuum. Stances the reader took toward the characters might be affected both by the filter through which the characters were revealed as well as the reader's personal view of the world. These conjectures about the interactive process between text and reader were confirmed in the talk among the eighth-grade students. One reader in particular illustrated how he built his view of a character by drawing on various sources of information distributed throughout the text. Other students supported this reader's perception by elaborating on the points he made, drawing on textual support. This was illustrated in the following exchange. Paragraphs in which the text is referred to by the reader are noted in parentheses.

Mike:	I hate the fox. I hate the fox.
Teacher:	You hate the fox?
Paul:	The fox, he's so sly.
Neal:	Like they said—no mercy or pity. (15) Leave the cat alone, I mean.
Paul:	He must have had a big feast with that polar bear.
Teacher:	Why did you hate the fox?
Mike:	Well, like the fox was, he sat there like whenever the bear jumped, the fox jumped away and sat there licking his paws very calmly and cool. (22)
Neal:	Like a cat, like a cat.
Mike:	Right.
Neal:	You know, like a cat, you know, like a cat misses a mouse you know, and says, well, I didn't want it. (22)
Mike:	Right, but the polar bear's sitting there starving. He's like on the verge of dying, you know, and the fox is sitting there licking his paws.
Teacher:	The fox is starving too.
Amy:	Yeah.
Neal:	You also don't expect the fox to give up his life just for the polar bear's hunger.
Amy:	Yeah.
Mike:	That's true, but uh, the fox really didn't react to all that hunger, you know, cause the fox wasn't doing any of the work. I mean the polar bear—all the fox had to do was to follow the polar bear. (11)
Amy:	Right, and the bear would kill the seals. (6)
Teacher:	The fox was basically living off the polar bear.
Mike:	Right, and then like when they talked about when the bear was eating and the fox would come along and just take his food out of his mouth, you know. It makes you really hate the fox. It was so cruel. (19)

Several aspects of the discussion merit attention. First, the students linked up different units of information to construct their view of the fox. Mike referred to information in paragraphs 22, 11, and 19 as he articulated his view. In the first utterance (paragraph 22), the action of jumping away was stated in the text; however, licking paws "calmly and cool" is added by the reader. Textual references were made regarding the fox sitting on his paws and staring at the bear "with calculating eyes" so the embellishment made by the reader is somewhat text-tied. He rephrased the text to correspond to his evolving view of the characters. Another trait of the fox noted by Mike is linked to paragraph 11 in which the fox was described as able to survive "as long as the bear walked before him." The consistency of the construct that Mike was building is evident in that he brought in textual support to make his case. This support, however, was not always borne out in the text. For example, Mike described the fox in paragraph 19 as taking "food out of the bear's mouth", and he commented further about the cruelty of this behavior. In this paragraph, however, these actions were described in a flashback to the bear's early years when the arctic foxes would snatch food from his mouth. Thus the fox itself had not performed this action.

The selection of information, then, was text-based, though the reader might have misread the text. This was evident in Neal's responses which also connected textual references that were used to support Mike's view. Neal indicated his agreement about the fox as an unappealing character by commenting on the text reference to his lack of mercy or pity. Actually, this occurred in paragraph 15 and referred to the specter of hunger that walked beside the bear, much nearer than the shadow of the arctic fox. This shadow was more powerful than the fox: "It had neither pity nor mercy." It is understandable how a reader on a first reading might have confused the two shadows. Neal also identified the analogy that the fox was "like a cat"; this point might have been evoked by the text passage in paragraph 22 describing the fox "like an inquisitive kitten." Mike's and Neal's talk support the view that the reader combines various bits of information to construct character.

Another aspect of the discussion was notable. In the context of a discussion, opportunity was provided for readers to influence one another's view. While Mike remained fairly consistent in his construct of the fox, others adjusted or firmed up their own views as a result of the discussion that "the fox is starving too." Neal apparently saw another side of the issue at this point, indicating that the fox should not give up his life for the bear. Similarly, another student, Amy, followed a pattern somewhat similar to her earlier one. Uncertainty about her own views came through as she confirmed points made by the teacher and Neal which contrasted with Mike's view of the fox. Later she seemed to support Mike's point that all the fox had to do was to follow the bear. It was, therefore, more difficult to ascertain Amy's construct of character.

In the small group discussion, the students seemed to be sensitive to the filter through which the characters were represented. Earlier, point of view was discussed as a potentially influential text feature. The role of point of view in shaping readers' constructs was evident in the small group discussion. It seemed that the polar bear would invite a greater association with the reader that the other characters, because his view was presented first and it was his story being told. From the beginning of the discussion and at various points throughout it, the readers' stance, particularly that of one reader, toward the bear was demonstrated:

Mike: It had a lot of feeling to it, you know, what the bear thought, you know, and how the bear felt as he'd go along . . .

Paul: Felt sorry for the bear . . . I wanted the polar bear to kill the guy. I wanted the polar bear to survive . . . the guy was not—I didn't like the guy—he was out for money and adventure.

In another way, Mike's stance toward the bear was clearly a positive one since he saw the fox as a cruel character who took the bear's food and watched him dispassionately. We might infer that Mike dislikes the fox because he displayed qualities other than those held by the bear; that is, he did not do any work to solve his dilemma, and he lived off another animal's efforts.

The effect of beginning with the bear's perspective and gradually shifting to the fox's created for the reader an illusion that the story concerned their survival alone. When the viewpoint shifted abruptly to the Eskimo's, this illusion was challenged and the students addressed this in the following ways:

Amy: At first where he had the people, I was wondering what happened to the bear.

Paul: Yeah, I know.

Teacher: Right, it causes a real break there in the story.

Mike: Yeah, like the bear's going along starving, and suddenly he's talking about this other dude, and I thought, who's this?

Teacher: At that point did you realize it would all meet?

All students: Yeah.

The teacher's question evoked the students' response that the text perspectives would eventually meet. Later in the discussion, the teacher raised a question which seemed designed to elicit how each character's point of view differed, yet the students seemed more interested in finding commonality among the characters. This was illustrated in the following exchange:

Teacher They were very different approaches to life, the polar bear, the fox and the man.

Mike: Well, they were all the same too. They all had the same approach but it was also different.

Teacher: In what ways were they the same?

Mike: Well, they were all out there for one thing.

Neal: Survival, they were all trying to survive.

Mike: They were all out there, but, you know . . .

Teacher: But they went at it differently.

Mike: The guy's thinking about being the famous dude in the village. (27)

Neal: And the bear's thinking about how his mother killed all the foxes. (16) (discussion continues on whether they were foxes or wolves)

The attempt to unify the characters' perspectives moved the discussion in the direction of exploring the theme of the story as survival. The teacher's questions regarding differences in appoaches was not picked up by the students immediately. Exploration of this idea was begun by Mike who referred to the motivation of the Eskimo for being out there. Neal linked into the character's thinking and related what the bear was thinking about. A digression on straightening out a fact then ensued and that particular thread was lost. The segment did provide another illustration of how characters' points of view are a critical feature of the text which contribute to the development of the construct of character.

The role of readers in constructing character has been explored in terms of how bits of information are connected and how they are interpreted. This analysis as well as the discussion on formulating expectations provides one approach for examining how readers and text interact in the construction of an aesthetic work.

SUMMARY REMARKS

The preceding analysis has illuminated several aspects of the reader–text interaction in the construction of the aesthetic object. The perspectives on both reader and text which have evolved provide insights into our understanding of aesthetic experiences as well as implications for future research. The principal findings and their relevance to the transaction between reader and text include these four points.

1. *The literary text is a potential sign generating numerous cues which are embedded in the expression plane.* The linearity of the text requires that units of information be dispersed along the linear text and remain unconnected without multiple ideational operations performed by the reader. These textual cues serve as guides for the construction of narrator, characterization, plot, and the reader in the text.

This observation implies that it is important to continue to explore the particular nature of the organized linear text plane, if we are to understand its contribution to the construction of the aesthetic object or actual sign. The textual guides, then, do play a role in the interactive process. In an aesthetic text, it might be arqued that the textual cues generate more plausible interpretations on the part of the reader. The text, then, is polysemous in nature. While multiple interpretations are possible, the range should be constrained somewhat by the textual guides; otherwise the text has no intrinsic quality generated by the author in his/her choice of surface cues. To return to Iser's contention, we judge the quality of a literary work in terms of the balance of contributions made by the text and the reader. Perhaps informative texts on one level share the same attributes of didactic literary texts by controlling the number of interpretations that are possible.

2. *The reader is actively engaged in the process of constructing the meaning and structure of the literary work.* Guided by cues in the text and information he/she brings to the text, the reader performs a series of ideational operations upon the text such as connecting information units, filling in the blank spaces of the text, and formulating and modifying expectations about the text. The construction of the aesthetic work is dependent upon these operations in which the reader engages.

The implication of this observation is that it is necessary to explore the ideational activities that a variety of readers utilize in order to discover both similarities and differences in reader's strategies. Similar to discoveries about text cues in different texts evoking different readings, it is useful to consider how different readers may construct the text. Since a text is polysemous in nature, the implication is that multiple readings are plausible; however, there is still the notion of whether some readings are better than others. The idea that more idiosyncratic, or, perhaps, more extratextual references during reading suggests that the reader relies on personal experience more than on what the text contributes to the process. It is important, therefore, to investigate further the contributions made by the reader. The processes of constructing the text, on the one hand, may be consistent across readers, but the kind of aesthetic object created, on the other hand, may differ across readers.

In addition, the concept of the evolving life of the literary work, as described by Ingarden (1973), merits attention. The nature of the readers' contributions to the construction of the text in this study focused on what a small group of readers did when the particpants built the text together during a discussion. These readers were involved in a retrospective look at the processes they participated in as well as constructing the literary text in a social context. The discussion enabled readers to articulate processes and to formulate their constructs of the text. Talk functioned as a means of bringing the constructed text to the level of articulation. This activity suggested parallels to what individual readers had been described as doing by literary critics. It should be emphasized, however, that this process was another phase in the development of the work. The meaning and structure created in this discussion might evolve into another level, if individuals read the text a second time. One student in the study, for example, observed that she had some ideas about the text after reading it herself and expected these to be changed during the discussion. Readers' roles, then, in a variety of contexts must be explored, if the interaction process is to be more fully understood.

3. *Related to the second point regarding the life of the text, the notion of the construction of meaning as a social process should be addressed.* A text can be said to be read differently according to the context in which it is read. A text is read differently by a reader for the second time, by readers in different historical and cultural settings, by readers who read individually or in groups, and so forth. To consider one reading as representative of the literary sign constructed by the reader is to ignore the dynamic evolution of a text in multiple readings.

The implication of this statment is that we should consider how texts are read in different contexts. The processes involved in a small group discussion suggested how social interaction plays a critical role in the construction of a literary work. Participants modified, challenged, extended, and clarified one another's textual perceptions. Together they built a group text, which might differ from the text they constructed as individuals. Further study on the construction of the text as a social process, then, is needed in order to appreciate this kind of interaction.

4. *The aesthetic work is created during the process of reader—text interaction, and meaning lies at the intersection between text and reader.* The aesthetic work,

then, cannot exist without contributions of text cues and the reader's operations. While multiple meanings are possible in literary work, certain text cues and reader strategies seem to be constant. That is, the reader combines textual perspectives, connects units of information, and formulates expectations about the text. The literary text has certain characteristics which are reflected in the kinds of cues it offers.

Universal traits of literary texts, as opposed to other texts, as well as the operations that readers perform in common when reading literary texts, should be investigated. Comparsions of the different aesthetic objects created in these processes can be made to determine how one text can generate different meanings and how these meanings can vary in what is an acceptable reading.

REFERENCES

Denzin, N.K. (1978). *Sociological methods: A sourcebook* (2d ed.). New York: McGraw-Hill.

Donelson, K.L., & Nilsen, A.P. (1980). *Literature for today's young adults.* Glenview, IL: Scott, Foresman.

Eco, U. (1979). *The role of the reader: Explorations in the semiotics of text.* Bloomington: Indiana University Press.

Golden, J.M. (1983, March). *The reader's construction of character in Fitzgerald's Josephine stories.* Paper presented at the Northeast Modern Language Association, Philadelphia.

Hrushovski, B. (1976). *Segmentation and motivation in the text continuum of literary prose.* (Papers on Poetics and Semiotics, No. 5). Tel Aviv: Tel Aviv University.

Hrushovski, B. (in press). Integrational semantics: An understander's theory of meaning in context. In H. Byrnes (Ed.), *Contemporary perceptions of language: Interdisciplinary dimensions.* Washington, DC: Georgetown University Press.

Ingarden, R. (1973). *The literary work of art: An investigation on the borderlines of ontology, logic, and theory of literature.* Evanston, IL: Northwestern University Press.

Iser, W. (1974). *The implied reader: Patterns of communication in prose fiction from Bunyan to Beckett.* Baltimore, MD: Johns Hopkins University Press.

Iser, W. (1978). *The act of reading: A theory of aesthetic response.* Baltimore, MD: Johns Hopkins University.

Iser, W. (1980). Interaction between text and reader. In S.R. Suleiman & I. Crosman (Eds.), *The reader in the text: Essays on audience and interpretation (pp. 106-119).* Princeton, NJ: Princeton University Press.

Kjelgaard, J. (1975). Blood on the ice. In G.R. Carlsen (Ed.), *Perception: Themes in literature* (pp. 249-254). New York: McGraw-Hill.

Patton, M.Q. (1980). *Qualitative evaluation methods.* Beverley Hills, CA: Sage.

Pratt, M.L. (1977). *Toward a speech act theory of literary discourse.* Bloomington: Indiana University Press.

Riffaterre, M. (1978). *Semiotics of poetry.* Bloomington: Indiana University Press.

Rosenblatt, L. (1968). *Literature as exploration.* New York: Noble and Noble.

Stierle, K. (1980). The reading of fictional texts. In S.R. Suleiman & I. Crosman (Eds.), *The reader in the text: Essays on audience and interpretations* (pp. 83-105). Princeton, NJ: Princeton University Press.

Suleiman, S.R., & Crosman, I. (Eds.). (1980). *The reader in the text: Essays on audience and interpretation.* Princeton, NJ: Princeton University Press.

9 Teaching Writing as Communication: The Use of Ethnographic Findings in Classroom Practice*

Luis C. Moll

University of Arizona

Rosa Díaz

University of California,
San Diego

The work reported here summarizes classroom research undertaken as part of a larger literacy study conducted in a bilingual community in San Diego, CA (Trueba, Moll, & Díaz, 1982). This larger project had two related goals: to collect ethnographic data to profile writing occurring in homes and other community settings, and to explore ways of using this information for the teaching of writing in schools, specially to limited-English-speaking students. We developed the activities described in this chapter to provide maximum information about this latter goal—the procedures for turning community ethnographic data into usable information for classroom practice.

Our basic strategy centered around the development and implementation of a series of writing "modules." These modules consisted of planned writing activities designed to bring understandings from the *community* into the organization of writing instruction in the *classroom*. A concomitant aim of these modules was to produce observable change in the students' writing within a relatively short time. To accomplish these twin goals, we recruited a dozen teachers from three secondary schools in the community to participate in the project. These teachers' efforts to improve the writing of their students form the basis of the classroom research described herein.

Cazden (1983) pointed out that most ethnographically informed educational studies described existing conditions but only a few implemented instructional change. She praised two projects, the Kamehameha Early Education Project (KEEP) in Hawaii and Heath's work in Appalachia, because researchers in these studies worked with teachers to produce concrete change in classroom conditions. Indeed, the incorporation of a native Hawaiian speech event, the "talk story," into KEEP reading lessons is the most famous example of teachers adapting classroom practice to accommodate cultural elements identified through ethnographic research (see e.g., Au, 1980; Tharp, 1982). But the KEEP reading program had two additional, somewhat overlooked, nonethnographic features which contributed to its

*The research reported herein was supported by the National Institute of Education Contract No. 400-81-0023; we are grateful for the Institute's assistance. Our sincere appreciation is extended to our colleagues, Stephen Diaz, Michael Cole, and Donald McQuade, who provided helpful comments on earlier versions of this manuscript.

success. One was a shift in the focus of instruction from decoding to comprehension; the other was the inclusion of the children's experiences as part of lessons' reading discussions. Combined, these two elements facilitated comprehension by making the children's experiences relevant to their understanding of the reading content.

Au's (1980) close examination of KEEP reading lessons revealed that the integration of children's life experiences and comprehension was helped by the native Hawaiian teachers who allowed, as part of the lessons' discussion, social interactions intuitively comfortable for them and for the students. These ways of interacting contained structural properties very similar to the aforementioned talk story. The talk-story lessons differed from routine lesson interactions in that they not only elicited individual participation as nominated by the teacher but also permitted mutual or joint participation by the students in the discussion of text. KEEP researchers used ethnographic information about the talk story to *interpret* lesson changes on cultural grounds. Therefore, in the KEEP project, at least initially, community information was not introduced directly into the classroom to modify lessons; instead, lessons were transformed by the teachers on the basis of sound pedagogical practice. Community data were used after the intervention to make sense of the effectiveness of the new reading lessons. As Cazden (1983) put it, the ethnographers' primary role was that of "agreeing on a particular plan of action for cultural reasons while psychologists and educators agreed to the same actions on other grounds" (p. 35).

In the second project mentioned by Cazden (1983), Heath (1983) worked cooperatively with parents and educators to modify the classroom lessons of black children having academic difficulties. Through ethnographic observations, Heath analyzed how black adults talked to their children in home and community settings as well as the children's responses and compared these verbal strategies with ways of interacting in the classroom. Classroom analysis revealed that teachers' questions were markedly different from ways of questioning in the community. Heath's intervention concerned having teachers incorporate into their lessons interrogatives used by the children's parents in nonschool settings as a way of increasing the children's participation in lessons. For example, teachers began social studies lessons with questions that asked for personal experiences and analogic responses such as "What's happening there?" "Have you ever been there?" or "What's this like?" The use of these questions in early stages of instruction were productive in generating active responses from previously passive and "nonverbal" students. Once the teachers increased the participation of students in lessons using home questioning styles, they were able to move them toward the use of school-type questioning styles necessary for academic development in those specific classrooms.

Heath suggested that two components were necessary to bring information about the community into the classroom. One was for teachers to become researchers. As part of her work, Heath asked the teachers to do research on their own families and in classrooms. In so doing, the teachers explored and discovered "how and why data on everyday behaviors—their own and that of others—can be useful in bringing about attitude and behavior changes" (Heath, 1982, p. 126). The teachers' data collection activities, when combined with data from the community, "led them to ask questions of their own practices and to admit other practices which would not necessarily have emerged otherwise" (Heath, 1982, p. 127). The second component was the collection of community data that was *credible* for classroom use. That is, were the interrogatives used in instruction the ones that "made sense" within the lesson context? What forms of questioning could be justified for classroom use "in terms of good pedagogy" (Heath, 1982, p. 124)? As such, ethnographic findings influenced the conduct of lessons only in so far as the findings were considered pedagogically relevant and useful by the teachers.

In yet another study, Heath (1981) used community information to motivate students to write by making lessons relevant to their interests. Once the students started writing, the researchers, which included teachers, implemented instructional procedures to help the students develop their writing. In contrast to KEEP's and Heath's own work which capitalized on specific sociolinguistic events, here Heath used ethnographic data to establish for the students the social relevance of writing. Through ethnography the researchers explored social and community settings for information that would be relevant to transfer to the classroom for instructional purposes.

The research described in the following pages contains elements similar to the already-mentioned studies, but with important variations given our schools' and community's characteristics and the goals of the project. We start by discussing the theoretical perspective that guided our efforts, in particular our adaptation of Vygotsky's (1978) concept of a "zone of proximal development," used to organize the writing modules. Our theoretical perspective, as we will discuss, influenced the formulation of the research problem and shaped our research procedures. We then present the design of the study. Here we emphasize our collaboration with teachers in developing and conducting the research.

With the conceptual framework as preface, we devote the bulk of the chapter to detailing the writing activities. These activities include a discussion of ethnographic findings that influenced the conduct of the study; descriptions of research meetings with teachers and of how writing activities were implemented; and several samples of student writings. We conclude with a discussion of the role of ethnography in influencing classroom practice, particularly with limited-English-speaking students.

CONCEPTUAL FRAMEWORK

In this project we set out to create a system of activities that would help secondary school students from a bilingual community to master writing as a tool of communication and thought. There have been significant advancements in recent years in systematic knowledge relevant to the teaching of writing (see, e.g., Whiteman, 1981; Nystrand, 1982; Graves, 1983; Frederiksen & Dominic, 1981; Scollon & Scollon, 1981). Our choice among these various lines of thought was guided by our search for a synthesizing viewpoint that could meet the very real needs of the secondary school population in this study.

The central premise of our approach was, that in order to enhance or modify intellectual skills such as writing, the skills must first be understood in their social and cultural context (Laboratory of Comparative Human Cognition, 1983; Scribner & Cole, 1981; Vygotsky, 1978). Applied to the problem of writing among secondary school students, this position required that we consider the contexts and contents of writing relevant to our students' lives. Hence we adopted a position that committed us to look at the social conditions within which writing occurs in order to know more about how writing activities were put together in the home and community. Using these ethnographic observations as a base, we then set about to discover ways in which we could use features of that one context (the community) to assist in another context (the classroom).

Some Guiding Principles

Our approach built on the ideas of sociohistorical psychologists (see Wertsch, 1979, for a review). These psychologists emphasized the critical importance of the social environment in intellectual development. The basis of this position is that human beings are inescapably social beings; and as social beings all learning occurs in social (and historical) environments. It follows then that social environments play critical roles in an individual's learning and development.

But human beings themselves, through their social interactions, create the social environments in which they function and in which they learn. Vygotsky (1978) expressed this relationship between social activity and individual learning in his general law of cultural development. He proposed that any higher psychological function appears "twice or on two planes. First on the social plane and then on the psychological plane. First it appears between people as an intrapsychological category and then within the individual child as an interpsychological category" (p. 57). Thus, social interactions are a principal mechanism through which human beings create and change environments, and, as a consequence, change themselves.

These interactions, however, are rarely direct: humans use verbal behavior, reading and writing—what Vygotsky called psychological tools—to mediate their interactions with the physical and social environment (Vygotsky, 1978; Wertsch, 1985). Moreover, and central to our work, is the fundamental social characteristic of these tools. That is, these tools (be it speech or writing) are social in two important ways. First, they are products of sociocultural evolution, created by human action in response to sociolcultural forces (Cole & Griffin, 1983). Second, they are primarily a means of communicating with others; that is, tools are used in the service of social interaction and communication. Ultimately, they are used to mediate our interactions with self, as we internalize their use and they become part of our behavioral repertoire. Thus, a strong connection is posited between external, practical, communicative activity and intellectual activity.

The point, however, is not simply that all learning takes place in social contexts and that tool use is a prominent characteristic of human beings. As already implied, sociohistorical psychologists have also suggested that the path of intellectual development moves from the social to the individual. Vygotsky (1978) held that the intellectual skills acquired by children are directly related to *how* they interact with adults and peers in specific problem-solving environments. Children first perform the appropriate behaviors to complete a task (e.g., writing) with someone else's guidance and direction (e.g., the teacher) before they can complete the task competently and independently. In so doing, children internalize the help they receive from others and eventually come to use the means of guidance initially provided by others to direct their own subsequent problem-solving behaviors.

Therefore, an important pedagogical implication of this theoretical approach is that the specific social organization of problem-solving environments is critical. The claim is not simply that children learn from participating in social activities, but that the manner in which an activity (e.g., writing) is represented to children is important, because there is a strong connection between how a given task is accomplished in social interaction and how children will eventually accomplish a similar task independently. In Vygotskian terms, the same mediational means are used on both the interpsychological and the intrapsychological planes (Wertsch, 1985).

The Zone of Proximal Development. Vygotsky elaborated the instructional implications of the connection between how a task is represented in social interaction and individual psychological action through the concept of a zone of proximal development. The zone is simply the *distance* between what children can accomplish independently (which he called the "actual developmental level") and what they could accomplish with the help of adults or more capable peers (which he called the "proximal developmental level"). Vygotsky suggested that performance at the proximal level reveals, in a real sense, the child's future, the skills or behaviors that are in the process of developing and maturing. In order for instruction to be effective it must be aimed at children's proximal levels, at the future, and social interactions within the zone need to be organized to guide and support children's performance at the proximal level until they are able to perform independent of help (what he called "internalization"). He argued that instruction aimed at the actual developmental level is ineffective, because it is aimed at behaviors that have already "matured," that children have already mastered. Similarly, aiming instruction below the actual developmental level or extremely beyond the proximal level is equally ineffective. The teaching goal, then, is to aim instructional activities proximally, while providing the social support or help to facilitate students' behaviors at those levels, so that, as Cazden (1981) noted, performance appears before competence (for examples of practical applications, see Griffin & Cole, 1984; Moll & Díaz, in press).

This conceptual framework influenced our research approach in several ways. Instructional activities were seen as systems of interaction that should be organized purposely to facilitate a shift from collaborative activity to individual action. Therefore, in the study of any learning activity, the unit of analysis became the act or system of acts by which learning was composed (Leont'ev, 1973; Talyzina, 1981). For this study's purposes, rather than studying the students' classroom writing independent of the conditions in which they were asked to write, we focused on the child–adult classroom interactional system which comprised "writing." Additionally, we studied child–adult interactions (the writing activities) in relation to the content and objectives of specific lessons. It was the relationship among the social organization of lessons, content, and the student's entering skill level that created effective zones of proximal development. In analyzing the classroom activities which we implemented we sought to (a) discover what kinds of community information teachers used to create effective zones for promoting writing, and (b) accumulate evidence about the effectiveness of specific interventions to see which activities provided the kinds of interaction that promote learning.

STUDY DESIGN

In accordance with the study's objectives and our theoretical perspective, we organized a teaching/research arrangement to help us explore how ethnographic data could be applied to various classroom conditions. We moved our research operations from our respective universities to a residence located in the heart of the community. A centrally located field office allowed us to hire and train community residents—including teachers and graduate students—as researchers to collect home and community observations (see Trueba et al., 1982). The same field office also became the place where we conducted all meetings with teachers as well as where we housed the data collected during the study. Working out of such an office facilitated interactions between the people conducting the ethnography and the teachers responsible for implementing instructional innovations. Our procedures enabled us to create and implement, in collaboration with teachers, writing activities that attended to both the teachers' and students' writing needs while making contact with the community issues and concerns documented by the ethnographic component of the study. As much as possible, we utilized existing school and classroom resources to minimize time and expense and to avoid disrupting daily classroom routines in any extraordinary way. We now describe specific components of the design.

Design Components

The success of the design depended on securing the active involvement of teachers. Although several teachers had expressed interest in the study, their level of participation was uncertain. As a means of linking our research interest to the teacher's need for training and career advancement, we arranged for the Multicultural Education Department of the School of Education at San Diego State University to give 12 teachers graduate credits for their involvement in the project. Further, the department awarded the teachers a small stipend to defray most of the cost of enrollment, registering, etc. This arrangement not only provided good incentive and remuneration but helped to develop an ongoing, positive relationship with the teachers who were to be our research collaborators.

The 12 teachers agreed to participate in the study in four ways.

1. *Teachers' Seminars.* The teachers attended formal class/research seminars held at the field office every other week for a semester. Usually, two separate meetings were held—on Wednesdays and Thursdays; the teachers could attend either day at their convenience. These meetings lasted 2½–3 hours each. A few days prior to each meeting an agenda was distributed which outlined upcoming activities and issues for consideration as well as any required readings.

From the beginning these seminars were intended to become the "theoretical context" (Freire, 1970); that is, a setting in which to discuss the development and implementation of fundamentally new classroom writing activities in the light of information that was being gathered from the community. At these meetings we presented specific aspects of the ongoing field study (e.g., parental attitudes toward schooling) to the teachers and related the information to their classrooms. These discussions allowed the field staff to understand what community data the teachers found relevant as well as what information could be relevant for classroom use.

2. *Writing Modules.* Every teacher agreed to implement a minimum of six writing modules. These modules consisted of a series of relatively well-specified instructional activities intended to facilitate utilization of community ethnographic data in the classroom. As such, module activities were the vehicle for linking the community data with teaching-learning practices. The specifics of the writing modules and the social factors that influenced their content and organization will be discussed separately. Each module was structured to take into account the limits and possibilities of individual teachers, subject matter, student characteristics, and school constraints. All modules were implemented under regular classroom conditions, and they represented instructional innovations by and for the teachers. The modules were "experimental" in that both teachers and students were participating in activities fundamentally different from the writing instruction offered by the curriculum. The modules were also sequential in that each module formed part of a series that provided the participants with experiences of a connected sort.

3. *Observational Journals.*   We sought not only to foster instructional change but also to document teaching practices that make such changes possible. Therefore, a central feature of the design was the collection of data by the teachers in the form of a self-observational journal. These journals provided both researchers and teachers with data on the organization of instruction in the writing modules and provided the teachers with a running log of their experiences in the project, a way to contrast their thinking and teaching over time. These journal entries became an important focus of discussion; they were submitted during each teacher seminar, treated as regular field notes, and returned with comments on their completeness and usefulness. Moreover, they also represented important data for our analyses; we found ourselves turning repeatedly to what the teachers' wrote as an important source of insight. We describe the modules in a later section and include excerpts from teacher journals to illustrate our points.

4. *Classroom Observations.*   Every week that the modules were implemented, at least two different teachers were observed in action. These observations were conducted by the researchers and were intended to supplement the teachers' observations. As with the teachers' observational journals, these field notes also became an important topic of discussion during the seminars. Information from the class-rooms also helped determine the nature of the seminars.

COMMUNITY AND SCHOOLS

The study was conducted in what is generally referred to in San Diego as South Bay. The community consists of an approximately 60 square-mile area adjacent to the border between Mexico and the United States. The South Bay is bounded on the west by the Pacific Ocean, extends about 8 miles to the east, and ends near large tracts of undeveloped land. Its northernmost boundary is a line paralleling the border about 8 miles to the north.

A distinctive demographic feature of the South Bay was the large concentration of ethnolinguistic minorities within the area. Most of the Latinos live in the south-ernmost regions of South Bay. Although this population distribution did not consti-tute barrios or ghettoes (in the strict sense of a small, isolated, ethnically homogene-ous population pockets), it was nevertheless clear to the observer that the area possessed the special character of an ethnically distinct community. It might be more appropriate to classify these communities as suburban barrios, where the specific ethnic characteristics of the population were not as marked as in an urban barrio. In the community one could hear a great deal of Spanish spoken, see a vari-ety of ethnic groups shopping in stores, and find stores that catered to the needs of specific groups. The Filipino population formed the second largest ethnolinguistic group, concentrated in a small area of the South Bay region. The Anglo population was scattered throughout South Bay, particularly in the north and northeast. To some degree, there was a gradual decrease of ethnolinguistic minorities in the South Bay as one moved northward away from the border and toward the more affluent areas of San Diego.

The proximity to Baja California, Mexico, accounted for a large number of Mex-icans residing in the South Bay, and numerous businesses catered to the Mexican consumer. In spite of peso devaluations (from 27 to 120 pesos per dollar during the project duration), the South Bay continued to be in many respects a binational com-munity with common social and economic interests. Until a few years ago, busi-nesses geared to the Mexican consumer were relatively small and independent. In the last five years, several national chains of grocery, drug stores, and department stores had built new facilities near the border to attract the Mexican shopper, and had bilingual staff, supervisors, and managers.

The residential area in the South Bay was composed of single-family homes, du-plexes, and large apartment complexes. In some cases, these residences were lo-cated next to small businesses, so that a resident of a single-family home might have as a neighbor a bakery or even a junkyard.

School Communities

At the outset of the project, we selected three junior high schools to participate in the study because of their ethnolinguistic minority populations: Western, Ocean

Park, and Montclair. The first two schools had a large Latino population, the third also had a large concentration of Filipino students. Owing to reasons unrelated to the project, we concentrated our work at Western and Ocean Park.

The Ocean Park community came the closest to resembling a barrio than any other community in the South Bay. Latinos accounted for about 37% of the total population of the area. The students were drawn in great part from residences located among and between large commercial zones. The area had a distinctive Mexican barrio atmosphere, with typical corner markets and fruit and taco stands that catered to local residents and patrons of the businesses in the area's main boulevard. In contrast to the Western community, the low-income units around the school were rundown and the streets less well kept. Because it was near the center of the commercial section, there was a great deal of traffic around the school.

The Western community area covered the northeastern portion of the South Bay and extended south to the international border. The immediate surroundings of the school were conspicuously more affluent when compared with that of Ocean Park, and the area was predominantly residential. The Latino population accounted for approximately 40% of the total population.

Ethnographic Findings

We concentrated our observations on 27 students from eight different families in the area. Most of the families were poor. Practically all qualified for some kind of aid to supplement their income, ranging from free lunch for their children at school to subsidized housing. Some heads of household were unemployed; others lived on small retirement benefits. For the most part, these families lived in small houses, apartments, or trailer homes.

The parents had a low level of education; most did not receive more than three to five years of schooling in Mexico. The language background of these families was predominantly Spanish, with some family members being fluent bilinguals. In general, the families communicated in Spanish at home and maintained many of the traditional Mexican customs.

What follows is a summary of specific factors that influenced the implementation of the writing activities. The majority of these factors resulted from the ethnographic observations conducted in the community, although classroom characteristics are also included in the summary.

Diversity. Despite the apparent homogeneity of the study population, our observations revealed the diversity that characterized social life in the community. Several factors, specially immigration patterns, constantly molded the specific social configuration of the community. This diversity was most evident in the familial organization. Field observations documented the different social arrangements as families attempted to adjust to the social and economic realities of life in the community. These arrangements ranged from the so-called "traditional" families with clearly demarcated roles and responsibilities for the family members to families where the father was missing with one of the offspring assuming the adult role. But perhaps more important for our purposes, family roles and responsibilities were often assigned on the basis of English-language fluency. For example, in families where the children were fluent (or near fluent) in English but the parents were Spanish monolingual speakers, the children took responsibility for conducting transactions that involved literacy in English such as paying bills or answering school-related queries. Although the parents would monitor what went on, the transactions were conducted by the children. These children, by virtue of their linguistic status, assumed a great deal of control and power within the family system usually reserved for adults, because they mediated the family's communication with important social institutions. Thus the social, economic, and linguistic demands of life in the community were usually met with familial flexibility in adjusting roles and responsibilities for survival.

Paucity of Writing. Another factor that influenced the implementation of the design was the information generated by the community observations regarding the nature and frequency of writing. Findings indicated that, in general, not much writing was taking place. Most of the writing observed in the homes was functional and practical including such things as shopping lists, phone messages, an occasional letter, and for the most part, students' homework assignments and other school-related materials (cf. Heath, 1983). This writing seemed to be less demanding in several respects than writing required of secondary school students. It did not look like a promising base from which to *raise* classroom writing skills.

Moreover, teachers were concerned that adoption of community writing events in class could prove time consuming and disruptive to classroom routine. We were told that, although it would make sense for an elementary school teacher to adapt, let's say, methods for assembling a shopping list as a writing exercise, such a direct transfer of nonschool-related writing into the secondary school classroom would be dysfunctional given the students' age and the more advanced academic goals at this level. The one exception noted was practice in filling out employment and other types of forms.

What was indeed clear from the home observations, however, was the important role of homework in creating opportunities for family literacy. Most of the observed literacy events were organized around homework activities. Other school-related materials such as survey notes also prompted many literacy activities in these homes. Homework, however, more than any other factor, set the occasion for literacy to occur; it brought school into the homes.

Values About Education. The lack of observable, extended writing events in community life notwithstanding, parents and other community members repeatedly expressed their belief in the great value of education and their concerns about the educational training of the children in the community. They viewed the development of writing both as an essential element of a good education and an indication of being cultured (*bien educado*). As documented in the field notes, some families moved to San Diego for the expressed purpose of having their children attend school there. They perceived the children's chances for an education better in San Diego than in Mexico. So, although not much writing was observed in the homes and other settings, it was clear that writing in particular and literacy in general were valued as important components of schooling. From the community's point of view, writing and schooling were inseparable and vital for educational and personal advancement.

Social Issues. A different aspect of the research problem became clear during initial home visits. Parents, students, and others all impressed us with their concern for social issues that permeate community life. Virtually every conversation that began as a discussion of writing eventually turned to the problems of youth gangs, unemployment, immigration, the need to learn English, and so on. Hence, at the outset of the study it became apparent that writing, schooling, and social issues were complexly *related* phenomena. As a result, we were no longer thinking of merely developing writing lessons using the community findings. Instead, the instructional component needed to be organized in relation to the complex social order that we encountered.

Student and Teacher Characteristics. Our procedures were also influenced by the characteristics of the students and teachers. As a group, the students scored among the lowest in tests of writing achievement. This fact caused widespread concern throughout the school district and was one reason for community support of the research study.

Not only were the students considered poor writers, but most teachers reported that they themselves had received little or no formal training in the teaching of writing and, for the most part, felt unprepared to teach it. In addition, the majority of teachers reported that writing instruction was an infrequent classroom activity. Most classroom writing was in response to tests or homework assignments with the teacher as the primary audience and and evaluator. Writing was rarely used as a broader tool of communication—to convey opinions and ideas to others or to oneself or to analyze and explore the world. This suggested that to succeed we needed to provide the teachers with specific techniques for teaching writing that they could practice, learn, and adapt to various subject areas. So long as writing was considered beyond what the students could accomplish and was subordinated to other curricular demands, there would be few opportunities for classroom instruction to interact with the information generated by the ethnography.

Finally, despite the obvious bilingual character of the surrounding community, the schools *excluded* Spanish from the curriculum. No bilingual classes were offered, thereby eliminating the possibility of using the students' Spanish literacy skills as a bridge to English-language literacy. In addition, most teachers were English monolingual speakers and lived outside their teaching community, putting them out of touch with everyday community dynamics. This pointed out the need to familiarize teachers on a regular basis with community issues. The innovation we developed was more than just a matter of providing the teachers with a "bag of tricks" or techniques to teach writing. We organized writing instruction that was responsive to the community dynamics we were uncovering while also addressing the teachers' training needs and the students' writing problems.

TEACHING WRITING AS COMMUNICATION

The Initial Modules

The initial modules organized classroom circumstances to connect with the community information. We emphasized the teaching of expository writing related to school performance because of the parents' overwhelming concern with their children's education. As the first step of our intervention, we introduced the teachers to our theoretical notions to maximize their understanding of and participation in our research activities. We encouraged the teachers to use theory to shape the design of the writing activities and interpret their teaching efforts. Throughout the project, we stressed the following notions:

1. *Writing as communication:* Writing is essentially a communicative activity and should be taught and understood as such.
2. *Writing as a tool of analysis:* Writing activities can be used as a way for students to explore and examine social, academic, and student-relevant issues; otherwise, writing is reduced to a mechanical and trivial (not to mention boring) task for students and teachers alike.
3. *Writing for intellectual development:* The higher-order goal of classroom writing is the elaboration of thinking; the mechanics of writing should be taught in the service of this goal. These mutually complementary activities should be combined as part of the same framework.
4. *Writing performance before competence:* Teaching involves establishing levels of performance in advance of what the students can do by themselves. These levels are sustained by the way the teacher structures (organizes) help, and this teacher help is eventually appropriated by the students to become part of their writing strategies. A key to successful instruction is establishing conditions (including goals) for writing that are, in a sense, "futuristic," provide guided practice to help students perform under these conditions, and monitor how students move toward performing independently what they can initially only do with help.

This move from outside regulation to self-regulation is reflected in the students' acquisition of the writing process, accompanying changes in the type of help the teachers provide, and in the improvement of the writing product. Our evaluation of success was based on evidence of these changes in the students' writing and the teachers' teaching.

A key to the success of the initial modules was that the teachers and students experienced immediate success in producing writing. This success established the credibility of using community information to teach writing. We provided the teachers state-of-the-art teaching strategies (e.g., Graves, 1983) for systematically implementing writing activities while exploring ways of using the community information. These strategies included prewriting discussions to generate and clarify ideas about writing and about the community, the production of drafts, evaluation of feedback from teachers and peers, and the revisions of drafts and final copy. At the outset we used social content provided by the ethnography as motivating themes for writing. Given the lack of extensive writing activities in the community, we chose to transfer information from the community for classroom use rather than any specific writing or sociolinguistic event.

In the following pages we review the initial modules. For the sake of brevity, we only present a summary of the teachers' seminars, review one module implementation, citing from the teacher's journal to illustrate points of interest, and provide examples of changes in the students' writing over this time span.

Modules 1–3

Teachers' Seminars. These were key sessions. We oriented the teachers to the nature of the study and provided practical suggestions for the implementation of writing instruction. We decided that the best way for the teachers to understand the types of writing activities we were asking them to implement in their classrooms was to have them perform the activities and then discuss the principles underlying the writing activity they had just experienced. In particular, we emphasized the utility of prewriting discussions (see, e.g., Applebee, 1981; Graves, 1982) as a vehicle to eventually introduce and implement additional writing activities based on the ethnographic data and the classroom observations. We also emphasized the use of student response groups. These groups consisted of small, peer groups which provided writers with feedback and a sense of audience. The goal of these groups was for the students to assume responsibility for helping out with the composing process, a role usually reserved for the teachers. The teachers' seminars usually concluded with teachers discussing and then writing about how they would implement a similar activity in their classrooms. This pattern—going from performing or reviewing a concrete activity, to theoretical discussion, to planning a practical classroom application—characterized these seminars.

For example, the first seminar's goal was to get the teachers writing. We introduced as a writing topic the pervasive community phenomenon of "low-rider" car clubs. This was a topic the students knew more about than the teachers, most of whom lived outside of their teaching community. These car clubs, perceived often as gangs, was one of the student- and community-relevant issues identified by the ethnography. For our purposes, we introduced the topic by showing a videotape about a local, low-rider club. The teachers' task was twofold: first, to take notes during the showing of the tape and then to use these notes to *describe* the events on the tape in as much detail as possible—a task similar to keeping observational journals in their own classrooms; second, they were to write a brief essay analyzing differences between themselves and the people on the tape.

The purpose of the latter task was to require the teachers to "act" on the information given, i.e., to analyze the information critically and to use writing as the tool of analysis. We also suggested that they write freely, spontaneously, and disregard editing or grammatical concerns.

Upon the conclusion of a few minutes of "free" writing, we paused to discuss the process and product of the writing. First, the group read and analyzed descriptions of the tape and provided suggestions for improving the quantity and quality of the notes. Following this exercise, the group read aloud their essays about the tape. Several points of view were introduced and discussed. Some teachers found the exercise easy and wrote several paragraphs without difficulty; others were hesitant to write about a community phenomenon they hardly understood.

The teachers were then instructed to rewrite and expand their essays on the basis of the discussion, but this time to write about similarities between themselves and the people on the tape. Once again, they were encouraged to write freely, but this time to use each other as resources for ideas. As expected, the teachers' performance differed. Some who had no difficulty in specifying differences from the "low riders" were at a loss when thinking about what similarities might exist. The group examined how the ideas of the previous discussion were incorporated into the writing, and some teachers were asked to read to the group what they had written and explain the thinking underlying their conclusions.

At this point we performed a joint analysis of the *procedures* implemented including a rationale for the use of a socially relevant issue as a theme for writing, characteristics of the lesson, component skills needed to perform competently in the activity, assessment of product, and so forth. Conducting these discussions *after* the teachers had engaged in the activity instead of as preparation for writing created optimal conditions for discussing how to conduct similar writing activities in their classrooms. The introduction of a community activity or issue to create a context for discussing classroom adaptations became the main strategy for developing plans and ideas for interventions.

To conclude the first session, we asked the teachers to develop a plan to implement a similar lesson in their classes. We encouraged them to treat writing as a process that might include several states such as prewriting discussions, drafts, revisions, editing, and final composition. They were to think of prewriting discussions as a teacher-student dialogue that would precede all subsequent teaching efforts. The teachers reported having used similar techniques before (e.g., brainstorming, small group discussions, exchanges), but not in the teaching of writing. Hence, prewriting was introduced as a way to actively involve the students in talking about writing and to help guide the thinking involved in writing as well as a way in which teachers could identify the knowledge that students bring into the classroom and organize activities to help them apply that knowledge to the writing process. We also encouraged the teachers to select writing themes relevant to their students and classroom goals. We were unsure if one session would suffice to help the teachers use community issues identified by the ethnography as part of their lessons. Therefore, we left the initial selection of writing themes up to their discretion. Finally, they were to observe and document in detail their implementation of writing activities.

Module Implementation.   Ten of the 12 teachers reported positive results with the use of prewriting discussions: Students had "increased enthusiasm"; there were "no moans from students when they were finally assigned to write"; and "students who had not written anything all year stayed after class (on their own) to complete the assignment." In general, the use of prewriting was successful in eliciting writing from the students, a major goal of our initial efforts.

As it turned out, however, most teachers selected safe school-related themes for the students' initial writing modules. These themes included "My Worst Grade," "Afternoon Vs. Night School Dances," "Detention," "P.E. Requirements," "Open Campus," and "Cafeteria Food" as well as "My Best Friend," "My Favorite Animal," and the timely "Jupiter Effect."

Clearly, the most powerful examples of student writing occurred in classes that used community-related themes. In one particular class, for example, the teacher aide had been killed just two months earlier; this murder of a person known to the entire class led the teacher to select "violence" as the writing theme. Rather than describe this module, we quote lengthy passages from the teacher's observations. Note how she introduced a prewriting discussion to organize the students' *thinking* as she prepared them for writing. (The passages were continuous; several sentences were omitted for brevity.)

> Normally our topics are light, i.e., favorite things to do, what friendship is, and so on. When I wrote "violence" on the board, I got some raised eyebrows and students shifting in their seats . . .
>
> I gave them a dictionary definition of violence and then asked them what came to mind when they thought, violence. These are the responses I initially received: killing, fighting, mugged, drugs, and guns. That was it. It was dead silent as I waited. Uncomfortable students prevailed . . .
>
> I went back and sat in my chair in the circle. I began recounting the previous week's Chula Vista trailer incident (a shooting in which five people were murdered) . . . I started to ask them why they thought it happened. Most felt the man just "snapped." There were many suggestions as to why, but that explanation was the prevalent one . . .
>
> I then asked them if Mrs. P's murder affected them more. She was my adult aide and was killed by her husband (earlier this year). Many of the students knew her on a personal basis. This was a difficult subject for me because she was my dear friend. The kids fell quiet when I brought up Maria. They obviously had been deeply affected by this violence. They began to relax when someone said, "Of course it affected me more, I knew her." What followed was an emotional discussion. It was like they had been waiting for a chance to analyze how this could've happened to someone they actually knew. . . . I then went to the board and said, "Now, after our discussion, what is violence to you?" the following are their responses:

Violence:	killing	jealousy
	fighting	depression
	mugged	fear
	drugs	hate
	guns	sadness
	revenge	bad
	stupid	paranoid
	crazy	terrified
	disappointed	prejudice
	insane	loneliness
	anger	depression
	confusion	rejection
	frightening	confined
	feelings	

I concluded by asking them to look over our "brainstorming" results to find a common strain. They easily did. I got words like "negative," "out of control," "confusing."

The next day the students wrote. The teacher provided three questions to help them structure their writing. We quote again from the teacher's journal.

They were slow in starting as they were in the discussion. I knew this would be the case due to the powerful emotions involved. I also tried to encourage each student to zero in on the writing problems they had on the (pretest sample) such as capitalization, proofreading, even paragraph form. At the same time I refreshed their memories by writing on the board some of the key words from our previous day's discussion. The writing began. Many wrote frantically to pour it out.

Writing Samples. Our design allowed us to collect writing samples from students over time. Writing samples collected from two students illustrate the writing that the students produced in the first module.

Student A:

I think the man in the trailer court shouldn't have just took out his anger out on innocent people. If he was mad about the dogs barking then he should have shot the dogs or either complained to the man with the dogs. He shouldn't have just shot out of every direction. I also think that the man should get special care and also be sent to jail for doing such things that he did. Furthermore, I think he really needs help. Finally, I hope he gets the help he needs and goes to jail.

Student B:

I never had a violent life. But one thing did happen, that effected my very bad. A couple of years ago, I found out my Uncle and Aunt had a divorce. My Aunt got the kids. Candy and Tammy where their names. My Aunt went into singing Country. She got pretty good, but she wasn't no Christal Gale. She had a affair with her chauffeur. After it was over she was going to get married to another man. The chauffeur was still in love with her, so he stabbed her. When I found out I flipped. It was so creepy. After a while I asked my cousins how they felt about the whole thing they said they were happy she died cause she had no time for them. The oldest Tammy said, she saw her mom dead on the floor and she started laughing. That has effected me very much. How can her own daughters feel that way. I felt confused about the whole thing. What triggered it was jealousy. The more I think about it the more I'm glad I'm alive and treasure my life.

To facilitate contrast with the students' usual classroom writing, we present pretest samples obtained from the same two students before the modules were implemented. In collecting the pretest samples we replicated the usual classroom conditions for assessing writing. The topic "Junk Food" was selected from the district's suggested list of topics.

Student A:

There are a variety of reasons why junk food shouldn't be sold on campus. First, junk food is very expensive. Second, junk food is not very nutritious. Also, junk food gives you zits. Furthermore junk food also, gives you cavities. For these reasons junk food shouldn't be sold on campus.

Student B:
Yes, I think schools should be allowed to sell junk food. They don't have a lot of junk food in the first place. Junk food tastes good and feels you up when your hungry. It really wouldn't do any good if they stopped selling it. Because they would bring it to school from home. Plus the school gets profit off of it.

Contrast the pretest writing to what the *same* children wrote during module 1. Note the increase in the amount of text written as well as the improvement in coherence and organization; also notice the dramatic content. But note in particular the students' use of writing to make connections between real world events and themselves. We have here the beginnings of their use of writing as a tool of thought and communication. And this from students that days before were judged as incapable of producing text of any consequence.

The prewriting discussion of the writing topic increased the students' understanding of the goal of the writing activity and greatly facilitated the production of text. It also created many opportunities for the teacher to teach and to encourage further writing. The teacher evaluated the results:

I was impressed with the results. As I went around and discussed each paper with the students I got interesting statements—I had never questioned them directly—regarding how much easier this topic was to handle regardless of the emotion, seriousness, and so on . . . Virginia, who wrote about a close call in a gang fight, stated, "Don't they know it's easier for us to tell how we feel when we've been there?" I gave so many more positive strokes this time around. Most knew their papers were better. I got no "Really?'s" when I pointed out specially good areas . . .

This was a very successful lesson for me in many ways. I enjoyed the time to really talk with my kids. It also furthered my belief that if what's taught is important in the mind of the learner, much more will truly be learned.

The success of the initial modules created conditions favorable for further experimentation during the final modules.

The Final Modules

The goal of the final modules was to capitalize further on the ethnographic information to extend the teachers' and students' writing activities. One ethnographic finding very important for our purposes was that students' homework assignments created the most frequent opportunities for writing to occur in the homes. With this finding in mind, we set out to purposely structure homework assignments that not only produced literacy-related interactions in the home but also involved the parents and other community members in the development and conduct of the classroom writing activities. At the same time, we wanted to retain the main academic goal of the writing modules: to develop the students' expository writing.

We had advanced rapidly in the initial modules. We provided the teachers with ways to think about and teach writing; through the teachers we got the students involved in writing activities that included by now a familiar routine: prewriting discussions to generate and clarify ideas about a writing theme and composing process, the production of a draft, some sort of evaluative feedback either from teacher or peers, and then revisions of the draft for final copy. We now wanted to provide both teachers and students with more challenging writing activities; in our terms, we wanted to create more advanced zones of proximal development by using writing assignments to make more direct contact with the world outside the classroom.

We proposed to the teachers that they implement three interrelated modules. These modules consisted of three different writing assignments that formed part of an integrated writing activity. More specifically, during the fourth module the students would write their opinions or ideas about a specific topic. This type of writing predominated in the initial modules, so we figured it would be a good takeoff point. In the fifth module the students were asked to obtain information from home, community, or school sources in order to expand the statements written in the previous module into an "explanatory" piece. The purpose here, as will be described in more detail, was to have the students branch out and use extracurricular information to enhance their writing. The sixth and final module had the students use the information gathered previously to persuade someone to adopt their specific point of view.

As in the previous modules, a key element was the selection of writing themes. We wanted each class to hold the theme constant over time so that students could practice modifying the writing in the service of different goals. We also wanted the teachers to make explicit to the students the process by which text could be modified depending on the goals of the writing activity.

Modules 4–6

Teachers' Seminars.   During the previous modules we had introduced the idea of organizing the teaching of writing proximally but had postponed formally presenting the Vygotskian idea of a "zone of proximal development" until the teachers had previous experiences (modules 1–3) which they could interpret from this perspective. We discussed the practical applications of this theoretical notion and showed the teachers a series of videotapes gathered in classroom situations (Moll & Díaz, in press) in which lessons were manipulated along the lines suggested by the theory. We emphasized that it was not a new curriculum that we were suggesting they implement but rather a principled way to organize instruction utilizing existing classroom and nonclassroom resources available to teachers. To make these ideas more relevant to the teaching of writing, we read excerpts from the teachers' journals that represented instances of creating effective zones. We supplemented our presentation by giving the teachers an article written by Graves (1982) that proposed a similar idea: "stretching" the students' writing by strategically helping them perform tasks ahead of their current level of writing. Combining these three resources we were able to provide the teachers with numerous examples of what we meant by a zone of proximal development.

In addition to the theoretical discussion, we also updated the field findings. In particular, we discussed how different families used literacy as part of their daily routines and the implications of this information for classroom writing activities.

We emphasized both how the creation of text could help the children understand their community and how understanding the community could facilitate the production of text.

In the following module implementation the teachers had to organize ways to access resources outside the classroom for use in developing the students' classroom writing. One goal was for the students to use, as systematically as it could be organized, extracurricular information to enhance and advance their thinking about what and how to write. Our motivation for developing this module was the field finding regarding the role of homework as central to literacy in the homes. With this in mind, we tried to bring family interactions into the classroom writing system as one of the prewriting steps necessary to complete the assignment.

We also felt that the teachers would benefit from this module's activities, because they provided a lesson-related vehicle that the teachers could use to gather knowledge about the children and their community as well as additional issues and ideas to bring into lessons as writing content. Although we had time to implement only one such module with the teachers, we emphasized that this type of writing activity could, given the teaching system they were implementing, become a regular feature of writing instruction in their classrooms. That is, the teachers could purposely use homework assignments to provide a regular "link to the external world," in lieu of the ideal—an ongoing ethnography to inform their teaching.

Module Implementation

This section reviews a remarkable module conducted in one of the English as a second language (ESL) classrooms. We selected this particular module to describe in detail, because it illustrates one good way, given the unfortunate lack of curricular emphasis on Spanish literacy development, to capitalize on extracurricular sources to help develop the English writing of limited-English-speaking students. The ESL teacher employed the same system being used by other teachers in their "regular" classrooms with fluent English speakers; that is, the same principles of instruction were being applied under different language conditions. From our perspective, individual differences between ESL and non-ESL students referred to the different ways in which students entered the writing activity and the nature of the help they needed to perform at the most advanced level possible. Whether fluent or nonfluent in English, instruction was organized for students to engage in the same basic educational activity: *writing for communication and intellectual advancement.* Given their English-language difficulties, ESL students might contribute differentially to the completion of the activity than regular students, and the teacher might have to provide more structured help, but both sets of students participated in comparable intellectual activities.

Day One. In this module, the theme for writing was bilingualism, because the teacher and students had expressed so much interest in this topic and had written about it in a preceding module. We quote at length from the teacher's journal.

Today, half way through the period, we began this 5th module by reviewing the writing we had done. I spent most time asking them about their last "bilingualism" papers, module 4, and they remembered a lot about them. We reviewed, and I listed on the board that that paper had been expressive in nature, *their* own feelings and opinions. That was readily accepted.

I told them the (next) module was going to be concerned with information, opinions, feelings, etc., that would be gleaned from *other* sources besides themselves. They looked at me with blank faces. Then I started to discuss and probe the meaning of "survey" and "questionnaire" with them. *They loved that!*" I gave examples of TV polls, of Cola tests, etc. Jorge and Lisa called out, "Does that mean we're going to do that?" They all were kind of excited or at least interested when I said "yes."

I "fed" them the beginning questions for their questionnaires, ones I wanted to make sure *all* asked. I gave them three they *had* to use, and two more samples they could choose. The assignment was explained as follows:

These three questions *all* must ask:

A.   What language do you speak best?
B.   What language do you read and write best?
C.   Do any members of your family who live with you speak another language besides English?

Two other questions were optional:

D.   Would you be willing to take classes to become bilingual?
E.   What career do you foresee in your future in which you would benefit by being bilingual?

Each student was required to ask:

A.   Two adults not working on campus.
B.   Two adults who do work on campus.
C.   Three students whose first language was English.
D.   Three students whose first language was other than English.

Homework for tonight was to invent three additional questions related to bilingualism and people's opinions about it.

Day Two.   The module continued the next day as the teacher got the students to generate additional questions to use in the survey.

Today's whole period was devoted to the project. Five students—Jacqueline, Amanda, Juan, Abelardo, and Rita—got double zeros. Abelardo didn't understand. Hector, who hastily scribbled down some questions by the time I got to him, came in moaning he didn't understand. I had him seek help from others. He's a very dependent 7th grader!

I walked around the room, reading each student's questions and putting checks next to ones I wanted put on the board. A few I helped reword a bit. Surprisingly, after such a shaky start with my questions, there were 10 questions I felt were good enough to be examples to everyone, with several duplicates. By the time I finished checking, all ten were on the board, and we began to discuss and reword for accuracy, each one. I told students they may choose 3 questions from these—their own or anyone else's—to use on their surveys.

Their homework tonight is to prepare their questionnaires on large construction paper (samples with the work turned in) and try out the questions on 2 people by tomorrow. I spent 10–15 minutes at the end of the period sitting with about 8 students showing them how I'd do one—and example—and I posted it for all to see. They were anxious to get started—borrowed rulers, chose paper colors, talked over question choices with each other.

These seemed to be the best:

1. Would you prefer to live around bilingual people in a bilingual community?
2. Are your closest friends bilingual?
3. a. Would you like to go to the University?
   b. Do you know that the best university require four years of 2nd-language training?
4. Which language do you like the best of the ones you don't speak?
5. What language do you speak with your friends? Why?
6. How many teachers do you have that speak some Spanish?
7. Do you think you would like to return to live where your learned your first language?
8. Which language does your closest friend speak with you?
9. Do you think speaking another language is important?
10. Is it comparatively hard for you to learn another language?

Day Three. Knowing her students would need further guidance in conducting the survey, the teacher spent part of the lesson clarifying examples and general concerns. Note the interest generated by the students interviewing adult respondents.

This is a minimum day with only about 25 minutes to the period, but I used the time today to share some good (visually) examples of questionnaires and to address some general concerns. First, as I looked around, I recognized the handwriting of Jeff (my principal), Gloria S. (The AP), and other adults. The students had handed the questionnaires to the person and told them to answer them. I instructed them that all future entries must be in students' own handwriting and that they were to ask the questions orally, explicating if necessary, since a few answers were not directed appropriately. The students didn't even moan at that; they thought that was logical for practicing oral English. Second, I asked the students to come up with at least one person who did not value bilingualism. So as not to have totally biased results, I asked the students to come up with at least *one* person who did *not* value bilingualism. Also, students must identify the person questioned with full name.

The students were buzzing when they came in and they buzzed all along! Some had never had occasion to speak to adults other than their teachers here, and a few, especially Hector C. and George (come to mind), were itching to show me Dr. S's responses, etc.

The teacher then structured some more help to move the students along and to maintain their interest in quite an involved writing activity.

The projects are shaping up and they seem to have a clear idea of what they are doing at this step, so I decided today to introduce the next step. Most had time in class to start formulating a "results" page. I just put a suggested format on the board and explained that after they had gotten their results, they could fill in the results chart. My sample looked like this:

Results

Questions	Agree (Yes)	Disagree (No)
1.		
2.		
3.		
4.		
5.		
6.		

Since we had a cultural fair in the afternoon, I gave no homework other than to complete the questioning of a minimum of 10 people by class tomorrow. They didn't feel hard-pressed to get this done.

The teacher spent much time on the module and at each step of the way she made sure that the students were in contact with the goal of the lesson. That is, the several tasks necessary to complete the module were done to accomplish a specified and mutually understood goal; at no time were the students relegated to doing writing exercises unrelated to the purpose of the writing activity that made up the module.

Day Four. As the module continued, the students showed signs of taking over the activity without the need for highly structured supervision. Noticing this change, the teacher decided to be less directive and had the students assume most of the responsibility for completing the necessary tasks. This shift in the control of the task is mentioned in the next excerpt.

Not too many completed rough drafts in class today, but they certainly were well on their way. I allowed them to take them home over the weekend, hoping to get polished work back on Monday.

In class, there was a lot of constructive communicating going on—students asked each other "how to say" this and that, and asked me (usually), "How do I do it?" After I had already explained the questions they had a difficult time getting going, but I decided not to handfeed them this time, but instead to let them muddle through. I answered specific questions today, but I didn't volunteer the questions, if you know the difference. I sent them home to finish by Monday.

The students returned Monday with their papers in different stages of completion. The teacher selected one of the more complete papers and placed it on an overhead projector to show it to the class. They then proceeded to edit the paper together and to clarify the requirements of the paper called for in the module. The balance of the class was used to write more drafts and to revise those already turned in.

Writing Samples. Three *unedited* examples of limited-English-proficient students writing in their second language follow. Despite the many mistakes, writing these essays created exceptional opportunities for teaching that otherwise would not have existed in this classroom.

Student A:
The people in my community think that being bilingual is bery important for several good reasons. Firts, I felt very proud doing the Survey. the people in our commuinity feel very proud at them self that they speak Spanish and Eanglish because they can talk with there friends in any of those two lenguages. Secondly, the people I ask Some were bilingual students and adults 60% were bilingual people and 40% weren't bilingual people. Also, I ask a teacher and a student if they would be willing to work as a bilingual person and they said no and then I ask a Student this qiestion Do you think Speaking Another lenguage is important and he said no that amazed me because I never herd one person that thinks that speaking another lenguage ain't important. finally, I ask a teacher that What career was he interested in that would require a 2nd language and he said no common and he told this I don't know What lauguage I'm interestes that would require a 2nd lenguage because I don't know it and I ask two Students this question what career are yo interested in that would require a 2nd lenguage and 50% said Fransh 10% said Germen 10% said Italian and 20% said no coman as you can see I was having fun.

Student B:
I found that people in our community feel good about belingualism for several good reasons. They think it is very important because they can communicate with other people. The people I asked are 60% students, 40% adults, 70% are Spanish speakers, 20% were English speakers, 70% can write and read English, 20% can write and read Spanish well. Most of the people told me that in there house can speak English and Spanish. The people I ask the questions, answers me very polite and they said the questions were very interesting. Some person said that these project was very good for me and interesting for him. when he said that I feel very good about the work I was doing. The most interesting thing that I found wat that the people like the project. Most of the people said that they were willing to take classes to become totally belingual because it could help them right now and in the future. The students I ask said that they have only friends that speak only Spanish and English not othey language. The adults I ask said that been belingual is very important for them because they can communicate with more people and they can have more opportunities for some jobs that othey people do I feel very good about the way people answer me.

Student C:
First, In my school, I asked some students and aduls. If they are bilinguals, some people are bilingual and someones are not in my school. Some of them tall me they are bilinguals. somea——they're not bilinguals about the 50%. Seconly, In my community some people is don't intersting about to be bilingual because they think, they don't need toher lenguage because they are in America and in America only speak English. Thirth, I don't felt good, because I think they are a little dum people because they think to be a bilingual person is waste them time. Also, I think the people who's don't interesting to be them selfs bilingual are going to the wrong way because the persons

who speak two languages or more have the opportunity to know other culture and lenguages or more have the opportunity to know other culture and lenguage. Finaly, In my family think to be a bilingual is to important because they learn other culture and language, And we speak spanish and we need speak English because we live in the U.S.A. but like in diferent countries is important to know other lnguages for we can talk with other persons.

This ESL teacher, as did other teachers, used formula paragraphs to get the student to write. Most felt, and we agreed, that the added structure facilitated participation and performance in writing activities that the students otherwise could not have done because of their oral language limitations. Of course, as students gained fluency in English the teacher moved them away from the tight structure of the formula paragraphs toward greater flexible and independent writing.

This module illustrates the idea of creating zones of proximal development for writing. The goal was to motivate shifts in the control of the task from teacher to student. A major role of the teacher was to capitalize on those skills that the students had developed in their first language and put them to good use in the service of academic goals in their second language. In the "regular" classrooms, prewriting, free writing, and response groups were combined in several ways to get the students actively engaged in writing as well as being prepared for more advanced efforts. In the ESL classrooms the same strategies were used to bring into the classroom the students' experiences and skills, and the formula paragraphs were used as the "crutch" to get and keep the students on task. Obviously, the students' difficulties in English verbal expression, reading, and vocabulary development needed remedy, but the "trick" was to organize lessons in ways that accommodated these difficulties and minimized their constraining influence while, at the same time, maximizing the use of the resources that the students did possess such as knowledge of the topic and other experiences. These three examples show that this goal was being accomplished: Students who would otherwise have done little or no classroom writing, wrote essays in their second language that incorporated information collected from the community as resources for the production of text.

DISCUSSION

Our results strongly suggest that for ethnographic research to be pedagogically useful it must provoke critical analysis and reorganization of classroom instruction. Although we started the project committed to the principled importation of community data into classrooms, we did not anticipate how much our use of field information would depend upon constraints imposed by the way instruction took place. Generally, most classrooms are structured in ways that *do not* facilitate experimentation and change; the conditions for change have to be created as part of the ethnographic enterprise. During the course of this project, we spent much time preparing the classrooms to interact with the ethnographic information—opening the door, so to speak, for the ethnography to have some effect. Doing so convinced us that without a strong theory of what constitutes effective instruction, ethnographic observations are very difficult to link in any useful way to practice.

Instructional change may occur in several ways. In our experience, it started by making the researchers, and through the researchers, the teachers, aware of the importance of explicitly shaping instruction through the social issues identified by the ethnographic interviews and observations. The introduction of these issues into lessons and their exploration in writing qualitatively changed the conditions for writing: It changed both the goals of writing and the means of writing. In so doing, it involved the teachers and students in a different kind of educational activity in which writing functioned properly in its role as a tool of the intellect in the service of social and academic goals. In this context, prewriting discussions acquired new meaning; they became "thick descriptions" that supported entry of student goals, experiences, and opinions into the activity of writing. As changes in the students' writing occurred, motivation and interest in writing increased.

In addition to classroom-specific factors, our "insider" status in the community helped to determine what we identified as relevant data for classroom use; that is, our insiders' perspective led to our emphasis on the social realities of the community and the content of the families' interactions as the critical source for writing activities. We did not find any literacy practices specific to "Chicanos," or for that matter, document any social conventions similar to the Hawaiian talk story or to Heath's forms of questioning. Furthermore, even if we had spent our time documenting a specific sociolinguistic event, it is unclear, given the classroom characteristics and parental concerns about academic achievement, whether such data would have become "credible" information for our English monolingual teachers to use in their classrooms. We are not arguing against the usefulness of sociolinguistic data; we are merely stating that because of this study's constraints and characteristics, we found it more profitable to focus on social content to organize writing activities. In other words, the classroom and community realities we encountered dictated what counted as data for classroom application.

But how we went about studying those realities also influenced what information we identified as relevant. For example, our decision to establish a field office in the community had very practical consequences for the study. Centralizing our efforts facilitated interactions between the people conducting the field study and the teachers responsible for taking the information generated by the field study and making sense of it through their teaching. These interactions, in turn, caused the two project components to become part of a single, unified teaching/research activity: It became difficult to view the field research activities independent of the classroom realities, and, conversely, to view the classroom teaching independent of the community needs and issues. This empirical link between field ethnography and classroom teaching shaped the nature of the research procedures and the nature of the findings.

As others have reported (e.g., Cazden, 1983), the key activity in this link between ethnography and classroom practice turned out to be teachers assuming the role of researchers. This research role went beyond viewing teachers as research subjects or, at best, as research consumers, and instead viewed teachers as full-fledged research collaborators (cf. Heath, 1983; Florio & Walsh, 1981). We accomplished this adaptation in roles by purposely creating conditions favorable to involving teachers in all aspects of the research. Particularly important, we believe, was getting teachers to write as part of their research responsibilities. All teachers involved in the project regularly collected and submitted field notes on their teaching. Writing field notes produced two important results: It helped teachers to analyze how they were organizing instruction to achieve specific writing goals, and through the analysis of their notes, to evaluate the effectiveness of their teaching. As the project progressed, the teachers became consciously aware of changes in the social organization of their lessons. Examining data that they collected on themselves in action demonstrated to the teachers in a very convincing way that they could, indeed, teach writing effectively, that their students could, indeed, develop their writing skills, and that there were numerous resources in both the classroom and the community which they could use to enhance their teaching. We should mention that one other consequence of requiring field notes was that it made teachers write while they tried to teach writing. It may well be that to teach writing effectively teachers must write along with their students.

Each new writing module created more favorable classroom conditions for exploring how to capitalize further on the ethnographic findings. We discovered, as Heath (1981) did, the need to make writing instruction more ethnographic as part of our basic research problem. This strategy of research/instruction makes writing a process that included exploration, discovery, and the critical analysis of social life. The consequence of this strategy is that it fosters mastery of writing as communication. As such, we believe that schools can make strategic use of the fact that classroom activities mediate the relationship between the school and the community. A strategy that builds on this mediating aspect of classroom activities has several advantages. It builds transfer of community information into a broad range of writing activities. It also can build transfer of school (writing) activities into a broad range of social encounters. We argue that this is achievable using extant classroom resources. What is needed is an orientation to the relevance of social life for learning and a system of writing instruction (interactions) that permits continual contact with the real world.

Along these lines, during the final modules we developed a plan that would help turn the teaching strategies that were introduced during the initial modules into a theory-driven system that could be adapted to different writing activities. A higher-order goal of this system, one that would help organize the purpose and process of writing, was to use community practices discovered through the ethnography in the service of teaching. As one way to extend this generalizing strategy, we attempted to include as part of one of the modules a homework assignment that would bring parents or other community members into the classroom writing system. We purposely chose a homework assignment as the vehicle because of field reports identifying homework as an important family literacy event. The idea was to have the students collect information from their elders about a specific topic and then use this information to increase the students' and teachers' knowledge about the topic. The homework assignment served as one of the mediating steps to writing and illustrated the utility of extracurricular sources for the development of writing to both teachers and students. In this way, homework (i.e., the survey research) was not an end in itself and quickly forgotten but an activity that could be repeated often to enhance the students' writing and to help the teacher explore the world outside the classroom to uncover resources to improve instruction. This ethnographically influenced writing activity provided the teachers and students with something important to communicate about while maintaining the academic orientation of the lessons.

Nevertheless, establishing community and student concerns as objects of study is, by itself, insufficient to provoke writing development. It may help orient teachers and students to the importance of going beyond the classroom make writing relevant and effective, but instruction still has to be organized insofar as writing is going to be a means to achieve this goal. This is where the concept of a zone of proximal development is of major utility. It provides an interactional frame to turn classroom writing into communicative activities that not only address social issues but into which we can embed the basic writing skills the teachers were interested in teaching. In the example with limited-English-speaking students, the students were required to interview adults and other children regarding their views on bilingualism. This information was needed to expand a paper written by the students in the preceding module by including additional details not immediately available within the classroom. The activity of collecting extra curricular information for use in writing was clearly an advanced task for secondary school students, regardless of English-language proficiency. However, this task could be accomplished with the assistance of more knowledgeable persons, in this instance, the teacher and parents. The teacher could "bridge the distance" between what the students were able to do individually and what the task required by providing them with strategic help to facilitate a capable performance at the higher levels.

The teacher in our example helped the students put together a questionnaire to structure data collection and gave them suggestions on how to gather data. Once the data were collected, she organized classroom discussions to assist the students in extracting relevant information and helped them include this information in their writing. This teaching activity is what we mean by aiming instruction at the proximal level. The goal of instruction was calibrated to be in advance of what the students were individually capable of doing. This proximal goal was established and achieved by linking instruction to the real world through ethnography and by providing students the instructional support necessary to perform at the highest levels possible. The theory predicts that with practice the students will appropriate this help and eventually perform what was previously an overwhelming task, independently and competently. It is this interaction between the organization of instruction and the social world that holds promise for developing effective academic writing programs for students such as those in our study: students who, from the point of view of the school, appear to have overwhelming constraints which restrict their ability and opportunities to write. The results of this study proved otherwise.

REFERENCES

Applebee, A.N. (1981). *Writing in the secondary school: English and the content areas.* Urbana, IL: National Council of Teachers of English.

Au, K.H. (1980). Participation structures in reading lessons with Hawaiian children: Analysis of a culturally appropriate instructional event. *Anthropology and Education Quarterly, 11*(2), 91-115.

Cazden, C.B. (1981). Performance before competence: Assistance to child discourse in the zone of proximal development. *Quarterly Newsletter of the Laboratory of Comparative Human Cognition, 3*(1), 5-8.

Cazden, C.B. (1983). Can ethnographic research go beyond the status quo? *Anthropology & Education Quarterly, 14*(1), 33-41.

Cole, M., & Griffin, P. (1983). A socio-historical approach to re-mediation. *Quarterly Newsletter of the Laboratory of Comparative Human Cognition, 5*(4), 69-74.

Florio, S., & Walsh, M. (1981). The teacher as colleague in classroom research. In H. Trueba, G. Pung Guthrie, & K. H. Au (Eds.), *Culture and the bilingual classroom: Studies in classroom ethnography.* Rowley, MA: Newbury.

Frederiksen, C.H., & Dominic, J.F. (Eds.). (1981). *Writing: Vol. 2. Writing: Process, development and communication.* Hillsdale, NJ: Erlbaum.

Freire, P. (1970). *Cultural action for freedom* (Monograph No. 1). Cambridge, MA: Harvard Educational Review.

Graves, D. (1982, February). How do writers develop? *Language Arts, 59*(2), 173-179.

Graves, D.H. (1983). *Writing: Teachers and children at work.* Exeter, NH: Heinemann Educational Books.

Griffin, P., & Cole, M. (1984). Current activity for the future: The Zoped. In B. Rogoff & J.V. Wertsch (Eds.), *Children' learning in the "Zone of Proximal Development"* (pp. 45-64) (New directions for child development, no. 23), San Francisco: Jossey-Bass.

Heath, S.B. (1981). Toward an ethnohistory of writing in American education. In M.F. Whiteman (Ed.), *Writing: Vol. 1. Variation in writing: Functional and linguistic-cultural differences* (pp. 25-45. Hillsdale, NJ: Erlbaum.

Heath, S.B. (1982). Questioning at home and at school: A comparative study. In G. Sprindler (Ed.), *The ethnography of schooling: Educational anthropology in action* (pp. 102-131). New York: Holt, Rinehart & Winston.

Heath, S.B. (1983). *Ways with words: Ethnography of communication in communities and classrooms.* New York: Cambridge University Press.

Laboratory of Comparative Human Cognition. (1983). Culture and cognitive development. In W. Kessen (Ed.), *Mussen's handbook of child psychology: Vol. 1. History, theory, and method* (4th ed., pp. 295-356). New York: Wiley.

Leont'ev, A. (1973, Summer). Some problems in learning Russian as a foreign language (Essays on Psycholinguistics). *Soviet Psychology, 11*(4).

Moll, L.C., & Diaz, S. (in press). Bilingual communcation and reading: The importance of Spanish in learning to read in English. *Elementary School Journal.*

Nystrand, M. (1982). *What writers know: The language, process, and structure of written discourse.* New York: Academic Press.

Scollon, R., & Scollon, B. (1981). *Narrative literature and face in interethnic communication.* Norwood, NJ: Ablex.

Scribner, S., & Cole, M. (1981). *The psychology of literacy.* Cambridge: Harvard University Press.

Talyzina, N. (1981). *The psychology of learning.* Moscow, Soviet Union: Progress.

Tharp, R.G. (1982). The effective instruction of comprehension: Results and descriptions of the Kamehameha Early Education Program. *Reading Research Quarterly, 17*(4), 503-527.

Trueba, H., Moll, L.C., & Diaz, S. (1982). *Improving the functional writing of bilingual secondary school students* (contract No. 400-81-0023). Washington, DC: National Institute of Education.

Vygotsky, L.S. (1978). *Mind in society: The development of higher psychological processes* (M. Cole, V. John-Steiner, S. Scribner, & E. Souberman, Eds.). Cambridge: Harvard University Press.

Wertsch, J.V. (1979). *A state of the art review of Soviet research in cognitive psychology.* Unpublished manuscript, Department of Linguistics, Northwestern University.

Wertsch, J.V. (1985). *Vygotsky and the social formation of mind.* Cambridge: Harvard University Press.

Whiteman, M.F. (Ed.). (1981). *Writing: Vol. 1. Variation in writing: Functional and linguistic-cultural differences.* Hillsdale, NJ: Erlbaum.

PART FOUR

LITERACY AT SCHOOL AND AT WORK

10 Literacy at School and Literacy at Work

Barbara A. Hutson

Virginia Polytechnic Institute and State University

The major assumptions in this chapter are (a) that literacy at work differs in a number of ways from literacy at school; (b) that there is a discontinuity between literacy in school and literacy at work, both in practice and in research emphasis; (c) that research on literacy in school and on literacy at work can both be categorized in terms of a model of reader–text–task interaction within varying contexts; (d) that just as school-based literacy research has contributed to research and, to a limited extent, to practice in literacy at work, aspects of current research on literacy at work can contribute to study and practice in school-based literacy; and (e) that awareness of this research can help to diminish discontinuities between literacy at school and literacy at work and can enrich our vision of what students need to learn about literacy.

CHARACTERISTICS OF LITERACY AT WORK

The term *literacy* is sometimes used to include reading, writing, oral language, math, and other skills. The emphasis here will be on reading, although writing and oral language will occasionally be mentioned. Literacy can be used to refer to several types of reading which are appreciably different, though they share a number of features. Chall (1975) pointed out that "literacy covers a wide spectrum of capabilities—all the way from, say, being able to decipher a want ad in a newspaper to being able to enjoy a novel by Thomas Mann or read a scientific treatise with understanding" (p, 6).

Definitions of Literacy

One type of literacy often discussed is basic literacy. This places greatest emphasis on the lower levels of traditional academic literacy, with or without direct application to life tasks. Most definitions of basic literacy specify a grade equivalent or skill level, but the criterion differs from one source (and one historical period, as Fletcher, 1977, and Clifford, 1984, have noted) to another. Criteria have ranged from having the ability to write one's name to having a fourth-grade reading level, a sixth-grade level, a ninth-grade level, etc.

Academic literacy, including the higher levels of literacy (and especially literature) taught in school, is undoubtedly a useful acquisition. Academic literacy not only has intrinsic value but also has implications for work settings. For example, the human dynamics studied by major writers are broadly generalizable and the tactics that make an essay clear are also applicable and too seldom used in technical manuals. But the relevance is seldom apparent to students, and academic literacy development seldom deals with some of the types of reading encountered at work. Students who are well-trained for academic literacy may be narrowly trained for life.

Content area reading skills, now commonly taught in secondary schools, include a number of features helpful in literacy at work, but the tasks are very frequently read-and-remember-for-the-test. As Diehl and Mikulecky (1980) observed, "Reading at work and reading in school settings may be quite different from each other"; moreover, "the decontextualized nature of reading-to-learn tasks requires different cognitive processes than are required in reading-to-do tasks" on the job, which are often completed in "an information-rich context" (pp. 226–227). Even effective training in content area reading is unlikely to prepare students for many aspects of literacy on the job.

Perhaps the most confusing term in literacy is functional literacy. This term has three common meanings. One use is coextensive with the term basic literacy. A second use refers to those literacy skills needed to cope with daily life. Functional literacy in this sense has received considerable attention but is marginally relevant to this discussion, because, as typically defined (cf. Northcutt, Selz, Shelton, Nyer, Hickok, & Humble, 1975), it has emphasized nonacademic and largely nonjob-related applications. These include survival skills—reading the directions on aspirin bottles, filling out an application for a driver's license—usually the very lowest levels of reading, oral language, and math skills as they relate to coping with various tasks in adult life. For this, Kirsch and Guthrie (1977–1978) used the term "functional competency," arguing that it "should be kept distinct fro m functional literacy, which is a more inclusive concept. Literacy, whether general or functional, should not be used to represent skills or behaviors beyond those with printed materials" (p. 491). These authors also noted measurement problems, stating that "estimates of [functional] literacy vary as widely as the measures employed" (Kirsch & Guthrie, 1977–1978, p. 504).

The third common use of the term functional literacy is to refer to job-relevant literacy, including but not always limited to basic literacy. One reason for this extension of the meaning of functional literacy is the growing awareness that many jobs require more than basic literacy. Duffy (1977), for example, noted that though few Navy recruits lacked basic literacy, half had "a reading deficiency relative to their job-reading demands" (p. 34). Similarly, Fletcher (1977) commented that "despite the universal attainment of literacy by Navy personnel, some men (and women) may fail to perform because they do not read well enough to meet the requirements of their jobs; there may exist, in effect, a literacy gap" (p. 86). While the more complex literacy skills required for more technical jobs are just as functional as are the basic literacy skills required for unskilled jobs, the term functional literacy seems strained and subject to misinterpretation when used to refer to the more complex skills.

The Need for Advanced and Continuing Literacy Development

Mikulecky and Diehl (1980) examined the thesis that literacy demands are relative. That is, the degree (and perhaps the kinds) of reading skill sufficient for an unskilled job or even a narrowly specialized, repetitive skilled job (such as that of a welder on an assembly line) might be insufficient for a more highly skilled job or one with frequent changes of task or technology. In addition, Hutson and Stump (1980) pointed out that literacy adequate for one stage of a career may be inadequate for continuing job mobility. An upgrade to supervisor or manager may bring reading and writing demands not only greater in quantity but different in kind from those previously faced.

The reading demands during training or in preparation for licensure, on the other hand, may be greater than in the entry-level jobs attained following training. In fact, the report of the National Academy of Education's Task Force on Education and Employment (1979) suggested that in some cases licensure is made artificially difficult by reading demands that exceed those encountered on the job.

This contention is to some degree supported by Diehl and Mikulecky's (1980) interesting argument that "many of the literacy demands of a job are not really demands at all; rather, literacy materials are used, not so much out of necessity as because they make the job task easier or more efficient" (p. 224). Nonetheless, they reported that workers at various occupational levels read job materials on the job about 2 hours per day. (Miller, 1982, reported that workers in a high-tech industry spent a third to a half of their work week on job-related reading materials, which were both important and frustrating.) Mikulecky and Diehl stated that opportunities to use print are increasing as technology changes. Some users of technical materials might resist calling this experience an opportunity.

Kirsch and Guthrie (1977–1978, p. 504) also noted the differentiation of *kinds* of literacy demands in various occupational specialties. Guthrie (1982, p. 494) reported that, for many companies, basic skills included interpretation of flow charts, tables, diagrams, and ledgers. O'Donnell (1982) listed "instructions, specifications, codes, manuals, employee contracts, memoranda, occupational journals, employment notices, and the like" (p. 474). Thornton (1980) pointed out that these sources of difficulty were often present in training as well as on the job. The occupational training literature, he said, ranged in difficulty depending upon task, amount of technical vocabulary, complexity of sentence structure, use of diagrams, the ratio of language to diagrams, etc.

Elfenbein (1983) commented recently that "major advances in technology are beginning to affect virtually every office and factory job, making it increasingly necessary for employees to demonstrate higher levels of literacy for entry-level jobs and for job advancement . . . The use of new technology requires additional, more complex skills" (pp. 5–6). As Paul Delker (1983) pointed out:

> Functional literacy is a construct which is meaningful only in a specific societal context. A corollary of this is that, just as functional literacy is culture-bound, it is even more closely bound to the technological state of a particular society. The person who is functionally literate in one society may be illiterate in another. Furthermore, as technology changes, the requirements for competency, or literacy, change. (pp. 31–32)

Guthrie and Kirsch (1984), in fact, suggested that "As society becomes more complex—socially, economically, and technologically—the literacies that must be taught in schools will inevitably multiply" (p. 355). David Smith (1983, p. 1), discussing "the new—or newly discovered—illiterates," also stressed the human costs of social change. He introduced his thesis by stating that:

> The new unemployed are not the barely employable fringe—minorities, young people, and women. They are increasingly the highly unionized and consequently highly paid, blue-collar middle class. For many the only hope of good reemployment lies in the new high-tech industries. [Unfortunately,] they are unable to read or write well enough to do the necessary paper work for the job transfers or to take advantage of proffered training opportunities. (p. 1)

These concerns were underlined in a recent analysis of trends in the work place: "The growth of high technology industries will carry high costs in terms of skill obsolescence . . . Skill obsolescence and changing production processes will raise the need to retrain and relocate displaced workers" (American Council of Life Insurance, 1984). It seems appropriate to extend to job-related literacy the Task Force on Education and Employment's (1979) suggestion that "much of what is now taught to youths would appropriately be provided at later points in life" (p. 139).

Needs are not limited to those at lower job levels. Chall (1975) said that "the most persuasive argument for literacy is that an individual cannot fully participate in modern society unless he can read, and by this we mean reading at a rather high level of literacy" (p. 9).

Henry (1983), reporting results in a survey by the Center for Public Resources, noted frequent reports of skill deficiencies (relative to job demands) not only among secretarial, clerical, and service workers but among supervisory and managerial personnel. He also noted a discrepancy in ways the problem was viewed by the school and by industry, and suggested that "the problem is not one of poor teaching in the schools, but rather what is being taught, due to the communication gap between industry and schools" (Henry, 1983, pp. 23–24). Donald Mann (1983) of the Prudential Insurance Company pointed out that

> workers will not only have to be able to read, but read better . . . It's clear that we will be needing people who can read and write, who can do needed arithmetic and analysis. And we will need fewer of them, so we're going to concentrate on getting the best. (pp. 27–28)

Contrasting views on the value of literacy are surveyed by Clifford (1984).

The "slipperiness" of the definition of functional literacy, the lack of attention in basic or academic literacy to some of the special features of literacy encountered in technical occupations, and the increasing need for advanced and continuing job-related literacy urge more focused attention to technical literacy.

Features of Technical Literacy

The subset of literacy called technical literacy was defined in Hutson (1982) as *"skills and strategies required to learn and to use high-concept density material (in print or in other visual modes) during training or performance for skilled, semi-*

skilled or professional employment'' (p. 2). This same source also suggested that technical literacy and academic literacy were not dichotomous but differed in distribution of certain characteristics. That is, there are few features that are found exclusively in one of these fields, but some features are much more common in technical literacy than in academic literacy. These features of technical literacy include the following:

1. *Content:* The content of technical literacy is often unfamiliar, though occasionally numbingly repetitious.
2. *Format:* There is greater use of graphics, less use of unbroken blocks of text, and more use of typographic cues to the structure of content.
3. *Semantic structure of materials:* There is often high density of unfamiliar concepts, with little redundancy; the structure, however, is often signaled explicity.
4. *Task structure:* The purpose is reading to do or to evaluate more often than it is reading to learn; memory is less likely to be a limiting factor in early stages, because the reading is often done with the task materials in hand.
5. *Mode of delivery:* While hard copy (print on paper) will continue to be used, an increasing proportion of technical literacy will be delivered by means of computers.
6. *Resources:* There may be, in addition to text and graphics, other allowable sources of information (including asking someone or getting feedback from the nontext materials used in the task).
7. *Problem formulation:* In complex or difficult tasks or materials, the role of the technical reader is often setting the problem, selecting, coordinating, and evaluating information from all relevant sources rather than attempting to solve a problem set by someone else.
8. *Criterion:* The success of the job task rather than mastery of the reading process or content per se is what matters; the criterion for adequacy is relative to current job demands, career aspirations, and personal meanings of the task.

There seems to be a discrepancy between the types of literacy for which schools prepare students and the types of literacy they will need on the job or in job training or licensure preparation. In today's society, basic literacy will equip students to join the unemployment line, functional literacy will help them fill out the unemployment insurance application, and academic literacy will prepare them to entertain themselves while standing in the line.

Very bright students, if they are able to get a job or job training, are likely to be able to size up the technical literacy requirements and to organize their resources in order to meet those requirements. Very weak students are likely to have great difficulty getting into or surviving training for many of the technical jobs potentially available. In between, however, are many students who are likely to fare better, *if* they are given a hint about the nature of technical literacy and the skills required.

Research and practice in school-based literacy have generated some insights useful for studying and facilitating literacy at work. There is, however, a valuable body of research on literacy at work, too little known to most educators, that can guide efforts to provide greater continuity between school and work. In order to provide a perspective on similarities and dissimilarities of research on school-based and work-based literacy, the next section will present a framework useful for viewing work in both areas.

THE INTERACTION OF READER–TEXT–TASK IN VARYING CONTEXTS

In order to find the threads that unite or should unite literacy at school and literacy at work, it is useful to categorize research in both fields in terms of a framework of reader–text–task interaction within varying contexts. Figure 1 presents such a framework. The three central areas of focus are The Reader, The Text (which can include oral or graphic information as well as written verbal material), and The Task. Included under the cluster of reader factors are skills, abilities, background knowledge, attitudes, and concepts about the role of the reader. Aspects of the text include the topic, format, underlying ideational structure, technical vocabulary, text structure, readability, etc. Aspects of the task include purpose, input and response modes, cognitive processes required, degree to which the task is explicitly stated and the appropriate strategies signaled, the criteria applied, presence of task materials, etc.

These three areas, however, intersect, representing interactions between the central factors. The intersection representing interaction between reader and text suggests that a given reader may find one text or type of text considerably more difficult than another. For example, Mason and Kendall (1980) found that elementary school students tended to impose upon expository text the expectations appropriate to more familiar narrative structures. Similarly, reading Gothic novels has little transfer to reading auto parts guides or word processor manuals, though Thurber (1957) provided a unique example of the projection of one genre (murder mystery) upon an example of another (Macbeth).

The intersection of reader and task suggests that a given reader may find one kind of task (e.g., comprehension of substantive knowledge) more difficult than another (e.g., application of procedural knowledge). The implication is that it may be useful or necessary to train readers to adapt their reading strategies to the task demands. Clinical observation suggests that students who have comprehension problems despite adequate decoding skills often do not recognize the difference in task demands for literal and inferential comprehension tasks. They may also fail to note the differential demands of tasks that require recall of detail versus tasks that require memory for higher-level organization. While such readers succeed on some types of reading tasks, they may fail on others.

The intersection of text and task represents the fact that a particular text may be more effectively organized for one task than for another. For example, in Zen and the Art of Motorcycle Maintenance, Pirsig's (1974) description of the components

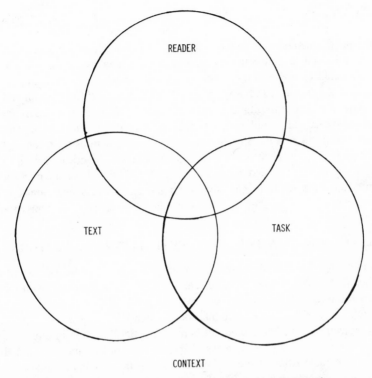

Figure 1. Framework of reader–text-task interaction.

and functions of a motorcycle is a piercingly clear explication of the relevant substantive knowledge. (The connotation of pain in my choice of the word "piercingly" is not unintentional—Pirsig's discussion is so absolutely clear that there is no room for negotiation of meaning—there is no need for me.) Yet this very clear text organization is not especially well designed for the procedural task of applying maintenance and repair procedures. On the other hand, another text might offer step-by-step, clear procedures without giving the user a sense of the overall structure, or a text might be designed to facilitate both kinds of tasks.

Any interaction of reader, text, and task, however, occurs in a distinct context that may affect the meanings and the outcomes of the literacy event. For example, the same student who lounged through reading assignments in school may snap to when comparable assignments are given during military or job training, especially if the reading-skill training and job-skill training are integrated or presented in functional contexts (Finch & Falls, 1981).

The chapters in this volume differed in emphasis on the three major factors, their interaction with one another and with the personal/social context. Several emphasized reader/text interaction, and Barr emphasized text/task interaction. Chapters such as those by Gilmore, Smith, Moll and Diaz, Barr, and Collins relate learning to its social context. These chapters represent a subset of the larger field of research on literacy at school. That larger field gives greater emphasis to characteristics of the reader such as content schema, story schema, metalinguistics, and metacomprehension, and to characteristics of the text such as readability or discourse structure. It also studies the interaction of reader and task, as in strategies for teaching students to use different approaches for various kinds of reading tasks (e.g., Hansen & Pearson, 1982; Raphael, 1980) or studies of differences in oral and written literacy in certain cultural groups (Tannen, 1982). That broader field of school-based literacy also studies the interaction of reader and text, as in Meyer's (1983) analysis of the relative difficulty of various text structures for readers of different ability levels. In recent years the context of school-based literacy has been more explicitly studied (cf. Bloome & Green, 1982). Although, as the next section documents, the work on technical literacy ranges across these same areas and in some cases has obvious parallels, it differs in relative emphasis on various aspects.

AREAS OF EMPHASIS IN STUDIES OF LITERACY AT WORK

The schematic used to describe studies of literacy at school can be used to categorize studies of literacy at work. This discussion will stress the three main factors more than the intersections and the context.

Although many of these topics are interlocking concepts, only a few of the more obvious connections will be pointed out here. Analytic dissection of any complex phenomenon loses some of the richness of the whole. For example, a given study might stress characteristics of literacy materials, but those materials interact with particular tasks carried out by a group of readers who have definable characteristics, all operating in a given context. Yet dissection of the whole may clarify the structural elements and interrelationships. It will be obvious that many of the reports cited here could be discussed under more than one category (and a few of them are); the arrangement here is in terms of major implications. Occasionally the distinction between school-based and work-based literacy is blurred, as in the work of Frederiksen and associates on components of reading; that study employed school-aged subjects but was funded by the Office of Naval Research as well as by the National Institute for Education because of its potential applicability to processing complex technical material.

The criterion for selection of studies mentioned in this section was potential applicability both in school and at work. Not all of the studies are *on* literacy, but they are all relevant *to* literacy. The attempt here was not to provide an exhaustive review of all relevant sources or an in-depth treatment of a few but to point to a number of interesting ideas, and, in some cases, to speculate on the applicability of these constructs to research and practice on literacy at school. It was sometimes necessary to focus on just one aspect of a complex study, and the wide span covered necessitated skimping on details. But then the reader who seeks out the primary sources and their cross-references will find enough details to expand each of these paragraphs into a chapter.

While some of these sources are available through the Documents Repository of selected libraries, other very attractive bodies of work are disseminated primarily to a small network of research contractors. Those persistent enough to master the literacy task of ordering such reports through National Technical Information Service will then probably experience delays, but since some of this work was designed to be several years ahead of its time, it will still be fresh when received.

Reader Characteristics

Obvious characteristics of the reader are reading ability and general mental ability, but measures need to be calibrated to fit the types of readers. For example, in groups of adults with very low reading ability and/or mental ability, standardized tests yielding reading grade levels and IQ scores are sensitive to important differences related to acquisition of basic literacy. In technical literacy, however, readers are more likely to range from low average to high in both reading and general mental functioning, and the measures appropriate for low-skilled readers may not tap differences at higher levels.

In reading at work, relevant characteristics of the reader are not so much decoding, common vocabulary, and literal comprehension as inferential comprehension, technical vocabulary, strategies for constructing meaning, and mental representations of text structure and the content of the reading. For these reasons, this section will deal, only too briefly, with inferential processes and with reader as thinker. Strategies will be discussed more fully as task demands.

Some of the most powerful research relevant to literacy at work has analyzed the nature of knowledge and the form in which it is held by the reader/worker. The core of this approach is well summarized by Glaser (in press):

> The focus on cognition makes salient the fact that human beings not only behave overtly in the course of performing their work, but also understand and have beliefs about what they are doing that influence their behavior and determine the adaptability of their performance. As they work on a task, they have certain knowledge, beliefs and understanding about it. This understanding influences the results of their work, how they control it, how they prevent errors, and how they predict what will result from the ways in which they perform.

The overlapping areas of research on problem solving, mental representation, and expert–novice differences have, I think, special implications for studying higher levels of reading that can bridge the gap between literacy at school and literacy at work.

The aspects of research on mental processing most pertinent to literacy at work have not all focused on reading per se and have as yet been examined relatively little in school-age students. In some cases, there are obvious parallels to or extensions of constructs more familiar in research and practice with younger readers, but even where this is not the case, these approaches have been selected because they have implications for analyzing and facilitating literacy in school. Discussed briefly here are problem solving (including problem representation and information search) and expert–novice differences as they apply to general gathering and organization of information through technical literacy. Also discussed are mental representations or schemata as they apply to expectations about the contents of literacy tasks.

One construct from research on adults that could well be applied and studied in school settings is the distinction between substantive knowledge (knowledge *about* a content domain) and procedural knowledge (knowledge of how to *apply* the content to carry out required procedures). This has implications for school settings, especially in monitoring the match between instruction and evaluation. Among the procedures taught (or at least tested) in schools are not only vocational skills and lab procedures but academic tasks such as organization of research papers. There is need, I think, to consider (a) whether there are instructional methods to help the learner move from knowing to doing; and (b) whether instruction is well chosen in light of the desire for substantive or procedural learning and well matched to evaluation.

A major source of understandings applicable to technical literacy is the field of problem solving. Hayes (1981), building on earlier work by Newell and Simon, suggested that the characteristic phases in problem solving are:

1. Finding the Problem: recognizing that there is a problem to be solved.
2. Representing the Problem: understanding the nature of the gap to be crossed.
3. Planning the Solution: choosing a method for crossing the gap.
4. Carrying Out the Plan.
5. Evaluating the Solution: asking "How good is the result?" once the plan is carried out.
6. Consolidating Gains: learning from the experience of solving. (p. 1)

Aspects of problem solving deserving special attention include problem representation and information search (primarily an aspect of carrying out the plan). Reading strategies such as inferential comprehension involve planning and carrying out the solution. Self-monitoring of learning, which has been better studied in school than at work, is a form of evaluation, carried out recursively.

While an external representation of the problem, such as the matrices or diagrams discussed later, can be helpful, Hayes (1981) stated that such external representations *"can't help us at all unless we also have an* [adequate] *internal representation of the problem"* (p. 3). Forming an internal representation involves an active process of selecting information from, adding information to, and interpreting information in the problem as presented. The overall picture of the task thus gained influences the strategies used and the information selected. The problem representation can be clarified or modified as an individual works through a problem.

One of the other approaches to problem solving is that of Anderson, Greeno, Kline, and Neves (1980), who suggested, "The outcome of learning is a schema that provides a structure for understanding a problem situation in general terms, as well as guiding problem-solving performance" (p. 12). A schema thus provides a framework with slots for organizing information, procedures to be performed, and context clues that signal how and when the schema can be applied in various contexts. The learner, whether human or computer, can learn to generalize a schema to a new problem domain, add new structure to an existing schema, and synthesize a simple schema into a more complex or comprehensive one. Anderson et al. (1980) also suggested that learners often apply declarative knowledge (substantive knowledge) slowly and fragmentarily at first, but that with repeated use this gradually develops into smooth, automatic procedural knowledge. Although their work was based on a specific domain (geometry), a small number of students, and a computer simulation, I believe some aspects of this work are highly relevant to understanding and facilitating literacy.

The term *problem representation* is sometimes used to refer to the problem *structure;* it may also be used to include understandings about the *content* of the problem. Another term, used primarily to refer to the content (not always in problem-solving contexts) is *mental representation,* which might be equated to schema (Gentner & Stevens, 1982). A mental representation, if accurate and sufficiently detailed, can facilitate comprehension or work, but if, inaccurate or sketchy, can lead to systematic errors. Examples of the application of such an approach are Kieras and Bovair's (1983) study of the role of a mental model in working a control panel and work by Brown and Burton (1980) and by Van Lehn (1982) on systematic and less systematic errors in math. The approach is also applicable to problems in technical literacy.

Experts have not just more knowledge but better structured problem representations—quickly sizing up the nature of the problem. In contrast, novices have incomplete and less well-organized knowledge structures (Chi, Glaser, & Rees, 1981). While novices tend to focus on the objects in a situation, experts organize their understandings around basic principles. In addition, once experts hit upon an appropriate problem representation, that suggests potential solutions, procedures to apply, and conditions under which these procedures are appropriate. Not all novices, however, will become experts.

Larkin's research emphasizes the importance of the way in which people represent to themselves the problem to be solved. While Larkin's work has usually emphasized expert–novice differences in approach to content such as physics problems (e.g., Larkin, 1980), one recent study looked at problem-solving strategies used by experts and novices in reading physics text books. These readers differed, for example, in what they considered important information. Another example of the application of a problem-solving approach to literacy is Linda Flower's (1983) extension of her work on writing as problem solving (Flower & Hayes, 1980) to an examination of expert readers' problem-solving behaviors as they construct meaning from text plus their own prior knowledge.

Another aspect of problem solving, often influenced by problem representation, is information search. This topic has been studied in areas as diverse as medical diagnosis and electronic trouble-shooting. Stone and Hutson (1983, 1984) studied the information search aspect of problem solving in a job-related literacy task. Subjects, following directions in a computer-based job aid for assembling an object, touched a light pen to the screen to select any additional information. The frequency and patterning of requests for definitions, graphics, and rechecks of previous text were automatically recorded. This made it possible to reconstruct at least some aspects of the on-line problem-solving process.

Once an individual has gathered some information relevant to the problem representation, he or she needs to *do* something with it in the steps (frequently cyclical rather than sequential) Hayes described as planning the solution and carrying out the plan. A central aspect of these steps in any literacy task is the reader's skill in inferential comprehension. For text there are a number of approaches to analysis of inferential comprehension too complex to be presented briefly. One that should be mentioned, however, is the attempt by Frederiksen, Weaver, Warren, Gillotte, Rosebery, Freeman, and Goodman (1983) to develop computer games to train on component skills in reading. While interesting results have been reported, qualifications are necessary. First, although their most complex training task, Ski Jump, involved some degree of inference, it did not seem so demanding as most measures of inferential comprehension. Second, although their outcome measure of inference clearly required some inference, the measure also tapped some difficult logical and linguistic concepts, making interpretation precarious.

There is a more basic problem. Although generally applicable, most work on inferential comprehension has focused attention on carefully controlled information in the text plus information from the reader's prior experience, which may or may not have been explicitly activated. Yet in technical literacy at work, there are *multiple* sources of information, and it may be necessary to integrate and infer across these sources, responding to a problem less well defined. Under these circumstances inferential comprehension may need to be defined and operationalized more broadly. Most existing work on inferential comprehension would thus be viewed as definitive only for some subsets of literacy at work and suggestive for others.

One of the resources frequently available in technical material is graphics, which may include pictures, tables, flow charts, diagrams, etc. The impact of this information source, though, depends upon the reader's skill. As Kolers (1973) has noted, "Literacy is required for pictorial interpretation as much as it is for textual interpretation" (p. 40). Schallert (1980), suggested that "Pictures help the reader learn and comprehend a text when they illustrate information central to the text, when they represent new content that is important to the overall message, and when they depict structural relations mentioned in the text" (pp. 513–514). She reviewed several less overtly graphic tactics as well. Reviewing literature on pictures, concrete examples, and analogies, she concluded:

> All three of these elicit in the reader an internal representation of the way the concepts being learned are structurally related. Structural relations lend themselves to spatial representation, which in turn lends itself to illustration, whether internal (as in imagery) or external" (Schallert, 1980, pp. 512–513)

There are many similarities in the kinds of processing skills needed in interpreting text, graphics, and oral information.

A conceptualization of reading as problem solving within a context of multiple information sources and studies based upon it might resolve questions such as how some readers in the job setting are able to read materials that are several years above their reading level, while others with higher tested reading levels fail. For the moment it is enough to say that relevant characteristics of the reader considered at work include but extend beyond those usually considered in school settings. Implications of the kinds of research reviewed here are described by Glaser (in press):

> The strong assumption is that problem solving, comprehension, and learning are based on structural knowledge and that people continually try to understand and think about the new in terms of what they know. If this is indeed the case, then it seems best to teach such skills as solving problems, performing complex procedures, and correcting errors of understanding in terms of knowledge domains and concepts with which individuals are familiar.

Text Characteristics

The salient cues in any situation can be judged relative to a given task and criterion. In schools the literacy task is frequently independent comprehension and memory for verbal printed material. The relevant aspects of the text, most narrowly considered, are verbal information in the printed text and the organization of that information. A slightly broader view also takes into account the interaction of text and task characteristics or the interaction of text and reader characteristics, as in the reader's skills in and concepts about how to process text of a given kind.

At work the literacy task frequently serves a broader task such as application of a complex procedure to immediately present physical objects, satisfying some criteria of accuracy, efficiency, safety, and, perhaps, personal satisfaction. In such a task the relevant text characteristics include both the verbal and graphic components of printed materials. Auditory input and material in hand may also contribute information. Because the work setting often legitimizes seeking information from peers (an activity sometimes carried on sub rosa in schools, as Wilkinson and Spinelli, 1985, have documented) a full specification of the characteristics of the "text" available might include a description of such resources. Thus, given a broader definition of task, a broader range of text characteristics may deserve study.

Written Text. Much of the work on the effects of text structure familiar in school-based literacy (e.g., Meyer, 1983) has in fact employed adult subjects and technical materials, though the criteria have usually been comprehension and recall rather than application. That work, surveyed by Meyer, will not be repeated here.

One of the text features studied in both arenas is readability, which is often estimated by using measures of vocabulary difficulty and sentence length. Caylor, Sticht, Fox, and Ford (1973) developed the FORCAST system for assessing the readability of job-related reading materials such as those used in the military by cooks, repairmen, and supply clerks. Recognizing that such material often includes non-sentence text, and evaluating the benefits of various formulas, they based their formula on the number of one-syllable words and found that such a formula was reliable. When the FORCAST formula was applied to materials used in the Army for job training and for support on the job, Vineberg, Sticht, Taylor, and Caylor (1971) found that the readability (difficulty) of the materials was well above the level of reading skill in both low- and high-aptitude workers.

Harrison (1980, p. 133) noted that in Lunzer and Gardner's (1979) British study,

The Effective Use of Reading, the FORCAST formula was not highly correlated with readability formulas that included sentence length. He suggested, however, that FORCAST might be particularly helpful in assessing technical materials such as forms, which seldom contain conventional length sentences. Jacob (1982) reported that forms were the most common reading material in the job setting she studied.

It is recognized in technical literacy as in academic literacy that comprehensibility (cf. Curran, 1977) involves more than readability as it is usually operationally defined. Williams, Siegel, and Burkett (1974), for example, examined the comprehensibility of training materials in the Air Force. They attempted to go beyond "mechanical readability factors" to reflect "what the text forces to happen inside a reader's head" (Siegel, 1976, p. 205).

Kieras (1978) examined characteristics of technical materials. He found, for example, that when the topic sentence was deleted from a paragraph or when a paragraph contained more than one topic, reading time increased. Later studies (Kieras, 1979) examined other factors that affect the difficulty of inferring the macrostructure (i.e., judging from the individual sentences what the larger passage is about).

Smith and Goodman's (1983) work on understanding and executing instructions is also pertinent. Among the steps of a trouble-shooting task, those containing more propositions (idea units) took longer to read, and those propositions that specified an action to be taken were recalled better than those that either identified an object or described its location.

It may be that for task-embedded literacy the real criterion should be *usability,* which overlaps but is not limited to comprehensibility. The information may be understandable yet inefficient to use, scattering critical information across several sources or camouflaging it in dense prose. The construct of usability is discussed and illustrated by Kern (1976). *Simply Stated in Business,* the newsletter of the Document Design Center, August 1984, provided a consumer-oriented checklist for battered consumers to consult in assessing the expected usability of any technical manual ("Before You Buy," 1984). Their final criterion was "Did perusing the manual increase your confidence in yourself as an intelligent human being?" In looking at texts in school, it may be useful to consider "What will the student be asked to *do* with this information?" and to evaluate potential difficulty of the text in terms of the intended use.

Suggestions for improving technical writing range from consideration of typography (Marcus, 1984; Rehe, 1974) to consideration of rhetorical issues such as purpose and reader's probable knowledge base (Sorrentino, 1985). Relatively few of the suggestions, however, are based on research, and it is quite difficult to study the simultaneous, possibly interactive, effects of many aspects of technical text.

The importance of increasing the readability/comprehensibility/usability of technical text is brought home every day to those who must use manuals such as those for complex software. There is increasing recognition by industry of this problem and opportunity. This is reflected, for example, in General Electric's recent series of more readable manuals for home repair of appliances, which appears to have the commercial advantage of inducing consumers to buy replacement parts, or IBM's attempts to design manuals for less technically sophisticated users. (See also the discussion by McDonnell, Osburn, and Hutson, 1983, of *expected* comprehensibility/usability of technical materials as a factor in purchase of expensive technology.) Computer manuals can be made more usable by organizing them around what the user must do rather than around a description of the system. This is a distinction between materials designed to facilitate procedural knowledge and materials designed to facilitate substantive knowledge. Similar issues in design of user-oriented manuals are discussed by Burkett (1976) and by Kern (1976; in press).

The economic importance of usable manuals is underlined by the increasing attention to documentation in reviews of computer hardware and software. :The January 1985 issue of *Creative Computing,* for example, used phrases ranging from "confusing," "inadequate," or "inconsistent" to "designed in a logical and consistent fashion" in describing product manuals.

One of the most demanding uses of technical materials recently discussed was in training purchasers' employees to program industrial robots to perform complex tasks. Gorman and Oltrogge (1984) of American Robot Corporation reported that while complex reference documentation and expert instruction for a few users at a given site were important, this was best integrated with the provision of simpler documentation designed for novices. They reported that "documentation aimed at the novice does pay off . . . Because of novice documentation, the novices (and the success of our strategy to reduce training costs) do not have to depend entirely on the availability of the on-site experts or the experts' patience and ability to answer questions" (Gorman & Oltrogge, 1984, p. 2).

Although the other text features to be discussed here undoubtedly have impact (which may vary in potency depending on the task), it seems likely that in most applications a central characteristic of the text will continue to be the clarity and organization of written information and its match to the reader's purpose and prior knowledge.

Oral Input. When adults in job settings read poorly or when it would be awkward to read, presentation of technical information orally is an alternative to be considered. The supply of qualified candidates for armed forces training has fluctuated with the economy, the total manpower pool, and military manpower requirements (Fletcher, 1977). During one low period, 100,000 men with lower than usual scores were admitted. One of the areas explored was the oral transmission of information. Sticht (1972) reported, however, that men with low reading levels "may learn equally [as] poorly by listening as by reading" and that "what can be comprehended by listening sets a limit to what can be comprehended by reading" (pp. 288, 294). The effect of compressed speech as a substitute for reading was assessed. High-aptitude subjects could comprehend at all rates of speech tested. The low-aptitude subjects could comprehend easy materials (5th-grade readability) at slow rates, but comprehension decreased even for these materials as speed increased, and for difficult materials their comprehension did not exceed 20% at any rate of speech. The Air Force also explored the usefulness of presenting information orally, in this case *supplementing* written text with oral material presented through headsets. Burkett (1976, p. 204), however, listed a number of qualifications to the effects of this approach, many of which made it appear less useful for moderate to high-skilled readers dealing with technical text.

A different approach to oral input was taken by Kern and colleagues (Kern, in press) based on their study of technical manuals and their use. They studied "task-extrinsic information sources" including seeking information both from manuals and from other workers by mechanics during maintenance activities. This information search appears to interact both with prior experience and with workers' ability to recognize their *need* for information. Close observation and interviews revealed that much of the information search

> represented an attempt to resolve the discrepancy between their expectations and the observed effect of their action. For example, mechanics described the observed effect, however well or poorly articulated, to another person and these two proceeded interactively to interrogate one another in an effort to identify the problem and a solution. (Kern, in press)

Even oral communication has hazards. Levin and Kareev (1980) described group problem solving by children in a computer club:

> There are sometimes "helping problems" in which the helper and the help seeker miscommunicate about the problem because each is conceptualizing the task in a different way. Then they have to solve jointly this meta-problem, renegotiating the ways to think about the situation, before helping can proceed. (p. 52)

Similar mutual oral problem solving may be observed in truckers exchanging directions on CB, computer bulletin boards, or dissertation advisement sessions, so work along these lines has the potential for broad applicability.

The frequent mention of oral information seeking on the job raises the question of why schools offer so little help to students in doing this *well*. The available research, though, makes it clear both that formal or informal oral information transmission is no panacea and that its interpretation shares many cognitive characteristics with interpretation of text and graphics.

Graphic Information. The importance of graphics as an element of reading material at work is underlined by Mikulecky and Diehl's (1980) finding that 33% of the material reportedly used at work was graphic. Graphic information has been extensively used in the design of job aids, which may be used in training but are primarily designed to assist workers in performing on the job, frequently in procedural tasks or in rapid information retrieval. (For useful reviews of earlier developments in this field, see Burkett, 1976; Kern, 1976).

One of the considerations in design of user-oriented manuals is that technical illustrations be closely integrated with succinct text. Stone and colleagues analyzed the information content of technical illustrations and designed verbal text with the same discourse structure. Subjects followed directions for a procedural task (assembly of a model loading cart) presented as text, graphics, or a combination. Although the directions were designed to be clear, Stone and Glock (1981) reported that 60 of the 90 subjects made uncorrected errors in assembling the cart. Subjects who viewed both text and illustrations, however, made far fewer errors than those who saw either text only or illustrations only.

A later series of studies (Stone & Hutson, 1983, 1984; Stone, Hutson, & Fortune, 1983) presented a computer-assisted job aid for the same procedural task with the set of core directions supplemented by a rich variety of optional verbal and graphic information, instantly available if the user touched the screen. Task performance was considerably better than in other studies using the same instructions and materials but without the Hypertext feature of hierarchical organization of supplemental information, combined with a high degree of learner control of the mode and amount of supplemental information.

Confirmation was inadvertently provided by Schorr and Glock (1983) who used the same task and materials and basically the same verbal and graphic text but without the Hypertext organization of supplemental information. They modified both verbal and graphic text slightly to provide more explicit procedural (how-to) information. Although these authors found that users of explicit operational information made fewer construction errors than users of the original text, errors were still substantially higher than in the computer-based Hypertext display used in the Stone and Hutson studies. Mudrick and Hutson (1984) raised the possibility that the advantage of the Hypertext arrangement of verbal and graphic information in computer-based job aiding is that it provides a *balance* between *program control* of the *core* information and *user control* of the *supplemental* information. The notion of balance seems worth further examination.

Bieger and Glock (1982) examined effects not only for mode (text vs. graphics) but for type of information displayed. They studied communication of spatial, contextual, and operational information in both text and graphics. When subjects constructing a felt wall hanging had only operational (process) information, the mean score was 19 errors per subject. Reanalysis of their tables shows that when both operational and contextual information were provided, either in text or in graphic form, mean errors were reduced, to a range of 13–15. And when both operational and spatial information were provided, either in text or in graphics, mean errors were sharply reduced, to one or less. A very similar pattern was found for assembling a model loading cart.

While these studies presented graphics to the reader, it is also possible for a reader to turn verbal text into graphic representations. Schwartz (1971) pointed out the advantages but noted that readers seldom spontaneously use matrices. Sticht (1977) trained readers to transform verbal text into graphic formats, and found that skill in such representation increased with reading ability. He pointed out that spatial displays of written text made it easier to guide attention and show relationships between features.

Geva (1981) had first-year community college students transform a verbal representation of meaning into a graphic representation of at least the higher levels of that meaning structure. Readers, given expository text, were trained to create treelike flow charts to depict the hierarchical relationships between major propositions and some of their relations to the passage and to other propositions. The study attempted to teach students "to uncover text structure. In other words, it was expected that students would learn to apply a top–down, cyclical, framework-seeking approach when they read a variety of texts" (Geva, 1981, p. 7). This was achieved through various tasks including identifying the conjunctions and noting their role in signaling logical structure. There were significant increases in comprehension, and, especially in awareness of higher-level text structure.

Another approach to transforming verbal text into a graphic form was developed by Dansereau, McDonald, Collins, Garland, Holley, Diekhoff, and Evans (1979). Networking was one of the primary strategies for understanding complex text in a learning strategy system called MURDER (moodsetting, understanding, recall, digest, expand, and review). As in Geva's flow charting, readers were trained to transform text into a graphic representation. Where Geva emphasized depicting hierarchically *what* was related to what, however, Dansereau et al. (1979) emphasized depicting *how* ideas were related, using different symbols for different types of relationships or links in a network map: "The networking process emphasizes the identification and representation of hierarchies (type-part), chains (lines of reasoning-temporal orderings-causal sequences) and clusters (characteristics-definitions-analogies)" (p. 9). It was difficult to evaluate the effect of this procedure, both because the tests at various points were apparently not equal in difficulty and because this complex strategy was only part of a still more complex learning system. Nonetheless, it represents one interesting alternative either for the design of learning tasks or materials or for modifying readers' strategies for processing complex verbal or graphic text.

Armbruster and Anderson (1982), applying notions of content schema (a reader's organized knowledge of the world) and text structure, developed a simple approach to analysis of text, adaptable to graphic presentation of information. They started from the assumption that much of the substance of content area texts can be "formulated in a relatively small number of generic structures or generalized plots [frames], each with a set of content categories [slots]" (Armbruster & Anderson, 1982, pp. 3–4). The two major types of story grammars considered for history texts were goal frames and problem/solution frames. A "frame map" was used to analyze excerpts from history texts into the slots labeled goal, plan, action, and outcome, depicted as a chain of boxes. Although this approach was developed primarily to guide evaluation and writing of text, Armbruster and Anderson suggested that it could also aid learning by providing students with purposes for reading and guides for self-monitoring of comprehension.

It is not clear whether these authors intended students to use frame-slot questions or actual graphic frames, but the general approach is adaptable to presentation of information in a way that guides development of strategies for processing text in work settings. The strategy, in fact, overlaps with those used in job performance aids. Other graphic procedures are among the formats that Berry (1982) described for aiding users in following procedures. Among the formats she discussed were decision trees and decision logic tables. Berry analyzed relative advantages of various formats for different tasks.

When text is even more "intense," with complex logical (conditional) relations such as those needed in filling out many legal forms, flow charting may be even more important. The article "If you write or use erasers and drive to work daily or sometimes have headaches . . . then read this . . . maybe" (1982) cites Holland and Rose as recommending that flow charts (after training) be used for especially difficult instructions and that prose questions be used to guide users through simpler series of directions. Earlier work by Wright and Reid (1973) explored similar tactics. Schwartz and Fattaleh (1972), presenting a different type of problem in the form of sentences, networks, or matrices, found matrices to be especially helpful.

Interactions of Text and Task. In addition to effects for text characteristics, there may be effects for the interaction of text characteristics and task characteristics. This is true not only for the verbal aspects of text but for the graphic aspects and their integration with verbal aspects. Kern (1976), discussing and illustrating the need for user-oriented or performance-oriented technical manuals, reviewed literature on this topic and offered concrete criteria by which to gauge the usability of printed material relative to a given task. Among the criteria were the ease of comprehending specific procedures and the ease of transforming information or procedural directions to the form required to aid task performance. Rogers and Thorne (1975), for example, reported that technicians using a trouble-shooting manual designed to meet such criteria performed noticeably better and faster than those using standard materials.

Siegel (1976) pointed out, however, that while text may be comprehensible yet hard to use, a text-based job aid may be quite useful in a given operational context, even if low on comprehensibility, if the text is supplemented by other features in the environment. He stated that comprehensibility and utility (usability) should not be confused.

Schorr and Glock (1983) found that making procedural details more explicit in text and graphics aided performance on a procedural task. On the other hand, provision of procedural details alone is not optimal. Kieras and Bovair (1983) found that performance on a complex procedural task was better if preceded by mastery of a mental representation (in this case, a schematic of the working of a control panel) than when rote training alone was provided. Similarly, Smith and Goodman (1983) have been examining the benefits of organizing instructions not linearly but hierarchically, thus providing a *reason* for the procedural steps to be taken during assembly of an electric circuit.

In addition to the static graphics discussed here (see also Hutson, 1985), dynamic graphics such as use of a computer videodisc to simulate panel conditions before and after steps in a trainee's maintenance procedures (Katner, 1984) show great promise. The effect, however, might be considerably less for another type of task or on another criterion measure for the same task. For example, Schorr and Glock pointed out that while graphics improved general location and orientation in the object assembled, text (with or without graphics) reduced errors in fine detail such as omission of parts.

In describing potential benefits of multimedia presentations, Collins (in press) suggested that "we can render into voice what verbal description best transmits (e.g., reasons why, abstract ideas) and render into animation what visual description best transmits (e.g., processes and relations between components, concrete ideas.)"

It seems clear that graphics can, under some conditions, contribute to comprehensibility and usability of technical materials. The effect of the graphics may vary, though, depending on the task (the type of information to be grasped and the use to be made of it) and perhaps on the user's experience with the content or format as well as his/her inferential ability and preference for various learning modes. Difficulty of the verbal text may also be a factor—very easy text may not require graphic augmentation, though a graphic alternative format might be more efficient for some tasks.

In clarifying the effects of graphics it will be necessary to sort out some very different ways of using graphics. Among the options are to present material in graphic form, to train readers to decode graphically presented materials, to allow users to use graphic notations as they read (if they choose), to request (with no pretraining) that users transform verbal text into a specified graphic form, or to train them to transform text into specified graphic forms. This list does not even include the possibilities of transforming graphics into text, a useful strategy in writing.

Still more basic is the need to define "graphics." It might even be possible to define a rough continuum: unadorned verbal text with little hint of structure, verbal text with more explicitly signaled structure and highlights, visuo-spatially-arrayed verbal text such as charts and procedural checklists, simplified graphics or schematics, and complex technical illustrations. Along another dimension these same formats may range from full text forms (verbal or graphic) to those compressed forms in which the critical information has already been abstracted and highlighted for the users.

Task Characteristics

Task factors have been studied in literacy at work more often, and perhaps more imaginatively, than in studies of literacy at school. Many approaches emphasize differences in a task's purpose or cognitive demands or the effects of task conditions.

Purpose. A primary determinant of task demands is purpose. Bormuth (1975) pointed out that "people differ in the kinds of occupational choices they make . . . Each of these pursuits involves different kinds of reading tasks and different amounts of reading" (p. 96).

The purposes of reading tasks encountered at work often differ from those encountered at school. In addition to reading to learn, the task most common in school, job-based literacy often includes reading to do, with or without incidental learning. Sticht (1977), in fact, reported that this was the most common type of reading on the job. Examples include reading the directions for maintenance and repair of vehicles or safety procedures in nuclear power plants. Mikulecky and Diehl (1980) also included a category of reading to evaluate, which they defined as involving "strategies aimed at quickly going through material in order to reach decisions about its use" (p. 84). They found that this category accounted for 25% of the reported purposes of reading at work.

Some of these functions of reading may be more common in school-based reading than is usually recognized. For instance, reading the directions for assignments is a form of reading to do, and effective readers learn to survey the text and to listen during lectures for cues that help them anticipate what material is likely to be included on exams, a form of reading to evaluate. Nonetheless, these other types of reading tasks are more common on the job than in school.

Because reading at work is seen as an adjunct to the job, reading skill can be evaluated relative to the job's literacy demands (Mikulecky & Diehl, 1980). Bormuth (1975) suggested that we "think in terms of models that regard a person as literate when he can perform well enough to obtain the maximum value from the materials he needs to read" (p. 98). This notion applies in school settings as well. A student who can read relatively brief text selections (and longer selections are seldom included on standardized tests) may use strategies that break down in longer selections, and the student who has adequate command of language for personal communication may lack guiding concepts for gathering and organizing research papers. The "jobs" are different, and the level or kind of skill observed in one school-based literacy task may be inadequate in another. There are many students (and not a few teachers) who lack clear concepts of the differences in demands from task to task.

The criterion for technical literacy tasks is not comprehension per se but the ability to gain the information needed to get the job done, at least effectively, and perhaps efficiently. Duffy (1977), overviewing literacy efforts in the Navy, stated that

> The goal is not to produce more literate men, but rather to give them the skills necessary to effectively perform the reading tasks required of them in the service. These skills involve an ability to find information readily in manuals, to read and comprehend procedural directions and instructions, to determine the relative importance of information on a system, etc. The vocabulary requirements and the reading strategy required in these tasks differ considerably from the requirements in general literacy. (p. 144)

In response to this same need, Sticht and colleagues at HumRRO developed for the Army a Functional Literacy program, which included three strands: (a) helping an individual apply existing skills to the types of tasks and materials that would be encountered on the job; (b) delivering direct instruction on both reading skills and job concepts; and (c) providing more practice and training in general reading (Sticht, Fox, Hauke, & Zapf, 1977). One version of this program was delivered before entry to military occupational specialty training and another was integrated with this training (Caylor, 1976). Although the functional literacy program was designed for trainees with lower reading levels, the general notion of training on job-relevant literacy tasks and of integrating such literacy training with job training has wide applicability.

An approach to studying the effect of task purpose is Antos and Bourne's (1982) study of reading for problem solving (which is a form of reading to do). They asked college freshmen and sophomores to read text containing facts about the value of stock in a hypothetical company, and assessed the kind of processing done when students were or were not asked to decide whether to buy a certain stock. They reported that, when reading for the explicit purpose of making decisions, subjects read the material at a deeper level of processing. This involved organizing facts into a coherent framework, thus recognizing (and remembering) discrepancies and resolving them in order to reach a decision. While competent readers adapt their processing to the demands of various reading tasks, others may need to be helped to assess task demands and to vary their strategies.

Even when individuals read the same materials, they sometimes read for different purposes. Miller (1982) found that "technical people read to analyze problems, propose solutions, and carry out research," while in the same organizaton "managers and supervisors read to review, advise, assign, develop organizational procedures and policy, and so on" (p. 112).

Task Conditions. Because reading at work usually serves as subcomponent in a larger task, reading often takes place in the midst of a task, with relevant materials in hand (Sticht, 1977, p. 235) and other sources of support in the environment. As Mikulecky and Diehl (1980) suggested: "Because most of the tasks involve the application of information to a particular job task, the job task itself provides a number of extralinguistic cues that help the reader in gaining information quickly and with a minimum of attention" (p. 61).

Baggett (1982) analyzed the ways in which learning technical vocabulary was affected by the task conditions. College students saw a film introducing the names and uses of pieces in a model. The narration was presented before, during, or after the visual presentation of a given piece. Recall of names and pieces was greatest when the visual presentation was synchronous with or a few seconds before the auditory presentation. One explanation Baggett offered for the benefit of presenting the visual first is that visual concepts are "bushy," permitting formation of more associations to them, while verbal concepts (that is, verbally presented concepts) are "skimpy," permitting relatively few new associations. Thus, she suggested that presenting the "bushier" concept first provides more branches to which the later-presented "skimpier" concept can be attached.

While more technical vocabulary and academic vocabulary is increasingly likely to be presented by means of technology that allows close control of the timing of visual and verbal presentations, it is probably too early to generalize widely the specific findings of this study. The proposed explanation, though, is provocative. It may be that the formulation as posed is too specific and that the broader principle is to call up first whatever type of concept the learner has most fully developed and then to present the new concept to be associated with the first. This notion is testable within a broad range of school settings as well as in work-based literacy tasks.

One relevant task condition may involve the contingencies for success or failure. Some young people in military or job training have stronger motivation to succeed or to avoid failure than they had in high school. If skills or strategies for a given literacy task are not well developed, however, the low probability of payoff is likely to diminish motivation for that task.

Another important task condition is the relevance and potency of feedback. Brown and Campione (in press) discussed this in the context of computer-delivered training at work:

> Computer technology has advanced to such an extent that it is already feasible to envisage simulated miniature job worlds in which the expert can teach and the novice practice and make errors with little cost. Novices can engage in *consequential tasks;* i.e., make moves and see the outcomes of those moves, before they are let loose in the work place. Such systems can also be programmed to present to the novice problem situations geared to their current level of understanding and modeled on common bugs or errors to provide realistic job-related experiences of a highly motivating and responsive kind.

The general notion of consequential tasks has a much broader application, as Brown and Campione (in press) noted later: "If the learner is attempting to read for a specific purpose, the failure to decode is a consequential activity—the reader can tell immediately that he cannot understand the text and, therefore, cannot complete the task."

Cognitive Demands. One of the major determinants of task difficulty is the degree to which the structure of the text must be inferred. A source of task difficulty recognized both with adults and with children is inferential comprehension. Many adults have adequate inferential ability and yet have difficulty with technical literacy because they lack familiarity with the content or with the genre. But others, even when they think well in other areas, may have difficulty inferring relationships between propositions in text. In such instances, tactics like those described by Hansen and Pearson (1982) for children or by Frederiksen et al. (1983) for adolescents may be useful for adults.

Another approach to considering cognitive demands of tasks is the distinction between learning static knowledge systems and learning dynamic skills, a distinction made by Munro, Fehling, Blais, and Towne (1981). By knowledge systems they mean organized bodies of "essentially propositional knowledge," the kind of knowledge stressed in most academic settings as well as in overviews that may guide literacy at work. By dynamic skills these authors mean "bodies of knowledge that coordinate perception, motor skills and decision making in real time driven environments" (Munro et al., 1981, p. 1). They exemplified this in a task that involved tracking fast-moving radar-detected objects on a computer display screen.

Although tasks like air-traffic controller training are rare in public schools, many important school tasks are, optimally, dynamic. This is true not only for psychomotor tasks such as driver education and physical education but at least metaphorically for abstract cognitive/academic tasks. For example, the revision process in writing involves moving language around; this may, through concrete external actions, lead to more abstract internal operations. In reading, too, the expert reader dynamically *acts* upon text, pulling out ideas and organizing them in a structure designed by the reader. If this deceptively simple notion has validity, it may have implications for sharing with novice readers and writers some radically different understandings of the tasks and for evaluating effects of such instruction upon learners' concepts of the nature of reading/writing tasks. On the other hand, specific findings on dynamic learning such as those by Munro et al. may apply only to fast-paced psychomotor learning.

Several topics discussed in other sections also have relevance here. For example, it seems a cognitively more demanding task to *infer* the structure of a text than to *use* a well-marked structure. It is also more difficult to infer the context or content of a passage about an unfamiliar topic than to use one's schema about a familiar topic to guide comprehension and use of text. Although the author or designer of technical materials can use tactics such as graphics or spatial array of text to aid processing, not all texts will be organized in this way, and some texts will serve as resources for several quite different tasks. Literacy tasks at work, then, are likely to vary in the degree to which the reader must transform text overtly into another modality (even written to oral) or covertly into another structure. It is possible, though not yet clear, that the need to integrate information from several sources may also increase the cognitive demands of a task.

Interaction of Task and Reader Characteristics.   In all of these instances the difficulty of a task is likely to be relative not only to the difficulty of the materials but also to user characteristics. One reader may find two tasks roughly equal in difficulty, while another finds one task much harder than another. Especially relevant in this interaction are the reader's inferential comprehension skill, general verbal abstraction ability, experience with the particular task, and concepts about the task.

This interaction is illustrated in the article "How Users Learn through Training Manuals" (1983). The article summarizes Mack, Carroll, and Lewis' studies of initial contacts with a word processing program and its manual. These researchers found that people actively tried to make sense of their experience, forming hypotheses about why the word processor worked as it did, though some of the hypotheses were wrong, interfering with the training. Learners' expectations were shaped by previous experience with office equipment, but when those expectations were not congruent with the operation of the word processor, error or confusion ensued. There was thus an interaction between task conditions and the adequacy of learners' concepts about the task.

Social Context

The interaction of reader, text and task occurs in a specific context, which can shape that interaction. Context, though analyzed deeply by some (e.g., Jacob, 1982), has been given less emphasis in work-based studies of literacy than in many school-based studies of literacy. While studies of technical literacy have explored a range of reader characteristics, tasks, and text features, there is room to look more deeply at the meanings of work-based literacy events for the participants, to analyze the social contexts of such events, and to study the differences in approaches and support systems preferred by various subgroups.

Some of the earlier studies (Sticht, Caylor, Kern, & Fox, 1971) of adults in workplaces were quite informative, although they examined the outward behaviors rather than the personal meanings. Exploring both are some of the more recent studies of adults (Lave, Murtagh, & de la Rocha, 1984; Jacob, 1982), but on the whole, the richest body of literature on people working together on literacy-related tasks has been based on observation in schools (cf. Bloome, 1983; Wilkinson & Spinelli, 1985) and in the home and community in varied cultures.

David Smith's chapter (this volume) focuses primarily on readers and their personal definitions of reading and their roles as readers, though he studied adults in a school setting rather than a work setting. A secondary emphasis was on the interaction of reader and task; that is, the way in which the reader gauged his own ability in relation to a given type of reading task. Smith studied these issues within the broader societal context of poverty culture and of male/female roles and relationships. In some recent studies of literacy at work (e.g., Warren & Jacobson, 1983), the analysis and exploration of personal meanings are not so deep as in many of the school-based studies such as those reviewed in Green and Smith (1983).

The Winter 1984 issue of *Review of Educational Research,* however, provided not only a review of some of the most pertinent recent studies of literacy, but thoughtful conceptual overviews such as Erickson's (1984) conclusion that "human learning as well as human teaching needs to be seen as a social transaction, a collective enterprise" (p. 543).

David Bloome's chapter in this volume, for example, emphasizes the interaction of reader and task, his/her understanding of the nature of the task, and the role he or she needs to play in reading in such a task. The social context of these activities was described with an implicit contrast to other contexts such as the approach that would be required on the job. Bloome's (1983) earlier work provides a conceptual framework for understanding reading as a social process, undertaken jointly with others.

The work-reading setting may be rich in social resources, and, as Cole (1980) pointed out, "thinking is a rarely a solitary activity" (p. 45). While sharing of information is often defined in school as cheating (Shulman & Carey, 1985, p. 517), the same kind of activity in job training is often defined as one of a number of equally acceptable means of gathering needed information (Sticht et al., 1971). Cole (1980) pointed out that "In attempting to solve a problem together, people represent intellectual resources for each other" (p. 45). Perhaps we need to help students in school recognize when use of social resources (Levin & Kareev, 1980) is and is not an acceptable strategy and help them to evaluate the short-range and long-range advantages and disadvantages of such strategies.

One area of school learning in which recognition of the value of peers as resources has emerged, largely accidentally, is in learning on computers. Although there is a widespread stereotype of an individual alone and totally involved with a computer, a number of studies of children in school settings (e.g., Levin, 1983; Rubin, 1983) have indicated the value of peer learning on computers, and Levin and Kareev (1980) have described group oral problem solving, especially information seeking and division of labor. Moreover, Hutson and Thompson (1985) described the ways in which community college students who composed and revised in small groups on the word processor seemed able to pool resources and to make use of different kinds of expertise possessed by various group members. The same phenomena can occur in reading tasks at work or at school. These and other observations (cf. Cole & Traupmann, 1981) and the earlier comments by Sticht and by Diehl and Mikulecky suggest that it would be useful to study both in school and at work individual and group differences in preference and skill in use of social resources for literacy tasks as well as the ways in which various media support or affect group involvement in literacy tasks.

Although the group work described here involved face-to-face contact, it is also possible to organize literacy tasks for groups that are geographically dispersed. Reasonably common today is oral group work via conference phone and, increasingly, via computer networking of verbal text. One user can respond to another's message immediately or at some later time. In addition, Lipinski and Plummer (1980) have described various ways in which graphic communication via computer can assist dispersed-group problem solving.

Considering these very positive aspects, however, brings us back to some of the difficult issues embedded in the larger societal context. Ethnographic studies of the beginnings of literacy show discontinuities between the kinds of literacy promoted in the home and community for some social groups and the kinds valued in schools. It seems likely that there are also discontinuities between the kinds of literacy taught and rewarded in schools and those required in many work settings.

There appears to be unequal access to text-based literacy instruction in schools, because of devaluing of the kinds of literacy some students display (Gilmore, chap. 5, this volume), because of lack of opportunity to view students in contexts where they are clearly competent (Moll & Diaz, chap. 9, this volume), or simply because of some limiting concepts of what counts as literacy or readiness for certain types of literacy experiences. Such unequal access may be exacerbated as more school tasks become computer based, an expense borne badly by poorer families and poorer school districts. For example, when college entrance tests include computer skills, students from districts that provide no training or provide only less cognitively demanding data processing may be greatly disadvantaged. The larger societal contexts of literacy in school may affect both success in school and readiness for the literacy demands encountered at work or in training.

CONCLUSIONS

From the sources and topics reviewed in this chapter emerges a picture of literacy at work as involving *information* to be selected and organized in terms of a problem formulated by the worker. The information is varied in form, including but not limited to verbal and graphic text delivered primarily on paper or, increasingly, on computer terminal. The information ranges in adequacy, in degree of structure, and in match of its current form to the form most useful for a given user in a given task.

The literacy task is also varied, including quick information location, gathering the gist or a detailed understanding of a system, immediate guidance through a procedure, etc. Factors affecting the difficulty of the task include familiarity with the content and with the structure of the support material and the number of times the worker has previously done that same task. Effectiveness and efficiency of the reader on the job are determined not just by reading ability, general intelligence, and schema for the content, but by conceptions about text and strategies for detecting and inferring structure and by conceptions about literacy tasks and strategies for selecting, seeking, analyzing, and integrating information from varied sources in order to solve a problem. Many of these descriptions could also be applied to school-based literacy.

The fields of school-based literacy and work-based literacy have mutual implications. Some issues (such as those concerning discrepancies between literacy at school and at work and unequal access to literacy training) need to be addressed as ethical or sociological issues. Information about students' typical levels of competence in a greater variety of literacy tasks and about the effects of training, however, can guide policy and implementation. Some information is available in national achievement studies, but the tasks sampled only partially overlap the literacy tasks encountered on the job or in training for technical occupations.

School-based literacy studies (especially qualitative studies) have implications for study of adult literacy in work settings. For example, there is room to look more deeply at the meanings of work-based literary events for the participants, to analyze the context of such events, and to study differences in approaches and support systems preferred by various subgroups. One caution must be kept in mind—notions developed in academic literacy cannot simply be transplanted to the work context. Scribner and Cole (1981) stressed that literacy ''is not simply learning how to read and write a particular script but applying this knowledge for specific purposes in specific contexts of use'' (p. 236), and Erickson (1984) concluded that reasoning abilities (the central aspect of reading) ''appear to be domain-specific rather than generalizable across task domains that differ in surface forms'' (p. 528). Yet performance in complex tasks is likely to have both task-specific and generalizable components. The attempt in this chapter has been to draw attention to those features of literacy at work that have greatest potential for enriching understanding and practice of literacy in school.

The theory-based literacy training programs such as those designed by Ann Brown (Brown & Palincsar, 1982), David Pearson (Hansen & Pearson, 1982), and colleagues have many features that could be adapted to development of comprehensive programs of technical literacy. One of the constraints on training programs at work, though, is that time is quite literally money when employees are given released time for training. The benefits of the training must outweigh the costs, and training must usually be concentrated in short bursts as in the functional literacy programs described by Sticht (1975) or Sticht et al. (1977).

Studies of technical literacy, in turn, might well influence studies of the school-based reader to give greater attention to several aspects of reader characteristics—ability to process and integrate text and graphic information effectively, ability not just to solve prestated problems but to formulate problems, selecting and organizing information for a purpose, and ability to transform information from one mode into another. Other areas for further study in school are analysis of the effects of training on such skills and of various text characteristics such as the purpose and features of the text that might prompt or inhibit adequate mental representations of the topic discussed in the text. And notions about task characteristics such as the difference between substantive and procedural knowledge could clarify problems in school-based literacy.

Although Perez and Seidel (in press) spoke in the context of military training, their words outline the task for elementary and secondary schools as well:

> What is required is an approach to training that integrates knowledge gained from cognitive and computer science in the design of instruction. That includes the content structure of a task, knowledge representation, prerequisite abilities and the interaction between procedural knowledge background and a conceptual knowledge from which to teach generic skills. Therefore the task to be undertaken is to develop an instructional model that makes use of previously acquired mental models and utilizes them to teach models that represent the "skills" needed to operate and maintain complex equipment.

Some issues in technical literacy cannot be studied within either school-based or work-based literacy, because the issue is continuity across home/school/work boundaries. Among the issues that need to be studied across school/work boundaries are these:

1. What kinds and degrees of literacy will be required for work in the near future?
2. Is there school-based inequity in access to job tracks (even if unintended) based in part on differential literacy instruction for students in various social groups?
3. Is there discontinuity between the aspects of literacy stressed in school and those required for literacy at work?
4. If there is a discontinuity, should all responsibility for training in technical literacy be left to industry and individual workers, or should the school act to develop students' technical literacy?
5. If the school takes responsibility for technical literacy, can approaches suggested by conceptualizations and tactics in the study of literacy at work be applied to literacy in school to reduce this discontinuity?

Research along these lines may deepen our understanding of the long-term development of basic processes that apply to academic literacy and to technical literacy, to verbal material and to graphic material, and to information delivered orally, in printed form, or via computer terminal.

REFERENCES

American Council of Life Insurance. (1984). *The changing work place: Perceptions—reality.* Washington, DC: Author.

Anderson, J.R., Greeno, J.G., Kline, P.J., & Neves, D.M. (1980). *Acquisition of problem-solving skills* (Technical Report No. 80-5). Pittsburgh, PA: Carnegie-Mellon University.

Antos, S., & Bourne, L.E., Jr. (1982). *Reading under the influence of decision making* (Technical report No. 114-ONR). Boulder: Institute of Cognitive Science, University of Colorado.

Armbruster, B.B., & Anderson, T.H. (1982). *Structures for explanations in History textbooks: Or so what if Governor Stanford missed the spike and hit the rail?* (Technical report No. 252). Champaign: Center for the Study of Reading, University of Illinois.

Baggett, P. (1982). *The role of temporal overlap of visual and auditory material in dual media comprehension* (Technical Report No. 113-ONR). Boulder: Institute of Cognitive Science, University of Colorado.

Before you buy: Is the manual clear? *Simply Stated in Business,* August (6), 2, 1984.

Berry, E. (1982). How to get users to follow procedures. *IEEE transactions on professional communication,* PC-25 C1.

Bieger, G.R., & Glock, M.D. (1982). *Comprehension of spatial and contextual information in picture and texts* (Technical Report No. 6). Ithaca, NY: Cornell University.

Bloome, D. (1983). Reading as a social process. In B.A. Hutson (Ed.), *Advances in reading/language research* (Vol. 2). Greenwich, CT: JAL.

Bloome, D., & Greene, J.L. (1982). The social context of reading: A multidisciplinary perspective. In B.A. Hutson (Ed.), *Advances in reading/language research* (Vol. 1). Greenwich CT: JAI.

Bormuth, J.R. (1975). Reading literacy: Its definition and assessment. In J.B. Carroll & J.S. Chall (Eds.), *Toward a literate society: The report of the Committee on Reading of the National Academy of Education.* New York: McGraw-Hill.

Brown, A.L., & Campione, J.C. (in press). Application of cognitive science principles of education in the military: Expert systems, interactive learning and dynamic assessment. In T.G. Sticht, F. Chang, & S. Wood (Eds.), *Cognitive science and human resource management. (Advances in Reading/Language Research, Vol. 4).* Greenwich, CT: JAI.

Brown, A., & Palincsar, A. S. (1982). Inducing strategic learning from texts by means of informed, self-control training. *Topics in Learning and Learning Disabilities, 2* (1), 1-17.

Brown, J.S., & Burton, R.B. (1980). Diagnostic models for procedural bugs in basic mathematical skills. *Cognitive Science, 4,* 379-426.

Burkett, J.R. (1976). A review of research and development on literacy and technical writing in the Air Force. In T.G. Sticht & D.W. Zapf (Eds.), *Reading and readability research in the armed services.* Alexandria, VA: Human Resources Research Organization.

Caylor, J.S. (1976). Ongoing R&D in Army literacy training. In T.G. Sticht & D.W. Zapf (Eds.), *Reading and readability research in the armed services.* Alexandria, VA: Human Resources Organization.

Caylor, J.S., Sticht, T.G., Fox, L.C., & Ford, J.P. (1973). *Methodologies for determining reading requirements of military occupational specialties* (Technical Report 73-5). Alexandria, VA: Human Resources Research Organization.

Chall, J.S. (1975). Report on the Committee on Reading, National Academy of Education. In J.B. Carroll & J.S. Chall (Eds.), *Toward a literate society: The Report of the Committee on Reading of the National Academy of Education.* New York: McGraw-Hill.

Chi, M.T.H., Glaser, R., & Rees, E. (1981). Expertise in problem solving. In R.J. Sternberg (Ed.), *Advances in the psychology of human intelligence* (Vol. 1). Hillsdale, NJ: Erlbaum.

Clifford, J.G. (1984). Buch und lesen: Historical perspectives on literacy and schooling. *Review of Educational Research, 54*(4), 472-500.

Cole, M. (1980). Introduction. *Quarterly Newsletter of the Laboratory of Comparative Human Cognition*, 2(3), 45-46.

Cole, M., & Traupmann, K. (1981) Comparative cognitive research: Learning from a learning disabled child. *Minnesota Symposium on Child Psychology* (Vol. 14). Hillsdale, NJ: Erlbaum.

Collins, A. (in press). High pay-off research in the cognitive sciences for military application. In T.G. Sticht, F.R. Chang, & S. Wood (Eds.), *Cognitive science and human resource management. (Advances in Reading/Language Research, Vol. 4)*. Greenwich, CT: JAI.

Curran, T.E. (1977). Readability research in the Navy. In J.D. Fletcher, T.M. Duffy, & T.E. Curran (Eds.), *Historical antecedents and contemporary trends in literacy and readability research in the Navy (Final Report)*. San Diego, CA: Navy Personnel Research and Development Center.

Dansereau, D.F., McDonald, B.A., Collins, K.W. Garland, J., Holley, C.D., Diekhoff, G.M., & Evans, S.H. (1979). Evaluation of a learning strategy system. In H.F. O'Neil, Jr. & C.D. Spielberger (Eds.), *Cognitive and affective learning stategies*. New York: Academic Press.

Delker, P. (1983). Defining adult functional literacy. In *Functional literacy and the workplace*. Washington, DC: Educational Services, American Council of Life Insurance.

Diehl, W. A., & Mikulecky, L. (1980). The nature of reading at work. *Journal of Reading*, 24(3), 221-227.

Duffy, T. (1977). Literacy training in the Navy. In J.D. Fletcher, T.M. Duffy, & T.E. Curran (Eds.), *Historical antecedents and contemporary trends in literacy and readability research in the Navy* (Technical Report No. 77-15). San Diego, CA: Navy Personnel Research and Development Center.

Elfenbein, I.M. (1983). Introduction to the proceedings. In *Functional literacy and the workplace*. Washington, DC: Education Services, American Council of Life Insurance.

Erickson, F. (1984). School literacy, reasoning, and civility: An anthropologist's perspective. *Review of Educational Research*, 54(4), 525-546.

Finch, C.R., & Falls, S.S. (1981, December). *Functional context methods of instruction in the military*. Paper presented to the annual conference of the American Vocational Association, Atlanta.

Fletcher, J.D. (1977). Historical perspective on literacy training in the Navy. In T.G. Sticht & D.W. Zapf (Eds.), *Reading and readability research in the armed services* (pp. 68-88). Alexandria, VA: Human Resources Research Organization.

Flower, L. (1983, December). *The writer's planning process and the hidden logic of text*. Paper presented at the National Reading Conference, Austin, TX.

Flower, L., & Hayes, J.R. (1980). The cognition of discovery: Defining a rhetorical problem. *College Composition and Communication*, 2(3), 21-32.

Frederiksen, J.R., Weaver, P.A., Warren, B.M., Gillotte, H.P., Rosebery, A.S., Freeman, B., & Goodman, L. (1983). *A componential approach to training reading skills: Final report* (Technical Report No. 5295). Cambridge, MA: Bolt, Beranek & Newman.

Gentner, D., & Stevens, A.L. (Eds.), (1982). *Mental models*. Hillsdale, NJ: Erlbaum.

Geva, E. (1981). *Facilitating reading comprehension through flowcharting* (Technical report No. 211). Cambridge, MA: Center for the Study of Reading, Bolt, Beranek & Newman.

Glaser, R. (in press). Cognitive science, selection and classification and technical training. In T.G. Sticht, F. Chang, & S. Wood (Eds.), *Cognitive science and human resource management. (Advances in Reading/Language Research, Vol. 4)*. Greenwich, CT: JAI.

Gorman, H., & Oltrogge, E. (1984, August). Novice documentation reduces training costs. *Simply Stated*, 48 1-2.

Green, J.L., & Smith, D.C. (1983). Teaching and learning as linguistic processes: The emerging picture. In B.A. Hutson (Ed.), *Advances in reading/language research* (Vol. 2). Greenwich, CT: JAI.

Guthrie, J. (1982). Corporate education for the electronic culture. *Journal of Reading*, 25(5), 492-495.

Guthrie, J.T., & Kirsch, I.S. (1984). The emergent perspective on literacy. *Phi Delta Kappan*, 65(6), 351-355.

Hansen, J., & Pearson, P.D. (1982). *An instructional study: Improving the inferential comprehension of good and poor fourth-grade readers* (Technical Report No. 235). Champaign: Center for the Study of Reading, University of Illinois.

Harrison, C. (1980). *Readability in the classroom.* Cambridge, England: Cambridge University Press.

Hayes, J.R. (1981). *The complete problem solver.* Philadelphia, PA: Franklin Institute.

Henry, J.F. (1983). Basic skills in the U.S. workforce. In *Functional literacy and the workplace.* Washington, DC: Education Services, American Council of Life Insurance.

Hutson, B.A. (1982, March). *Studying technical literacy in today's society.* Paper presented to annual conference of the American Educational Research Association, New York.

Hutson, B.A. (1984). Bridging the gap between literacy at school and literacy at work. *Greater Washington Reading Journal, 9,* 18-19.

Hutson, B.A. (1985). Developing students' technical literacy as a tool for work. *Delta Kappa Gamma Journal, 51*(2), 26-32.

Hutson, B.A., & Stump, R. (1980, October). *Job-related literacy: Broad and narrow definitions and their implications.* Paper presented to the annual conference of the Northeastern Educational Research Association, Ellenville, NY.

Hutson, B.A., & Thompson, D. (1985). *Gaining power over the written word: Group word processing.* Paper presented to the South Eastern Conference of English Teachers in the Community College, Greenville, SC.

If you write or use erasers and drive to work daily or sometimes have headaches . . . then read this . . . maybe. (1982, January). *Simply Stated,* pp. 2-3.

Jacob, E. (1982). *Literacy on the job: Final report of the ethnographic component of the industrial literacy project.* Washington, DC: Center for Applied Linguistics.

Katner, W. (1984, September). *Microprocessor-controlled video disks and computer graphics for skills training and maintenance.* Paper presented at Defense Computer Graphics conference, Washington, DC.

Kern, R.P. (1976). U.S. Army research and development on readability and useability of printed materials. In T.G. Sticht & D.W. Zapf (Eds.), *Reading and readability research in the armed services.* Alexandria, VA: Human Resources Research Organization.

Kern, R. (in press). Modeling information processing in the context of job training and work-site performance. In T. Sticht, F. Chang, & S. Wood (Eds.), *Cognitive science and human resource management. (Advances in Reading/Language Research, Vol. 4).* Greenwich, CT: JAI.

Kieras, D.E. (1978). Good and bad structure in simple paragraphs: Effects on apparent theme, reading time, and recall. *Journal of Verbal Learning and Verbal Behavior, 17,* 13-28.

Kieras, D.E. (1979). *The role of global topics and sentence topics in the construction of passage macrostructure* (Technical Report No. 4). Tucson; University of Arizona.

Kieras, D., & Bovair, S. (1983). *The role of a mental model in learning to operate a device* (Technical report No. 13). Tucson; University of Arizona.

Kirsch, I., & Guthrie, J.T. (1977-1978). The concept and measurement of functional literacy. *Reading Research Quarterly, 13*(4), 485-507.

Kolers, P.A. (1973). Some modes of representation. In P. Pliner, L. Kramer, & T. Alloway (Eds.), *Communication and affect: Language and thought.* New York: Academic Press.

Larkin, J.H. (1980). *Understanding, problem representation, and skill in physics.* Paper presented at NIE-LRDC Conference on Thinking and Learning Skills, Pittsburgh.

Lave, J.A., Murtagh, M., & de la Rocha, O. (1984). The dialect of arithmetic in grocery shopping. In B. Rogoff & J. Lave (Eds.), *Everyday cognition: Its development in social context* (pp. 67-94). Cambridge, MA: Harvard University Press.

Levin, J.A., & Kareev, Y. (1980). Problem solving in everyday situations. *Quarterly Newsletter of the Laboratory of Comparative Human Cognition, 2*(3), 47-52.

Levin, J.A. (1983, November). *Muktuk meets Jacuzzi: Computer networks and elementary school writing.* Paper presented at National Reading Conference, Austin, TX.

Lipinski, R., & Plummer, R.P. (1980). *Graphic communication in a group setting.* Paper presented to the annual conference of the American Society for Information Science, Anaheim, CA.

Lunzer, E.A., & Gardner, W.K. (Eds.). (1979). *The effective use of reading.* London: Heinemann.

Mann, D.C. (1983). Basic skills in financial services. In *Functional literacy and the workplace.* Washington, DC: Education Services, American Council of Life Insurance.

Marcus, A. (1984). Display users now making type decisions. *Computer Graphics Today*, *1*(3), 7, 18.

Mason, J.M., & Kendall, J.R. (1980). *Prose comprehension: Analysis of task and passage*. Paper presented to the annual conference of the American Educational Research Association, Boston.

McDonell, G.M., Osburn, B., & Hutson, B.A. (1983, December). *Communication in the real world*. Paper presented at National Reading Conference, Austin, TX.

Meyer, B.J.F. (1983). Text structure and its use in studying comprehension across the life span. In B.A. Hutson (Ed.), *Advances in reading/language research* (Vol. 2). Greenwich, CT: JAI.

Mikulecky, L., & Diehl, W. (1980). *Job literacy: A study of literacy demands, attitudes, and strategies in a cross-section of occupations*. Bloomington: Reading Research Center, Indiana University.

Miller, P.A. (1982). Reading demands in a high-technology industry. *Journal of Reading*, *26*(2), 109-115.

Mudrick, D., & Hutson, B.A. (1984, September). *Hypertext as a component in computer based training*. Paper presented to the annual conference of the Defense Computer Graphics Conference, Washington, DC.

Munro, A., Fehling, M.R., Blais, P., & Towne, D.M. (1981). *Intrusive and non-intrusive instruction in dynamic skill training* (Technical Report No. 97). Redondo Beach, CA: Behavioral Technology Laboratories, University of Southern California.

Northcutt, N., Selz, N., Shelton, E., Nyer, L., Hickok, D., & Humble, M. (1975). *Adult functional competency: A summary*. Austin: University of Texas.

O'Donnell, H. (1982). Reading and the vocational education student. *Journal of Reading*, *25*(5), 474-478.

Perez, R.S., & Seidel, R.J. (in press). Cognitive theory of technical training. In T.G. Sticht, F. Chang, & S. Wood (Eds.), *Cognitive science and human resource management. (Advances in Reading/Language Research, Vol. 4)*. Greenwich, CT: JAI.

Pirsig, R. (1974). *Zen and the art of motorcycle maintenance*. New York: Morrow.

Raphael, T.E. (1980). *Improving question-answering performance through instruction* (Reading Education Report No. 32). Champaign: Center for the Study of Reading, University of Illinois.

Rehe, R.F. (1974). *Typography: How to make it most legible*. Carmel, IN: Design Research International.

Rogers, J.P., & Thorne, H.W. (1975). *The development and evaluation of an improved electronics troubleshooting manual* (Technical Report No. 65-1). Alexandria, VA: Human Resources Research Organization.

Rubin, A. (1983, November). *What did I do to deserve this? Teachers' views of writing with computers*. Paper presented at National Reading Conference, Austin, TX.

Schallert, D.L. (1980). The role of illustrations in reading comprehension. In R.J. Spiro, B.C. Bruce, & W.F. Brewer (Eds.), *Theoretical issues in reading comprehension: Perspectives from cognitive psychology, linguistics, artificial intelligence, and education*. Hillsdale, NJ: Erlbaum.

Schorr, F. L., & Glock, M.D. (1983). *Comprehending procedural instructions: The influence of comprehension monitoring strategies and instructional materials* (Technical Report No. 10). Ithaca, NY: Cornell University.

Schwartz, S.H. (1971). Modes of representation and problem solving: Well evolved is half solved. *Journal of Experimental Psychology*, *2*, 347-350.

Schwartz, S.H., & Fattaleh, D.L. (1972). Representation in deductive problem solving: The matrix. *Journal of Experimental Psychology*, *2*, 343-348.

Scribner, S., & Cole, M. (1981). *The psychology of literacy*. Cambridge, MA: Harvard University Press.

Shulman, L. S., & Carey, N.B. (1984). Psychology and the limitations of individual rationality: Implications for the study of reasoning and civility. *Review of Educational Research*, *54*(4), 501-524.

Siegel, A.I. (1976). Research on the comprehensibility of Air Force technical materials. In T.G. Sticht & D.W. Zapf (Eds.), *Reading and readability research in the armed services*. Alexandria, VA: Human Resources Research Organization.

Smith, D.M. (1986). The anthropology of literacy acquisition. In P. Gilmore & B. Schieffelin (Eds.), *The acquisition of literacy: Ethnographic perspectives*. Norwood, NJ: Ablex.

Smith, E., & Goodman, L. (1983). *Understanding and executing instructions: The role of explanatory material* (Technical Report AD# A119762). Cambridge, MA: Bolt, Beranek & Newman.

Sorrentino, P. (1985). Let's be technically right about technical writing. In B.A. Hutson (Ed.), *Advances in reading/language research* (Vol. 3). Greenwich, CT: JAI.

Sticht, T.G. (1972). Learning by listening. In J.B. Carroll & R.O. Freedle (Eds.), *Language comprehension and the acquisition of knowledge*. Washington, DC: Winston.

Sticht, T.G. (1975). *A program of Army functional job reading training: Development, implementation, and delivery system*. (Final report HumRRO-FR-WD(CA)-75-7). Alexandria, VA: Human Resources Research Organization.

Sticht, T.G. (1977). Comprehending reading at work. In M.A. Just & P.A. Carpenter (Eds.), *Cognitive processes in comprehension*. Hillsdale, NJ: Erlbaum.

Sticht, T.G., Caylor, J.S., Kern, R.P., Fox, L.C. (1971). *Determination of literacy skill requirements in four military occupational specialties*. (HumRRO report 71-23). Alexandria, VA: Human Resources Research Organization.

Sticht, T.G., Fox, L.C., Hauke, R.N., & Zapf, D.W. (1977). *Integrated job skills and reading skills training system* (NPRDC Technical Report 77-41). San Diego, CA: Navy Personnel Research and Development Center.

Stone, D.E., & Glock, M.D. (1981). How do young adults read directions with and without pictures? *Journal of Educational Psychology, 73*(3), 419-426.

Stone, D.E., Hutson, B.A., & Fortune, J.C. (1983). *Information engineering: On-line analysis of information search and utilization* (ONR Technical Report No. 9). Ithaca, NY: Cornell University for Office of Naval Research.

Stone, D.E., & Hutson, B.A. (1983, April). *Computer based job aiding: Problem solving at work*. Paper presented to the annual conference of the American Educational Research Association, Montreal.

Stone, D.E., Hutson, B.A. (1984, April). *Using the computer to study on-line information selection processes*. Paper presented at American Educational Research Association, New Orleans.

Tannen, D. (1982). Oral and written strategies in spoken and written narratives. *Language, 58*, 1-21.

Task Force on Education and Employment, National Academy of Education. (1979). *Education for employment: Knowledge for action*. Washington, DC: Acropolis.

Thornton, J.L. (1980). *Review and synthesis of reading in the post-secondary occupational education*. Harrisburg: Pennsylvania State Department of Education, Bureau of Vocational and Technical Education.

Thurber, J. (1957). Macbeth murder mystery. *The Thurber carnival*. New York: Modern Library.

Van Lehn, K. (1982). *Empirical studies of procedural flaws, impasses, and repairs in procedural skills* (Technical report ONR-8). Palo Alto, CA: Xerox Palo Alto Research Center.

Vineberg, R., Sticht, T.G., Taylor, E.N., & Caylor, J.S. (1971). + iEffects of aptitude (AFQT), job experience, and literacy on job performance: Summary of HumRRO Work Units UTILITY and REALISTIC (Technical Report No. 71-1). Alexandria, VA: Human Resources Research Organization.

Warren, J.W., & Jacobson, S.H. (1983, December). *An ethnographical look at information processing in the military: Phase I*. Paper presented at the National Reading Conference, Austin, TX.

Wilkinson, L.C., & Spinelli, F. (1985). Using requests effectively in peer-directed reading groups. In B.A. Hutson (Ed.), *Advances in reading/language research* (Vol. 3). Greenwich, CT: JAI.

Williams, A.R., Siegel, A.I., & Burkett, J.R. (1974). *Readability of textual materials—A survey of the literature*. Lowry AFB, Colorado: Air Force Human Resources Laboratory.

Wright, P., & Reid, F. (1973). Written information: Some alternatives to prose for expressing the outcomes of complex contingencies. *Journal of Applied Psychology, 2*, 160-166.

11 Workbooks: What They Can Teach Children About Forms*

Deborah Keller-Cohen
Jane Heineken
University of Michigan

INTRODUCTION

For many years now scholars have documented the transition made to literacy (Goody, 1968, 1977; Havelock, 1982; Graff, 1981; Lockridge, 1974; Ong, 1982; Pattison, 1982). We have come a long way from the time when oral patterns of communication mediated most interactions and the functions of writing were restricted. These days it is inconceivable that societies once could have managed themselves successfully without mountains of paperwork. Clanchy's (1979) elegant treatment of England's transition to written records (from the Norman conquest to the demise of Edward I) made clear that even when familiarity with written records became more widespread, the records were still often treated as objects to be spoken, that is, read aloud, rather than perused in silence. "Thus in 1219 in an action of warranty of charter in Lincolnshire William of Well, defendant, is reported in the plea roll to 'have come and claimed a hearing [auditum] of his father's charter' and it was duly heard" (pp. 215–216). It is similarly difficult to fathom that important information could be presented orally rather than assimilated visually. Vestiges of these traditions remain today in several areas. The conferring of honorary degrees is typically done aloud with the written confirmation presented later. Poetry readings also reflect the oral primacy of the material; indeed, the writing down might be thought of as a mnemonic device for a basically auditory phenomenon.

And yet, we in America fundamentally are creatures of paper in a way that perhaps is unparalleled in history. We make use of paper records as never before. We initiate service through paper (applying for benefits, opening charge accounts, registering for classes); we acknowledge achievements (diplomas, report cards, commendations); we limit or regulate activities (drivers' licenses, numbered cards to reflect one's place in line); we record events (we send letters "as per our conver-

---

*Figures 3, 11, and 18 from *Starflight Workbook* (Teacher's Edition), by Carolyn Pantazelos (pages 54, 71, and 82); Figures 7, 14, and 15 from *Crystal Kingdom Workbook* (Teacher's Edition), by Joanna Cairns, Elizabeth Galloway, and Robert Tierney (pages 58, 46, and 61). Both copyright © 1981 by Scott, Foresman and Company; used with permission.

Figures 2 and 16 from *Skillpack* (Teacher's Edition) for *Little Dog Laughed* (pages 1 and 15); Figures 4, 6, 10, 12, and 17 from *Skillpack* (Teacher's Edition) for *Give Me a Clue* (pages 62, 91, 88, 52, and 54); Figures 5, 8, 9, and 13 from *Skillpack* (Teacher's Edition) for *Flights of Color* (pages 93, 92, 102, and 69). All are parts of the Ginn Reading Program by Theodore Clymer and others, copyright © 1985, 1982 by Ginn and Company; used with permission.

sation yesterday, I am enclosing . . . ''); we file reports; and we sign waivers of liability. These paper-centered activities are so much a part of our lives that it is difficult to imagine a day where we make no contact with the written word. Indeed, some would even call us literacy junkies.

While much attention has been paid to reading in recent years, writing is less well understood. The study of writing is difficult because of the heterogeneity of things written. We write lists, business letters, fill out job applications, record inventories, read recipes, newspapers, and mysteries. And yet despite the diversity of formats and functions there is a genre that plays an increasingly prominent role in interactions in American society—and that is the form.

Forms are more readily illustrated than defined. Accident reports, inventory records, loan coupons, benefits applications, sales agreements, health care service receipts, and requests for insurance reimbursements are all examples of forms. These all share the following characteristics: Some information is preprinted on the paper and other information is filled in by hand, typewriter, or, perhaps, even at a computer terminal. On a form the questions may be few such as when you fill in the amount paid on a charge account stub that is returned with your payment; or forms may be lengthy, requesting a range of information across a formidable series of questions. One illustration of the demands a form can place is the Michigan Department of Social Services Assistance Application/Redetermination. It is used to apply or reapply for social service benefits ranging from food stamps to medical assistance and must be completed by anyone applying for any such benefits. It is 22 pages long with as many as 90 items per page.

Wright (1980a) proposed a useful step toward a definition of forms: ''a structured question and answer dialogue, in which the questions are written and the kinds of answers permitted may be highly constrained'' (p. 151). Indeed, the interrogative function is at the heart of forms since their primary function is to elicit information. Even so, Wright's description needs some refinement because forms are not genuine dialogues. Specifically they share with dialogue the participation of two parties, that is, the person/unit/institution that has formulated the questions and the party or parties responding. They differ from dialogue in the absence of feedback as a central characteristic, because the questioner generally cannot provide corrective feedback to a particular answer while the respondent is answering the questions, except where a representative of the questioner (e.g., an employee) assists. The respondent, on the other hand, may make comments about the question asked by using parenthetical statements, but the distance between the questioner and the respondent crucially differentiates a form from the traditional conceptions of dialogue.

Additionally, forms have some of the characteristics of a highly structured interview where the questions are established ahead of time and are controlled by one side. Fillmore's (1973) metaphor of interaction as a ball game makes this clearer. He characterized conversation as a game in which participants take turns by throwing a ball back and forth. In forms, one player has a bag of different colors/types of balls. The game consists of the player with the bag throwing one ball at a time at the other player, who then throws it back; the first player selects a second ball, throws it, and it is returned, and so forth. This characterization of the type of interaction in forms captures the central role the first player has in controlling information on a form. Thus our definition of a form might be *a structured question-and-answer exchange in which the questions are predetermined and written and the kinds of written responses permitted may be highly constrained.*

Despite the importance of forms in American society, we know very little about how forms became so prominent, nor do we know how individuals become literate with the form genre. The purpose of our project was to take a preliminary look at the possibility that the workbooks used in our schools could teach children about forms. It was also part of a much larger plan to conduct experimental work in the schools to evaluate what children actually do know about formatted information. As such, it made sense to look first at the two reading workbook series used in a local public school system: the Scott, Foresman and Ginn series.

Both Scott, Foresman and Ginn produce a complete basal reader series from kindergarten through eighth grade. Both the 1981 Scott, Foresman and Ginn series have 16 workbooks. We sampled them by selecting workbooks at particular intervals along the K–8 continuum. It seemed sensible to choose workbooks that were different enough from each other to reveal changes in format as broadly defined (including types of questions and responses in addition to variations in the use of graphics). To this end we selected three workbooks from each series as the core of our analysis. The first workbook selected was the first of each series in which written instructions are directed to the students. In the Scott, Foresman series this was first grade, level 2. Since there were three level-2 workbooks, we selected the middle book, *Going Up*. The comparable Ginn workbook was *Little Dog Laughed*. Ginn rated this a preprimer located in the series between kindergarten and first grade. To complete the intervals in our series we selected a second- and sixth-grade workbook. The second-grade workbooks were near the middle of the 16-book series, and the sixth- grade workbooks near the end. These were Scott, Foresman: *Crystal Kingdom* (2nd grade), *Star Flight* (6th grade); Ginn *Give me a Clue* (2nd grade), and *Flights of Color* (6th grade). The first workbooks in our sample (*Going Up* and *Little Dog Laughed*) each were 50 pages. In order to sample equally from the other workbooks which were greater in length we examined the middle 50 pages in the second- and sixth-grade workbooks.

THE FEATURES OF FORMS

In order to ask whether children can learn about forms from school workbooks, we needed a more general view of the characteristics of forms. Regrettably, there was much we did not know about forms. Some of our knowledge was drawn from research on more general aspects of texts and how they were understood, while other work offered important insights specific to forms but did so without developing a synthetic view. Despite this, there was some important work on the characteristics of forms, the most prominent of which was by Wright (1980b, 1983). She proposed that we think of the design of forms in three ways: "the language on the form, the overall structure of the form, and the substructures within the form such as the questions themselves" (Wright, 1980b p. 157). By language, Wright meant the choice of words, whereas "substructures" was used to capture the syntactic patterns that were used to elicit responses. As an example of the language of forms, Wright compared the consequences of alternative ways of requesting the same information such as "When did you leave school?" versus "How old were you when you left school?" By the overall structure of forms was meant the general organization of the form, i.e., how information was sequenced and how the various subsections of a form were arranged and related to each other. This chapter concentrates on the overall structure of forms and the substructures but does not consider the choice of words as such. The words one chooses to ask questions are in part dependent on the information being sought as well as assumptions made about respondents' reading levels. For example, the wording of questions about the number of people living in your household, your date of birth, your home address, or your choice of flight time would be unrelated to the wording of questions in children's workbooks because the content focus of the latter was different.

The overall structure of forms consists of several characteristics. First, a form can be divided into more than one section on a single page. This is illustrated in Figure 1, the Michigan Department of Social Services Assistance Application/ Redetermination, which contains one section that asks questions about the applicant's vehicles and another that inquires about absent spouses or parents.

Second, sections of forms may be related to changes in the type of information requested or the type of response desired. Forms are often organized into sections to communicate that the respondent is being asked for different types or categories of information (e.g., Fig. 1). We can also see that changes in information category are often, but not always, accompanied by changes in the way the questions or items are organized on the page and by changes in the type of question asked. Recognizing this cue is an important part of learning to use forms. There are a plethora of signals used to communicate changes in section. These include the introduction of a new set of instructions, alternations in color and shading, and variations in question or response type.

Third, forms also differ in the type of substructures utilized. In terms of function, there are two broad types of substructures: those which elicit responses and the responses themselves. There exists no complete taxonomy of either of these so it will not be possible to compare precisely those substructures which elicit responses in forms for adults and those which exist in children's workbooks. It is important to note, however, that a single page of a form may include a range of both elicitation and response types.

Just how extensive this can be is illustrated in a travel agent record form offered in Wright (1980a). There the range of responses requested on a one-page form included free response, fill in the blank, yes/no, and multiple choice. It is equally important to note that responses can be elicited by questions or nonquestions. For example, in the travel agent record none of the responses were elicited by a syntac-

Figure 1

VEHICLES

1. Do you own a motor vehicle? Yes (Complete the rest of this section)   No (Please go to the next section)

2 Vehicle No.	Describe each vehicle Make and model, year and type (car, truck, motor home, motorcycle,)	3 Enter vehicle owner's name.	4 Is vehicle licensed?		5 Is vehicle used to produce income?		6 Is vehicle used in person's work or to get to work?		7 Is vehicle used as your home?		8 Amount owed on vehicle.
1			Yes	No	Yes	No	Yes	No	Yes	No	$
2			Yes	No	Yes	No	Yes	No	Yes	No	$
3			Yes	No	Yes	No	Yes	No	Yes	No	$
4			Yes	No	Yes	No	Yes	No	Yes	No	$
5			Yes	No	Yes	No	Yes	No	Yes	No	$

ABSENT PARENT(S) AND/OR SPOUSE

Complete this section if absent parent(s) and/or spouse are alive but are not in the home. If this section does not apply to you, go to the next page. PLEASE NOTE: If you do not disclose the name(s) of and information about the absent parent(s) and/or agree to assist in taking court action against the absent parent(s), if necessary, assistance for yourself will not be granted unless you have good cause not to give information. However, eligibility for the children will still be evaluated.

	1. 1st Absent Parent or Spouse Name	1. 2nd Absent Parent or Spouse Name	1. 3rd Absent Parent or Spouse Name
2. Last Known Address (No., St., P.O. Box, RR)	3. City	2. Last Known Address (No., St., P.O. Box, RR)	3. City	2. Last Known Address (No., St., P.O. Box, RR)	3. City

2. Last Known Address (No., St., P.O. Box, RR)	3. City
4. State	5. Zip Code	6. Social Security No.	7. Date of Birth
8. Did Parent and Child(ren) Ever Live Together? Yes - When did parent leave (date) No
9. Were Parents Married To Each Other? Yes   No
10. If Yes, Are They Now Divorced? Yes   No
11. If Parents Were Never Married To Each Other, Was Paternity Legally Established? Yes   No
12. Has A Court Ordered Parent To Pay Support? Yes   No
13. If Yes, What Court?
14. Has A Court Ordered Parent To Pay Medical Expenses For The Child(ren)? Yes   No
15. Name(s) of Children
16.

(The above block — items 2 through 16 — is repeated identically for the 1st, 2nd, and 3rd Absent Parent or Spouse columns.)

Figure 1.   The Michigan Department of Social Services Assistance Application/Redetermination

tic question. In each case, the interrogative function of the elicitation item was implied. One can find examples of forms where syntactic questions are used, but it is only one of a range of structures used to elicit information on forms for adults.

Just as elicitation substructures are seldom syntactic questions, responses are seldom full sentences. Indeed, responses are often words or phrases rather than clauses. The reason for the syntactic simplicity of questions and responses on forms is economy. A form is often designed to elicit a variety of information in a limited space. Fuller question and response structures would be counterproductive.

This briefly introduces the organization and structural characteristics of forms that seem most relevant to our discussion of children's workbooks. In the section which follows we explore the organizational and structural properties of children's workbooks to see whether they could lead children to make certain generalizations about this genre that would prepare them for using forms when they grow older. Before plunging into our analysis, however, it is useful to point out that workbooks have been little studied. Osborn (1983) observed that the existing work failed to examine "the design, relevance, and efficacy of workbook tasks" (p. 46). Similarly, workbooks have not been examined to assess what contribution they might make to the acquisition of knowledge about the form genre.

But are workbooks central and frequent enough in grade school classrooms to be available as an important source of information about forms? In Osborn's (1983) study workbooks were observed to be used regularly as part of the instructional process in the teaching of reading. In fact, students spent "as much time reading and writing in their workbooks as they do interacting with their teachers" (Osborn, 1983, p.51). Of course there were other uses of time ranging from reading primers to fooling around. But the point is that when one examines the use of workbooks in the school classroom, they are as central an activity as any. This would suggest that they are used frequently enough to be a source of input for many things, including learning about forms. The purpose of this chapter is to suggest some preliminary thinking about what sorts of information workbooks might supply about forms. Whether children have acquired these details is a question we plan to assess in the future.

THE STRUCTURE OF WORKBOOK PAGES

In the discussion which follows, particular workbooks pages are referred to using a 3-term mnemonic: the series to which they belong (e.g., SF = Scott, Foresman or G = Ginn), the grade level of the workbook (PP = preprimer, 1, 2, or 6), and the particular page of the workbook under discussion. For example, page 95 of the Ginn grade-2 level would be G2–95. Our approach is first to describe the structure of workbook pages; then, where appropriate, we compare workbooks to forms.

Major Components of Workbook Pages

In order to understand the contents of workbook pages, let us examine two sample pages, one from the preprimer level of the Ginn series, GPP–1 (see Fig. 2) and the

VOCABULARY: word identification in context
BASIC WORDS: come, not

Level 2 "Come to the Play"

Figure 2. Sample page GPP–1.

other from the sixth-grade level of the Scott, Foresman series, SF6–54 (see Fig. 3).

At the top of each sample page is a space in which the student is to write his/her name. Below this space are the instructions. In the case of Figure 3 and the other pages of the Scott, Foresman series, a short title for the exercise is located in this area as well. With Figure 2 and most of the other Ginn pages, the instructions are set off by a heavy black line.[1]

In the area below the instructions, we find numbered units which evoke responses from the student and spaces in which the student is to write those responses.

---

[1]There are 8 pages in the Ginn series where instructions are not set off by dark lines.

Reuse of page: Have pupils list any pronouns they can find on the page and tell to whom each pronoun refers.

Commas

Read the paragraph. Write answers for the questions.

This year, Felicia, Ann is going to a special summer camp, Challenges, that meets in a wooded area near her school. Ann and her fellow campers, sixth-graders from Durban School, meet challenges like crossing a stream on a fallen log, scaling a high wall, sailing down a "zip wire," and crossing a rope bridge.

1. Who is going to a special summer camp? Ann

2. Who were her fellow campers? sixth-graders from Durban School

3. What was the camp called? Challenges

4. How many challenges are listed? four

5. Who was spoken to? Felicia

Read the paragraph. Write answers for the questions.

A few weeks ago, Kenny, Richard had to say goodby to Jerome, the guide dog pup he has been caring for and training for a year. Guide dogs used to be trained in kennels, but people found that it was better for the dogs to be with a loving family. During the training period Richard had to take Jerome for brisk walks into stores and restaurants, and on and off buses. Richard and Beth, Richard's sister, were sad to say goodby to Jerome but are looking forward to welcoming Cleo, a new guide dog puppy.

6. Who was spoken to? Kenny

7. Who was Jerome? a guide dog pup

8. How many things did Richard do with the dog? two or three

9. Who is Beth? Richard's sister

10. Who is Cleo? a new guide dog puppy

Assess Commas: of address, series, apposition

© 1981 Scott, Foresman and Company

Figure 3.   SF6–54.

We have termed the first *elicitation items* and the second *response slots. Elicitation items* are words, groups of words, sentences, groups of sentences, illustrations,[2] or any combination of these, which, in conjunction with the exercise instructions, require the student to formulate and write down one or more responses. In addition to the variation in the nature of elicitation items, the pages also differ in the frequency of such items per page. There may be as few as 1 elicitation item or as many as 16 on a single page. For example, Figure 2 has 5 numbered elicitation items, each of

[2]We use illustrations here to mean all color or black-and-white drawings, photographs, maps, and graphs.

which is an unfinished sentence to be completed by the student, whereas Figure 3 has 10 numbered elicitation items, each a direct question about a reading passage on the same page.

A significant difference between the elicitation items in Figure 2 and those in Figure 3 is the presence and absence, respectively, of response choices. Thus, we can speak of elicitation items as giving the student varying amounts of response latitude. Where an elicitation item includes or refers to a list of response choices from which the student is to choose the correct one, we say that the item has *limited response latitude*. The student's responses must come from the alternatives listed on the page, and once he/she chooses a response, the elements of that response are provided for him. In Figure 2, each elicitation item allows limited response latitude because it provides the student with two words as response choices. Another example of a workbook page with elicitation items allowing limited response latitude is shown in Figure 4 (G2–62). Here each item offers three response choices.

An elicitation item may also allow *open response latitude* as shown in Figure 3. On this page, the topic or focus of response is controlled by the elicitation item, but the content of the response is entirely up to the student. An additional example of elicitation items allowing open response latitude is shown in G6–93 (see Fig. 5) where the student must produce his or her own members for certain categories.

Midway on this continuum of response latitude is *semilimited response latitude*. Elicitation items with this latitude provide the student with some or all of the response elements, but these elements are not presented as mutually exclusive alternatives, and often the student must hunt for them or make certain decisions in order to

Name   62

Read each sentence. Then fill in the circle next to the word that goes into each sentence.

1. Lee liked to _____ stories.
   ○ white   ● write   ○ right

2. Joe _____ ask his friends to lunch.
   ● would   ○ wood   ○ weed

3. Sometimes Will _____ books about trains.
   ○ red   ● read   ○ reed

4. Rosa had _____ pet rabbits.
   ○ fur   ○ for   ● four

5. Would you like to go, _____?
   ○ to   ● too   ○ two

Figure 4. G2–62.

Name

Read each category and the item listed below it. Then write two
more items for each category. **Answers will vary. Examples are given.**

---

1. Animals that Live in Water

   whales

   seals

   lobsters

2. Sports

   volleyball

   tennis

   basketball

3. Things Used to Measure

   barometer

   ruler

   thermometer

4. Sticky Things

   glue

   adhesive tape

   molasses

Figure 5.   G6–93.

---

compile his/her own list of possible response choices. An example of this can be found on G2–91 (see Fig. 6). On this page, the student is given a mock shopping list which contains the elements needed to respond to the elicitation items below it. However, the student must independently extract the most pertinent information from each of the shopping list articles. For example, in elicitation item 4, the student must determine that the key word in the information provided about the flour is "small." Because she/he must refine response elements given, we say that the elicitation item allows a semilimited rather than a limited response latitude.

It is clear from this discussion that the topic, focus, and often the very elements of the student's response are directed by the elicitation item. But the way in which the student represents this response on the workbook page is governed by the response slot. A *response slot* can be defined as the space provided for the written response to an elicitation item. On Figures 2, 3, 5, and 6, the response slots are blank lines upon which the responses are to be written. However, pages in workbooks vary greatly in form. In addition to blank lines, response slots can be empty circles next to a list of response choices (e.g., SF2–58; Fig. 7), rows of boxes in crossword puzzle exercises (e.g., G6–92; Fig. 8), or even the space around a sentence that is to be circled or underlined (e.g., G6–102; Fig. 9).

Therefore, we can speak more specifically about *slot types,* the conventionalized ways in which responses are written on workbook pages. A single response to an elicitation item can be represented by many different slot types. For example, the elicitation item may call for the choice of one word, phrase, or sentence over another, but this choice can be represented on the workbook page by underlining the correct item, circling it, writing it in a specified space, or by filling in a circle next to it. This is illustrated on Figures 2, 4, 9, and 10. In each case the elicitation items require that the student choose the appropriate word to finish the sentence. Yet, the

Name

Jeff's mother has left a note for him. Read the note.
Then write the correct answer to each question.

Dear Jeff,

I am going to visit Grandma for the morning Remember
the surprise dinner we are going to cook for Dad's birthday
tonight? Please go to the store and get these things

2 small melons   1 dozen eggs
4 ears of corn   1 small bag of flour
1 bunch of grapes   1 jar of pickles
2 cans of tuna   4 potatoes
1 large chicken

1. How many melons should Jeff get? _____ 2 _____

2. Should the chicken be large or small? _____ large _____

3. How many eggs should Jeff buy? _____ 1 dozen _____

4. What size bag of flour should he get? _____ small _____

5. How many cans of tuna should Jeff buy? _____ 2 _____

From Ginn Reading Program Level 8 Skillpack copyrighted by Ginn and Company

LIFE SKILLS: consumer information (shopping list)

Level 8 "Life Skill: Shopping List"

Figure 6. G2–91.

9 Crystal Kingdom
Use with Reinforce 2, Skills Unit 9   NAME

Word Grab Bag

Fill in the circle next to the word your teacher says.

1. ⓐ hobby   2. ⓐ act   3. ⓐ dark
   ⓑ hungry   ⓑ arm   ⓑ dime
   ⓒ hurry   ⓒ aunt   ⓒ dry

Figure 7. SF2–58.

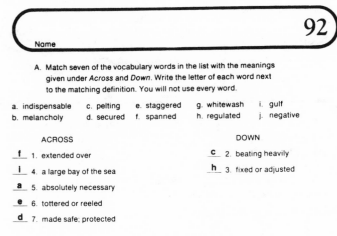

A. Match seven of the vocabulary words in the list with the meanings given under *Across* and *Down*. Write the letter of each word next to the matching definition. You will not use every word.

a. indispensable   c. pelting   e. staggered   g. whitewash   i. gulf
b. melancholy   d. secured   f. spanned   h. regulated   j. negative

ACROSS

f 1. extended over
i 4. a large bay of the sea
a 5. absolutely necessary
e 6. tottered or reeled
d 7. made safe; protected

DOWN

c 2. beating heavily
h 3. fixed or adjusted

Figure 8. G6–92.

response is represented on paper in four different ways, that is, with four different response slots.

Of course, certain slot types are not suited to certain elicitation items. An elicitation item with open response latitude, for instance, cannot have a corresponding response slot in which response choices are to be circled. Where an elicitation item allows open response latitude it is most common to have blank lines as the accompanying slot type (see Fig. 3). However, in general semiopen and open response latitudes permit a great variety of slot types.

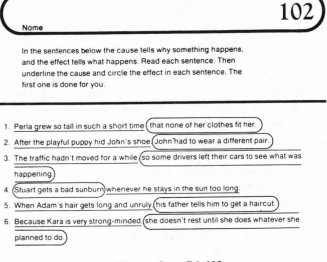

In the sentences below the cause tells why something happens, and the effect tells what happens. Read each sentence. Then underline the cause and circle the effect in each sentence. The first one is done for you.

1. Perla grew so tall in such a short time that none of her clothes fit her.
2. After the playful puppy hid John's shoe, John had to wear a different pair.
3. The traffic hadn't moved for a while, so some drivers left their cars to see what was happening.
4. Stuart gets a bad sunburn whenever he stays in the sun too long.
5. When Adam's hair gets long and unruly, his father tells him to get a haircut.
6. Because Kara is very strong-minded, she doesn't rest until she does whatever she planned to do.

Figure 9. G6–102.

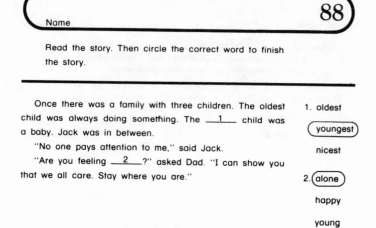

Read the story. Then circle the correct word to finish
the story.

Once there was a family with three children. The oldest   1. oldest
child was always doing something. The ___1___ child was
a baby. Jack was in between.   youngest
    "No one pays attention to me," said Jack.   nicest
    "Are you feeling ___2___?" asked Dad. "I can show you
that we all care. Stay where you are."   2. alone

                                                               happy

                                                               young

Figure 10. G2–88.

We have now identified many of the components found on a typical workbook page: the instructions, elicitation items (each allowing limited, semilimited, or open response latitudes), and the response slots (each having a particular slot type). An additional component is the reference material. As shown in Figure 4, the student can formulate a response to each elicitation item based solely on the information provided with that item. In Figure 3, however, the student must leave the elicitation item to refer to one of the reading passages located elsewhere on the page in order to obtain the information needed to respond to that item. When material is spatially removed from an elicitation item and yet must be referred to in order to complete that item, we term it *reference material.*

Reference material may also consist of graphics such as illustrations (e.g., SF6–71; Fig. 11) and tables as well as simulated articles or real-world materials (e.g., G2–91; Fig. 6).

Instructions, elicitation items, response items, and response slots (plus reference material) are organized as sets. One set, or section as we have termed it, generally occupies the space of one entire workbook page. In some cases, however, more than one section occurs on a single workbook page (often divided by a dark line or by extra spacing; e.g., G6–69, Fig. 12). While multiple sections on a page are related to each other topically or thematically (they may even share reference material), one or more section components may differentiate one section from another. For example, in Figure 12, one section is differentiated from another in terms of the skills required by the instructions and elicitation items, even though the response choices and slot types are similar in both. In A on Figure 12, the student must correctly combine a root and a prefix, whereas in B the newly formed words must be used appropriately in a sentence.

Graphs

Study the graphs and answer the questions.

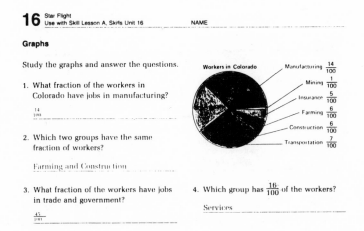

1. What fraction of the workers in Colorado have jobs in manufacturing?

$\frac{14}{100}$

2. Which two groups have the same fraction of workers?

Farming and Construction

3. What fraction of the workers have jobs in trade and government?

$\frac{45}{100}$

4. Which group has $\frac{16}{100}$ of the workers?

Services

Figure 11. SF6–71.

In contrast, the two sections in Figure 3 share similar instructions, elicitation items, and slot types, but are set apart by different reference material.

We found it significant that a unit with consistent structure such as the "section" unit appears to be basic to the workbook page. Thus, we have used the "section" rather than the page as the basic unit of analysis in our discussion. To facilitate reference to a particular section in a multisection page, hereafter we refer to sections with roman numerals. For example, SF6–54II refers to the second section on page 54 of the Scott, Foresman sixth-grade workbook.

Organization of Page Components

One of the most striking features of the workbook pages we studied was the consistent top-to-bottom orientation of the exercises. Where a page had more than one section, the sections were always arranged vertically, as in Figures 3 and 12. Within sections, there were three dominant arrangements. In the simplest, elicitation items were placed in a single column and numbered from top to bottom (see Fig. 4) or unnumbered (see Fig. 13).

In a variation of this, elicitation items were embedded in a text, and students were to complete the items as they proceeded through the text in the standard left-to-right, top-to-bottom direction (e.g., SF2–46; see Fig. 14).

A third dominant pattern occurred where there were two or three columns of elicitation items (we never encountered more than three columns). Within this third pattern there were two variations. One can be seen in G6–93 (Fig. 5) and the other on SF2–61 (Fig. 15). In the first, the student proceeds left to right across the columns until the end of the line, then moves downward to the next line and repeats this process. In the second, the student proceeds from top to bottom in the left-most column, then moves right to the top of the next column, moves downward in this column, and so on to the next column, if there is one. In all three cases, the major

271

A. Look at the meaning of each prefix found in the box. Then use these meanings to help you add the correct prefix to a word to give it a particular meaning. In the blank write each word you form.

Prefix	Meaning
inter-	between; among; with
intra-	within or inside
extra-	beyond or outside

1. Add a prefix to *state* to make a word that means "within a state." __intrastate__

2. Add a prefix to *weave* to make a word that means "weave between." __interweave__

3. Add a prefix to *ordinary* to make a word that means "beyond or outside what is normal or ordinary." __extraordinary__

4. Add a prefix to *stellar* to make a word that means "between the stars." __interstellar__

5. Add a prefix to *curricular* to make a word that means "outside the normal curriculum." __extracurricular__

B. Now in each of the sentences below use one of the words formed above.

6. Drama club, dance club, and the school newspaper were among her **extracurricular** activities.

7. Aretha always seems to have __extraordinary__ stamina when she races.

8. I will try to __interweave__ the threads that have come loose.

9. The new popular movie deals with __interstellar__ travel.

10. The smaller trucking companies make only __intrastate__ deliveries.

From Ginn Reading Program Level 13 Skillpack. Copyrighted by Ginn and Company

DECODING: prefixes inter-, intra-, extra-

Level 13 "Weird and Wacky Inventions," "How Can I Improve It . . . ?"

Figure 12. G6–69.

progression involves one or more top-to-bottom passes. Only 7 of a total of 322 sections in all the examined workbooks were exceptions to these arrangements.[3] All other sections conformed to one of the three top-to-bottom arrangements.

---

[3]SF1–59, SF1–89, and GPP–28 had multiple columns and unnumbered elicit ation items. Thus, the student could proceed in any direction. SF6–71 and SF6–72 were sections b roken up in the center by reference material and thus had a slightly different arrangement; and G2–56 and G2–94 were sections in which the final elicitation item was located adjacent to its predecessor rather than below it.

7 Crystal Kingdom
Use with Reinforce 2, Skills Unit 7 NAME

A Good Blend

Read the story. Draw a circle around the word in dark print that makes sense in the sentence.

Martha was sitting in a **(cling, swing)** when she saw the spaceship. It fell from the **(true, blue)** sky like a **(flake, snake)** of snow. Martha watched in wonder as the spaceship landed behind a big raspberry bush.

A little door in the ship opened very slowly. Two tiny space people **(truck, stuck)** their heads out. They waved to Martha with their red and **(pint, pink)** arms.

"Hi," said the space people together. "Is this earth?" Martha nodded.

"Finally!" the space people **(cried, tried)**. "You **(just, junk)** can't imagine how **(long, lock)** we've been looking for this planet! May we have one of these raspberries?"

Figure 13. SF2–46.

COMPARING FORMS AND WORKBOOKS

Sections

Now that we have developed an overview of the features of workbooks and forms, we can begin to compare them directly. One of the characteristics of forms used by adults is that their pages often contain more than one section (see Fig. 1). That is to say the reader is often confronted with more than one set of instructions, more than one type of elicitation item, and more than one type of response slot. We wondered whether children's workbooks displayed a similar degree of complexity. In our analysis of the components of workbook pages we observed that there was a tendency for sections, instructions, elicitation items, and response slots to covary. That is, each section tended to have its own set of instructions, elicitation items, and response slots. So it made sense to look at the number of sections per page and use this measure as an indirect means of assessing the internal complexity of workbook pages.

Table 1 describes the average number of sections per page at the various grade levels. As can be seen, each page had an average of one section in the early grades; by sixth grade there was a modest increase. Those pages with more than one section per page all consisted of two sections only with the exception of two pages with three sections per page in the Scott, Foresman workbook. These findings suggest that pages with multiple sections are not common in children's workbooks. However, the data indicated that by the time a child had reached junior high school, she/he should have begun to encounter the multiple-section page.

Figure 14. SF2–46.

Instructions

Forms prepared for adult readers vary in the nature of instructions. Sometimes instructions are very general, often consisting of a global request that the reader complete the item. By *global request* we mean a directive to complete a form that does not at the same time specify the type of response desired. This is illustrated in the following example. "Thank you for purchasing a Hamilton Beach product. In order to provide you better products and services in the future, we would greatly appreciate your completing this card and returning it to us." In other cases, there are *explicit* instructions as in "Please check your choice in the appropriate box," or

Roots and Endings

Write the root word of each word in dark print on the line.

1. Oliver Tribble **owns** a music store.
   _____

   _____

2. He thinks that music is the **sweetest** sound in the world. But, alas, Oliver cannot play a single instrument.
   _____

   _____

3. One night, Oliver discovered that he had left his **glasses** in the music store. It was very late when he returned to the store.
   _____

   _____

4. The moon was **golden** in the sky.
   _____

   _____

5. Oliver's glasses were **resting** beside a violin.
   _____
   --------------------- ----------------
   _____

6. As Oliver reached for them, his fingers brushed the **violin's** strings. Then Oliver had a funny feeling.
   _____

   _____

7. He **picked** up the violin and began to play.
   _____

   _____

8. He played as if he had been **playing** all his life.
   _____

   _____

9. The next morning the magic was gone. Oliver could no **longer** play.
   _____

   _____

10. But Oliver **says** he will never sell that violin. Perhaps some night the magic will happen again.
    _____

    _____

Practice Root words, Endings

Figure 15.   SF2–61.

Table 1.   Sections in Each Page

Grade level	Series	N sections	N pages	M
PP	G	44	44	1.0
1	SF	52	52	1.0
2	G	50	50	1.0
2	SF	51	50	1.0
6	G	58	50	1.2
6	SF	69	50	1.4

"Write directions to your home below." Still other forms include instructions that are far more *implicit*. In these, the type of information requested is expressed explicitly, but the request itself is implicit. this is illustrated in the following example:

Name _____

Address _____

Phone _____

Experienced readers interpret such a format as a request for information, even though an explicit request is absent. And it can be argued that form writers depend on adults' familiarity with forms when they draft forms without explicit instructions.

Although forms may have global, explicit, or implicit instructions, often one finds that forms for adults are a combination of global and implicit or explicit and implicit instructions. For example, the University of Michigan uses a form for reporting characteristics of applicants who were seriously considered for positions involving a national search. Some parts of the form explicitly describe what is required of the individual completing the form e.g., "Below list the names of all the applicants who were seriously considered for the position. . ." However, other parts use the implicit format, as in a column headed "Field of Specialization."

While form writers can or do assume that their audience has had sufficient experience with forms to understand global or implicit instructions, such references cannot be made so readily when children are the audience. Hence, it is not surprising that the workbooks we sampled included instructions on every page.[4] Moreover, the instructions in each series were largely explicit in telling the child what is required. Indeed, these instructions not only told the child what type of response was required but also directed the child to the response slot. Here are examples illustrating just how explicit these instructions tend to be.

Pick the word that best fits the picture. Write the word in the blanks. (SF1–56)

Read the story. Then fill in the circle next to the best answer to each question. (G2–62)

Put an X in the square before the sentence that best states the main idea. (SF6–14)

It seems clear that the writers of workbooks regard instructions as something students need in order to know how to respond to a workbook page.[5]

While we found instructions primarily to be explicit, there was some variation in the degree of explicitness. First, let us view explicitness as a continuum with the most explicit instructions on the left and the least explicit on the right. In each series both the earliest workbook examined and the second-grade workbooks could best be described by locating their instructions at the leftmost end of the the continuum.

---

[4]The first readers in a series have no instructions. Instead, the teacher is to provide the childlren with directions regarding how to complete a page. Apparently, those involved in writing workbooks assume that children do not have the working vocabulary, syntactic knowledge, or experience with forms to be able to interpret written instructions.

[5]Whether instructions are needed as often as they appear in a particular workbook is debatable, given the repetition in types of responses required over the course of a single workbook.

Instructions described what to do, how to do it, and where to record the response. By sixth grade, however, one began to find instructions that told the student what type of response was required but did not detail its location.

Consider the following examples from the sixth-grade workbooks.

Use each word above to complete the following sentences. (G6–7III)

Now complete the puzzle using the words whose meanings are given above. (G6–92II)

Use the mileage table below to answer the questions. (SF6–93)

In the first example the student learns that a word is to be used to complete a sentence, but the instructions do not specify that the word is to be written on the lines below. In the second example, the student is told to finish the puzzle, but this does not include the directive to put the words in the boxes of the puzzle. Similarly, the student is told to answer questions in the third example but is not instructed to write the answers on the lines. So while the sixth-grade instructions are far more explicit than the global instructions "Complete the items below," they lack specific information about the location of the response. Thus, they would fall somewhere toward the middle third of the explicitness continuum. Table 2 describes the percent of explicit instructions at each grade level.

As shown in Table 2, the general pattern at all grade levels was the use of explicit instructions. Even so, there was a noticeable decline in the use of explicit instructions in the sixth-grade sample. In the Scott, Foresman series this decline is accounted for largely by an increase in the frequency of instructions which ask the student "to answer the questions."

Who is going to a special summer camp? _____ (SF6–54)

(In an exercise about personification)
What is talked about as if it were a person? _____ (SF–103II)

In the Ginn series, no single instruction type accounts for the decline in explicit instructions. Therefore it can be seen that students are gradually provided with less explicit information in instructions as they move into the upper grades.

Elicitation Items and Responses
If one wishes to compare workbooks and forms, characteristics of the items used to elicit information are central to this matter. If you skim a page of a form, you often

Table 2. Explicit Instructions by Grade

Grade level	Series	N sections	% explicit
PP	G	44	100
1	SF	52	88
2	G	50	100
2	SF	51	94
6	G	58	81
6	SF	69	75

find a number of different sections, each consisting of a series of elicitation items requesting various types of information. If workbooks are potential sources of information about forms, then they ought to provide similar multiple opportunities on a single page to request information from a reader. In Table 1 we saw that workbook pages typically consisted of a single section. In that regard, they demanded much less of the child than a form often did from an adult and did not offer an opportunity to prepare for the multisection character of forms. Although workbooks might not present the same overall level of difficulty when the entire page is taken into account, within sections we might still find the child challenged by a series of elicitation items. So we examined the within-section composition of workbooks to see what they asked of a child.

We were first interested in determining whether page sections consisted of one or more than one elicitation item. Table 3 describes the number of elicitation items per section. Like the sections on forms, Table 3 suggests that workbook sections consist of multiple elicitation items. So in both cases the reader is asked a variety of questions. The frequency of multiple questions appears to increase with grade level, although the data are suggestive more than conclusive. At any rate, the major structural component of workbooks—the section—can be said to present a student with a context for eliciting information that bears some similarity to forms.

What signals help a child proceed through the elicitation items in a section? One obvious cue is the frequent top-to-bottom orientation of the page, and this orientation is similar to that used on forms. But children do not have the same level of experience as adults do, so it would not be surprising to find other cues available to children to guide them through the exercises. Another possibility is numbering. In examining forms, one discovers that elicitation items are often unnumbered. This is no doubt because adult readers are assumed to have sufficient experience to make their way through the items without a great deal of difficulty. Children would not be as experienced and so might benefit by the numbering of workbook elicitation items. Table 4 summarizes the percent of sections with numbered elicitation items. A section was viewed as consisting of numbered elicitation items if all of the items in that section were numbered.

As shown in Table 4, the numbering of elicitation items appears at all grade levels. Indeed, nearly all sections have numbered elicitation items. So we have seen that workbook sections consist of multiple elicitation items that are, for the most

Table 3. Elicitation Items by Section

Grade level	Series	N sections	N elicitation items	M
PP	G	44	254	5.8
1	SF	52	235	4.5
2	G	50	334	6.7
2	SF	51	289	5.7
6	G	58	402	6.9
6	SF	69	508	7.4

Table 4. Percent of Sections with
Numbered Elicitation Items

Grade level	Series	% sections
PP	G	97.7
1	SF	90.4
2	G	100.0
2	SF	90.2
6	G	93.1
6	SF	91.3

part, numbered. Having touched on the organizational characteristics of elicitation items, it seems appropriate to turn now to their structural properties.

When we think about children's workbooks as potential sources of information about forms, the way workbook items elicit information and the type of responses required are at the very core of the matter. One of the characteristics that sets forms apart from other spoken and written genres that elicit information is the frequent use of simplified syntactic structures in elicitation items. One is struck by the frequent use of phrasal or lexical requests for information or forms such as: date of accident; name; years at current address; age if under 18 on date of departure (Wright, 1980); and explanation of other work expenses. The presence of syntactically reduced structures is not restricted to forms, but it seems to account for a good deal of their language, particularly when one focuses on the structures used to request information.

We wondered whether the sampled workbooks shared this characteristic with forms. While there is no statistical information available on the frequency of lexical and phrasal elicitation items, we can still ask whether workbooks offer examples of such elicitation items. If workbooks provide a model for the elicitation items of forms, one would expect either that workbooks would elicit information using phrasal or lexical elicitation items or that they would do this increasingly as the children become more sophisticated users of workbooks. In the former view, phrasal or lexical forms would be present throughout the workbook; in the latter view they would become more frequent over time.

To address this question we examined the syntactic structure of the elicitation items in the workbook samples at each grade level. Elicitation items that were pictures and consequently had no syntactic structure were excluded from analysis (e.g., GPP–15; Fig. 16).

In Figure 16, the elicitation item is the picture on the left and the response slot is the circle to be filled in which accompanies the correct description of the picture. While we could evaluate the syntactic structure of the textual component of items such as in Figure 16, the full elicitation item could not be said to consist of text only. In these cases the picture was intimately tied to the text and necessary for formulating a response. Accordingly, we excluded such items from our analysis.

In the remaining elicitation items, we determined which consisted of reduced

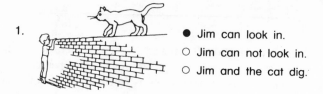

Name   15

Look at the picture. Then read the sentences.
Fill in the circle next to the sentence that goes
with the picture.

1.
● Jim can look in.
○ Jim can not look in.
○ Jim and the cat dig.

Figure 16. GPP-15.

syntax, that is, of lexical and phrasal elicitation items. We looked for instances in which information was elicited through the use of a word (see Fig. 17) or a phrase (see Fig. 8).

Table 5 describes the percentage of elicitation items that were lexical or phrasal in structure.

The data in Table 5 show that the two workbook series differed in the relative frequency with which they used lexical and phrasal elicitation items with Ginn employing these structures much more often throughout the sample studied. Despite this difference, there were important similarities. First, the frequency with which a series used phrasal and lexical elicitation structures varied moderately at most. Second, as a consequence, there was no apparent increase in the frequency with which syntactically reduced elicitation items were used through the grade range studied in both series. Accordingly, students did not receive increasing exposure to elicitation items that were structurally similar to those used in forms. More importantly, in no sense could workbooks be said to consist of phrasal and lexical elicitation items as the basic structural device for eliciting information. They certainly did provide some opportunity to work with such structures, although the magnitude of this opportunity varied considerably by series.

'While workbooks requested information from children, they also offered the opportunity for children to provide that information and they constrained the type of response required. As we described earlier, an elicitation item allowed the student a certain degree of response latitude, i.e., freedom to formulate the content of his/her response. While response latitude lies on a continuum from completely limited to completely open, it was possible to characterize the response latitude of a particular elicitation item as highly constrained (limited), partially constrained (semilimited), or relatively unconstrained (open).

A response of limited latitude consisted of selecting a response from a predeter-

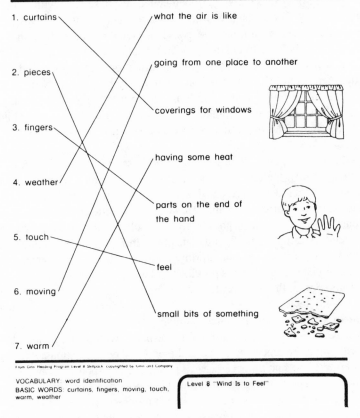

VOCABULARY: word identification
BASIC WORDS: curtains, fingers, moving, touch, warm, weather

Level 8 "Wind Is to Feel"

Figure 17. G2–54.

Table 5. Lexical and Phrasal Elicitation Items by Grade

Grade level	Series	N excluded	% lexical, phrasal
PP	G	171	24.1 (20/83)
1	SF	107	9.4 (12/128)
2	G	11	13.3 (43/323)
2	SF	15	1.8 (5/274)
6	G	0	21.1 (85/402)
6	SF	0	5.9 (30/508)

mined set that appeared on the page. In forms, responses with limited latitudes were often used when the range of responses from which the set was drawn was limited by the nature of the set. For example, an individual completing an order blank for tickets to a performance might be presented with a set including all days of the week on which the performance was to be held. Since the performance was to be held on those days and only those days, an open-ended response (one with item response latitude such as "When would you like to see this performance?") would be inappropriate. Thus, the use of limited response latitude reflected real-world constraints on the possible choices. In children's workbooks, limited response latitudes were often used when knowledge of particular information was being tested. In this regard, the members of the set were constrained only by what the writers wished to test rather than the sort of real-world limits that might be found on forms. Another reason for the use of limited latitude responses in workbooks was that children had limited knowledge and might not be able to generate appropriate answers without assistance.

In contrast to responses with limited latitude, semilimited and open latitude responses constrained the child's response to a lesser degree. When a response was semilimited, the child was presented with a predetermined body of material from which to select the correct response. However, in contrast to limited responses the child must select his or her responses from a "field" in which the correct response is embedded. SF2–61 (Fig. 15) illustrates this. In Figure 15, the child is asked to write the root of each word in dark print on the lines below each sentence or set of sentences. While the full word is provided and displayed in boldface type, the child does not know what the specific alternatives are. So she/he knows that the root must be drawn from the letters of the word, but various options are not set out in the way they are in a response with limited latitude.

In a typical elicitation item calling for a response with open latitude, the child is presented with a reference paragraph and then is asked a question about that material. Often the information necessary to produce the response is obtained inferentially from reading the reference material. Most importantly, however, the range of responses is not packaged for the child as it is in responses with limited latitude. In this respect, one can argue that responses with open latitude place the greatest demands on the child. In such responses, the child must generate the response on his/her own. This can be seen in Figure 18 (SF6–82).

Figure 18 illustrates the type of material a child must utilize in order to generate an open response and the type of elicitation item employed to elicit that response. In most cases the child must pull together information presented in the paragraph with other world knowledge he/she possesses. For example, in the Juan paragraph in SF6–82 (Fig. 18), Juan is doing homework when his mother asks him to set the table. In order to answer the question about the time of day, the reader must put together the facts about homework and table setting with knowledge of the time of day such things generally occur based on his/her own experience.

With this view of the degree of response latitude, how might responses of different latitude be employed in workbooks at different grade levels? One would predict

House of page Have pupils reread the paragraph about Juan and
underline the exact words spoken by Juan's mother.

Time and Place Relationships

Read each paragraph below. Then answer the questions about
when and where the actions or events took place.

Ruth got off the ski lift. She decided to
ski down Boomer Trail for her last run of
the day. The sun was so low in the sky
that long tree shadows snaked across the
trail. It had been a beautiful day of
skiing—bright and sunny. And the snow
was almost perfect. Ruth hoped that the
rest of the week would be as nice.

1. What season of the year is it?

   winter _____

2. What time of day is it?

   late afternoon _____

Beryl went over to visit with Mrs.
Dwight after school. She checked at the
nurses' station for the room number, and
then went up to room 504. Mrs. Dwight
was looking much better and told Beryl
the doctor had said she could go home
tomorrow. Beryl went home feeling happy.
In fact, she was singing as she set the table
for supper.

3. Where did Beryl visit Mrs. Dwight?

   in the hospital _____

4. When did she visit?

   after school _____

Tom and his parents were on a small
bus that was winding its way steadily
upward into the California mountains. It
was late afternoon on a September day
and Sequoia National Park was beautiful.
Tom breathed deeply of the scent of the
forest on both sides. Then he saw the
giant sequoias. He could scarcely believe
any trees could be that huge!

5. In what national park is Tom?

   Sequoia National Park _____

6. What season of the year is it?

   fall _____

Juan sat at his desk, trying to
concentrate on his social studies
homework. It was not easy. His sister and
a friend were in the next room giving each
other dancing lessons. Finally, his mother
called, "Time to set the table, Juan. It's
your week." Juan was glad to set the
homework aside and glad his dad would
be home soon.

7. Is Juan at home or at school?

   at home _____

8. What time of day is it?

   almost dinnertime. _____

Scott Foresman and Company

Figure 18. SF6–82.

that limited latitude responses would be more prevalent in lower-grade workbooks
and open responses would be more prevalent in higher-grade workbooks. For each
section, we determined the nature of the response latitude. In eight sections, there
were two response latitudes. In those cases, we counted each latitude. The result
was that the number of latitudes slightly exceeded the number of sections; hence the
marginal total in Table 6 are greater than 100%.

Two patterns are worth noting in Table 6. First, limited response latitudes are the
preferred type at all grade levels. At the lowest level over 90% of all sections utilized limited responses in both series. By sixth grade the series differed in the extent
to which they employed limited response latitudes, although in both cases it re-

Table 6. Response Latitude by Grade Level

Grade level	Series	Latitude type	% sections with this latitude
PP	G	Limited	97.7
		Semilimited	2.3
		Open	—
1	SF	Limited	94.2
		Semilimited	9.6
		Open	—
2	G	Limited	98.0
		Semilimited	2.0
		Open	—
2	SF	Limited	78.4
		Semilimited	19.6
		Open	7.8
6	G	Limited	79.3
		Semilimited	6.9
		Open	13.8
6	SF	Limited	44.9
		Semilimited	36.2
		Open	23.2

mained the latitude of choice. Second, responses with open latitude did not appear with regularity in both series until the sixth grade in our sample. What this suggests is that workbooks offer a child practice in responding to questions by selecting from a range of predetermined responses and that this remains a major characteristic of the nature of responses required of children until late in their elementary school years. By then, children are asked to generate their own answers in response to elicitation items.

We have discussed the latitude of responses but have not examined the types of response slots themselves. In a visual comparison of adult forms and children's workbooks, response slots were the most obvious shared feature. Many of the slot types found on workbook pages are easily recognized by the adult as typical of everyday bureaucratic paperwork. To capture the utilization of slot types in workbooks, we calculated the average number of slot types per section. Then we recorded which slot types were present in each section and how often they occurred relative to all slot types in that particular workbook.

As can be seen in Table 7, workbooks rarely mixed slot types within a single section. This simplicity might well provide the student with clear, early lessons about slot types. Over an entire workbook, however, there might be as few as 5 or as many as 11 different slot types used, as shown in Figure 19.

The slot type "Write the answer on the line" occurred most often in all the workbooks we studied: roughly one third to one half of the sections use this slot type. The next most common types were "Draw a circle around," "Fill in the circle next

Table 7. Slot Types in Each Section

Grade level	Series	Total	Average
PP	G	44/44	1.0
1	SF	66/52	1.3
2	G	50/50	1.0
2	SF	54/51	1.1
6	G	59/58	1.0
6	SF	76/69	1.1

to," and "Underline." The great variety of slot types used both within each workbook and within each series suggests that children should have encountered many of the slot types they would see on adult forms by the time they were at the sixth-grade level.

DISCUSSION

Workbooks are central to reading programs for the school-age child, and yet little attention has been paid to the possible contribution they might make to how children go about learning to read a major genre of contemporary American life, i.e., forms. The purpose of this chapter has been a first effort in this direction. Our ability to generalize from the findings reported here is, of course, limited by the size of our sample and the idiosyncracies of the individual workbook series we studied. Even so, our analyses were aimed at drawing a rough sketch of the characteristics of workbooks that might provide children with clues to the nature of forms. A next step in addressing this situation would be to collect more direct information by studying teacher and student behavior with workbooks and forms in naturalistic or laboratory settings.

When we asked what workbooks taught children about forms, the picture that emerged was complex. Our analyses pointed to some striking similarities and some important differences between workbooks and forms. Many of the differences could be explained by the different functions of workbooks and forms. Workbooks are a pedagogical tool (whether they do this effectively is a question that is outside the scope of this chapter); forms are not. They are used to record and report information. Some of the very important characteristics of workbooks noted in our analyses are a consequence of this pedagogical function. First, consider the components of workbooks. Workbooks were found to consist of instructions, elicitation items, response slots, and reference material. Forms contain the first three components but generally do not include reference material. If we think about the function of reference material as essential to the pedagogic function of workbooks, it is easy to understand why workbooks would have reference material and forms would not. Typically, reference material provides the student with the opportunity to learn new information, practice prose reading, or develop skills in reading and understanding graphic displays such as tables, maps, and graphs. The goal is learning. In forms,

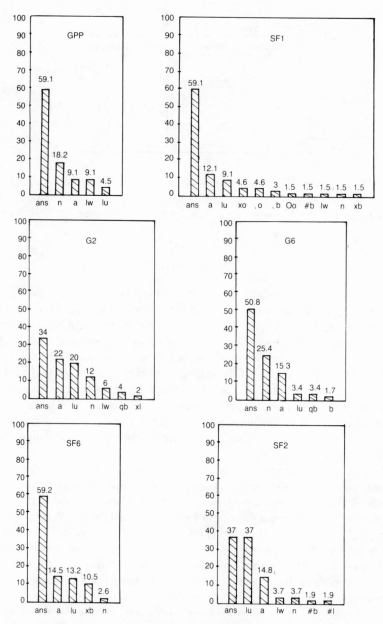

Figure 19. RESPONSE SLOT TYPES

ANS, write answer on line; N, fill in circle next to; A, draw a circle around; LU, underline; LW, draw a line between; B, put a in the box; XL, put an X on the line; XO, put an X on; O, put a on; OO, put an O on; #B, put the number in the box; QB, put letter(s) in the box(es); #L, write number on the line; XB, put an x in the box.

the user is providing information for the record and is presumed to have the necessary skills and information to do this.[6] As such, we would not expect reference material to be a common component of forms.

The teaching function of workbooks also helps explain why highly constrained responses (those with limited latitude) were the response type of choice in our sample. If you are interested in testing specific knowledge, you maximize the probability of eliciting reactions directly relevant to it, if you preselect the range of responses. When the range of responses is not constrained, as in open latitude responses, there is increased opportunity for answers that fall far from the mark.

Another factor which accounts for the differences between workbooks and forms reported here is the audience to which the material is directed—adult versus child readers. Children are presumed to be less experienced readers and to have more limited knowledge of the world. Accordingly, workbook writers seem to make the assumption that children will have difficulty reading and understanding the syntactically reduced elicitation items typically found on forms. This may explain the use of full sentences rather than lexical and phrasal elicitation items. Similarly, the use of limited response items can be seen as a device to compensate for the child's limited knowledge. By offering explicit alternatives to choose from, possible gaps in what the child knows are filled. Similarly, children are also expected to know less about the workbook genre, and workbooks are designed to take this into account. For example, recall that workbooks contained one section per page and generally one type of elicitation item and one type of response latitude. Similarly, nearly all instructions used in our sample were explicit, that is, they told the child exactly what was required. Explicit instructions go along way toward helping the child figure out what is required in a workbook exercise and as such can be viewed as responsive to the child's inexperience. Whether workbooks continue to provide explicit instructions beyond the developmental point where they are needed is a question that must be addressed separately. Suffice it to say that they would seem to provide additional guidance for the inexperienced reader.

There are other differences between workbooks and forms that we did not have the opportunity to cover in this chapter. One in particular must be mentioned. Forms often contain many sections on a page. In addition, sections on forms include complex matrices that tax even the most experienced user. The processing demands of pages with many sections and with graphically demanding contexts is strikingly absent from the workbooks we studied. Since workbooks are aimed at teaching content and, we hope, do so using tools that support rather than impede access to the content, it was not surprising that the matrices and multiple sections of forms were absent from workbooks. The workbooks we studied offered very little in the way of preparation for the difficulties adults encounter in some of the forms they must complete.

---

[6]Recently, there had been considerable concern over the inability of many Americans to use the written materials of modern American life such as phone directories, bus schedules, and forms. This skill known as functional literacy, therefore, is not something we can assume all readers possess.

Despite the differences between workbooks and forms, we have noted many similarities especially in the area of structure and organization. Workbooks require that students learn to understand and relate the major components of the workbook pages. Since most of the major components of workbooks are also found in forms, the set of skills learned through interacting with the structure of workbooks will serve the student well when it comes to using forms later on. They also provide the child with a variety of elicitation items and response slots and so expose the child to the frames for eliciting and responding to information that will be compatible with the elicitation-response character of forms.

A good deal of criticism has been leveled at workbooks. It has not been the purpose of this chapter to address these. It has been our goal, however, to assess the possible contributions workbooks might make to exposing children to a genre with which they must interact on a routine basis as adult participants in this society. The task remains to appreciate the differences between workbooks and forms and then to exploit their similarities in classrooms.

REFERENCES

Cairns, J., Galloway, E., &Tierney, R. (1981). *Crystal Kingdom: Workbook*. Glenview, IL: Scott, Foresman.

Clanchy, M.T. (1979). *From memory to written record, England 1066-1307*. London:Edward Arnold.

Clymer, T., & Venezky, R. (1982). *Give me a clue: Skillpack* (Teacher's Edition). Lexington, MA: Ginn.

Clymer, T., & Venezky, R. (1982). *Little dog laughed: Skillpack* (Teacher's Edition). Lexington, MA: Ginn.

Clymer, T., Venezky, R., & Indrisano, R. (1982). *Flights of color: Skillpack* (Teacher's Edition). Lexington, MA: Ginn.

Fillmore, C. (1973). *Deixis, I*. Unpublished lectures, delivered at the University of Southern California, Santa Cruz.

Goody, J. (Ed.) (1968). *Literacy in traditional societies*. Cambridge: Cambridge University Press.

Goody, J. (1977). *The domestication of the savage mind*. Cambridge: Cambridge University Press.

Graff, H. (1981). *Literacy in history: An interdisciplinary research bibliography*. New York.: Garland.

Havelock, E. (1982). *The literate revolution in Greece and its cultural consequences*. Princeton: Princeton University Press.

Lockridge, K.A. (1974). *Literacy in colonial New England*. New York: Norton.

Ong, W.J. (1982). *Orality and literacy: The technologizing of the word*. New York: Methuen.

Osborn, J. (1983). The purposes, uses and contents of workbooks and some guidelines for teachers and publishers. In R.C. Anderson, J. Osborn, & R.J. Tierney (Eds.) *Learning to read in American schools. Basal readers and content texts*. Hillsdale, NJ: Erlbaum.

Pantazelos, C. (1981). *Star flight*. Glenview, IL: Scott, Foresman.

Pattison, R. (1982). *On literacy*. New York: Oxford University Press.

Wright, P. (1980a). Strategy and tactics in the design of forms. *Visible Language*. 14(2), 151-193.

Wright, P. (1980b). Usability: The criterion for designing written information. In P. Kolers, M. Wrolstad, & H. Bouma (Eds.), *Processing of visible language* (Vol. 2). New York: Plenum.

Wright, P. (1983). Writing and reading technical information. In J. Nicholson & B. Foss (Eds.), *Psychology survey no. 4*. London: British Psychological Society.

PART FIVE

POLICY IMPLICATIONS

12 Literacy, Language, and Schooling: State Policy Implications

Cynthia Wallat

The Florida State University

During 1983 a spate of educational policy reports heightened an interest that began several years ago to improve schooling at the state level. Since 1980, at least 140 new state-level commissions on education have been sponsored by all branches of state government (governor's office, educational departments, state boards of education, and state house and senate legislatures); 54 new state-level commissions were created in 1983 (Walton, 1983).

Instructional content, use of instructional time, and competence in speaking, listening, and reasoning in addition to competence in reading, writing, mathematics, and science lead the list of policy targets recently established by either state legislatures or state boards of education (cf. Task Force on Education for Economic Growth 1983; Task Force on Educational Quality 1983).

The subject of this chapter is the identification of several recent policies legislated in one state and a discussion of policy implications in recent research on literacy, language, and schooling in upper elementary, middle, and secondary classrooms. Two questions will be considered: What values become educational law? What is the place of research after a bill becomes a law (cf. Bardach, 1977)?

Although concern for adolescents has been reflected in national policy studies for at least two decades (Ianni, 1983), a new intensive and focused interest is influencing state and local institutional efforts to achieve excellence. This interest is reflected in a spate of state policy commissions concerned with instructional scope, use of instructional time, and the establishment of legally binding content requirements for the completion of elementary and secondary school. Presented in this chapter are (a) a sample of some state policies about literacy and language which reflect the current upsurge of concern for schooling during the adolescent years; (b) a discussion of some ideas implicitly or explicitly conveyed in these policies; and (c) a map of some suggestions to advance adolescent education from recent research on literacy, language, and schooling. The last will be referred to as effective learner and effective teacher implications.

DEFINING POLICY

By *educational policies* we mean value decisions outlining the most effective and efficient solutions perceived by a corporate body, be it a government, an enterprise, or an organization (cf. Mayer & Greenwood, 1980).

Recent reviews of educational and social policy highlighted a range of diverse approaches to developing an understanding of the ways various problems are handled (Glenny & Schmidtlein, 1983). However, Dye (1984) recommended that researchers concerned with understanding public policy avoid elaborate academic discussions of definitions of policy. Instead he recommended a simple definition: "Public policy is whatever governments choose to do or not to do" (p. 2). Note that Dye (1984) focused not only on government action, "but also on government inaction, that is, what government chooses not to do" (p. 2). The contention here is that government inaction can have just as great an impact as government action. Taking a similar stance on relying on simple images such as what educational and social values become law, and, what may happen afterward, Wildavsky (1977) capriciously reminded us: There are only a few simple questions to consider when attempting to analyze the research implications of a particular policy. First, "What is the problem?" And, second, "How is a problem distinguished from a puzzle?" (Wildavsky, 1977, p. 13).

THE RELATIONSHIP BETWEEN POLICY AND RESEARCH

Before beginning a detailed account of current state-level literacy, language, and schooling policies and the effective learner and teacher implications suggested by these policies, several myths about policy and research need to be addressed. Let me briefly overview a few contributions from past work which may clear up these myths and clarify the relationship between policy and research. The purpose of the overview is to consider the kinds of research that can inform future educational policy. In other words, after a bill becomes a law, how can research help to point the way to modifications in that law which will enable to to fulfill in practice the purposes for which it is intended?

Until recently, public policy was considered to be the end point in analysis of the actions of public institutions and as such was treated quite negatively by educational researchers. Critics of early Head Start, bilingual, and remedial reading policies bemoaned the fact that the implementation of educational policy during the '60s and '70s generally preceded support for the development of an empirical research base (Takanishi, 1977; White, 1972). Analysis of this view of the relationship between policy and research led to the creation of models such as Figure 1 (cf. Shuy, 1977, p. 22). Discussion of the direction of the arrows in Figure 1 generally end with the indictment that educational research is not valued because it tends to follow legislated policies rather than precede it.

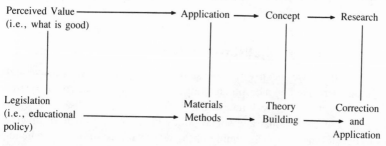

Figure 1.   A Development Model of Policy and Research (cf. Shuy, 1979)

Those of us who have studied the slippery, transparent phenomenon called language or "reading as a social process" can recognize the prematurity of negative judgments about the value of research during policy implementation. We would agree with Bardach (1977) that design can only go partway, and, as such, policymakers probably need researchers more during the implementation stage than at other times. For example, one important conclusion that emerged from language and literacy programs in the '60s and '70s, was that:

> the character and degree of any implementation policies are inherently unpredictable. Even the most robust policy—one that is well designed to survive the implementation process—will tend to go awry. The classic symptoms of under/performance, delay, and escalating costs are bound to appear. As they do, someone, or some group must be willing and able to set the policy back on course. (Bardach, 1977, p. 5)

In other words, rather than lamenting the fact that language and literacy policies have never been quite right, researchers should consider alternative interpretations to that presented in Figure 1. One such premise is that the most profitable policies for research are those which stay in effect long enough to support clarification and understanding of the problem (cf. Bardach, 1977, p. 4). Datta (1982) suggested that the fact that some policies have led to support for research should be read as a sign of the growing maturity of the study of teaching and learning. This premise suggests that the direction of the arrows can be read as a positive sign of legislative appreciation of research as an expedient as well as a scientifically attractive solution to evaluating whether a perceived value such as literacy is achieved (Datta, 1982, p. 144). As Datta (1982) reminded us, one of the most striking developments since about 1977 in government-financed educational policy has been the recognition by many legislators that evaluations of a perceived good such as literacy cannot be limited to analysis of test performance or aptitude/treatment interactions. Her review of support for research by policymakers suggested that the direction of the arrows in Figure 1 was a positive sign that policymakers were no longer content with null findings which were unable to reveal why massive amounts of support for literacy achievements produce no measurable effects.

Louis (1982) agreed that policymakers have begun to look to research as a means to improving their understanding of next steps. She contended that some federal-level policymakers had a deep-seated skepticism about the impact of their policies. They remained skeptical, unless implementation information was available from which a path could be followed to the point of understanding what the events meant to members of the social structure.

As reflected in Table 1, policy and research questions, answers, and outcomes can look quite separate, unless we remind ourselves how one side of the page can build on the other.

While oversimplified in Table 1, the comparison points serve to highlight potential communication points between policy personnel and educational researchers. As Meyer and Greenwood (1980) reminded us: The intent of research is to expand understanding of social processes. The intent of policy is to make us capable of influencing these processes. It seems to me that the similar concern for identifying processes of teaching and learning can overcome some of the potential areas of

Table 1. Policy and Research Frameworks on Literacy, Language, and Schooling: Classification of Typical Questions, Answers, and Outcomes[a]

Factor	Policy	Research
Primary questions	What is the desirable state of affairs?	What is the state of affairs generally?
		Why is the state of affairs the way it is?
Forms of answers	X's are good (e.g., general or specific value claim)	X is true; X is true because of . . . ; S is perceived as true by . . . (e.g., explanation, illustration)
Outcomes	Are the expected effects achieved?	What are all the effects?
	What are the most efficient programs?	What does the program look like to different people?
	Are the students achieving the objectives?	
	Is the teacher producing?	
	Are institutions, programs, and people meeting numerous objectives?	
Overriding concerns (i.e., potential areas of communication difficulty)	Efficiency	Professional acceptance
	Productivity	Inquiry
	Accountability	Conceptual analysis
	Effectiveness	Longitudinal experimental studies or field research
	Improved standards	
	Resolution	

[a]Cf. House (1978), Smith (1980), and Stufflebeam and Webster (1980).

communication difficulty outlined in Table 1. One way to help keep in mind the positive research possibilities of state policies is to remind ourselves that both policymakers and educational researchers face the same dilemma. That dilemma has been succinctly captured by Bardach (1977):

> It is hard enough to design public policies and [research] programs that look good on paper. It is harder still to formulate them in words and slogans that resonate pleasingly in the ears of political [and educational] leaders and the constituencies to which they are responsive. And it is excruciatingly hard to implement [either a policy or research design] in a way that pleases . . . all, including supposed beneficiaries and clients. (p.3)

Policy on Literacy and Schooling in Florida: Implications for Research

What is the state of affairs in education? Why is the state of affairs the way it is? What is the desirable state of affairs? These questions have been addressed by both policymakers and educational researchers in Florida. The State of Florida has gained national media attention several times in the past two years because of several firsts in an attempt to reach a desirable state of affairs. The functional literacy exam required of all students for high school graduation is one example that will be used to explicate the potential usefulness of current research on literacy, language, and schooling. Second, third, and fourth examples of Florida's "firsts" in middle and secondary schooling policy are (a) the RAISE law (Raise Achievement in Secondary Education); (b) the Gordon Writing Act; and (c) the Florida Meritorious Instructional Program.

Inasmuch as I was a close observer of the policy process that led to the passage of the RAISE law and the Merit bill in 1983, I chose the subsequent history of these educational reform statutes as a primary source of data for considering teaching and learning implications from six papers presented at the conference. In addition, current functional literacy policies, the Gordon Writing Act of 1982, and the Educational Accountability Act of 1978 have many facets that can be informed by recent research during legislative oversight and implementation hearings in the years to come.

Functional Literacy.[1] A landmark ruling by a U.S. district judge on May 4, 1983, allowed Florida to deny diplomas to high school seniors who failed the state functional literacy test.[2] The legislative origins of the test reached back several years. In 1978, the Florida legislature approved an amendment to the Educational Accountability Act of 1978, which required uniform testing for grades 3, 5, 8, and 11. The intent of this uniform testing policy was to provide a mechanism for moni-

---

[1]This section is largely drawn from *Memorandum Opinion and Order* No. 78–892. Civ. T. GC. (Middle District of Florida, Tampa Division. May 4, 1983.)

[2]During the 1983 graduation ceremonies, approximately 1,200 seniors received certificates of completion instead of diplomas because they failed the test. This total represents approximately 1% of the class of 1983.

toring whether basic mathematics and communication skills were included in the official curriculum in all 67 school districts.

The functional literacy test covered 30 basic skills. Of these, 15 were designated as communication skills and 15 were designated as mathematics skills. The communication skills included determining the main idea stated in a paragraph, identifying the cause or stated effect stated in a paragraph, following written directions, identifying an appropriate conclusion or generalization for a paragraph, obtaining appropriate information from tables, graphs, or schedules, and including the necessary information when writing messages to make a request, to supply information, or to note an assignment.

The events between 1978 when the policy was adopted and 1983 when the U.S. district judge ruled that the functional literacy requirement for high school graduation was constitutional serve to highlight the premise that educational research had become a valuable part of policy decisions. For example: Shortly after its enactment in 1978, Florida high school students filed a class action challenging the constitutionality of the literacy test requirements. A Court of Appeals ruled that the test would be constitutional, if it were instructionally valid. Specifically, the Court of Appeals directed the U.S. District court in Tampa to make further findings on whether the test covered material actually taught in Florida's classrooms. Of specific interest were students who would be high school seniors during the 1982–1983 school year.

Between 1981 and 1983 several educational research steps were taken to determine whether the test was instructionally valid. First, a questionnaire was sent to all 82,000 teachers in Florida. The survey asked both elementary and secondary teachers whether they provided instruction relating to the skills tested in the functional literacy exam. Second, a set of six survey forms were sent to all 67 school districts asking the districts to estimate the grade levels at which the students received the preparation; to report any major instructional variations among the schools in the district; to describe any remedial programs specifically related to attaining mastery of the functional literacy skills; to identify any staff development activities to promote student mastery of the communication and mathematics skills; to list instructional materials that specifically prepared students for any of the skills; and to identify any programs directed specifically toward helping students pass the functional literacy exam. Other effort to determine instructional validity included a site visit to each district and a student survey administered by the three-member site-visit team to one or two eleventh-grade social studies and English classes. The site visitors spent two days in each district interviewing administrators and teachers and comparing the instructional materials used in the district with those listed in the district report. The student survey asked the students to state whether they had been taught how to answer 24 sample questions. The sample questions included all the original 24 communication and mathematics skills.

The instructional validity trial was held in February, 1983. the results of the analysis of the data were presented as evidence that Florida was indeed teaching what it was testing. The teacher survey indicated that students were given an average of 2.7

opportunities to attain mastery of the functional literacy skills. According to the expert educational research witness for the State of Florida, a student need only be exposed once to mastery-level instruction for the test to be instructionally valid. The results adduced from the remaining data were that students were receiving remediation as needed and that suitable instruction was being offered.

Educational research experts for the plaintiffs attempted to argue that the instructional validity of the test could not be established by survey information. Although the plaintiff's educational research experts admitted that they had no problem with the survey procedures used by the defendants, they suggested that the survey was hearsay and not a reliable indicator of what actually went on in classrooms. In particular, the survey was not checked with actual visits to classrooms in which communication and mathematics skills were taught. Moreover, the survey covered only the 1981–1982 school year rather than a twelfth grader's entire school career.

The judgment offered in May, 1983 was instructional for literacy, language, and schooling research for several reasons. The judge recognized that the argument against the survey data had merit. Although he rhetorically asked, "How can we view videotapes of every child?" the final judgment rested on data that was reducible to manageable size. The judge ruled that the basic facts were proved. What was required constitutionally was that the tested skills be included in the official curriculum and that the majority of teachers recognized them as something they should teach. The proper focus was judged to be legally maintained through clear demands, fair testing, and appropriate sanctions.

While subsequent appeals might affect later use of the functional literacy test as a high school requirement, the ruling on clear demands, fair testing, and appropriate sanctions seemed to have influenced the legislation passed in the session immediately following this ruling. During the 1983 legislative session, state statutes were passed regarding standards of student achievement, student performance, and teacher performance evaluation. Section 232.246 of the Florida Statutes required that by the 1984-85 school year, ninth- through twelfth-grade students must have taken 22 credits as a requirement for graduation. By 1986–1987, completion of the 24 credits outlined in Figure 3 will be required for graduation.[3] In addition to content scope and content time requirements, the legislature also addressed how time on language and literacy tasks would be more accountable. For example, according to what was known locally as the Gordon Writing Acts, tenth graders were required

---

[3]Compared to national averages of year of completed course work by high school seniors, these additional credit hours represent significant additions:

	National Average	Florida
English	2½ – 3 yr	4 yr
Math	1½ – 2 yr	3 yr
Science	½ – 1 yr	3 yr
History or Social Studies	1½ – 2 yr	3 yr

to write a paper every week, and freshman and sophomores in college were required to write 28,000 words before moving on to upper-division status.

The writing acts as well as the 24 credit requirements were subject to further accountability legislation called Student Performance Standards. This legislation called for standards to be adopted for each program in ninth through twelfth grade by July 1, 1985. Unlike the early functional literacy standards, the 1983 legislated standards recognized the teacher's function in setting clear demands and appropriate sanctions. For example, the description of student performance standards included the following sentence: "Teacher observation, classroom assignments, and examinations may be considered appropriate methods of assessing student mastery" (State of Florida, Department of Education, 1983, p. 330).

The reason for considering the functions of teacher observation and classroom observation appropriately is tied to the final "first" in recent state policy in the State of Florida: The Florida Meritorious Instructional Program, or Merit law.

The Florida Meritorious Instructional Personnel Program. The legislative language included in the State Statutes for the Florida Merit Program underscores the importance of addressing the topics of literacy, language and schooling policy implications. For example, this legislation called for the documentation of superior performance evaluation. By law, the State Board of Education was charged with developing and adopting rules for school districts to follow in order to document how they determined what was an effective performance and what was an ineffective performance. The law required that for each teacher who was nominated for merit, the results of a performance evaluation team should be included as documentation. In other words, in order to be considered that year and in future years, any performance observation instrument that was used by the team must be documented in terms of how it was normed and how each element within the performance measurement system was documented in terms of a valid knowledge base.

Table 2.   **Standards of Student Achievement by 1986—1987**[a]

N credits	Subject
4	English (with major concentration in composition and literature)
3	Mathematics
3	Science
1	American history
1	World history
½	Economics
½	American government
½	Practical arts, vocational education, or exploratory vocational education
½	Fine arts
½	Life management (i.e., nutrition, drug education, consumer education, cardio-resuscitation, and hazards of smoking)
½	Physical education
9	Electives
24	Total

[a]7 instructional periods per day, or equivalent, to allow each student to successfully complete 7 credits per school year.

The eight-word phrase, "documented in terms of a valid knowledge base," is, I believe, the richest opportunity teacher educators and educational researchers have ever been offered in policy language. Our challenge will be to keep alive the recognition that educational research has led to a valid knowledge base.

All 67 school districts that were required to begin the merit application process on April 20, 1983 had few choices in adopting a normed performance evaluation system. The one system that met the State Board Rule of having a cadre of trained observers was known as the FPMS, or Florida Performance Measurement System. This observation system for noting effective and ineffective behaviors currently includes 21 behaviors. As shown in Table 3, the behaviors represent a set of activities that have been documented in past work on student achievement. These achievement-related behaviors were extracted from the literature by a B.O. Smith and small group of researchers at the University of South Florida. The instrument represents an extraction from a longer document called *Domains: Knowledge Base of the Florida Performance Measurement System* (Florida Coalition for the Development of a Performance Measurement System, 1983). As stated in the preface:

> There is no expectation that the system is or ever will be "finished." As there is nothing static about human behavior, so there must be growth and development in systems which study human behavior. As new research is conducted, particularly in areas and at levels where present research is fragile, it is expected that the FPMS will be regularly updated to reflect the best professional knowledge. (p. iii)

Identifying Policy Implications

Given the legal reality of functional literacy currently being reduced to 15 skill areas as a requirement for high school graduation and the political reality that a majority of school districts in Florida adopted the instrument of 21 effective teaching behaviors in Table 3 to determine merit, I reviewed six of the classroom research chapters included in this volume in light of the following questions:

1. What are the implications from current research in terms of adding to our knowledge base about effective learning of literacy and language?
2. What are the implications from current research in terms of adding to a valid knowledge base about effective teaching?

In order to address these questions, a short review of each of the chapters may be helpful. Table 4 presents the issues considered by each author, the strategies by which each author proposes to deal with each issue, and the anticipated outcomes of these strategies.

Rebecca Barr's study of *"Classroom Interaction and Curricular Content"* (chap. 7, this volume) granted that interaction is an important part of instruction. However, she argued that exploration of effective teaching behaviors needed to move beyond the literature represented in performance evaluation systems such as Table 3. Building on past work which demonstrated that children's reading achievement was significantly influenced by the content they covered, she examined the relation between teacher questions and student responses and the content of the

Table 3. Florida Performance Measurement System

Domain		Effective Indicators	Frequency	Frequency	Ineffective Indicators
3.0: Instructional organization and development	1.	Begins instruction promptly			Delays
	2.	Handles materials in an orderly manner			Does not organize or handle materials systematically
	3.	Orients students to classwork/maintains academic focus			Allows talk/activity unrelated to subject
	4.	Conducts beginning/ending review			
	5.	Questions: academic comprehension/ lesson development	asks single factual (Dom 5.0) requires analysis/ reasons		Poses multiple questions asked as one, unison response
					Poses nonacademic questions/nonacademic procedural questions
	6.	Recognizes response/amplifies/gives corrective feedback			Ignores student or response/expresses sarcasm, disgust, harshness
	7.	Gives specific academic praise			Uses general, nonspecific praise
	8.	Provides for practice			Extends discourse, changes topic with no practice
	9.	Gives directions/assigns/checks comprehension homework, seatwork assignment/gives feedback			Gives inadequate directions/no homework/no feedback

4.0: Presentation of subject matter	10. Circulates and assists students	Remains at desk/circulates inadequately
	11. Treats concept-definition/attributes/examples/nonexamples	Gives definition or examples only
	12. Discusses cause-effect/uses linking words/applies law or principle	Discusses either cause or effect only/uses no linking word(s)
	13. States and applies academic rule	Does not state or does not apply academic rule
	14. Develop criteria and evidence for value judgment	States value judgment with no criteria or evidence
5.0: Communication verbal and nonverbal	15. Emphasizes important points	Uses vague/scrambled discourse
	16. Expresses enthusiasm verbally/challenges students	Uses loud-grating, high pitched, monotone, inaudible talk
	17.	
	18.	
	19. Uses body behavior that shows interest—smiles, gestures	Frowns, deadpan, or lethargic
2.0: Mgt. of std. conduct	20. Stops misconduct	Delays desist/doesn't stop misconduct/desists punitively
	21. Maintains instructional momentum	Loses momentum—fragments nonacademic directions, overdwells

Table 4. Implications From Current Research: Adding to Our Knowledge Base About Effective Learning of Literacy and Language

Study	Strategy	Outcomes
Barr		
Will randomly selecting lessons for intensive study lead to unfortunate sampling bias?	Consider the question of how lesson unit fit into larger instructional units (e.g., over 100 class periods)	Understandings of how units of discourse or types of behavior fit together and are organized within a lesson Understanding of interconnections of what looks like different lessons from day to day
The development of interpretive reading comprehension: i.e., how does the nature of class discourse change when students are dealing with easy short stories vs. more difficult selections?	Consider the issue of change in light of evidence from 45 class sessions when four different short stories were read	Understandings of how the development of interpretive reading comprehension occurs (e.g., learning strategies of interpretation during the autumn minimized the problems of text-base comprehension during spring
How can we understand the difference between classes in which students learn a lot and those in which they learn a little?	Consider the issues in light of evidence of how instructional interaction consists of three-way interaction between text, teacher, and student	Analysis of question-answer units in relation to text content (i.e., documentation of content covered during instruction)
Golden		
How can we understand the nature of reader-text interaction?	Consider the analysis of textual cues and features from a variety of text types in order to specific similarities and differences among different kinds of discourse	Several constructs from literacy theory offer promising insights (e.g., formulating expectations about text; building characterizations)
Moll and Diaz		
How can observable changes in students' writing within a relatively short period of time be produced?	Identify useful ethnographic data for developing and implementing a series of writing modules (i.e., 27 students from 8 different families)	Identification of student and family literacy practices Creation of a system of activities that help secondary school students master writing as a tool of communication and thought
Bloome		
How can we identify nonovert aspects of reading and writing development?	Identify how learning to read involves the learning of classroom-bound ways of problem solving, inferencing, and conceptualizing	Identification of distinctions between teaching and learning constructs such as "procedural display," "analysis," "cataloging," and "catalog frame"

302

Gilmore

How can we formulate follow-up work to the body of ethnographic literature that illustrates that factors beyond academic competence affects judgments about student ability?

Focus on discrete linguistic and social behaviors that shed light on what the student must also know to display knowledge according to socially accepted rules of classroom interaction

Access to contexts where opportunity for literacy acquisition is maximized seems to be determined by appropriate displays of attitude

Collins

How can we account for the paradox that there are consistent class-related differences in literacy ability but not in language ability

Identify some of the aspects of children's conversational strategies which seem to affect their acquisition of reading and writing literacy skills (e.g., focus on ways in which connective ties between parts of a discourse are signaled)

Refine communicative, social background, and pedagogical variables that can help build more explicit models of the organization of conversation in lessons, i.e., variables that can inform:

a. How speakers and writers establish and maintain reference to major characters in their narratives

b. How speakers differ in use of syntactic and intonational cues, e.g., vowel elongation and rise-fall contours to signal definiteness; use of relative clauses to maintain identity of reference

c. How narrators make interpretive demands on their audience, e.g., are sentence boundaries more easily discerned by a casual adult listener?

d. How student may move through several stages of recognizing shifts in classroom contexts, e.g., assess referential antecedents and illocutionary intent of a given message

Consider constructs from sociolinguistics which offer promising insights of text-comprehension strategies of readers and/or communicative involvement:
turn disruption
uptake
shift in the reference of pronouns (i.e., ambiguous reference)
referential misfires
referential repairs

Focusing on episodes of apparent comprehension practices looks promising for drawing the most plausible connections between the nature of communication in the classroom and what is known about the text-comprehension strategies of the skilled reader, e.g., situations in which contradictory interpretations are assigned to a pronoun, with the result that two or more topics are simultaneously on the floor.

Table 5. Implications From Current Research: Adding to a Valid Knowledge About Effective Teaching

	Premises	Procedure	Barr	Golden	Moll & Diaz	Bloome	Collins	Gilmore
A.	Categories currently used to represent interaction need to be reconsidered in light of capturing effective elements of the interaction		Need to address larger instructional units in order to classify aspects of classroom discourse across instructional sessions (e.g., ways to capture the creative activities through which teachers' help students learn to: gather evidence of character's motives; draw conclusions; focus on author's intent or reader's understanding	Need to address how teachers link into students': formulating expectations about text; constructing elements in literacy text such as characterization	Need to address the act or system of acts by which learning is composed	Need to develop ways to capture the unitary aspects of social and cognitive processes rather than separate processes	Need to develop more specific models for classroom communities (e.g., the evolving relations between language use and literacy; the pedagogical and interactional demands of a particular message; the organization of conversation into lesson phases (i.e., antecedents and intent of a given utterance)	Need to consider not only teachers' academic rules, but classroom interaction rules for students to display that knowledge
B.	Other conditions as well as interaction must be studied, if one is to understand the effectiveness of instruction	Available curricular and classroom materials	+	+	+	+	+	+
		Students and their competencies	+	+	+	+	+	+
		Instructional time (i.e., content covered)	+	+		+	+	
		Characteristics of instructional group	+	+		+	+	+
		Interaction of teacher–text–student	+	+		+	+	
		Identify, build on, and/or expand upon out-of-school literacy practices			+	+	+	+

Interactional history of teachers with students and groups of students

Characterize difficulty of the material

Related tasks that may reinforce learning, e.g., opportunity for readers to influence each other's view of story, character perspective, interpretation

C. Observers judgments of effectiveness must be qualified in light of a particular lesson's learning goal and/or content

Understanding what the story is about rather than interpretive skills may be an appropriate and effective focus during some lessons

Personal opinion may be effective in constructing characterization

Consider whether the story is being read for the first or second, etc., time

Consider whether text cues have channeled the teacher and/or reader into a particular way of reading

Concepts of text production and cataloguing need to be considered in determining effectiveness

Concepts of comprehensive preparing strategy need to be considered in determining effects (vocabulary taught; information about text elicited through sight-reading and precise directions)

Judgments of ineffectiveness need to be qualified in light of differences between goals such as acquisition of literacy and/or admission to literacy success tracks

Issues of effective teaching ignore the fact that teaching styles may be part of a larger whole (e.g., administration policies on time and personnel evaluation procedures)

story being taught. As outlined in Table 4, the study addressed several effective learning dimensions. The issues of selection of lessons for study, development of interpretive reading comprehension, and differences in effective learning, guided the design of strategies for considering units of instructional and over-time analysis.

Joanne Golden's *"An Exploration of Reader–Text Interaction"* offered a summary of past approaches of literary theorists to the study of reader responses. As outlined in Table 4, the directions for research suggested by literary theory led to her development of several useful constructs of building an image of the cues both teachers and students might use to formulate expectations about text and build characterizations.

Luis Moll and Rosa Diaz (*"Teaching Writing as Communication"*) suggest that another effective learner question that needed further exploration through research is the extent to which the identification of out of school literacy practices might be used to produce observable change in student's writing. Also interested in focusing more sharply on variables that influence how students spend their time, David Bloome (*"Reading as a Social Process in a Middle School Classroom"*) and Perry Gilmore (*"Sulking, Stepping, and Tracking: "The Effects of Attitude Assessment on Access to Literacy"*) are guided by past ethnographic findings to direct our attention to nonacademic dimensions of effective learning of literacy and language. As described in Table 4, a similar outcome of Moll and Diaz, Bloome, and Gilmore's research is that effective teaching and learning does not have to limit its field of vision to a small portion of variables. Instead, researchers can use a range of constructs to help explain relationships among the social and academic development of effective learners. In other words, teachers' efforts to influence students' attitudes, norms, and social behavior need no longer be ignored because of a lack of constructs to define the way in which academic and nonacademic variables interact.

James Collins's interest is identifying discourse skills that students must learn in the process of becoming literate. He has also focused readers' attention on a range of discourse skills that are not specific to either a home, school, or community setting. The student's skill in eatablishing and maintaining reference is described in terms of group-specific discourse conventions and individual differences in discourse skill. Overall, the strategies described in *"Using Cohesion Analysis to Understand Access to Knowledge"* provide a model for assessing the overall ability of students to deal with the complexity of communicative events involved in acquiring the skills of literacy.

Table 5 states three premises that can frame further discussion of the 21 effective teaching indicators in Table 3. The first premise (A) is that the "interaction" categories do not enumerate specific elements of a desired teaching ↔ learning interaction. For example, the use of frequency counts gives no clue as to how teachers organize learning from the beginning to the end of a lesson. As Barr, Golden, Moll and Diaz, Bloome, Gilmore and Collins point out, there is a need to develop images of how teachers link all aspects of literacy and language teaching across time. Phrases and constructs such as "instructional units," "linking," "learning act or system of acts," "unitary aspects," and "evolving organization" imply that teaching and learning is not simply an additive process made up of separate actions. Rather, the "need" statements reproduced in Table 6 suggest that adding to a valid knowledge base about effective teaching depends upon developing analytic procedures which can capture the evolving nature of instruction and student development.

The second premise (B) includes a list of important components of the teaching situation such as "available classroom materials" which are not a part of the 21 indicators. How, for example, is a teacher to be evaluated with regard to indicator 8 ("provides for practice") without reference to the availability of classroom materials? How is a teacher to be evaluated with regard to indicator 5 ("requires analysis/ reasons") without regard to the "characteristics of the instructional group"?

Premise C states that "21 effective indicators" cannot be applicable to the presentation of all lessons. For example, with some groups it may be appropriate to discuss a story which is being read for the first time solely on the basis of *what happens* in the story. Trying to introduce questions of cause-effect, law or principle, analysis/reasons, etc., may be counter/productive at such a point.

Policy decision-making, exemplified by the "21 effective indicators," often results in measures which appear feasible but which can only be implemented arbitrarily. In such cases, recommendations from those who must do the implementing can be of the greatest value.

SUMMARY

As noted earlier, the subject of policy implications is a recent concern among educational researchers. The "implementation problem" has been perceived as an interesting social science problem only since 1970 (Bardach, 1977); the concept of utilization of research findings was rarely mentioned in educational literature before 1970 (Dickey, 1980).

Although teaching and policy as a subject has only recently become of popular interest, language and literacy researchers have been faced with answering hard policy questions since at least 1969. The earlier evaluation of Head Start suggested that the original goal of effecting language and reading development in a six-week summer program was an overpromise. Fortunately, policymakers were not content with null findings about preschool effects on the development of language and reading, and support for early language and literacy research was forthcoming. Hence, the overall results of research which followed legislation were far from negative.

Consider the following important implications that we learned from the evaluations of early childhood programs:

- the idea that behaviors that are physically identical may not have the same meaning; i.e., that observations of teacher and student behavior must be collected and analyzed in terms of their meaning for the participants (Shapiro, 1973).
- the idea that the testing situation must be considered from higher levels of analysis than scores; e.g., that students with incorrect answers were often

found to be performing the very cognitive operation being tested by the questions and that an "incorrect" answer might have resulted from a different interpretation of the testing material (Cicourel, Jennings, Jennings, Leiter, MacKay, Mehan, & Roth, 1974; Mehan, 1978).

- the idea that the impact of programs on the aspects of development must be considered; i.e., academic, social, and emotional (Almy, 1975; Consortium for Longitudinal Studies, 1983).

The hope is strong that more recent student effectiveness and teacher effectiveness legislation will lead to research which can rediscover an important set of additions to a valid knowledge base on literacy, language, and schooling in middle and secondary school years.

REFERENCES

Almy, M. (1975). *The early educator at work*. New York: McGraw-Hill.

Bardach, E. (1977). *The implementation game: What happens after a bill becomes a law*. Cambridge, MA: MIT Press.

Cicourel, A.V., Jennings, K.H., Jennings, S.H.M., Leiter, K.C.W., MacKay, R., Mehan, H., & Roth, D.R. (1974). *Language use and school performance*. New York: Academic Press.

Consortium for Longitudinal Studies. (1983). *As the twig is bent . . . Lasting effects of preschool programs*. Hillsdale, NJ: Erlbaum.

Datta, L. (1982). Strange bedfellows: The politics of qualitative methods. *American Behavioral Scientist, 26*(1), 133–144.

Dickey, B. (1980). Utilization of evaluation of small-scale innovative educational projects. *Educational Evaluation and Policy Analysis, 2*(6), 65–77.

Dye, T.R. (1984). *Understanding public policy*. Englewood Cliffs, NJ: Prentice-Hall.

Florida Coalition for the Development of a Performance Measurement System. (1983). *Domains: Knowledge base of the Florida Performance Measurement System*. Tallahassee, FL: Office of Teacher Education, Certification, and Inservice Staff Development.

Glenny, L.A., & Schmidtlein, F.A. (1983). The role of the state in the governance of higher education. *Educational Evaluation and Policy Analysis, 5*(2), 133–153.

House, E.R. (1978). Assumptions underlying evaluation models. *Educational Researcher, 7*(3), 4–12.

Ianni, F.A.J. (1983). *Home, school, and community in adolescent education*. New York: ERIC Clearinghouse on Urban Education, Teachers College, Columbia University.

Louis, K.S. (1982). Multisite/multimethod studies: An introduction. *American Behavioral Scientist, 26*(1), 6–22.

Mayer, R.R., & Greenwood, E. (1980). *The design of social policy research*. Englewood Cliffs, NJ: Prentice-Hall.

Mehan, H. (1978). Structuring school structure. *Harvard Educational Review, 48*, 32–64.

Nagel, S.S. (1980). *The policy studies handbook*. Lexington, MA: Lexington Books, D.C. Heath.

Shapiro, E. (1973). Educational evaluation: Rethinking the criteria of competence. *School Review, 81*, 523–50.

Smith, N.L. (1980). Federal research on evaluation methods in health, criminal justice, and the military. *Educational Evaluation and Policy Analysis, 2*(4), 53–59.

State of Florida, Department of Education, (1983). *Laws relating to Florida public education enacted by the 1983 legislature*. Tallahassee, FL: State of Florida, Department of Education.

Stufflebeam, D.L., & Webster, W.J. (1980). An analysis of alternative approaches to evaluation. *Educational Evaluation and Policy Analysis, 2*(3), 5–20.

Shuy, R. (1979). On the relevance of recent developments in socio-linguistics to the study of language learning and early education. In O. Garnica & M.L. King (Eds.), *Language, children and society: The effects of social factors on children learning to communicate* (pp. 21–36). New York: Pergamon Press.

Takanishi, R. (1977). Federal involvement in early education (1933–1973): The need for historical perspectives. In L.G. Katz (Ed.), *Current topics in early childhood education* (Vol. 1, pp. 139–163). Norwood, NJ: Ablex.

Task Force on Education for Economic Growth. (1983). *Action for excellence.* Denver, CO: Education Commission of the States.

Task Force on Education Quality. (1983). *Policy options for quality education.* Alexandria, VA: National Association of State Boards of Education.

Walton, S. (1983, December 7). Aiming for excellence: States' reform efforts increase as focus of interests shift. *Education Week,* pp. 5–17.

White, S.H. (1972). *Federal programs for young children: Review and recommendations.* Cambridge, MA: Huron Institute.

Wildavsky, A. (1977). Principles for a graduate school of public policy. *Urban Analysis, 4,* 3–28.

13 Policy Development in Reading Education: Implications of Naturalistic Literacy Studies

John T. Guthrie

University of Maryland

POLICY IMPROVEMENT

The challenge

Discussions of policy fire the imagination and arouse the missionary zeal of individuals who are usually regarded as sober scholars. Bevan (1982), in his presidential address to the American Psychological Association, raised an important question for scholars concerned with policy improvement. Bevan's commitment to moving the discipline of psychology into the public arena can be felt from the question he posed: "How do we stand as a body of citizens who share special skills, knowledge, and insights on those societal issues of transcendent national importance to which our competencies can make a useful contribution?" (Bevan, 1982, p. 1303).

Bevan contended that as scholars and professionals it was our obligation to dedicate ourselves to the improvement of policy in our respective fields. This improvement might, under ideal conditions, come through a threefold program of effort. First, *we must understand our intellectual foundations,* which is to say we must know what we know about the essentials of our discipline. Second, *we must be able to identify and articulate those social issues of abiding public interest to which we can make a concrete contribution through analysis and the utilization of knowledge.* Third, *we must communicate what we know and what we do to the policy-shaping community* with a simplicity that we have not been previously willing to attempt.

It is a challenge to determine how the accumulation of knowledge about facts and relations among facts which is the accomplishment of research will assist in the formulation of judgments about policy. Determining how to use research for policy improvement is complicated, for the situation consists of heterogeneous groups of individuals with diverse purposes all attempting to make meaning out of the same events, each in their own ways.

The Process

The process of formulating policy is regrettably not easy to pinpoint and observe. Indeed, searching for a widely shared meaning for the word *policy* can be a seemingly endless task. For example, reviewing several years of the AERA publication *Educational Evaluation and Policy Analysis* proves futile in deriving a shared meaning for policy. While not providing a shared definition, Yeakey (1983) stated that "Policy-oriented research stresses the need for articulation between the molar as well as the molecular, the need to accommodate the universal as well as the particular" (p. 278). A clearer statement is provided by Cronbach, Ambron, Dornbusch, Hess, Hornik, Philips, Walker, and Weiner (1980), who said that the term *policy* should be understood as "representing broad plans, general principles and priorities from which programs stem" (p. 101). In addition, Cronbach et al. (1980) suggested that, "By the term program, we mean a standing arrangement that provides for a social service" (p. 14).

However, policy is not simply an end and program the means to it. Policy may be the instrument to achieve societal values, and programs may be ends in themselves when objectives to attain them are under debate. Means–ends relationships depend on the level of discourse in a particular time and situation. The process of forming policy has been studied by Weiss (1980, cited in Husen, 1984), among others. Husen quoted Weiss as saying that

> decisions are seldom "taken," they emerge out of a complicated web of pressures and influences of interest groups, a process that often operates over quite some time between which no particular moment of a "decision" being made can be identified . . . The knowledge relevant to a particular policy issue most often derives from a multitude of pieces of research each of which contributes a portion to "knowledge creep." (Husen, 1984, p. 11)

It is vital to determine how the accumulation of knowledge which is the accomplishment of research can assist in the development of judgments about policy. The use of research in policy-making has been studied by Aaron (1978) from the perspective of the "Great Society" legislation. As a social scientist at the Brookings Institution, he pointed out that

> research and experimentation comes in many guises. It may consist only of tabulations of data not previously available or used; this form of R&E is the most consistently productive and valuable, because it is easily understood and can refute common misperceptions. R&E more frequently [is correlational, consisting] of statistical estimates of the impact of some variable (such as teacher characteristics or weeks of training) on some other variable (such as test scores or earnings). In this form R&E is harder to understand and results are usually subject to criticism and rejection. (p. 155)

Added to these two categories is a third, consisting of naturalistic studies. In these investigations, complex systems are observed and thoroughly described in their normal settings. Many policy studies that appeared in 1983 and 1984 take this form. Among them, Sara Lightfoot, in *The Good High School* (1983), presented detailed portraits of six high schools with an emphasis on social perceptions of students, community ethos, and academic life. Theodore Sizer's (1984) *Horace's Compromise* is an impressionistic account of students, teachers, programs, and structure. Both are replete with policy implications. John Goodlad's (1984) study, reported in his book entitled *A Place Called School*, consisted of visits as well as tests and tabulations of courses taken in 38 schools with over 1,300 teachers in 7 states. The report contained in *High School* by Ernest Boyer (1983) was similar in its degree of objectivity and examination of multiple variables. All of these are naturalistic studies.

NATURALISTIC LITERACY STUDIES

Findings

In March 1984, a series of naturalistic literacy studies was presented at the Literacy, Language, and Schooling Conference at the University of Michigan (this volume is based upon that conference). When viewed as a "whole," these naturalistic literacy studies provide part of a picture of literacy and schooling.

Golden (chap. 8, this volume) reveals literacy in one of its more glamorous manifestations, that is, aesthetic reading. A usual course of acquiring this accomplishment was charted by Barr (chap. 7, this volume). However, as Smith (chap. 3, this volume) pointed out, the zenith of interaction between reader and author is not reached by everyone. Smith described how being alienated from the literate community is a stigmatized source of anguish. The reasons for exclusion from literacy are complex, but one of them related to norms of social interaction that Gilmore (chap. 5, this volume) described as necessary for admission to the more desirable forms of literacy teaching. The processes of learning to read in school, particularly among low-income minority youth, are often marked by superficial uses of language and personal detachment, according to Bloome (chap. 6, this volume). And the opportunity for instruction in interpretive processes is frequently limited to a few students who begin school with advantages in traditional literacy skills, (Collins, chap. 4, this volume). Low-income, low-achieving youth who may be members of linguistic or ethnic minority groups can participate fully in educational programs, however, if teachers are able to follow the example of Moll and Diaz (chap. 9, this volume) who brought social issues of the community into active exercise in the classroom.

Findings from the naturalistic literacy studies presented at the Literacy, Language, and Schooling Conference are not easily extricated from the modes of inquiry used in the studies themselves. Many of the reports must be fully read and discussed to be assimilated, and they do not lend themselves to reduction into summaries. Nevertheless, I will attempt to distill the insights that have issued from these studies from the perspective of implications and cautions for policy development. Some findings can be embraced more confidently than others, but they are all sufficiently compelling to warrant consideration in the area of policy development.

The process of understanding written text was elegantly portrayed by Golden in her discourse on reader–text interactions. First, she documented persuasively that although text is inevitably linear in its external form, it must be addressed with multiple planes of cognitive processes. To perceive the author's point of view, characterization, style, plot, and symbolism demands a continual restructuring and reintegration by the reader. Second, Golden contended that because unique readers may bring distinctive perspectives to a text, the meaning derived from reader–text interaction can legitimately vary in radical ways. However, it is important to note that there are limits to the range of idiosyncratic interpretations that are possible for a given text. For example, the sentence "The goldfish is in the pond" cannot be identical with the sentence " 'African history is interdisciplinary,' said Mr. Curtin," outside of bizarre circumstances. The limits to the polysemy of text must be explored. Third, Golden pointed to the contextual quality of interpretations. What people gain from reading a short story the second time is quite different than what they experienced on their initial encounter, and reading in a group gives rise to meanings that are not possible when reading alone, and so on. The aesthetic experience of text comprehension itself is inalterably social as well as cognitive.

Barr introduced a potentially powerful research method in her study "Classroom Interaction and Curricular Content." She examined low-achieving juniors and seniors in an English course in an urban private school throughout one full academic year. She found, however, that the short story served as a useful unit of analysis for it represented a unit of teacher planning as well as student absorption.

Barr found that difficult materials such as *The Merchant of Venice* were the occasion for the teacher to use text-based questions rather than interpretive, thought-provoking, and comparative questions. In turn, easier texts such as *"First Confession"* by Frank O'Connor which had a readability of sixth-grade level were the occasion for interpretation and inquiries that get at the appreciation of the writer's craft. This finding suggests that the elaborate interpretations reported by Golden may occur for texts that are relatively easy materials.

Barr's account hypothesized that English teachers may approach text comprehension in a "bottom–up" fashion. They may expect that students will understand words before sentences and that sentences will be comprehended before passages and passages assimilated before themes may be extracted and analyzed. Teachers may behave as though they believe that if a student cannot comprehend the literal meaning of a sentence and illustrate such understanding through paraphrase that questions about the theme of the story in which the sentence is embedded are meaningless. While recent research in cognitive psychology illustrates "top–down" processes in which schema influence sentence comprehension, Barr's findings suggest that in meeting the instructional needs of lower-achieving students, teachers may approach learning in a "bottom–up" manner.

Barr illustrated that interpretive reading strategies were likely to be learned through a pedagogical sequence of (a) displaying the prototype strategy, (b) modeling the strategy by the teacher, and (c) frequent opportunities for using the strategy in small group work in classrooms. Although an independent measure of learning interpretive strategies was not used, the opportunity to use strategies was reported by students to be indispensable to understanding and applying them to new texts.

Golden and Barr described the phenomenon of reading comprehension in some of its finest manifestations. We now turn to the problems of learning and teaching literacy.

The role of literacy in most cultural contexts within the United States cannot be underestimated. As Smith claimed, being able to read is an issue of self-respect for most men and a tool of domestic necessity for many women. He noted that, for illiterate males, the process of learning to read would be valuable for its "redemptive" quality. However, although illiterate males who learn to read may experience social reconciliation and freedom from the stigma of ignorance or retardation, this benefit should not be overgeneralized. Individuals who use literacy widely as adults but did not have difficulty acquiring it describe its benefits in terms of knowledge acquisition, relaxation, specific information, regulation of behavior, and social interaction. The value of literacy for these individuals is not that it preserves them from estrangement and ridicule, despite the fact that it invariably fulfills those functions. The penalty of reading failure for the illiterate, then, should not be confused with the benefit of literacy for those who have learned it.

The extreme difficulty in acquiring reading to levels of proficiency that meet societal or educational criteria, however arbitrary and irrational they may be, is an urgent educational dilemma. People of the kind Smith described suffer; and families dependent on them are disadvantaged. Employers who rely on them face losses in inefficiency and productivity.

One of the challenges to educators, amply illustrated by Gilmore, is that the avenue to literacy is strewn with obstacles for individuals who are members of ethnic, linguistic, or racial minority groups. Gilmore studied black, urban, elementary school children in a low-income neighborhood. She reported that an academically accelerated program which took the top third of students contained a nonachievement-oriented basis for selection. Students entered the accelerated program if they possessed a "good attitude." This trait was marked in a negative form by two types of social interaction. That is, a "bad attitude" was said to characterize students who engaged in either (a) stylized sulking, or (b) doin' steps. Stylized sulking was a behavioral response by a student to teacher requests or demands; it featured a certain turn of the eyes and posture. Such sulking was regarded as hostile and uncooperative to the teaching effort. In turn, steps were rhythmic chants that were reported to be sexy, polished, "nasty," black, and banned from school. Students who engaged in either form of social interaction were regarded as having bad attitudes and were not to enjoy certain academic opportunities.

Gilmore contended that access to the best forms of literacy education required social interactions which conformed to certain norms. These norms were d efined by teachers in terms of white, middle-class behavior contours. Behaviors that defied these standards were rejected and, consequently, students who identified closely with their group communication patterns were excluded from some educational programs. These findings confirm Au and Mason's (1982) finding that social interaction patterns of Hawaiian children in school were a disadvantage in cases in which they conflicted with interaction patterns expected by majority group teachers.

The difficulty of accomplishing coherent and inspiring lessons in literacy was amply documented by Bloome. He illustrated that black, urban, middle school children from a working-class environment indeed struggle to comprehend instructional texts. He illustrated the attempts of teacher and students to jointly construct meaning from a story entitled "The Saint" by Pritchett. In his description of classroom interpretation processes there were four primary operations. The first consisted of "text reproduction" in which a specific word, phrase, or passage from the text was orally rendered, or in which assignments were copied off a blackboard, etc. A second category of activity consisted of "procedural display" in which students documented that they indeed were progressing through a lesson or a text. The third category of activity was regarded as "cataloging." This process consisted of listing features of an object such as the characteristics of a person or the exterior features of a building. Bloome also described a passive and alienated relationship to text taken by students. They refused to get engrossed and make themselves vulnerable to error, emotion, or learning.

The interactions surrounding text that Bloome found can also be viewed in terms of the "bottom–up" framework suggested previously in connection with Barr's study. The teacher Bloome described may have regarded reading as a process of moving from the simple to the complex in terms of word recognition, sentence comprehension, passage comprehension, text recall, and thematic interpretation. From this framework, the teacher in Bloome's study may be seen as: (a) attempting to ensure encoding of words and phrases; (b) attempting to control attention to printed language which is required for learning to read; and (c) beginning the first stages of concept building. These bottom–up processes may be manifested through the social, interpersonal processes of text reproduction, procedural display, and cataloging. Finally, students who were expected to write about what they had read would have incomplete responses to the degree that their processing of the text was inadequate and incomplete. The apparent "alienated" posture may have resulted from the absence of an available response repertoire. Text difficulty may have precluded constructive, interpretive questions from the teacher and processes from the students in Bloome's investigation.

The insights found in the study by Collins were plentiful and provocative. He endeavored to reexamine the age-old question of why literacy acquisition should be low for children, especially in the low-income groups, when language acquisition is not apparently deficient in these groups. He also pointed his inquiry toward the problem of how students use oral language surrounding their literacy events in school.

Collins first confirmed the finding of other investigators that students in a low reading group within a classroom tended to receive emphasis on decoding and vocabulary in comparison to students in high groups who tended to receive emphasis on syntactic and semantic cues for longer passages of material. He went on to point out, however, that intonation in oral reading for students in the high group included falling intonation in sentence-final locations, as observed in oral language, whereas students in the low group did not have such marked intonation contours.

A variety of findings were convincingly drawn from the comparison of second-grade and third-grade reading teachers. The second-grade teacher was able to switch her oral language code from standard to black English vernacular. She did not correct children who used black English vernacular during reading. She allocated approximately the same amount of time for reading to high- and low-achieving groups and gave well-devised preparation questions that set the stage for comprehension of text. A third-grade teacher, on the other hand, spoke standard English only and corrected students' occurrences of the black English vernacular. She had fewer stage-setting questions for comprehension and less instructional time for students in the low reading group. In this comparison, there was a positive correlation between the students' use of standard English and the teacher's allocation of time and opportunity for learning to read.

Collins reported that the low reading group was characterized by a variety of features that seemed to be disadvantageous for reading. First, they had less time for engaging in reading comprehension practice. Second, the low reading group had more occasions when the student who was reading aloud suffered a disruption, fewer occasions when the teacher used a student's words or message in formulating her next question, and perhaps, most importantly, more confusion about reference in discussing narratives. In other words, students in low reading groups were relatively unable to follow the thread of a story and contribute to the discussion when referents such as *he, she,* and *it* were used to refer to actors and objects within the story. This finding prevailed despite the adequate use by this group of reference during narration in oral language. It is possible that the students were unable to discuss the story clearly because their comprehension of it had been fuzzy from the outset. Nevertheless, Collins documented a host of factors that might plausibly impede learning in the lower reading groups and preclude access to full opportunities for interpretive comprehension by the children in these groups.

Collins made a policy recommendation. He suggested, based on his findings, that ability groups be abolished. However, the questions raised by his study are not whether there should or should not be ability groups but rather the nature of instruction provided to lower-ability or lower-achieving students. Certainly, opportunity for comprehension practice was smaller for low groups in his study. However, we need studies in which fully heterogeneous groups are investigated and data from individuals within these groups are defined. Individuals who are low in reading achievement in broad heterogeneous groups may have even less opportunity for comprehension engagement than they do in the homogeneous grouping program he observed. The fact is we do not know whether the results will be positive or negative. The question can be answered empirically but not otherwise.

Alternative policy recommendations based on Collins's study might be directly tied to the questions raised by the study; namely, the nature of the instruction provided to low-achieving students. For example, one policy recommendation would be to suggest that teachers should be educated to act constructively with low-achieving reading groups. Needless to say, empirical substantiation is needed here as well.

The impulse to ameliorate the problem of teaching literacy was followed and subjected to observation by Moll and Diaz. They devised a project with the purpose of developing expository writing in low-income, bilingual, middle school students. They attempted to import community content into the classroom to spark and sustain activities of written composition.

The program they developed contained four major phases: (a) teacher orientation in which teachers themselves actively wrote: (b) a program of community involvement in which students circulated a questionnaire on bilingualism to community members; and (c) writing assignments in which students composed a descriptive account of the results of their surveys. The authors concluded, quite rightly, that it was possible to shape instruction through engaging students in the social issues inherent in their own communities.

Variations on this technique have been described as the language experience approach to language development in the context of elementary school education. Its power to motivate writing and activate previously reluctant learners was amply documented by Moll and Diaz. Perhaps the dilemma of apparent passivity found by Bloome in his investigation may be addressed with this approach. Possibly, the alienation and exclusion experienced by students with "bad attitudes" in Gilmore's study can be ameliorated with this strategy.

Implications

The collective force of the studies presented at the Literacy, Language, and Schooling Conference and briefly discussed here may have a substantial impact on how the nature of a reading program is perceived and described. The studies posed important questions, descriptions, and insights in ways that were different from studies of data tabulation and correlation. The knowledge provided is extremely valuable in education, and regrettably, it is quite rare.

The questions, descriptions, insights, and ways of knowing provided in the naturalistic literacy studies need to be accompanied by studies in which variables are measured, comparisons are quantified, and replications of findings available. The studies described in this volume are meant to introduce new ways of looking at learning to read; that is, the studies provide findings from processes of inquiry in a discovery mode.

One prevailing theme in the studies from this volume is that learning to read in most schools is a social process as well a psychological accomplishment. It becomes clear from these investigations that engagement with the text at the interpretive level in classroom contexts requires: (a) the appropriate selection of material for the student group in terms of subject matter content and difficulty; (b) expert guidance by the teacher into the full spectrum of meanings that can be constructed in the reader–text interaction; (c) the use of oral language by teacher and student that extends the child's language structures and deepens the reach into text meanings; and (d) management of groups of children which assures that learning time is equal for all individuals or proportional to need.

This view of a program contrasts sharply with a perspective that is all too frequently held in education. If a teacher or school principal or superintendent is asked, "What is your reading program?" the answer will usually be the name of a commercial program such as Ginn 720 or the Laidlaw workbooks. Elsewhere I have documented how the study of reading programs has consisted of the study of materials in isolation from the other factors needed for learning (Guthrie, 1981).

If the view of learning to read as a social process is to be communicated to educators, how should such an effort be undertaken? Individuals who can benefit from such an insight are probably not policymakers such as superintendents, who ap-prove and disapprove program proposals but rarely are expected to initiate authentic innovations. Administrators of currently existing programs are not the most receptive audience, for their interests will be vested in the system for which they are currently responsible.

Teachers may in their own ways incorporate this perspective, although their space for maneuvering is often severely restricted. Teachers determine the essential quality of the social environment for learning, the social organization of the classroom. Grouping according to achievement levels has been shown to lead to deleterious effects for the low group, despite the efforts of dedicated teachers. Grouping by interest may be a more potent means to facilitate learning for all students. Developing reading activities around topics that students want to learn about or expect to enjoy may paradoxically foster the acquisition of reading skills more effectively than a skill-based system. Such organizational plans enhance the amount and depth of social interaction for teachers and students which may accelerate cognitive development as well as serve as a valued end in itself.

Education leaders who are in roles of program development are likely consumers of the message of this volume that learning to read is a social process as well as a cognitive achievement. New initiatives are continually undertaken in school districts, state departments of education, and national publishing houses that could profit from this perspective. Individuals responsible for policy at these levels will need to be persuaded, however, rather than merely presented with statements of conviction.

If educators were to embrace the obvious power of the social interaction perspective on literacy, implications for schooling would be twofold. First, a person could not simply be indexed as literate or illiterate or as a success or a failure in reading. The diversity of reading competencies and practices would preclude such simplistic classifications. New ways of describing a person's competencies in literacy will be imperative. The social interaction perspective, in addition, emphasizes that one goal of education is to acculturate students to the practices of reading in their communities. Reading and writing should be taught as processes and practices that enable self-improvement throughout life. These practices include reading a wide variety of materials for specific purposes. As society becomes more complex—socially, economically, and technologically—the literacies that must be taught in schools will inevitably increase.

CHALLENGES IN POLICY IMPROVEMENT

Communication Barriers

There are several reasons why research does not flow uninterrupted through an open channel to illuminate policy in education. First, the problems researchers find interesting are not the same problems thought to be important in the policy-shaping community. Researchers are oriented to causal accounts of how complex systems function. Policymakers, however, are more frequently oriented to questions of status such as how many handicapped children or reading disabled students exist in elementary schools. The first sort of problem is considered irrelevant by policymakers, and the second sort of problem is shunned as boring by many researchers.

A second obstacle is one of timing. Frequently, the political climate produces new research and new policies on the same issue at the same time. The "right to read" effort in the 1970s induced program starts and basic research simultaneously. As a result, the basic research had less than optimal opportunity to inform policy.

A third dilemma is that the literacy practices of researchers and policymakers are different. Policy people such as legislators, superintendents, senators, and others read newspapers and magazines. They rarely read books for information and never encounter professional journals, in education. Researchers, on the other hand, are enamored by professional journals and technical books. It has been documented that both practitioners and researchers read reviews of research, but their choice of topics is quite different. (Guthrie, Seifert, & Mosberg, 1983). As a result, the base of information and world views of those who produce knowledge and those who use it are quite divergent.

A fourth obstacle to policy improvement through research is that policy must be apparently sensible and cost effective. Research, however, is usually neither of these. Most research findings are not common sense; otherwise, they could not easily be justified as sufficiently original to be regarded as important contributions to knowledge. Rarely are research implications cost effective; they usually require a change in practice or program which is frequently expensive.

A fifth problem pertains to the unmet challenge of communicating knowledge that undergirds education to a broad public. There are peculiar pitfalls for writers who attempt to deal clearly with difficult or technical matters. They will be accused of oversimplification. A clear and simple exposition of complex matters has been considered, until quite recently, to be treachery among the community of scholars. One reason for this is that clear writing tends to expose unclear thinking. As a result, people who attempt to make sense of educational research are often at risk with their peers in the research community.

Problem Formulation

In addition to the communication barriers, a second challenge in policy improvement is suitable problem formulation. Regrettably, there is a dearth of well-formed problems in reading education. To illustrate the kinds of problem statements that shape policy, I will use an example from the field of mental health. This example was taken from an article written by Edward Roybal (1984) entitled "Federal Involvement in Mental Health Care for the Aged." He is the chairman of the House Select Committee on Aging, and my purpose here is to show how he constructs a problem and its solution. Roybal pointed out that over 11% of the American population are over 65 years of age and that proportion is growing rapidly. He continued by saying that the President's Commission on Mental Health reported that 15% to 25% of older persons have significant mental Health problems. In comparison, he pointed out that only 4% of the patients seen at public outpatient mental health clinics are 65 or older, suggesting that these statistics illuminate the lack of care in mental health services for the elderly population.

To address this problem, in 1976 Jimmy Carter created the President's Commission on Mental Health which was charged to report on the mental health needs of the nation with recommendations on how to meet those needs. Subsequently, the Mental Health Systems Act was passed in October 1980. Goals of the law were to emphasize federal funding for mental health care, create a national priority for the care of the chronically ill in the community, and create a federal-local partnership in the coordination of services. According to Roybal, Reagan subsequently decreased appropriations to the programs funded by this act by more than 24%. Despite this, however, he pointed out that 22 states provide direct reimbursement to psychologists for outpatient services for the aged. However, because Medicare coverage of outpatient mental health care is limited to $250 per person, there are economic barriers to quality care for the elderly who need mental health services.

In the case of reading education, the scenario of policy formation has taken the following course in many states and districts. First, the literacy of students in public schools is regarded as inadequate. This is usually based on a standardized reading test which reveals that a shocking proportion of students is below the mean. Second, a law is usually enacted which requires students to pass a test for promotion and graduation. Klein (1984) reported in the *Phi Delta Kappan* that 40 states now have mandated testing programs to ensure that all high school graduates attain some criterion of literacy. Third, educational administrators react to this law by increasing the number of courses or remedial programs designed to help students pass tests. For example, in California, 85% of the school districts in one survey increased their English programs and accelerated their staff development activities in response to minimum competency test legislation. Finally, curricula are usually adjusted to enable students to pass these tests, although I know of no quantification of how frequent and profound these adjustments are.

The consequences of this scenario are paradoxical in many schools. On one hand, frequently fewer students fail the minimum competency tests. On the other hand, many fewer students meet with success in fulfilling their potentials. This latter consequence reaches disastrous proportions in many schools and may vastly outweigh any other advantages to these programs.

POLICY-DRIVEN RESEARCH

To improve the applications of research and improve the common sense of education policies, I submit that what we need is policy-driven research. We begin by going back to the basics in the development of research questions. We need to ask simple, broad, fundamental questions—questions that are hard to answer but ones that strike toward the center of our real concerns. This kind of question was recently exemplified by Messick, Beaton, and Loard (1983). In the rationale for the new National Assessment of Educational Progress, they asked, ''Are today's students learning the skills necessary for productive functioning in America in the 1980s?''

(Messick et al., 1983, p. 12). They stated that it was part of the mission of the National Assessment of Educational Progress (NAEP), which is now under Messick's direction at the Educational Testing Service, to provide data relevant to this question.

It is right for the NAEP to address this issue as well as the question of how many students pass certain types of items. Knowing what percentage of 9-year-olds pass a literal comprehension item on hydroelectric dams is like knowing that a hummingbird can flap at 65 beats a second without knowing how many strokes are needed for actual flight. Previous NAEP efforts have told us something of what students are learning; now, I hope, we can discern whether this learning is useful or productive for them in school, work, or personal endeavors.

One of the lessons the International Reading Association learned from attempting to respond to *A Nation at Risk* is that many of the most obviously important problems have been essentially untreated by educational research (Guthrie, 1984). For example, one recommendation from the National Commission on Excellence in Education (1983) was that "The teaching of *English* in high school should equip graduates to . . . comprehend, interpret, evaluate, and use what they read" (p. 25). In addition, as you will recall, 4 years of English were recommended as a requirement for all high school students. To answer that question, it would be valuable to know the following:

1. Do 4 years of English in high school increase reading achievement as compared to 1, 2, or 3 years?
2. Are there different types of reading that should be taught such as comprehension, interpretation, critical evaluation, functional literacy, or reference reading?
3. What distinctions among types of reading are viable for testing purposes?
4. What evidence do we have about reading achievement and instructional variables in high school such as amount of time, use of tests for accountability, curriculum sequence, the presence of remedial programs, or the amount of homework assigned to students?

Needless to say, the answers and approaches to the answers are complicated, but the fact that we have such little information on these issues suggests that we have not engaged in policy-driven research.

In the last part of this chapter, I briefly discuss the roles of naturalistic, data tabulation, and correlation studies in the rationale, problem, method, results, conclusions, and dissemination of policy-driven research.

Rationale

Policy-driven research begins with the documentation of a social dilemma. As indicated in the example for mental health described by Roybal, the rationale must address many questions: what is the problem? How many people suffer from this problem? What segments of the population are involved? What is the cost in human or economic terms to the person or the social group afflicted by the dilemma?

While naturalistic studies tend to emphasize the first question posed in a rationale (What is the problem?), they also have a role to play in other parts of the rationale. They can accompany data tabulation and correlation studies to provide examples, description, and insights. Naturalistic studies do not replace data tabulations and/or correlation studies; rather when the three types of studies are taken together, they can persuasively communicate a rationale and the broad nature of policy issues.

Problem
The study must address a broad question or set of questions about the current state of things. I am referring to the following questions. What is a good high school? What is the literacy level in the U.S.A. today? How can students be taught to write more effectively? What kind of literacy should be taught to special populations such as retarded children or vocational education students?

Method
To examine problems of this breadth, studies must include many factors. The design of inquiry should not specialize in exclusion of variables and control of factors. On the contrary, it should incorporate as many factors as would likely affect the outcome of the questions stated in general terms. Controlled experiments will not provide maximum yield, and problems should be studied in situ despite the ambiguity and uncertainty this entails. A combination of qualitative and quantitative procedures will be likely to be optimal. Qualitative strategies including case studies, ethnographies, interviews, systematic self-reports, and linguistic analysis may be valuable for a variety of purposes and stages of investigation. However, qualitative methods should be accompanied by quantitative methods of testing and verification in which sufficient objectivity is achieved so that the given question is answered in the same way by independent observers. This combination of strategies is especially powerful in policy studies, but it is relatively rare in traditional educational research.

Results
The objectivity of conclusions in an important criterion. In the classical sense, different people should draw the same conclusions from the evidence presented in the study.

Results will be constrained by logic. Inductive or deductive reasoning and a discovery mode of inquiry across a small number of detailed examples may be valuable, but they are not a sufficient basis for proposing generalizations and/or conclusions. Such modes of logic need to be supplemented by more deductive methods. Quantitative measures of important variables should be taken and related to one another. Predictions should be made and tested within the data, if possible.

Conclusions
Distinctions should be made between summary propositions warranted by the data and implications of the findings for practice. Since the conclusions of policy-driven

research will relate to programs that have not yet been initiated, generalizations are imperative. However, the natural skepticism of an investigator should not be suspended when the person attempts to apply findings to a nearby domain.

Dissemination

There is a wide range of audiences within the policy-shaping community. In addition to communicating to scholars and peers, a research report that is policy-driven must penetrate the mass print media. Newspapers are frequently scorned and universally frustrating to scholars. However, their power to control policy should not be underestimated. According to Weiss, national leaders from 30 different categories such as the U.S. Senate, foundation presidents, and others, read most intensively from three sources: the *New York Times*, the *Washington Post*, and the *Wall Street Journal*. Unless the results of educational research are able to fill vehicles such as these, educational policy will no more fully be informed by research tomorrow then it is today.

REFERENCES

Aaron, H.J. (1978). *Politics and the professors: The Great Society in perspective.* Washington, DC: Brookings Institution.

Au, K., & Mason, J. (1982). Social organizational factors in learning to read: The balance of rights hypothesis. *Reading Research Ouarterly, 27* (4), 115–152.

Bevan, W. (1982). A sermon of sorts in three plus parts. *American Psychologist, 37,* 1303–1322.

Boyer, E.L. (1983). *High school: A report on secondary education in America: The Carnegie Foundation for the Advancement of Teaching.* New York: Harper & Row.

Cronbach, L.J., Ambron, S.R., Dornbusch, S.M., Hess, R.D., Hornik, R.C., Philips, D.C., Walker, D.F., & Weiner, S.S. (1980). *Toward reform of program evaluation.* San Francisco: Jossey-Bass.

Goodlad, J.I. (1984). *A place called school: Prospects for the future.* New York: McGraw-Hill.

Guthrie, J.T. (1981). How to recognize a reading comprehension program: An afterword. In J.T. Guthrie (Ed.). *Comprehension and teaching: Research reviews* (pp. 313–328). Newark, DE: International Reading Association.

Guthrie, J.T. (Ed.) (1984). *Responding to ''A Nation at Risk'': Appraisal and policy guidelines.* Newark, DE: International Reading Association.

Guthrie, J.T., Seifert, M., & Mosberg, L. (1983). Research synthesis in reading: Topics, audiences, and citation rates. *Reading Research Quarterly, 19,* 16–27.

Husen, T. (1984). Research and policymaking education: An international perspective. *Educational Researcher, 13*(2), 5-11.

Klein, K. (1984). Practical applications of research: Minimum competency testing: Shaping and reflecting carricula. *Phi Delta Kappan, 65,* 565–567

Lightfoot, S.L. (1983). *The good high school: Portraits of character and culture.* New York: Basic Books.

Messick, S., Beaton, A., & Lord, F. (1983). *National Assessment of Educational Progress reconsidered: A new design for a new era* (NAEP Rep. 83–1). Princeton, NJ: National Assessment of Educational Progress.

National Commission on Excellence in Education. (1983). *A nation at risk: The imperative for educational reform.* Washington, DC: U.S. Government Printing Office.

Roybal, E.R. (1984). Federal involvement in mental health care for the aged: Past and future directions. *American Psychologist, 39,* 163–166.

Sizer, T.R. (1984). *Horace's compromise: The dilemma of the American high school*. Boston: Houghton Mufflin.

Yeakey, C.C. (1983). Emerging policy research in educational research and decisionmaking. In E.W. Gordon (Ed.), *Review of research in education* (Vol. 10, pp. 255–301). Washington, DC: American Educational Research Association.

PART SIX

CONTEXTS OF LITERACY REVISITED

14 *Literacy in Society: Readers and Writers in the Worlds of Discourse*

Jay L. Robinson

University of Michigan

PROLOGUE

Writing is distinct from most other forms of communication in that its basic skills—putting words into a conventional material form and being able to read them—do not come necessarily as parts of the basic process of growing up in a society. A spoken language, in terms of an ability both to speak and to understand, comes as part of the normal process of growing up in a particular society, unless there are some individual physical disabilities. Writing, by contrast, has been from the beginning a systematic skill that has to be taught and learned. Thus the introduction of writing, and all the subsequent stages of its development, are intrinsically new forms of social relationship. There has been great variation in making these skills available, and this has had major effects on the relationships embodied in writing in diverse historical and cultural conditions. (Williams 1984, p. 3)

When I first began to learn to read, during the late years of the Great Depression, the process appeared neither complex nor difficult: the text was easy to locate—it was right there on the page in black print. Decoding the text seemed perfectly straightforward—a matter of matching sounds to letters until several came together to form a recognizable whole, an echo of what had been heard from the lips of parents and teachers. And interpretation was quite easy: Most stories had obvious morals for middle-class children, and those that didn't (and even many that did) had a moral or two printed at the end.

When I first learned to read critically, as a literature student at Berkeley during the late years of the Korean war, the process was a bit more—but only a bit more—complex and difficult. The text was still there, tangible and unchanging; and since our critical skills were honed on lyric poetry, it still made sense to think of letters as associated with sounds. Though interpretation was more problematic, because taste and apprenticeship to its dictates were involved, the text was still authoritative—it held its own meanings—and any context necessary to interpretation could be assumed to be bounded by the text's initial capital letter and its final period. And when the text was not authority enough for the apprentice critical reader, the critic-teacher was. His (and I use the pronoun deliberately) reading could be presumed at least to approximate the single meaning sometimes hidden in the authoritative text.

How things have changed since the thirties, since the fifties. Reading and writing—activities at the root of the more complex set of human developments comprehended by the term literacy, activities that are seen alike by professional educators and by the lay public as the most basic of the basics old and new—are now being seen, at least by professionals, as the complex phenomena that they really are.

As professionals, our research agendas become not only ever more lengthy but also ever more difficult because, when our research is into literacy, our very topic becomes problematic.

Take reading, for an example, as discussed by Golden in this volume. Reading is not, as was assumed in my day, a matter of a single reader decoding graphic symbols and then verbal cues to derive a determinable meaning from a fixed text. Reading is not a reactive process but an interactive one in which a reader beings at least as much to a text as the text offers. Readers are less well described as decoders than they are as co-creators of texts, since they are "driven" (Golden's word) by a need to find consistency and pattern in what they are comprehending, in which process they draw upon their own attitudes and feelings, their own knowledge of other texts and of the world, in order to construct satisfying wholes. Nor is reading a cumulative inductive process in which bits of information are linked together to form a single, unifying interpretive hypothesis once the text has been read through. Rather and crucially, reading involves prediction, since it proceeds through the formulation of expectations about where the text is going, then through expansion, modification, or negation of the expectations formulated. And readings are never final nor texts ever fixed. Re-readings produce not necessarily more accurate, but certainly new readings—different interpretations, since human beings change between readings; different interpretations, since readings can be modified in group discussions that negotiate the meaning of a text both for the group and for the individuals who comprise it.

To take present theories of language and language use seriously, as Golden does in her use of reader-response theory and text grammar, is to place ourselves as students of language use in a far more difficult world than most of us have occupied before. When some reader-response theorists assert that texts do not really exist, except as physical objects—that texts are really created by readers—they are only reflecting other trends in twentieth-century philosophy. All philosophers have rejected absolutes, and language philosophers argue that while language is referential, it does not refer to something tangibly real so much as to something rather more like itself, that it is a system of signifiers that signal other signifiers. The more philosophical of literary critics argue that literature refers only to itself, and other certainties go. Walter Ong (1977) finds that a "writer's audience is always a fiction" (p. 74)—something that the writer makes up as she goes along; and Michel Foucault (1979) claims that authors are things society makes up to limit and control discourse. A writer, a text, a reader: These used to be concrete identifiable points for those mapping communication. But the twentieth-century intellectual map cannot be drawn with fixed points: It has only constituents that keep changing shape and relations that keep shifting.

The dominant metaphors for research in our time are metaphors of interaction; they are in almost every domain of serious intellectual inquiry ecological metaphors capturing the notions of system and of systematic, symbiotic interrelationships of organisms. The emergent research focus in our time, when the topic is literacy, reading and writing, or any other human uses of language, is upon individuals and their interactions as participants in social groups—as participants in neighborhood activities or the activities of a classroom, or as members of discourse communities and intellectual communities, which are also, of course, social groups. The impulse behind the development and flourishing of ethnographic description of face-to-face interactions is not finally dissimilar to the impulse that produces reader-response theory, speech act theory, or certain forms of the so-called new rhetoric: All deal with interaction and with the various contexts in which interactions take place.

It will no longer do, I think, to consider literacy as some abstract, absolute quality attainable through tutelage and the accumulation of knowledge and experience. It will no longer do to think of reading as a solitary act in which a mainly passive reader responds to cues in a text to find meaning. It will no longer do to think of writing as a mechanical manipulation of grammatical codes and formal structures leading to the production of perfect or perfectable texts. Reading and writing are not unitary skills nor are they reducible to sets of component skills falling neatly under discrete categories (linguistic, cognitive); rather, they are complex human activities taking place in complex human relationships. These ideas are revolutionary in the field of pedagogy, we must recognize, just as they have been in the more abstruse domains of philosophical speculation, and just as they should be in the more conservative domains of academic inquiry and research.

On the occasion when the papers published here were originally presented, I was asked in response to them to address two main questions: What, from my perspective as a humanist—a linguist trained also in literature, a student of writing and its teaching—is it important to know and say about literacy and especially about "print literacy"? And second, what would I recommend as an appropriate research agenda for other students of literacy, especially those interested in the functions of language in schooling? I will deal first with some notions of literacy and then make suggestions about research.

THE DIMENSIONS OF LITERACY

The place of language in the cultural life of each social group is interdependent with the habits and values of behaving shared among members of that group. (Heath, 1983, p. 11)

The range of meanings attaching themselves to the term *literacy* in our culture and to the related terms *literate* and *illiterate* is at once an interesting semantic phenomenon and a barrier to clear thinking about the topic. In some of its uses, literacy is equatable with the terms *education* or *being educated,* especially in socially valued ways, as when we speak of a colleague whom we admire as "highly literate," by which we seem to mean well read in respected texts and able to discourse about them articulately. Such uses of the term literacy seem to offer tacit justification for what, when examined from a distance, seem to be rather questionable educational arrangements: for example, the assignment of sole responsibility for teaching literacy, to English departments in high schools and colleges or the assumption that literacy is taught in those departments, even though teachers in them most often teach only literature (Robinson, 1983a, 1983b).

Related meanings for the term *literacy* may be found in the increasing usage of compound terms like *computer literacy, scientific literacy, media literacy, mathematical literacy,* even—may the good Lord help us—*musical literacy,* in which literacy seems to mean either being knowledgeable about or adept in some domain, and, in some cases, being able to think critically about issues in that domain. Thus the report of the Commission on the Humanities (1980) asserted that:

> Our citizens need to become literate in a multiple sense. We all need to understand the characteristics of scientific inquiry and the repercussions of scientific research. We must all learn something about the use of the media and of new technologies for storing, transmitting, and expanding knowledge. Without this sort of literacy, our society as a whole will be less able to apply science and technology to humanistic needs, less able to measure the human effects of scientific achievements, less able to judge the information we produce and receive. (pp. 18–19)

Two significant lessons can be drawn from the range of usages I have discussed: Something called literacy permeates the culture we inhabit—in fact, to a large extent constitutes that culture; and second, whatever literacy is, our culture values it, and highly (Graff, 1979, 1981). The term *literate* is awarded in our culture as a badge of honor, but *illiterate* stigmatizes, and, in fact, is often applied to persons who know perfectly well how to read and write for perfectly useful personal and social purposes.

It is tempting to say, especially when our concern is language and schooling, that we must restrict the term *literacy* to its involvements with language in print, to discussion only of the activities of writing and reading scripted and printed material, and for certain purposes we probably should. But doing so, if the broader contexts of human interactions with texts are ignored, invites a reductive approach to literacy and its uses, a focus upon code and text that has bedeviled the teaching of reading and writing, the measurement of their acquisition, and the study of both. It is also tempting to assert that we must, at least for purposes of study and description, treat *literate* and *illiterate* as quasi-technical terms and strip them of their laudatory and pejorative overtones. But doing so will result in inadequacy, if our aim is to describe accurately the place and functions of literacy in society; doing so is unrealistic if our aim is to prepare students for a place in the society they will inhabit as adults. We must not lose sight of two well-established findings: The possession of fully functional literacy, a term whose meanings will be explored in the final section of this chapter, correlates with economic and social success in our culture, in spite of the fact that exceptions can be found; the terms *literate* and *illiterate* are reflective of how our society views and values people and how people in our society value themselves. Feelings and attitudes constitute a significant dimension of the contexts of literacy and cannot be ignored.

Restrictive definitions of literacy, fascination with the codes and forms of written communication, and failure to see reading and writing as interactive processes involving individuals and texts in context have all led to educational practices that have disadvantaged many students and left many ill-equipped as users of written language in academic and workaday settings.

> Social historians and critics of the development and role of formal schooling in industrialized nations have increasingly reexamined the content and methods of teaching and learning communication skills. Bourdieu (1973) and Graff (1978) point out that formal education systems tend to teach and promote the learning of only the barest of rudimentary skills for communicating. Proper spelling and grammar, varied vocabulary, and topic-sentenced paragraphs are not sufficient to make cohesive intelligent whole narratives or expositions. Schools teach and test to insure that students "absorb the automatic response and rule-of-thumb techniques," but neither teaching nor testing touches "the higher, active sense . . . [necessary to] set up an interchange between ideas, needs, and external reality" (Calhoun, 1970, pp. 130–31). Through mechanistic linguistic tasks, such as spelling tests and grammar drills, schools claim to impart communication skills. Yet, the academic discourse forms which lie at the heart of success in the higher levels of schooling—oral and written extended prose, sequenced explanations, and logical arguments—[rarely] receive explicit identification and discussion. (Heath & Branscombe, 1985, pp. 3-4)

Similar findings issue from other more recent reports on school practices (see, e.g., Goodlad, 1984, chaps. 5, 7).

To study literacy and its uses is to commit oneself to the study of contexts and relations. Literacy exists only as human activity in context, and our job as students of literacy is to decide which activities and which contexts are worth studying and what relations we must seek to establish between literacy, language, learning, schooling, and life both before and after schooling.

WORLDS IN THE UNIVERSE OF DISCOURSE

> If the critic wishes to produce new and subtle readings, he is at perfect liberty to entertain himself in this way, but he should not do so in the belief that he is thereby making important contributions to the study of literature. An understanding of literature, both as an institution and an activity, involves an understanding of the conventions and operations which enable works to be written and read. (Culler, 1981, p. 124)

> It is genuinely difficult for someone who has spent a working life with print, and has had access, through it, to writing in societies quite unlike his or her own, to take seriously the idea that the conditions the reader shares with those available writers, through the common property of the texts, are socially specific conditions, which cannot be simply read back as the central truths of all active writing and reading. (Williams, 1984, p. 4)

It is common in the literature on the acquisition and development of literacy to find written language and writing described as depersonalized and contextualized when compared to spoken language and speaking. Even a scholar so sensitive to context as Shirley Brice Heath used the terms to to describe contrasts between speech and writing and degrees of familiarity among writers and readers of letters:

> Writing to Shannon had bridged the highly contextualized letters of the upperclassmen [who attend the same school as their correspondents] and the more decontextualized,

nonpersonalized letters to Heath and ultimately the standard classroom assignments of interpretive essays. (Heath & Branscombe, 1985, p. 22)

When compared to the functions of speech in face-to-face interactions, the functions of writing are sometimes less personal, though not inevitably so. Some kinds of writing function to connect a writer with an audience of unknown others, but other kinds of writing—love letters, for example, or letters of condolence, or notes of reminder—presume far more personal relations and rely more heavily upon personally shared contexts between writer and reader than even those that obtain in face-to-face interchanges, especially those among speakers and hearers who do not know one another well. But even in the instances where it makes sense to talk of writing as depersonalized—when,for example, a writer and his or her readers do not know one another, or share contiguous geographical space (or ever intend to)—it is still misleading to think of written texts (or written language) as decontextualized, especially when that term is used by scholars less cautious than Heath to name an absolute, invariant quality of written language.

All texts exist in context. And while it is quite obvious that some written texts, like love letters, depend for their meaning upon shared contexts built through personal relationships, it is less obvious that all texts depend for their meaning either upon shared contexts or shared contextualization. Without sharing, there can be no communucation between a reader and a writer. The problem for us professionals in understanding this notion lies in the appearance of texts—especially printed ones—and in our unconscious behavior as professionals who are literate. There is an appearance of stability in printed texts, and because they are objects, neatly packaged into what always appear as neatly bounded wholes, we are tempted to think that texts contain all context necessary for their interpretation. And because we are professionals like those pointed to by Williams, who have spent a working lifetime with print, gaining access through printed texts to societies unlike our own, we have sometimes been led to think—because of the stable appearance of texts and our uses of reading—that texts are all we need: that we can understand societies unlike our own as would citizens of those unlike societies.

I want to argue in this and the following section that written texts are always richly and complexly contextualized. Some written texts—love letters, for example, or notes of reminder—are contextualized in the same ways as intimate conversations are; other written texts—essays, for example, or lab reports—are otherwise contextualized. But all texts have contexts; and communication, if it is to be successful, requires on the part of writer and reader either the pre-existence or the construction of shared contexts. I will also argue, in this and following sections, that learning to write and learning to read are not movements from personal, contextualized uses of language to depersonalized, decontextualized ones but rather movements from one set of contexts to other sets of contexts. Writing and reading, like speaking and listening, are social acts: Literature, Culler tells us, is both an institution and an activity.

To begin the argument, I will ask and then sketchily answer this question: What besides the code, the language used by the writer of the text, does a reader need to know in order to read a text successfully—to comprehend or construct a reading that is reasonably consistent with meanings constructed by other readers of the text and the meanings intended by the writer? Figures 1 through 3 sketch the categories of requisite knowledge that I will treat.

The Domain of Text

Simple models describing writing and reading as communicative activities place heavy emphasis upon code as the means of contact between writer and reader, and code is taken essentially as a signaling system; in the simplest models, *code* and *text* are taken as essentially the same thing. In the model of Figure 1, the notion *text* is represented by the circle and its five elements: code, writer-in-text, reader-in-text, text-as-argument, and text-as-structured-language. All five are to be taken both as textual elements and as constructs on the part of a reader. The status of the elements is probably best described as a response to these questions: What must a reader minimally perceive and construct in order to know that what s/he is reading is a text and not some random gathering of language? What must a reader perceive and construct to know that a reading for meaning is appropriate?

The term *code* is familiar, but it is used here in something other than its customary sense. *Code* is not a signaling system capable of conveying meaning; rather it is a mode of contact capable of being invested with meaning by a writer and a reader. The terms *writer-in-text* and *reader-in-text* are adaptations from various sources: text grammar, semiotics, the less easily classified work of Walter Ong. As used here the terms refer to text functions in the sense that they can almost always be connected with code and its structured use or with isolable characteristics in the argument; they are reader constructs in the sense that they are created by a reader to help guide both his or her sense that the text coheres and his or her interpretation of the text. *Writer-in-text* is similar to the familiar notion of *persona* and is an element of what is perceived and constructed as stance or style; *reader-in-text* is perceived and constructed as a set of instructions for response: it is also an element of style.

The term *argument,* in *text-as-argument,* is used not in its current but in one of its more common earlier meanings: the subject matter of discussion or discourse in

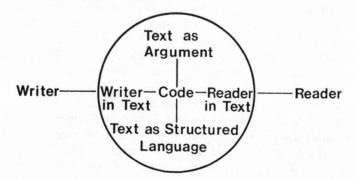

Figure 1. The notion of text and its elements

speech or writing; theme, or subject. The term refers to a reader's perception that a text is about something—that its messages cohere and are intentionally organized into a unified and potentially meaningful whole. The term *text-as-structured-language* refers both to formal aspects of organization and to the various links and connections that are described by linguists as grammatical and semantic elements of cohesion, as that term is used, for example, by Halliday and Hasan (1976).

Taken together, these terms are a specification of interconnected elements that comprise the notion *text*. They refer, and their presence can be illustrated by reference, to features of language and thought in a bounded stretch of written language; but they also refer to a reader's responses, to constructs formed by a reader interacting with a text, bringing knowledge and experience to bear in the task of reading it. The claims made here are these: that when a reader perceives that a text is present and thus that interpretation is possible, s/he sees in the text evidence of an author's control (writer-in-text), suggestions for how to respond to the text (reader-in-text), the presence of cohesive devices (text-as-structured-language), and the presence of propositions and assertions that are at least potentially connectable and thus meaningful (text-as-argument). These are reader percepts and constructs as are several other features customarily taken to be purely textural features: meaningfulness, unity, coherence, organization, for example. In talking about texts and the reading of texts, it is quite impossible to separate reader responses from the linguistic "facts" of a text and equally impossible to separate language from thought. A reader's judgment that a text is unified, coherent, well organized, is just that—a judgment; and it is as much a reaction to text-as-argument, to the perception that a text is about some one meaningful thing, as it is a reaction to the formal features of the text.

And what does a reader bring to this point of judgment? At least those categories of knowledge and experience named in the next concentric circle drawn in Figure 2.

Text in the Domains of Thought and Form

How does a reader perceive that an argument is present in a stretch of written language? It is possible, of course, to analyze a text, identify and isolate its propositions and assertions, and then describe their connections with reference to some system of inference and entailment. In order to do so, however, it is necessary to impose upon a text some abstract scheme, and then to extract from the text those features that seem to fit it. To perform such operations, in order to be able to claim that arguments are logical structures and that readers perceive them as such, relying when they do so upon general or specific congitive capacities, it is necessary to make another abstraction: The structure must be abstracted not only from the text and the verbal context the text provides, but also from the context of a real reader interacting with a text for some purpose in some particular community of writers and readers. The counterclaim made here (see Figure2) is rather that readers perceive the presence of an argument in a text when they find similarities to other arguments they have read, or heard, and have remembered, arguments that were offered in some likewise remembered domain of inquiry or representation.

Arguments are instances of discourse in some clearly or ill-defined *field;* they are instances of discourse that are recognized as arguments because they employ some clearly or ill-defined *mode* of inquiry or representation. The argument of ''Rose White, Rose Red'' is recognizable and potentially interpretable, because it, like other fairy tales, is narrative employing agents and events that are fanciful and implausible; the text you are now reading is interpretable, because it, like other essays, shapes speculative assertions into informal arguments, reminds its readers of pertinent arguments offered in commonly read texts, and tries to push for synthesis of thoughts and systems of inquiry not before connected. Arguments, in short, exist in history—in a reader's memory of other arguments, in a reader's knowledge of human domains and modes of inquiry and representation. Logic, too, is a matter of history.

Text-as-argument is a term in the domain of thought but not in the domain claimed by cognitive psychologists. Text-as-structured-language, obviously a term in the domain claimed by linguists, reaches past that domain to other ways of characterizing the human capacity to create and recognize form. A text is perceived as structured language, as organized, in part because of its linguistic features of cohesion but also because it is recognized as a text of some one kind—as an instance or realization of a genre: as a letter, or an essay, or a technical report, or a sonnet, or a recipe for baking a cake. Recognition of form is in part a matter of responding to linguistic signals, to features of code; but it is in larger part also a matter of memory, of seeing in a presented instance of organized language a resemblance to other instances similarly organized, a matter of having formed something like a gestalt

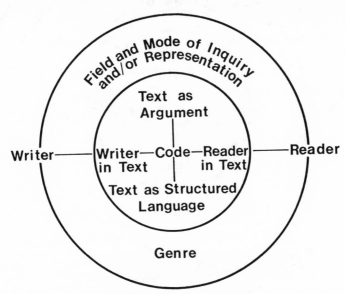

Figure 2. Text in Context: The notions of thought and form

that allows one to find resemblances in otherwise nonrelatable presentations of texts. A reader's sense of form, as referred to by the term *genre*, operates in concert with that reader's sense of field and mode of inquiry to create the notion that a meaningful text has been offered; both operate in concert to help a reader know what to do with a text, to guide, to the extent they can be guided, that reader's interpretations. A single text comes into existence, for an individual reader or an individual writer, in the context of similar texts, prior in history and stored in memory.

Text, Thought, and Form in the Domains of Knowledge and Discourse

Finally, in the outermost circle of Figure 3 which completes the diagram are placed two notions: both the notion of ''accumulated human knowledge and imagination'' (*the universe of discovered and represented meanings*) and the notion of ''functional forms of human expression'' (*the universe of discourse*).

An argument is recognized as such and gains value, in a reader's eyes and mind, as it fits into one or another field or mode of inquiry; and that field or mode is valued and validated as it fits into or adds to or modifies those meanings that constitute

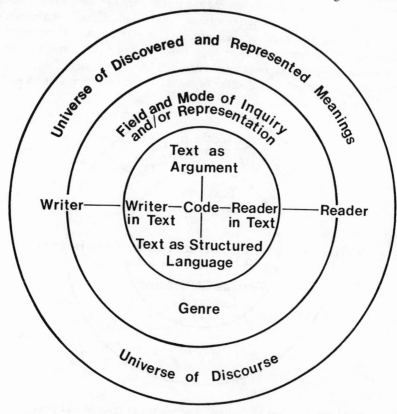

Figure 3. Text in Context: The notions of knowledge and discourse

human knowledge. Similarly, a text is recognized as an instance of some one genre, e.g., sonnet, and thus gains value as one contribution to human expression in that world of human discourse called "poetry," which world along with all others so far created and discovered constitute the universe of discourse. A sense of what is or may be known and a sense of form make thought and language meaningful for readers and for writers, because they enable them to find, validate, and make use of meanings: to act, in short, as human beings, as social beings, in communities made possible and, in fact, constituted by language written down and read. Community is established not merely through a code, not merely through the existence of texts as organized language, but through the common understandings, intuitions, experiences, and memories that readers and writers bring to the negotiations we call reading and writing.

And what of the two terms so far not described—writer and reader? Each of us, whether a 13-year-old ninth grader in Ms. Callisher's remedial reading class or an English professor in an elite university, finds existence in a universe bounded by language and made interpretable only through language, made manageable only through interchange of meanings where language is the coin of exchange.

Readers and writers are also human beings, of course, and as such have their own particular and unique material existences in the world as well as their own individual and unique complexes of impulses and intentions. But the terms *reader* and *writer* do not name solitary physical and psychic existences but rather social roles, for the terms have meaning only in reference to interchanges within the social institutions of written language.

In the next section, I want to make more explicit three arguments that have already been suggested: (a) that the communities formed by writers and readers within the universes of knowledge and discourse are essentially social in their character (to argue otherwise is to misunderstand the functions and importance of written language and literacy in modern societies); (b) that the links formed by written language in creation of these communities are in some ways the same kind and fully as functional as those formed in face-to-face interaction in communities created through speech; and (c) that education is usefully thought of as a movement from community to community, better thought of in this way than as a quasi-maturational process, as something akin to growing taller or developing secondary sexual characteristics.

INTERPRETIVE COMMUNITIES AND HOW TO JOIN THEM

Student writers must, however, learn for written communication—just as they have learned for oral language—that communication is negotiation. When direct response is not possible through a return letter, the writer must play the role of writer *and* reader, anticipating and hypothesizing the kinds of information the reader will bring to the text and the questions which, therefore, the writer must explicitly answer. This social interaction is similar to the process through which children acquiring oral language move as they learn to handle discourse topics—to adjust, clarify, expand, or abandon their efforts to communicate with listeners. Crisis in communication is a natural part of this learning process; at some point in learning to write, students must have the experience of an audience which responds, "I don't understand you. What do you mean?" (Heath & Brandscombe, 1985, p. 26)

One should stress that the whole institution of literary education depends upon the assumption . . . that one can learn to become a more competent reader and that therefore there is something (a series of techniques and procedures) to be learned. We do not judge students simply on what they know about a given work; we presume to evaluate their skill and progress as readers, and that presumption ought to indicate our confidence in the existence of public and generalizable operations of reading. (Culler 1981, p. 125)

To begin my arguments, I will use concepts identified in Figure 3 and apply them to a text, Lewis Thomas's essay "The Medusa and the Snail" (1979), as "operations of reading." Then I will ask how such operations might be both learnable and learned. The concepts I will use primarily are those of writer-in-text and reader-in-text.

Readers and Writers as Participants

Walter Ong (1979), a critic and a cultural historian, claims that "the writer's audience is always a fiction," and is in two ways: First, "the writer must construct in his imagination, clearly or vaguely, an audience cast in some sort of role— entertainment seekers, reflective sharers of experience . . . inhabitants of a lost and remembered world of prepubertal latency (readers of Tolkien's hobbit stories), and so on" (60–61). Second, readers must consent to fictionalize themselves in a way that corresponds to the writer's imaginative construction of their role: "A reader has to play the role in which the author has cast him, which seldom coincides with his role in the rest of actual life" (p. 61). Reader roles are best thought of, I will argue, as essentially social roles, mirroring those of actual life.

A specialist writing for a general audience undertakes difficult problems of exposition. Because he is a specialist, he has knowledge that his readers do not have, and he cannot presume their interest in his topic. Lewis Thomas (1979), biologist and physician, begins his essay on uniqueness and symbiosis in nature in the following way:

We've never been so self-conscious about our selves as we seem to be these days. The popular magazines are filled with advice on things to do with a self: how to find it, identify it, nurture it, protect it, even, for special occasion, weekends, how to lose it transiently. There are instructive books, best sellers on self-realization, self-help, self-development. Groups of self-respecting people pay large fees for three-day sessions together, learning self-awareness. Self-enlightenment can be taught in college electives.

You'd think, to read about it, that we'd only just now discovered selves. Having long suspected that there was *something alive* in there, running the place, separate from everything else, absolutely individual and independent, we've celebrated by giving it a real name. My self.

It is an interesting word, formed long ago in much more social ambiguity than you'd expect. The original root was *se* or *seu,* simply the pronoun of the third person, and most of the descendant words, except "self" itself, were constructed to allude to other, somehow connected people, "sibs" and "gossips," relatives and close acquaintances, came from *seu. Se* was also used to indicate something outside or apart, hence words like "separate," "secret," and "segregate." From an extended root *swedh* it moved into Greek as *ethnos,* meaning people of one's own sort, and *ethos,* meaning the customs of such people. "Ethics" means the behavior of people like one's self, one's own ethics. (pp. 1–2) [From "The Medusa and the Snail," by Lewis Thomas. Copyright© 1977 by Lewis Thomas. originally published in *The New England Journal of Medicine.* Reprinted by permission of Viking Penguin, Inc.]

Thomas's form of address is the inclusive pronoun "we," a form of address that involves and implicates both himself, as writer, and all of us, his readers, in a single perspective upon the subject matter he will treat. The role he creates for us is a role identical to his own: Both he and we are to look at things in the world, muse about the implications of observable phenomena, and try to find messages hidden in them. We as his readers are not fictionalized as his pupils, nor he as our teacher; Thomas as writer does not play the expert, nor are we imagined as lacking expertise in a collaborative search for things and their meanings. Rather, we and our companion who gently guides us are fictionalized as alert to our environment and curious about its meanings. In company with Thomas, "we" have read about "self" in popular magazines and instructive books (even if we have not); he and "we" are implicated alike even in the *naming* of the phenomenon: "Having long suspected that there was *something alive* in there, running the place, separate from everything else, absolutely individual and independent, we've celebrated by giving it a real name. My self."

By including his readers in his musings and assuming their curiosity, by reminding them of things familiar, and by treating difficult concepts in common language (there is "*something alive* in there"), Thomas prepares his readers to play the role *he* is playing as the author of his essay: an observer who tries to find meaning in what he sees—meaning that is personal but also shared, because it applies to all humans. The role Thomas assigns us is a flattering one. We are his colleagues, not his pupils; we are assumed to be as able as he is in identifying significant observations and in drawing important conclusions.

The role Thomas assigns *himself,* as writer, is as fictitious as the one he creates for his readers. In fact he is an expert, and in fact he must teach us because he is a biologist and we are not; in fact he must point us toward important phenomena and help us to see them, since that is his function as a biologist and teacher. But when Thomas instructs, he does so as one would inform a colleague:

> Beans carry self-labels, and are marked by these as distinctly as a mouse by his special smell. The labels are glycoproteins, the lectins, and may have something to do with negotiating the intimate and essential attachment between the bean and the nitrogen-fixing bacteria which live as part of the plant's flesh, embedded in root nodules. The lectin from one line of legume has a special affinity for the surfaces of the particular bacteria which colonize that line, but not for bacteria from other types of bean. The system seems designed for the maintenance of exclusive partnerships. Nature is pieced together by little snobberies like this.

Coral polyps are biologically self-conscious. If you place polyps of the same genetic line together, touching each other, they will fuse and become a single polyp, but if the lines are different, one will reject the other.

Fish can tell each other apart as individuals, by the smell of self. So can mice, and here the olfactory discrimination is governed by the same H_2 locus which contains the genes for immunologic self-marking. (p. 3)

Thomas does not pause in these three paragraphs to define terms that only a biologist might be presumed to know (glycoproteins, lectins, polyps, immunologic self-marking). Were he to do so, he would risk causing us to step out of our role as his companions and colleagues. And if as his readers we were to step out of this role, we might forget that we are engaged with Thomas in a search for something more important than mere detail: some sense of our place in nature and of our oneness with nature's many detailed manifestations. To enkindle this sense in his readers is Thomas's central purpose; and his creation of a role for his readers—the role of colleagues, fellow humans, who observe and wonder and try to find meaning—is essential to the achievement of his purpose.

Thomas's own musings are about manifestation of self in nature (beans, polyps, fish as distinct selves) and about opposite phenomena—symbiotic relationships in which self becomes a problematic concept. To illustrate symbiotic relationships between individual selves, Thomas tells a story about a snail and a jellyfish:

Sometimes there is such a mix-up about selfness that two creatures, each attracted by the molecular configuration of the other, incorporate the two selves to make a single organism. The best story I've ever heard about this is the tale told of the nudibranch and medusa living in the Bay of Naples. When first observed, and nudibranch, a common sea slug, was found to have a tiny vestigial parasite, in the form of a jellyfish, permanently affixed to the ventral surface near the mouth. In curiosity to learn how the medusa got there, some marine biologists began searching the local waters for earlier developmental forms, and discovered something amazing. The attached parasite, although apparently so specialized as to have given up living for itself, can still produce offspring, for they are found in abundance at certain seasons of the year. They drift through the upper waters, grow up nicely and astonishingly, and finally become full-grown, handsome, normal jellyfish. Meanwhile, the snail produces snail larvae, and these too begin to grow normally, but not for long. While still extremely small, they become entrapped in the tentacles of the medusa and then engulfed within the umbrella-shaped body. At first glance, you'd believe the medusae are now the predators, paying back for earlier humiliations, and the snails the prey. But no. Soon the snails, undigested and insatiable, begin to eat, browsing away first at the radial canals, then the borders of the rim, finally the tentacles, until the jellyfish becomes reduced in substance by being eaten while the snail grows correspondingly in size. At the end, the arrangement is back to the first scene, with the full-grown nudibranch basking, and nothing left of the jellyfish except the round, successfully edited parasite, safely affixed to the skin near the mouth.

It is a confusing tale to sort out, and even more confusing to think about. Both creatures are designed for this encounter, marked as selves so that they can find each other in the waters of the Bay of Naples. The collaboration, if you want to call it that, is entirely specific; it is only this species of medusa and only this kind of nudibranch that can come together and live this way. And, more surprising, they cannot live in any other way; they depend for their survival on each other. They are not really selves, they are specific others. (pp. 4–5)

In telling his story, Thomas ultimately becomes our teacher—inevitably, because he must tell us about unfamiliar things and make his point: The two creatures "are not really *selves,* they are specific *others*" (italics added). But he stops well short of explicit didacticism: "It is a confusing tale to sort out," he confesses," and even more confusing to think about." And he refuses to identify himself as an expert biologist. What he gives us is not evidence, data, but a "story," a "tale,"— "the best story I've heard about this . . ." Other experts, "some marine biologists," may search the waters for "earlier developmental forms"; for Thomas, it is enough to hear their narratives about what they have found.

In the concluding paragraph of his essay, Thomas in effect invites us to form our own conclusions:

The thought of these creatures gives me an odd feeling. They do not remind me of anything, really. I've never heard of such a cycle before. They are bizarre, that's it, unique. And at the same time, like a vaguely remembered dream, they remind me of the whole earth at once. I cannot get my mind to stay still and think it through. (pp. 5–6)

The writer is now "I," but still part of the community of the inclusive "we." Because "we," as Thomas's readers, have seen what he has seen, have heard the same tales, have shared his concerns, have pondered and mused and wondered with him, each of us as an individual reader understands the task: to act as a companion "I," to recall our own "vaguely remembered dream," and to find a meaning that is personally significant. "They are bizarre, that's it, unique," is a sentence that invites us to choose our own words, tentatively, knowing that they are replaceable by better ones should we find a surer truth. There is no final meaning in Thomas's essay, no sure and certain message, if Thomas's readers do not act the role he has created for them.

Lewis Thomas's essay is deliberately artistic, and it might be argued that the reading offered here is one appropriate only to belletristic texts; and in some respects it is, since operations of reading must to some degree be sensitive to the requirements of genre and argument. But I would argue that sensitivity to writer-in-text and reader-in-text is perfectly generalizable: that the systematic absence of personal address in scientific prose, for example, defines its reader's role as certainly as Thomas's personal address does in "The Medusa and the Snail." Explicitness, objectivity, and distance typically define the terms under which a negotiation for meaning may take place in scientific prose as certainly as tentativeness, subjectivity, and familiarity do in Thomas's essay. The textual domain, as identified in Figure 1, is a society in miniature with fictional writers and readers represented in familiar social roles. To enter that small domain writers must project for themselves a social role, for only by doing so can they convey their intentions and with them their proffered meanings; in agreeing to play a complementary social role, readers enter the same domain and in doing so consent to control their own particular intentions in order to negotiate a meaning for the text that approximates the meaning intended. As James Boyd White (1984) put it: "Whenever you speak [whenever you write], you define a character for yourself and for at least one other—your audience—and make a community at least between the two of you; and you do this in a language that is of necessity provided to you by others and modified in your use of it" p. xi). Text analysts, even literary critics, are coming to use a language familiar to those who describe face-to-face interactions mediated by language; some sociologists and sociolinguists even read literary criticism.

Students and Teachers as Participants

Classrooms, of course, are the larger and more tangible social environments in which the roles of writer and reader must be learned if they are to be learned functionally. If in reading, a text is mediative between the intentions of writer and reader so that meaning may be negotiated, in a classroom texts are even more importantly mediative as apprentice readers share their changing and enriching constructions of meanings with each other and with the teacher, reaching beyond their present conceptions of arguments, modes of inquiry, their present stores of knowledge— beyond their present sense of structure and form, their limited acquaintance with genres, and their present worlds of discourse toward the wider universe. Learning is finally social, and not only because it involves face-to-face interactions of students with students and students with teachers; it is social, because students interact within the larger historical contexts and structures made possible through written language.

The process that leads a serious though young student of literature to ever more satisfying readings of texts is at base similar to that which leads a marginally literate students to a more functional literacy. Both processes begin in the acquisition and use of spoken language; both proceed through stages in which meanings of texts are negotiated—stages in which formal education is vital; and the acts of reading and writing always imply, finally, a community of interpreters—even though that community may be (though it rarely is) entirely imaginary. Heath and Branscombe said this about the connections between the development of oral and written language:

> We maintain that just as the development of oral language depends on the context of the rich interaction between child and adults, so the development of written language depends on a rich responsive context. This context is especially critical for older students who have reached high school without opportunity to participate in any extended interactive writing. Young children acquiring language *search for units of symbolic behavior, construct systems of elements and relations, and try to match their production to those of selected others in recurrent situational contexts;* the new writer must follow similar steps to generate internal rules for writing to communicate. Responsive, interactive writing frequently occurring over a period of time provides the data from which students may search out meaningful units and systems in writing. (1985, pp. 29-30)

In the early stages of learning to write, personal, direct immediate response is certainly necessary and may differentiate the needs of an apprentice from those of an experienced writer. But all writers require a responsive context, all seek to participate in extended interactive writing and reading (What are learned journals for?), and all try to match production with that of selected others (What are style manuals for?): Literate societies, after all, devote a major share of their resources and modes of production to the maintenance and control of literate discourse. Literate communities are real communities, not imaginary ones, and they are rooted in social practices even if not always in person-to-person contact. Janice Radway's (1984a, 1984b) recently published works describe in detail one such community composed of readers of romance; hers is pioneering work in its description of institutions and forces binding a literate community together in a social compact formed by readers who have not necessarily even met one another.

The model of reading and writing touched upon in the immediately preceding discussion and treated more fully in the explanations of figures 1 through 3 implies these things about the development of reading and writing: (a) Once the rudiments of decoding are managed, part of the process of learning to read is reading—in an ever widening array of genres—so that memory may begin to apply functionally in the process of text interpretation; (b) Part of the process of learning to read is the accumulation of knowledge and experience so that these may be brought to bear in the comprehension and interpretation of texts. (c) Essential in learning is the opportunity to discuss with others what has been read, so that the social relations implicit in texts may be made explicit as readers share with others their own particular perceptions of their places in the textual world. Writers must have equal opportunity to have their works read and then discussed as contributions to communal knowledge, and to have their works reacted to by readers who share their social space and will grant them their intentions. In designing curricula for the teaching of reading and writing we have been all too eager to search for isolable constituent skills and to teach these as somehow basic: spelling, vocabulary building, grammar, problem solving, word attack skills, semantic analysis—activities of a sort that are easy to translate into drills and worksheets, activities that are easy to teach and to test.

The matter is a serious one. Goodlad (1984) reported, on the basis of perhaps the most comprehensive survey of schools and schooling done in recent years, that in elementary schools, junior high schools, and senior high schools:

> The dominant emphasis throughout was on teaching basic language use skills and mastering mechanics—capitalization, punctuation, paragraphs, syllabication, synonyms, homonyms, antonyms, part of speech, etc. These were repeated in successive grades of the elementary years, were reviewed in the junior high years, and reappeared in the low track classes of the senior high schools.
>
> Reading instruction in the junior and senior highs appeared to be a matter of remediation involving the mechanics of word recognition, phonics, and vocabulary development. In English, there was still a substantial emphasis on the basics of grammar and composition—punctuation, capitalization, sentence structure, paragraph organization, word analysis, parts of speech. *In line with the findings* [all emphasis mine]

*of our analysis of tracking reported in Chapter 5, lower track classes tended to empha-
size the mechanics of English usage, whereas high track classes were likely to stress
the intellectual skills of analysis, evaluation, and judgment, especially through literature. The low track classes were unlikely to encounter the high status knowledge dealt
with in the upper tracks and normally considered essential for college admission. (p.
205)*

Do we, either unknowingly or deliberately, design for failure in the curricula we
offer certain of our students?

To read and to acquire through reading (and other means) knowledge and experience *is* the crucial thing in the development of a reader; to write and to acquire
through writing the capacity to convey both personal intention and what can be
known or experienced by others is the crucial thing in the development of a writer.
In some sense these are "natural" developments in the academic world and in the
literate world. Part of our job as teachers is to design and put in place contexts in
which the processes of development take place naturally. If we want to intervene,
we might do so more effectively by paying less attention to skills and mechanics and
using the time saved to help our students perceive the various moves and strategies
employed in the various fields and modes of inquiry and representation, and then to
practice them.

James Boyd White (1983), lawyer, legal scholar, and rhetorician, claims that the
layman's difficulty in understanding legal discourse does not result from an ignorance of legal language—its vocabulary, its sometimes peculiar syntax—but rather
from ignorance of what he calls the "invisible discourse" of the law: "the unstated
conventions by which [legal] language operates" (p. 48):

> Behind the words, that is, are expectations about the ways in which they will be used,
> expectations that do not find explicit expression anywhere but are a part of the legal
> culture that the surface language simply assumes. These expectations are constantly at
> work, directing argument, shaping responses, determining the next move, and so on;
> their effects are everywhere but they themselves are invisible. (p. 49)

Each domain of inquiry and expression, each domain of endeavor, no matter how
modest, is held together by a system of invisible discourse. And in each case, it is
this system of invisible discourse that binds together readers and writers into an interpretive community, into a cohesive social group able to use language to find
meaning. Our job as scholars is to make the invisible visible, just as our job as
teachers is to do the same and thus invite our students to join our groups as full
participants.

SOME IMPERATIVES FOR RESEARCH ON LITERACY

Nevertheless, educational theory and practice have traditionally been dominated by
psychology. The reason for this seems clear enough to me. The logistic triumphs of
space exploration and of information management systems generally, added to an
earlier respect for the standardized achievements of mass production, consolidated the
belief among educators in authority that success would result from delivering to chil-

dren the right amounts of the right instruction at the right time, with constant monitoring and quality control. The belief still has not been totally discredited that learning is a simple matter of individual ability and effort applied to appropriately organized and presented subject matter. Thus for literacy, educators occasionally turned to linguists to ascertain what should be taught but primarily to psychologists for how the instruction should be delivered. (Smith 1984, pp. vii–viii)

It has come to be recognized, in recent years, that St. Augustine was an astute developmental psychologist, and in the *Confessions* he has something to say about language learning that is relevant here. He is contrasting the learning of Greek, which was for him a second language, with the learning of Latin, his mother tongue:

> Time was also (as an infant) I knew no Latin; but this I . . . (came to know) without fear or suffering . . . for my heart urged me to bring forth its own thoughts, which I could only do by learning words not of those who taught, but of those who talked with me; in whose ears also I gave birth to such thoughts as I conceived. (Donaldson 1984, p. 177)

The multitude of human activities in developed societies that are comprehended by the term *literacy* permeate every aspect of life—even the lives lived by those who are or are called illiterate. For the researcher this means there are rich fields to plow, but it means other things as well. Because literacy is so all pervasive, it has been and continues to be studied from a wide variety of perspectives; but because literacy is merely a term used in general reference to a complex of very complex human activities, no single perspective seems to reveal very much. Written language can be viewed as an artifact, or as a tool, or as a code, but it is more than any of these because it *is* language and because, in a real sense, as humans so are we, for humans are social beings. Reading and writing can be viewed as skills, but because they are human activities linked to social existence and the processes of coming to know, they are far more than that. To study literacy seriously is to commit oneself to interdisciplinary work—to the risk of stepping beyond one's comfortable academic domain. And to study reading and writing, because these are complex human activities taking place in some complex of real circumstances, is to commit oneself to a study of contexts and relations. Literacy is impossible to define, for whatever purpose, without reference to its nature and use in some one context—in some one delimited and clearly defined social context: To drive this point home has been a major contribution of ethnographers to the study of literacy in school and society. But to remind ethnographers that "literacy events" occur in the wider social contexts of literate communities linked together by the institutions of written language is the joint responsibility of sociologists of culture, social historians, rhetoricians, and certain kinds of literary theorists.

Raymond Williams (1981) employed the term *convergence* to speak of a coming together of different interests and methods applied to increasingly common issues and problems in formation of something approximating a new academic discipline (pp. 9–32). Those of us who study literacy have not yet reached convergence of this kind, but increasingly we are dealing with similar issues, similar problems, and learning from one another in the process. High on our agendas for study and research, even as we follow our own interests and employ our own methodologies, should be a search for new ways to share information about literacy. The amount of work coming out in books and journals is staggering, and some of it is even good and useful. Given societal needs and a proper, ethical sense of professional obligation, we cannot afford disciplinary parochialism; neither can we afford wasteful territorial disputes. We need to learn from speculative studies, from those scholars who rely on insight, from those who do careful analyses of historical documents, from those who propose general, integrative, and abstract theories as well as from those who go out and look, digest, and interpret. If as teachers we must construct classrooms in which reading and writing can happen, as researchers and scholars we must create forums for fruitful exchange.

To reach toward convergence as scholars in separate disciplines who would be interdisciplinarians we must meet three challenges of theory. The first is to engage in rigorous critical analysis of the methodologies that are dearest to our hearts and minds—the kind of analysis, for example, that Clifford Geertz (1983) offered in several essays in his collection *Local Knowledge*. In such analysis, I believe, outside and even alien perspectives can be useful. When I teach English grammar, as I sometimes do, I teach my students at least two systems of grammatical description, because I want them to see that grammar is not something given by God but rather something human beings construct as a system of discourse about language. I suggest that we will learn more about literacy if we apply multiple perspectives and explore differences and similarities among the discourse systems we construct, looking for their limitations and strengths. We need forums in which widely divergent positions can be stated and examined: forums, for example, in which ethnographers—with all their commitments to the particular—can talk fruitfully to cognitive psychologists—with all of theirs to generalization.

If we are to make further progress toward convergence, we will need to overcome the mutual unintelligibility of the discourse systems—the very languages—that we employ in our work. We badly need, if not theories of translation which may prove to be too abstract, at least methods or operations for translating one set of claims into another, for talking sensibly about similarities and differences between disciplinary approaches, some of which differences are sometimes exalted into a claim that different epistemological assumptions are at work. If they are, we need to know it; if not, we need to know their status. Committed sociologists can easily claim that the language used in earlier sections of this essay is far too figurative and fuzzy; but I would want to ask them if their language is less figurative, and if so on what theory of referentiality: and I would want to ask whether or not figurative and fuzzy language is a better or worse kind for describing indeterminate events and their relations to changing situations.

Third, and I think the most important of our theoretical tasks: If we are finally to reach convergence in the study of literacy, we will recognize that we are jointly engaged in the study of context and that we are rapidly moving toward, in our several disciplines, a usable general theory of context. In saying this, I am thinking about ethnographic work of the kind represented in this volume and in other places, much of it indebted to John Gumperz and Dell Hymes, which for all its particularity implies some generalizations about what counts as relevant context in descriptive work on interaction (Fetterman, 1984; Gilmore & Glatthorn, 1982; Goelman, Oberg, & Smith, 1984; Hymes, 1974; Wagner, 1983); I am thinking about work in conversational analysis and the analysis of other forms of talk (Goffman, 1981); I am thinking about work in speech act theory (Bach & Harnish, 1979; Coles & Morgan 1975; Searle, 1969, 1979, 1983), and in reader-response theory and semiotics (Culler, 1981; Eco, 1979; Iser, 1978; Tompkins, 1980); about work in rhetoric (White, 1984; Knoblauch & Brannon, 1984; Winterowd, 1975); and about sensitive new work by my colleague Alton Becker (1982, and in press) drawn from linguistics, rhetoric, and philosophy. References provided can only be suggestive, which is itself a measure of the volume of activity in study of this problem. Context is becoming, for those of us who study language and its uses, less a garbage-can term, a useful receptacle for the inexplicable, than one that we can use in principled ways to explain what needs explanation. We need, I think we all recognize, to explore the multiple contexts of literacy; we may, before too long, be able to explore together as a community of participant observers informed by theory and able to communicate intelligibly and usefully. It is right, and will be useful in future research, to treat literacy as a set of differing but related social phenomena, embedded in history and involving for individuals both linguistic and cognitive capacities. The challenge for us is twofold: Make sense of this notion and then apply it rigorously to understand such pressing social problems as school failure, high rates of illiteracy, and the relations between illiteracy and poverty.

SOME IMPERATIVES FOR RESEARCH ON FUNCTIONAL LITERACY

What then is "English literacy" for professional students and teachers of English? Is it their own condition and that of people much like them, currently and retrospectively applied? Or is it the diverse and changing conditions of their whole nominal people? To approach two centuries of English literacy means restricting our account to a bare majority. General literacy has a bare century, and within that many are still disadvantaged. In relation to what is seen as "our" literature, where then do students and teachers of English stand?

I have made my own awkward stand. By my educational history I belong with the literate and the literary. By my inheritance and still by affiliation I belong with an illiterate and relatively illiterate majority. It is said that as the whole society develops, and has for the past century been developing, these inherited problems and contradictions resolve themselves. I do not think so. Beyond our local and diverse histories there are major intellectual issues, of a fully objective kind, which need to be traced to this radical unevenness between literature and general literacy. Underlying them, always, are the complex general problems of language, and it is in how these problems are dealt with, in the coming years, that the success or failure of English studies will, in my view, be decided. (Williams, 1984, pp. 212–213)

The problem of a "radical unevenness between literature and general literacy" is not one only for those who think of literature as a particular body of imaginative writings. It is the problem of expertise in all complex modern societies, in which ever more specialized intellectual elites produce theories and information inaccessible and unintelligible to the general public while continuing to influence public policy. It is the problem of media control and access to the various media controlled by economic conditions as print sources become ever more expensive, leaving the less affluent dependent upon the more easily controlled electronic media. It is the problem of decisions made by those in control about the wishes and wants of the illiterate and relatively illiterate that lead to debased entertainment and to political debate that finds its most influential forms in 1-minute television commercials or 10-minute film biographies that resemble either the lives of saints or those of movie stars. The problem of the radical unevenness of general literacy and literature is as much these things as it is the more familiar problems associated with the term *functional literacy:* denial of access to jobs that demand an increasingly higher level of literacy, denial of access to training programs for such jobs because entrance tests demand a relatively high level of literacy. In thinking about the more obvious problems associated with illiteracy, we should keep somewhere in our minds the less obvious ones of access to something beyond economic sufficiency. Not to do so is to render ourselves as teachers and researchers into mere functionaries in a society we may not wish to leave unchanged; not to do so is, perhaps, to limit access through literacy for our students. I do not think, in our culture, that we can maintain that "illiteracy per se is not necessarily a problem" (Smith, chap. 3, this volume) just because some illiterates manage to get money.

Ethnographers of literacy and of schooling have made important contributions to our understanding of functional literacy by exploring the uses of reading and writing in particular social contexts, giving substance to such definitions of the term as UNESCO's—definitions that emphasize the relativity of the term. It is certainly right to say that the terms *literate* and *illiterate* find meaning only with reference to specific social contexts; it is no less right to say as Smith does "that the problematicality of illiteracy is contextually determined" (chap. 3, this volume). But who delimits the contexts that determine access to other contexts? Do we merely observe and describe, or do we act as participant observers? And in what roles should we participate?

I want to offer two simple and complementary definitions that may be useful in talking about functional literacy:

Writing is the ability to employ written language to create texts that are valued by readers in particular contexts.

Reading is the ability to act upon written texts to create meanings that are valued by one's self and by other readers joined in community in particular contexts.

And to these definitions, I would add one other dimension, borrowed from James Boyd White (1983):

Literacy is not merely the capacity to understand the conceptual content of writings and utterances, but the ability to participate fully in a set of social and intellectual practices. It is not passive but active; not imitative but creative, for participation in the speaking and writing of language is participation in the activities it makes possible. Indeed it involves a perpetual remaking both of language and of practice.

But to participate, of course, one must gain or be granted access; and because literacy, reading and writing, are as much group activities as individual ones, to exercise them fully—to develop "ability"—requires opportunity. Our instructional programs often fail because we fail to provide opportunities for our students to make best use of their abilities with written language; and our society in fact creates functional illiterates by denying many citizens the opportunity to participate in a broad enough range of social and intellectual practices. There is no reason to urge high literacy upon a person with dismally low prospects.

Ethnographers studying language and literacy in schools and schoolrooms have quite properly and usefully focused upon teacher-student face-to-face interactions, and sometimes—now increasingly—upon written texts as mediative in such interactions, an even more promising line of research. But because many such studies have produced negative results, there is growing reluctance in schools to having them done and increasing skepticism about their usefulness. Courtney Cazden (1983) reported having been told in Alaska that somewhere in the Alaskan State Department of Education there is a sign that says:

> WE DON'T NEED ANY MORE
> ANTHROPOLOGICAL EXPLANATIONS
> OF SCHOOL FAILURE (p. 33)

I think we do, when schools in fact fail, so that we may come to understand why. But more importantly, I think we need wider understanding of the reasons for failure; and to get this, we will have to study schoolrooms and schools in their various contexts. Along with Cazden (1983), I believe we need

> a broader view of research relevance. Exclusive concern with translating the outcomes of research into improved skills of the practitioner is too narrow; practitioners have not only skills, but also a view of reality, a vision of reality, a vision of the achievable, and a commitment to act; and social science knowledge can influence all four. (p. 33).

Humanistic knowledge can also influence all four, and perhaps even social scientists as well.

One of the more exciting developments within ethnography, and one that seems to promise productive change in practice, is the joining of teacher-practitioners with researchers in the model now known as "teacher-as-researcher." But after reading impressive reports of new curricula and student achievement (Moll & Diaz, Chap. 9, this volume; Heath, 1983; Heath & Thomas, 1984; Heath & Branscombe, 1985), one is left with a nagging question: Will these changes and gains last? The gap between research and educational practice is very wide, even when the research is into practice and even when it is done in schools; and for those who read history, even very recent history, the gap between research and educational policy often appears unbridgeable.

In these circumstances lie new opportunities for ethnographers interested in questions of education. Why is it that useful findings are so rarely used, while obviously trivial ones are so readily adopted and applied? Who and what forces control the flow of information from researchers to teachers? What are the impediments to information flow? Why are our institutions so impervious to change—even when change would seem to support and sustain their very continuation? Using various theories, we can offer various generalizations in answer to such questions, but we do not know very much in detail—perhaps because such study is inevitably depressing. I suggest that our first need in studying literacy, its uses, and acquisition is an ethnography of power and its uses, the kind of study that identifies agents and their actions rather than forces and their operations, and in doing so, perhaps makes change more possible. We need an ethnography of power at least as much as we need more of the useful studies now appearing that treat continuities and discontinuities between home and school, community and school, and work and school, important though these are.

I am struck by what we do know and believe that suggests what should and should not be looked at. Even granting that individual differences exist in the intellectual equipment of individual children, we do *know* that insofar as linguistic competence is involved in the acquisition of literacy, all people have a sufficient measure of such competence, as a birthright, to escape illiteracy, unless some kind of pathology intervenes; we do *know* that insofar as cognitive competence is involved in the acquisition of literacy, most people have that, and for the same reason. Given these articles of our mutual faith, we should be able to frame pretty good guesses about where to look for the causes of illiteracy. Students are often all too easy to blame when we focus upon the linguistic and cognitive competencies involved in writing and reading to the neglect of social interaction and the larger social forces that affect interaction and language use. Teachers are also all too easy to blame when we isolate their interactions with students for study while ignoring contexts that limit what they can say and how they can say it.

A final imperative for those of us who do research on questions in education is to meet a challenge made by Stephen Cahir of NIE to those of us who attended the conference reported on here: Append, he said, to all research papers a statement saying "This is what our findings are good for." He added, jokingly, what many others who fund research say seriously: It would also be good if we could later show results in upward changes of test scores. As researchers, we do have the responsibility to state the relevance of our research and to involve ourselves in making it work in practice. But in so doing, we must also have a voice in determining the means by which results will be evaluated. Test scores have contexts too.

When testing is the topic of research or the means of measuring outcomes of its application, what we should be after, in my view, is not always changes in test scores but as often changes in tests. If I understand the findings of ethnographic research about literacy, they lead to the conclusion that standardized tests are poor instruments for measuring such things as writing and reading: Certainly this is true of those national tests that are completely insensitive to local contexts of need and opportunity.

Let me speak briefly to a case. The University of Michigan has a writing program that offers some students who need it remedial preparation for an introductory course; the introductory course then leads in turn to a more advanced content-based course which all students must take. This final course is offered in each department in the college of Literature, Science, and the Arts and is intended to instruct students in how to write effectively in the discipline they are studying. Chemists teach chemistry students how to write like chemists do; art historians introduce students to the art of describing art; and economists teach acolytes the mysteries of economic discourse.

Those of us who work in the program and are responsible for it think it is a good one but would like to find out whether or not it produces results—for better reasons than to save our funding. But how do you test for learning and development in a complex and loosely organized program that is deliberately designed to produce diverse outcomes? We could easily test common mechanical features like spelling or verb agreement, but the results would be trivial; we could test writing correlates, but we would not be certain that, in fact, the correlates correlate; and if we were to build into the instructional program, for purposes of testing, constant tasks for purposes of comparability, we would waste our students' time and irritate them with irrelevances while contradicting the program's major assumptions and subverting its aims.

The simple fact is that although we are working on the problem, we do not know how to test for real rather than apparent growth in our program. (I would feel worse about this confession if I thought that anybody did.) We do not know how to test for real growth, because we cannot reconcile prevailing assumptions about testing with these two definitions:

Writing is the ability to use written language to create texts that are valued by readers in particular contexts.

Literacy is the ability to participate fully in a set of social and intellectual practices.

As we grope our way toward an adequate means of evaluation, we know these few things: We will not be able to decontextualize our tests; we will have more use for variables than for constants; and we had better be ready to involve human beings and to trust their informed, if sometimes subjective, judgments.

REFERENCES

Bach, K., & Robert M. Harnish. (1979). *Linguistic communication and speech acts*. Cambridge, MA: MIT Press.

Becker, A.L. (in press). *Correspondences: an essay on iconicity and philosophy*.

Becker, A.L. (1982). The poetics and noetics of a Javanese poem. In D. Tannen (Ed.), *Spoken and written language: Exploring orality and literacy* (pp. 217–238). Norwood, NJ: Ablex.

Cazden, C.B. (1983). Can ethnographic research go beyond the status quo? *Anthropology & Education Quarterly, 14*, 33-41.

Coles, P., & J.L. Morgan. (1975). *Syntax and semantics III: Speech acts*. New York: Academic Press.

Commission on the Humanities. (1980). *The humanities in American life: Report of the Commission on the Humanities.* Berkeley: University of California Press.

Culler, J. (1981). *The pursuit of signs: Semiotics, literature, deconstruction.* Ithaca, NY: Cornell University Press.

Donaldson, M. (1984). Speech and writing and modes of learning. In H. Goelman, A. Oberg, & F. Smith (Eds.), *Awakening to literacy* (pp., 122–130). Exter, NH: Heinemann Educational Books.

Eco, U. (1979). *The role of the reader: Explorations in the semiotics of texts.* Bloomington: Indiana University Press.

Fetterman, D.M. (Ed.), (1984). Ethnography in education. Beverley Hills, CA: Sage.

Foucault, M. (1979). What is an author? In *Textual strategies: Perspectives on post-structural criticsm* (J.V. Harris, ed.) (pp. 141–160). Ithaca, NY: Cornell University Press.

Geertz, C. (1983). *Local knowledge: Further essays in interpretive anthropology.* New York: Basic Books.

Gilmore, P., & Glatthorn, A.A. (Eds.) (1982). *Children in and out of school: Ethnography and education.* Washington, DC: Center for Applied Linguistics.

Goelman, H., Oberg, A., & Smith, F. (Eds.). (1984). *Awakening to literacy.* Exeter, NH: Heinemann Educational Books.

Goffman, E. (1981). *Forms of talk.* Philadelphia, PA: University of Pennsylvania Press.

Goodlad, J.I. (1984). *A place called school: Prospects for the future.* New York: McGraw-Hill.

Graff, H.J. (Ed.) (1981). *Literacy and social development in the west: A reader.* Cambridge, England & New York: Cambridge University Press.

Graff, H.J. (1979). *The literacy myth: Literacy and social structure in the nineteenth-century city.* New York: Academic Press.

Halliday, M.A.K., & Hasan, R. (1976). *Cohesion in English.* London; Longman.

Heath, S.B., & Branscombe, A. (1985). "Intelligent writing" in an audience community: Teacher, students, and researcher. In S.W. Freedman (Ed.), The acquisition of written language: Revision and response. Norwood, NJ: Ablex.

Heath, S.B., & Thomas, C. (1984). The achievement of preschool literacy for mother and child. In H. Goelman, A. Oberg, & F. Smith (Eds.), *Awakening to Literacy* (pp. 51–72). Exeter, NH: Heinemann Educational Books.

Heath, S.B. (1983). Ways with words: Language, life and work in communities and classrooms. Cambridge, England & New York: Cambridge University Press.

Hymes, D. (1974). *Foundations in sociolinguistics: An ethnographic approach.* Philadelphia: University of Pennsylvania Press.

Iser, W. (1978). *The act of reading.* Baltimore, MD: Johns Hopkins University Press.

Knoblauch, C. H., & Brannon, L. (1984). Rhetorical traditions and the teaching of writing. Montclair, NJ: Boynton/Cook.

Ong, W. (1979). The writer's audience is always a fiction. In *Interfaces of the word* (pp. 53-81). Ithaca, NY: Cornell University Press.

Radway, J. (1984a). Reading the romance: Women, patriarchy and popular literature. Chapel Hill: University of North Carolina Press.

Radway, J. (1984b). Interpretive communities and variable literacies: the functions of romance reading. *Daedalus, 113,* (3).

Robinson, J.L. (1983a). The social context of literacy. In P.L. Stock (Ed.), *Fforum* (pp. 2–12). Upper Montclair, NJ: Boynton/Cook.

Robinson, J.L. (1983b). The users and uses of literacy, In R.W. Bailey & R.M. Fosheim (Eds.), *Literacy for life, the demand for reading and writing* (pp. 3–18). New York: Modern Language Association of America.

Searle, J.R. (1969). Speech acts. Cambridge, England & New York: Cambridge University Press.

Searle, J.R. (1979). *Expression and meaning: Studies in the theory of speech acts.* Cambridge, England & New York: Cambridge University Press.

Searle, J.R. (1983).*Intentionality, an essay in the philosophy of mind.* Cambridge, England & New York: Cambridge University Press.

Smith, F. (1948). Introduction. In H. Goelman, A. Oberg, & F. Smith (Eds.), *Awakening to literacy* (pp. V-XV). Exeter, NH: Heinemann Educational Books.

Thomas, L. (1979). *The medusa and the snail: More notes of a biology watcher.* New York: Viking.

Tompkins, J.P. (Ed.). (1980). *Reader-response criticism: From formalism to post-structuralism.* Baltimore, MD: Johns Hopkins University Press.

Wagner, D.A. (Ed.) (1983). Literacy and ethnicity (special issue). *International Journal of the Sociology of Language, 42.*

White, J.B. (1984). *When words lose their meaning.* Chicago: University of Chicago Press.

White, J.B. (1983). The invisible discourse of the law: Reflections on legal literacy and general education. In P.L. Stock (Ed.), *Fforum* (pp. 46-59). Upper Montclair, NJ: Boynton/Cook.

Williams, R. (1981). *The sociology of culture.* New York: Schocken.

Williams, R. (1984) *Writing in society.* New York: Schocken.

Winterowd, W. R. (Ed.). 1975. *Contemporary rhetoric: A conceptual background with readings.* New York: Harcourt, Brace, Jovanovich.

15 Literacy Instruction in Secondary School Classroom Contexts

Gladys Knott

Kent State University

Recently, sincere and growing interest has been shown in secondary students' reading and writing performance. Some of this interest stems from traditional assessments of student progress across grade levels on a national scale (Dearman & Plisko, 1981; Tierney & Lapp, 1979). Particular interest in secondary students' literacy achievement derives largely from a number of reports on the general status of secondary education in American (Boyer, 1983: Sirotnik, 1982; Cuban, 1982). Although a critique of the reports is not the purpose of this chapter, it will suffice to state that they generally characterized students' achievement as mediocre (National Commission on Excellence in Education, 1983; Sirotnik, 1982). Findings varied across the reports, but the central and compelling recommendation was to initiate and implement educational reform in American schools.

Given the concern with literacy instruction expressed in many reports and the central role that literacy development plays in academic achievement, it is important to consider what is known about literacy development and instruction at the secondary school level. Specifically, attention needs to be focused on new directions and perspectives offered by recent theory and research from the fields of educational psychology, linguistics, sociolinguistic ethnography, anthropology, and educational sociology.

The purpose of this chapter is to highlight select advances in our knowledge of secondary students' literacy development and to suggest directions to improve student performance. Three sections comprise the discussion. The first section presents recent theoretical contributions in reading and writing and provides exemplary selections of research conducted with secondary students. Having illustrated that literacy achievement can be demonstrated with secondary students, the second section addresses present classroom practices and the role of literacy in secondary schools. The third section raises additional issues that preclude one-dimensional solutions to secondary students' literacy problems. Perspectives are suggested for talking about and learning more about qualitative aspects of secondary literacy instruction and classroom life.

READING AND WRITING DEVELOPMENT THEORY AND RESEARCH AT THE SECONDARY SCHOOL LEVEL

In general, secondary school literacy instruction has been guided by philosophical beliefs about practice, intuitive wisdom, and by the transfer of elementary school models of literacy instruction into secondary classroom (Early, 1973; Nelson &

Herber, 1982). Specifically, skills-building models of reading development and models emphasizing writing mechanics (e.g., punctuation, capitalization, etc.) have proliferated. Political and other nonresearch-based events and circumstances (for example, minimum competency standards for high school graduation) have yielded more recent alternative models of literacy instruction at the secondary level (Knott, 1985). In brief, with few exceptions, models and discussions of literacy development and instruction at the secondary level have lacked the research-based foundations that could have provided a basis for constructive, ongoing discussions leading to improved literacy achievement.

Early theoretical constructs in the field defined reading as a series of subskills that proceed linearly from sound to words, then phrases, and eventually to sentences to obtain meaning (Spearritt, 1972). Reading programs, materials, and instructional strategies train reading comprehension as a set of multiple skills (e.g., finding the main idea and sequencing narrative events). Several researchers have taken issue with defining reading comprehension development as the acquisition of discrete skills (Goodman, 1979; Smith, 1973; Goodman & Smith, 1971). Shafer (1978) has evaluated the extent and effects of skills-oriented models of reading and concluded that such instruction fails to result in improvement of secondary students' reading performance.

One alternative to subskill-based models has been psycholinguistic-based models of reading. Goodman (1976), Smith (1975) and Harker (1979), for example proposed models of reading comprehension development that emphasize the construction of meaning as an active process involving the reader's cognitive processing of linguistic information and world knowledge. Goodman, for example, defined reading as a "psycholinguistic guessing game" in which the reader used past experiences and knowledge of language to test hypotheses and/or make predictions about what would be discovered in reading text. However, empirical program evaluations of psycholinguistic applications to secondary students' reading are not readily available (in part, because of the dominance of subskills-based on models). Implications of the psycholinguistic view of comprehension remain to be ascertained with secondary students. As Artley (1980) cautioned, psycholinguistic approaches to literacy development and instruction are not a "panacea for all our reading problems" (p. 107).

Similar to psycholinguistic models, more recent reading development constructs have defined comprehension as an interactive process (Rumelhart, 1976). Simply stated, the reader brings cognitive, social, and linguistic resources to interact reciprocally with text data, thus resulting in comprehension (Adams & Bruce, 1982; Adams & Collins, 1979; Berger & Robinson, 1982; Brown, 1980; Langer & Nicolich, 1981; Singer, 1983; Spiro, 1980).

While the usefulness of schema-theory as an explanation of reading comprehension and development is still being debated, it does provide a heuristic for discussing reader resources and text features which may effect reader-text interaction. Both reader resources and text features are discussed in the next two sections. The placement of components in the next two sections is somewhat arbitrary; in certain instances a component may well be discussed as a reader resource, text feature, or some other categorization (e.g., self-regulation, study skills).

Reader Resources

Among the major resources a reader brings to interact with text information are cognitive and linguistic process and knowledge. Among the linguistic processes is the syntactic and semantic processing of text data. Difficulty with either syntactic or semantic processing may preclude the reader establishing relationships between major resources that can be brought to interacting with text information.

Readers may experience difficulty in structuring and organizing new concepts in relation to past experiences. An inability to form and/or access concepts to interact with text information may preclude comprehension, for example. Adams (1980) found, for example, that concept formation and utilization represent major obstacles to comprehension among secondary school students.

A study by Vogel (1981) also suggested the importance of the relationship between concept formation and utilization and literacy achievement. Achieving and underachieving ninth-grade students were administered a series of standardized tests of intellectual ability, reading, and concept formation. Differences were reported in the students' ability to advance in levels of reasoning, thinking, expression of problem solutions, and basic concept formation strategies (Vogel, 1981). Although the results from the investigation related primarily to the select sample, implications for literacy development with secondary students seem appropriate. Difficulty in verbalizing a concept may affect comprehension and production of text. Some secondary students may experience problems in categorizing and classifying information, attaching appropriate labels to represent past experience, and in integrating new concepts with old information through linguistic processing. These factors are important to consider in efforts to learn more about reading problems among secondary students.

Metacognition is a recent area of study in understanding reading development. Brown (1980) defined the term as "the deliberate conscious control of one's own cognitive actions" (p. 453). Brown's lucid explanation focused on the reader's awareness of what was known, when information was known, as well as when it was not known, and the reader's awareness of a need to seek intervention. This latter awareness included the reader's selection of active reading strategies, for example, self-testing and categorization of information. Much of the empirical research on metacognition has been conducted with young and middle school children; however, research with secondary students has begun to emerge.

In a recent study of metacognitive behavior, Bridge and Winograd (1982) investigated secondary students' awareness of referential, conjuctive, and lexical relationships in cloze comprehension. Students read passages and supplied missing words to establish cohesive relationships or meaning relations in text, but good and poor readers demonstrated different difficulties in their awareness of cohesive relations. With both groups, lexical deletions were easier to supply than were referential or conjunctive deletions. Instructional implications suggested by the researchers include teachers' recognition of students' difficulties and the need to adjust instruction to assist students to learn about cohesive cues in text.

Another type of resource the reader brings to text is termed *prior* or *background knowledge* (Adams & Collins, 1979; Bransford, Nitsch, & Franks, 1977; Brown & Campione, 1979). Recently, Adams and Bruce (1982) explained the importance of background knowledge in reading.

> To say that background knowledge is often used, or is useful, in comprehending a story is misleading . . . In fact, reading comprehension involves the construction of ideas out of pre-existing concepts . . . comprehension is the use of prior knowledge to create new knowledge. Without prior knowledge, a complex object, such as text, is not difficult to interpret; strictly speaking it is meaningless. (pp. 36–37)

The effect of background knowledge on secondary students' reading comprehension was demonstrated in two recent studies. Stevens (1980) assigned ninth graders of varying ability levels several high- and low-familiarity paragraphs and administered multiple-choice questions about the passages. For the different ability groups, background knowledge was a significant factor. Prior knowledge of paragraph content aided understanding of text.

In another study, researchers were guided by the premise that "text-specific concept and vocabulary knowledge affect the processing and recall of text and that a measure of this knowledge might assist teachers in determining whether a reader possesses adequate background to successfully comprehend and recall a particular text" (Langer & Nicolich, 1981, p. 374). High school seniors enrolled in an advanced placement English literature course were asked to free associate with specific content words taken from passages. Later, they were asked to read, recall, and write what they remembered from the passages. Two important conclusions were reached from this study: Level of prior or background knowledge was related to the ability to recall passages, and prior knowledge predicted recall independent of intellectual ability of normal and above-average students.

Although a few researchers have shown the value of considering students' prior knowledge in reading comprehension, important questions remain to be answered, particularly with secondary-level students. The issues include whether classroom-developed background knowledge increases the quantity and quality of information for use in novel situations. Another issue relates to variations in students' background knowledge (Singer, 1983) and how their information is structured for retrieval in appropriate situations. These and other topics are currently under investigation; results should lead to improved comprehension instruction with secondary students.

Text Features

The effects of text structure on comprehension and retrieval of information have been the subject of recent reading research. Several psychological correlates of text structure have been discussed by Goetz and Armbruster (1980). They maintained that connected discourse facilitates greater learning than groups of unrelated sentences or lists of isolated lexical items. Correspondence between the text and the reader's knowledge and expectations also facilitated comprehension. These researchers maintained that within texts, readers identify certain elements that were important to remember. Another research-based conclusion was that interaction of the reader, the context in which text occurred, and the text itself resulted in an internal representation of text. This text feature construct suggested that lists of information such as modes of transportation, plant species, or categories of print media were better retrieved when learned in a meaningful narrative context. Another suggested implication was that texts should relate to students' existing knowledge, and from these texts, main points rather than details were expected in retrieval.

Researchers have also been concerned with the effect of text structure on reading comprehension (Kreider, 1981; Meyer, Brandt & Bluth, 1980). Kreider (1981) investigated the effect of the presence, absence, and placement of topic sentences in paragraphs on secondary students' comprehension. Superior, average, and difference readers (students whose comprehension was average but whose vocabulary knowledge was above average) were subjects in the study. Findings indicated that regardless of topic sentence placement in text, the topic sentences improved reading comprehension, particularly main ideas. Significant differences between the groups were not found when topic sentences were placed in beginning, middle, or end positions, or when topic sentences were implied.

With a limited sample of students, researchers have also demonstrated that the expectations, knowledge of different text structures, and purposes that students bring to reading interact and effect comprehension. Clearly, the selection of well-structured texts and increasing students' awareness of text structure may result in improved reading comprehension. And, although available research has focused on prose or narrative text, future research involving technical and scientifically oriented information will have special significance for secondary students.

In summary, the construct of reading as an interactive process offers improvement beyond past formulation of reading. The research-based theories and constructs are useful and informative in stimulating further research with secondary students. However, the research to date on comprehension as interaction is not comprehensive enough to suggest thorough practical classroom strategies. A need exists to continue research and provide a scientific foundation on which secondary reading instruction can be applied.

WRITING DEVELOPMENT THEORY AND RESEARCH

"Teaching of Writing Gets New Push," the headline for the *New York Times* Winter Education Survey (January 8, 1984), attested to the need to address writing at all levels of American education. The urgency of the decline in thinking skills and effective writing was reinforced in several articles which also suggested that writing should become a central mission of the schools.

Recognition by researchers of the need to address a "writing crisis" (Dearman & Plisko, 1981; Scribner & Cole, 1978) in American education was evidenced by several recent volumes on writing (Deford, 1980; Frederiksen & Dominic, 1981;

Whiteman, 1981). Although strides have been made in fostering writing, the focus of most research has been the acquisition and development of young children's writing. The goal of this early research has been to examine various theoretical assumptions and perspectives and present a conceptual framework of writing and writing development.

Frederiksen and Dominic (1981) summarized four current research perspectives on the activity of writing. They viewed writing, first, as a cognitive activity, one in which the writer's reasoning/thinking skills, acquired knowledge, and processing capacities influenced written production. A second perspective on writing suggests that language form and use influence production. Syntactic and semantic processing capacity and the writer's awareness of appropriate use of language in different contexts are reflected in effective writing. A third perspective on the activity of writing incorporates the writer's sense of audience and function of written messages. Writers anticipate processing demands on readers as well as the effects of their communicated messages. The fourth perspective on writing suggested by Frederiksen abd Dominic (1981) involves writing as a "contextualized, purposive activity" (p. 2). The processes writers engage in while writing are influenced by the situations in which they write and the goals and functions of the writing activity. The perspectives on writing as an activity are interrelated; they represent multidisciplinary research approaches and offer promise in understanding writing acquisition and development.

With an emphasis on improvement of writing instruction, Bruce, Collins, Rubin, and Gentner (1978) explored writing from a cognitive science framework. Presented as a mechanism for generating ideas rather than a unified theory, these researchers view writing as a communicative process built on select principles of communication. One principle is comprehensibility which makes text easy to read; another is "enticingness" which holds the reader's attention. Other principles include persuasion techniques, designed to convince the reader that ideas are true, and memorability which assists the reader in retaining essential information.

Applebee (1981) conducted an extensive study of secondary school writing practices and commended several steps to guide effective writing. The primary objective was to provide students opportunities in which "writing can serve as a tool for learning rather than as a means to display acquired knowledge" (Applebee, 1981, p. 101).

Beginning efforts have been made in addressing the writing crisis at the secondary school level. However, more definitive research is needed to discover the nature of secondary students' writing in relation to recent theoretical assumptions, perspectives, and conceptual frameworks on the writing activity.

CLASSROOM INSTRUCTION AND THE ROLE OF LITERACY: CURRENT PRACTICES

Secondary school reading instruction is beset with difficulties originating in reading theory, the translation of theory into classroom practice for older students, and misunderstandings about what goes on in secondary schools. Various arguments and analyses of problems in secondary school reading instruction portray a picture of conflict.

Among prominent researchers' evaluations of reading instruction at the secondary level, Early (1973) wrote:

> In the past thirty years, the status of reading instruction in the secondary school has changed very little . . . we are still debating the merits of special reading services and urging the whole school faculty to teach reading in the content fields. (p. 364)

Presenting a general discussion related to the organization and management of secondary school reading programs, Nelson and Herber (1982) stated:

> In spite of the growing concern for the improvement of reading instruction, the organization and management of secondary reading programs has changed relatively little over the past two decades. The predominant mode of organization is the creation of special reading classes for limited groups of students. (p. 143)

More specifically, these researchers described three types of reading classes generally found in any given secondary school: (a) students who were severely deficient in reading achievement were enrolled in remedial classes; (b) students who performed a year or two below their potential were enrolled in corrective reading classes; and (c) average to above average students were occasionally offered developmental reading to assist in advancing their study skills and present reading achievement.

Given the declining status of secondary students' reading achievement (Dearman & Plisko, 1981; Tierney & Lapp, 1979), a close examination of the basic foundation of classroom practice seems necessary. An impending conjecture is that the problem rests in multiple facets of secondary reading instruction, all affecting the quality and success of classroom practice.

One immediate concern is the source of underpinning of secondary reading instruction. Numerous reading instruction practices, programs, materials, and achievement tests acknowledge and reflect product-centered reading theory, research, and literature of the past. Basically, the product-centered framework examined readers' responses to questions about text and inferred mental processes readers used to derive responses. Reading methodology (Early, 1973), classroom practice (Linquist, 1982; Stallard, 1976) and measurement of reading (Farr, 1969), followed this conceptual scheme.

New theoretical insights into reading processes have led to criticism of product-centered research and classroom reading practices. Simon (1971) investigated product-centered reading instruction and concluded that the research underpinnings revealed little about reading processes. Although product-centered reading instruction has been shown to be generally ineffective, one goal at the secondary level was "to increase students' proficiency in the identical basic reading skills taught in the elementary schools" (Nelson & Herber, 1982, p. 144).

In addition to the ineffectiveness of reading methodology found in many secondary schools, the quality of classroom practice is affected by misguided recommendations to improve reading. Consider, for example, the quality and type of recommendations in a recent edited volume, *Secondary School Reading* (Berger & Robinson, 1982).

> Students can skim through a whole chapter or even a whole book to find something that looks interesting, then stop and consider that for a while. (p. 33)

Use instructional dialogue to help both teacher and student reflect upon particular interpretations and responses. (p. 48)

The first recommendation failed to recognize that students bring interesting background resources to the classroom. Suggesting to some secondary students that they "find something" in a text reinforces apathy and negative attitudes toward school. The usefulness of the second recommendation is questioned in view of present conditions and contexts in many secondary schools. The average secondary class enrollment (25–35 students), teacher-student talk ratio (3 to 1) (Sirotnik, 1982), the minor or superficial emphasis many teachers place on reading-to-learn (Rieck, 1977), and the stress to cover content almost preclude meaningful teacher-student dialogue.

Thus far I have suggested that much secondary reading instruction is characterized by attempts to designate every secondary teacher a teacher of reading, the use of ineffective models or conceptual frameworks of reading instruction, and by questionable assumptions and recommendations to improve reading. These observations and difficulties in secondary school reading instruction support general findings on many students' reading achievement. They require investigation as they pertain to secondary students' reading performance in any school setting.

Inseparable from successful reading instruction is the necessity to build and foster purpose in reading. In contrast to the preceding discussion of classroom practices which appear devoid of meaningful purpose, a subsequent discussion in this chapter highlights the importance of purpose in conducting reading instruction. The gist is that not all secondary school reading instruction fails its primary goal—effective reading performance.

The state of writing instruction at the secondary level is similar to that of reading instruction. Although an increased interest in writing research and the teaching of written expression has been shown in recent years, the present status of writing instruction at the secondary school level is unsatisfactory. Type of writing tasks, responsibility for improving writing performance, differences among teachers in terms of writing expectations and "how" to teach writing are issues confronting the secondary school. With these and other difficulties, writing instruction results in short-answer responses, checks on ditto sheets, and other simplified forms, which primarily serve teacher grading purposes.

During recent years writing instruction has been described as being almost remiss in the secondary curriculum. Scribner and Cole (1978) explained:

> The kind of writing that goes on in school has a very special status. It generates products that meet teacher demands and academic requirements but may not fulfill any other immediate instrumental needs. (p. 35)

A comprehensive study (Applebee, 1981) of writing tasks secondary students perform, classroom instruction practices, and students' purposes in writing across secondary grades indicated that

> so much of the writing students do is assigned in a test situation, rather than an instructional one . . . it comes from a conceptualization of writing as a simple skill which a given student has or does not have. (p. 102)

This state of the art on writing instruction in secondary schools is an indicator of the need to nurture the topic. Several reports of writing projects funded by the National Institute of Education are expected in the professional literature. Whiteman (1980) described the objectives and goals of the projects and included researchers' studying secondary students' syntactical and rhetorical fluency in writing, teacher variation in writing instruction, and students' ability to engage in writing as an ideation or thinking process. Reports from these and other writing projects will serve and inform classroom writing instruction.

In summary, present literacy instruction practices in secondary schools warrant immediate and considerable attention. Although extensive research has resulted in improved knowledge of initial literacy acquisition, its continuing development through effective classroom instruction must be pursued.

THE ROLE OF LITERACY IN SECONDARY SCHOOLS

The function, role, or use of literacy by secondary students has been assumed to be important in school success. Greater emphasis and stronger assertions have been made on reading demands than writing. This circumstance exists particularly because writing demands on secondary students have been virtually nil in the past. In this regard, the role of literacy in the discussion relates primarily to reading.

Reading professionals' concern for improving secondary students' reading achievement has involved examination of kinds of reading courses and functions of reading in secondary classrooms. Investigations related to kinds of reading have yielded quantitative data on the number, classification, and grade levels of different reading courses. Greenlaw and Moore (1982) investigated specific types of reading instruction in middle and secondary schools; at the secondary level, remedial reading dominated course offerings, followed by developmental accelerated and "other" reading courses such as "Recreational Reading" (p. 535). Respondents to the survey indicated that reading instruction was not necessarily an integral part of any secondary subject area, but that reading instruction was relegated, in most instances, to English courses. In such courses classic and contemporary literature was used.

Two secondary school history classes provided Smith and Feathers (1983) insight into the role of reading aand the necessity to read for success in secondary classrooms. Quantitative data indicated that reading assignments were primarily textbook materials selected by the teacher. The majority of students indicated that they completed less than half of the assignments because the information could be acquired in other ways. Worksheets which followed textbook arrangements and required short answers were the primary mode of reading instruction. In this study, "the students" primary, often sole, purpose for reading was to locate specific answers to literal questions" (Smith & Feathers, 1983, p. 266).

Similar observations of the role reading plays in junior high and secondary school settings were discussed by Rieck (1977), Ngandu (1976), Knott (1979), and Bloome and Green (1982). The work of these researchers also suggested that reading to learn played an insignificant role in many students' academic programs.

Rieck's (1977) work captured the reality of the role of reading in many secondary schools. Across several content areas, including English, art, science, mathematics, and social studies, teachers and students were interviewed. Teachers (approximately 34) were conscientious and enthusiastic, but they conducted classes in a manner which suggested that "their students would learn better if they were 'told' about subjects rather than getting them involved in reading" (Rieck, 1977, p. 647). Most students indicated that they did not read their assignments, that tests covered mainly lecture and discussion, and that discussion of reading assignments was not required. In addition, the students' responses indicated that purpose in reading was not suggested by teachers, rather it was the number of pages to read that guided the assignments. Students noted that their teachers did not recommend interesting books or bring outside reading materials to class.

However, there are secondary schools in which literary instruction and the role of literacy are meaningful components of secondary education. Seifert (1978–1979) reported data which suggested that reading instruction and purpose in reading were integral to 34 secondary school academic programs. Seven factors were described as the focus of school practices: (a) academic rigor; (b) English curriculum; (c) mathematics; (d) guidance programs; (e) grouping and grade weighing; (g) teacher attitudes and expectations; and (g) parental and student attitudes and expectations" (p. 164). The data indicated that some secondary schools were characterized by high scholastic expectations and commitment to foster the development of students' communicative, cognitive, and social abilities. The data also indicated the necessary influence of effective home-school cooperation in developing students' ability and assisting them to reach educational and personal-social goals.

PERSPECTIVES ON IMPROVING SECONDARY STUDENTS' LITERACY

Evidence in the previous section suggests that the present structure, organization, and management of instructional contexts in some secondary schools is one reason for poor literacy performance. In this view, the nature of secondary school classroom life, including teacher-student interactional competences, requires investigation. Thus, the purpose of this section is to examine traditional secondary school classroom instruction and to relate theoretical constructs and conceptual frameworks which can serve to initiate change.

Traditional Secondary Classroom Instructional Contexts

In many traditional secondary school settings, students are viewed as individuals who attend classes to consume specific content knowledge and develop specific skills. This educational programming purports to enable students to pursue higher education, additional vocational preparation, or gainful employment on graduation. On a large scale in traditional settings, what students consume in the classroom is found in textbooks and other commercial materials such as workbooks and films. Generally, textbooks and complementary materials contain instructional designs, including how the information is to be consumed and evaluated. It is unnecessary for teachers to ask questions about what students need to be taught, how they individually or collectively learn, or what the students already know from previous everyday or school-related experiences. In a significant number of secondary classrooms across content subject areas, materials control instruction. The teacher's primary objective is "to cover the material"; therefore, teacher judgment and decision-making processes are rendered unimportant.

Other constraints and complexities support traditional instructional contexts. In some classrooms, smooth-flowing activity with materials is a facade to prevent disruptions by students who manifest difficult social and behavioral adjustment problems. In some classrooms, the drive for accountability lessens instructional options. Students are expected to demonstrate certain skills and scores on achievement and/or minimum competency tests. Therefore, specific materials which contain information on which students will be tested receive primary instructional attention. There are still other conditions which affect effective classroom instruction at the secondary level. Among them are parent demands, teacher guardianship, crisis counseling, administrative-type responsibilities and expectations, and clerical duties. In summary, there are traditional classroom instruction conditions and priorities which are persistent, interrelated, and serve to perpetuate, and perhaps, generate inferior achievement.

Explicit in this brief summary of traditional instructional contexts in some secondary classrooms is the need to effect change. Recent theoretical literature, constructs, and conceptual frameworks from the study of teaching (Bransford et al., 1977; Cazden, 1982; Goodlad, 1983b; Green & Smith, 1983; Mehan, 1979) offer insights into redefining secondary school classroom instructional contexts. In the following discussion, select contributions are presented in relation to teacher-student interactional competence in classroom instructional contexts.

Redefining Secondary School Classroom Instructional Contexts

Processes in transmitting and transforming knowledge as objective and reflective activity have concerned researchers in studies of educational settings and teacher-student interactions. From the traditional presentation of education processes as psychological phenomena, various recent constructs illustrate social dimensions of the educational process, including literacy achievement.

The Construct of Context. Several researchers have defined *context* in relationship to teacher-student academic and social interactions and expectations

(Cook-Gumperz & Gumperz, 1976; Green & Wallat, 1981; Mehan, 1979; Shultz, 1979). Although there are variations in researchers' illustrations of the meaning of the construct, characteristic or features of context are similar. Erickson and Shultz (1981) have suggested

> Context can be thought of as not simply given in the physical setting—kitchen, living room, sidewalk in front of drug store—nor in combination of persons (two brothers, husband and wife, firemen). Rather, contexts are constituted by what people are doing and where and when they are doing it. As McDermott (1976) puts it succinctly, people in interaction become environments for each other. (p. 148)

These researchers suggested that "interactionally constituted environments" might change from one situation to the next and "with each context change, the role relationships among participants are redistributed to produce differing configurations of concerted action" (Erickson & Shultz, p. 148).

The view that individuals create contexts between and among themselves and that the outcome may be the sharing of information and acquisition of new knowledge (Cazden, 1982; Green & Smith, 1983, Mehan, 1979) suggests rethinking and modifying present teacher-directed instruction in secondary classrooms. It is fundamental to note how recent constructs of context offer potential for rectifying the role of literacy for many secondary students, traditional secondary classroom contexts, and conservative estimates of teacher-student talk in secondary classroom instruction.

Contexts for literacy instruction include internal "contexts in the mind" and social contexts in the school, according to Cazden (1982). Students bring internal psychological contexts or representations of focused or simple as well as complex events related to literary tasks. That is, in classroom instruction activities, students bring different experiences with text to the activities. The experiences may differ in quality and quantity as they relate to literacy. Second, students bring internal psychological contexts of world knowledge that can be demonstrated, in part, through their lexicon or use of vocabulary. The internal contexts that students bring to classroom instruction represent assets; therefore implications for classroom instruction are appropriate: (a) teachers need to know more about what students have acquired from literacy activities outside the school setting; (b) knowledge acquired from outside literacy activities may serve as a base on which to build new information; (c) students' internal context of understanding minimal and larger meaning units of written discourse (e.g., sentences and multiple paragraphs) should receive attention; and (d) literacy instruction should be focused across the educational curriculum.

Teacher-student interactions in classroom instruction and interaction among students in literacy activities are characteristic of social contexts in the school setting. Cazden alluded to typical literacy instruction in classrooms (e.g., the traditional secondary classroom instruction context described earlier in this chapter) and cited problems that such teacher-student interaction patterns create. With few opportunities to participate in classroom instruction, students have few changes to demonstrate important skills. Consequently, "teachers have less information from which too diagnose their problems" (Cazden, 1982, p. 419). But Cazden cautioned that if students participated too much, disciplinary talk ensued and less time was available for academic activities. Thus a balance between minimal and excessive student participation is one goal in modifying traditional classroom instruction contexts. In addition, the quality of secondary students' classroom interaction during literacy activities warrants special consideration and further explanation. The overriding implication is that instruction should be more responsive in character and substance to what students bring to classroom literacy activity.

Teaching and Learning as Linguistic Processes. Representative findings from seeveral researchers' examination of educational settings and processes help to define teaching and learning from a linguistic perspective. Recently, Green & Smith (1983) summarized constructs common to several investigations related to teaching and learning in classroom environments.

Fundamental to the conceptualization of teaching and learning as linguistic processes is the view that classrooms are communicative environments in which several factors affect teacher-student interaction. As teachers and students engage in classroom activities, they attend to each others' verbal and nonverbal messages and behavior. Particularly, as students participate in classroom activities, they monitor, interpret, and infer messages and signals about teacher expectations and shifts in expectations from one activity, or segment of an activity, to another. Similarly, teachers monitor such processes, but they also set, support, examine, withdraw, and redirect student behavior to achieve instructional goals. Thus, teacher-learning processes are viewed from the perspective of participation in classroom activity, and the communication successes and/or failures of participants influence learning and achievement.

The identification of certain common variables has assisted researchers in ascertaining how teachers indicate their expectations for student performance and how, in turn, students interpret and participate in classroom communicative events. One variable suggests that "communication is a rule-governed activity" (Green & Smith, 1983, p. 357), meaning that in face-to-face activity, students and teachers interact in patterned ways. Such rule-governed behavior includes conversational turn-taking, gaining opportunity or access to conversation, and demonstrating group affiliation and appropriate interaction behavior. Rules which govern communicative events are dynamic; they are "signaled," and they may vary, depending on expectations for participation and the nature and goal of an activity. Although students play a major role in making decisions about communication behavior, the teacher, as instructional leader, dominates in establishing expectations for interaction in the classroom.

A second variable suggests that inferencing is required from students and teachers for conversational comprehension. In that communication consists of verbal and nonverbal symbolic behavior (gestures, facial expressions, distance behavior, voice tone, pitch, etc.), messages may be sent simultaneously, and they may contradict, restate, complement, or serve other functions. However, students and teachers use components of one communication channel, for example, lexical items and syntax of verbal behavior, to interpret components of nonverbal communication. Therefore, inferencing is a complex process requiring not only understanding of messages but also consideration of the functions that communication serves and goals and roles the participants assume.

A third variable infers that "meaning is context-specific" (Green & Smith, 1983, p. 359). Past experience may assist in interpreting messages, but their specific meanings depend on specific contexts. Not all communication behavior is interpreted the same way in different situations, or with different people. Rather, what precedes, what happens during, and what follows human interaction must be considered.

AA fourth factor related to teacher-student interactions suggests that "contexts are constructed during interaction" (Green & Smith, 1983, p. 360). Some communication behavior and expectations are established rituals, and teachers and students share many frames of reference in communicating. However, if incorrect predictions and discrepancies between expected and actual events occur, overt and covert "frame clashes" may be observed.

The fifth factor that underpins teaching and learning as linguistic processes involves the teacher's role in the communicative process. To achieve a variety of goals in different ways, the teacher "orchestrates" and manages numerous messages, contexts, and levels of classroom interaction. The teacher also has responsibility as an evaluator—monitoring and assessing students' participation, participation style, and academic performance on the basis of linguistic performance during classroom instruction.

This briief review of teaching-learning as linguistic processes offers considerable contrast to traditional perspectives of student-teacher classroom interaction. The discussion has shown that student participation is not only encouraged, but that student participation is an active, integral part of classroom instruction. The perspective permits systematic identification of what teachers and students do, analysis of their perceptions of classroom events, and rules and expectations that govern classroom performance.

Teaching Discourse in Learning. An awareness and understanding that some secondary students in mainstream classroom environments present language problems (Knott, 1980, 1981; Wiig & Semel, 1975, 1976, 1980) have been evidenced in recent literature. Such language problems include difficulties in the receptive, productive, and pragmatic uses of communicative behavior. Thus, these problems may interfere with all literacy and literacy-related classroom activity. For example, the language demands of the curriculum, instruction, and student-teacher interaction require competence in the same elements in which some students experience difficulty.

In this vein, Silliman (1984) presented several theoretical constructs which further suggested conceptual and social expectations for effective participation in the instruction context. Instruction and everyday discourse strategies are differentiated and serve to illustrate that some secondary students may fail to make appropriate distinctions. Citing Bronfenbrenner (1979), Silliman stated

Everyday discourse is that type of interaction serving social functions arising from the regulation of interrelationships among setting, participants, role expectations for participants, and the nature of joint activities or tasks. (p. 289)

Everyday discourse in characterized, therefore, by informal and cooperative turn-taking, common interest topics, and shared frames of reference about a particular topic. In contrast, instructional discourse serves "a primary cognitive function in the transmission of scientific or logically based knowledge" (Silliman, 1984, p. 289). In addition, one of its primary functions is to structure thinking processes as relating, reflecting, and reasoning activities which rely on internal language resources.

Everyday and instructional discourse can also be differentiated in relation to the general purposes they serve, the character of comprehension activities in each form of discourse, the coding complexities, and the assumptions participants present in communication interactions. The two modes of discourse are further differentiated in a description of interrelated components which are characteristic of both modes of discourse. Discourse is organized to include conversational acts or functions that language serve such as requesting, regulating, asserting, and responding; it includes turn-taking behavior in conversational interactions, sequencing behavior, and episodes which represent a composite of conversational acts, turns, and sequencing. Gossip, telling a story, and discussions of popular topics are episodes.

Teaching discourse is organized with respect to three types of teacher-student interactional competence. First, knowing how to mean suggests that teachers use various conversational acts to elicit different responses from students in an instruction activity. Choice elicitations function to gain a reply to question content or to elicit agreement or disagreement; product elicitations serve solicitation of factual information about events, actions, etc.; process elicitations invite opinions, ideas, and interpretations, and metaprocess elicitations require reflection on how response content is formulated. Second, knowing how and when to participate includes timing and regulation of turn-taking, knowing implicit participatory rules for gaining access to conversation, and knowing how to maintain attention during interaction. Finally, knowing how to be relevant, clear, and original suggests skill in constructing sequentially organized and related content and skill in repairing breakdowns in communication.

This review of how teachers and other educational personnel regulate and organize conversation illustrates conceptual and social expectations during classroom instruction. Suggested is a shift from the knowledge consuming and knowledge testing of students in the classroom instruction context to enabling students to learn and use language to achieve academic, social, and personal goals. The interactional process becomes the focus of ongoing teacher-student activity.

SUMMARY AND CONCLUSION

In recent years, outstanding contributions have been made in advancing our knowledge of literacy development and learning behavior. Although much of the researchers' attention has been focused on initial acquisition and early development of literacy, progress in nurturing ongoing development during adolescence is evident, though still in need of much attention. As illustrated by a few research efforts with secondary students, change in literacy achievement can be effected. Promising directions are provided by recent theory and research on the nature of interactional processes which may serve to redefine teaching-learning activity in secondary school classrooms.

REFERENCES

Adams, M. (1980). Failures to comprehend and levels of processing in reading. In R. Spiro, B. Bruce, & W. Brewer (Eds.), *Theoretical issues in reading comprehension*. Hillsdale, NJ: Erlbaum.

Adams, M., & Bruce B. (1982). Background knowledge and reading comprehension. In L. Langer & M. Smith-Burke (Eds.), *Reader meets author/bridging the gap: A psycholinguistic and sociolinguistic perspective*. Newark, DE: International Reading Association.

Adams, M., & Collins, A. (1979). A schema theoretic view of reading. In R. Freedle (Ed.), *New directions in discourse processing*. Norwood, NJ: Ablex.

Applebee, A. (1981). *Writing in the secondary school*. Urbana, IL: National Council of Teachers of English.

Artley, A. (1980). Psycholinguistics applied to reading instruction. *Reading Horizons, 20*(2), 106–111.

Berger, A., & Robinson, H. (Eds.). (1982). *Secondary school reading*. Champaign, IL: ERIC Clearinghouse on Reading and Communication Skills.

Bloome, D., & Green, J. (1982). *Capturing social contexts of reading for urban junior high school youth in home, school, and community settings* (Final report). Washington, DC: National Institute of Education.

Boyer, E. (1983). *High School: A report on secondary education in America*. New York: Harper & Row.

Bransford, D., Nitsch, K., & Franks, J. (1977). Schooling and the facilitation of knowing. In R. C. Anderson, R. Spiro, & W. Montague (Eds.), *Schooling and the acquisition of knowledge*. Hillsdale, NJ: Erlbaum.

Bridge, C., & Winograd, P. (1982). Reader's awareness of cohesive relationships during cloze comprehension. *Journal of Reading Behavior, 14*(3), 299–312.

Brofenbrenner, U. (1979). *The ecology of human development*. Cambridge, MA: Harvard University Press.

Brown, A. (1980). Metacognitive development and reading. In R. Spiro, B. Bruce, & W. Brewer (Eds.), *Theoretical issues in reading comprehension*. Hillsdale, NJ: Erlbaum.

Brown, A., & Campione, J. (1979). The effects of knowledge and experience on the formation of retrieval plans for studying from text. In M. Gruneberg & P. Morris (Eds.), *Practical aspects of memory*. London: Academic Press.

Bruce, B., Collins, A., Rubin, A., & Gentner, D. (1978). *A cognitive science approach to writing* (Technical Report No. 89). Champaign: University of Illinois, Center for the Study of Reading.

Cazden, C. (1982). Contexts for literacy: In the mind and in the classroom. *Journal of Reading Behavior* (Special Issue), *14+4(4), 413–427*.

Cook-Gumperz, J., (1976). Context in children's speech. In *Papers on language and context* (Working paper #46). Berkeley, Language-Behavior Research Laboratory, University of California.

Cuban, L. (1982). Persistent instruction: The high school classroom, 1900–1980. *Phi Delta Kappan, 64* 113–118.

Dearman, N., & Plisko, V. (1981). Test scores and attainment rates. *American Education, 17*(7), 15-20.

Deford, D. (1980). Learning to write: An expression of language. *Theory into Practice*, 19 (3).

Early, M. (1973). Taking stock: Secondary school reading in the 70s. *Journal of Reading, 16*, 364–373.

Erickson, F., & Schultz, J. (1982). When is a context? Some issues and methods in the analysis of social competence. In J. Green & C. Wallat (Eds.), *Ethnography and language in educational settings*. Norwood, NJ: Ablex.

Farr, R. (1969). *Reading: What can be measured?* Newark, DE: International Reading Association.

Fredericksen, C., Dominic, J. (Eds.). (1981). *Writing: Process, development, and communication.* Hillsdale, NJ: Erlbaum.

Goetz, E., & Armbruster, B. (1980). Psychological correlates of text structure. In R. Spiro, B. Bruce, & W. Brewer (Eds.) + lTheoretical issues in reading comprehension. Hillsdale, NJ: Erlbaum.

Goodlad, J. (1983). Research on teaching. *Elementary School Journal* (Special Issue), *83*(4).

Goodman, K. (1969). Analysis of oral reading miscues: Applied psycholinguistics. *Reading Research Quarterly, 5,* 9-30.

Goodman, K. (1976). Behind the eye: What happens in reading. In H. Singer & R. Ruddell (Eds.), Theoretical models and processes of reading, 2nd ed., Newark, Deleware: International Reading Association.

Green, J. (1982). Participation in classroom contexts: Teaching/learning from a sociolinguistic perspective. *New York University Educational Quarterly, 13*(4).

Green, J., & Smith, D. (1983). Teaching and learning: A linguistic perspective. *Elementary School Journal, 8*(4), 353–391.

Green, J., & Wallat, C. (1981). Mapping instructional conversations—a sociolinguistic ethnography. In J. Green & C. Wallat (Eds.), *Ethnography and language in educational settings.* Norwood, NJ: Ablex.

Greenlaw, M., & Moore, D. (1982). What kinds of reading courses are taught in junior and senior high school? *Journal of Reading, 25*(6), 534–536.

Harker, V. (1979). Implications from psycholinguistics for secondary reading. *Reading Horizons,* 19(3), 217–221.

Knott, G. (1979). Developing reading potential in black remedial high school freshman. *Reading Improvement, 16*(4), 262–269.

Knott, G. (1980). Communication competence and secondary learning disabled students. *Directive Teacher, 2*(3), 22–24.

Knott, G. (1981). Adolescent learning disabilities: Beyond phonics, punctuation, and popularity. In W. Cruickshank & A. Silver (Eds.), *Bridges to Tomorrow* (selected papers from the 17th International Conference of the Association for Children with Learning Disabilities). Syracuse, NY: Syracuse University Press.

Knott, G. (1985). Literacy in the secondary school. In J. Orasanu (Ed.), *A decade of reading comprehension: From research to practice.* Hillsdale, NJ: Erlbaum.

Krieder, K. (1981). The effect of topic sentences and their placement on the reading comprehension of groups of achieving eleventh grade male readers. *Dissertation Abstracts International, 4*(2), 631A.

Langer, J., & Nicholich, M. (1981). Prior knowledge and its relationship to comprehension. *Journal of Reading Behavior, 1*(4), 373–379.

Lanier, J. (1983). Tensions in teaching teachers the skills of pedagogy. In G. Griffin (Ed.), *Staff development* (Eighty-second Yearbook of the National Society for the Study of Education). Chicago: University of Chicago Press.

Lingquist, A. (1982). Applying Bloome's taxonomy in writing reading guides for literature. *Journal of Reading, 25*(8), 768–774.

Mehan, H. (1979). *Learning lessons.* Cambridge, MA: Harvard University Press.

Meyer, B.J.F., Brandt, D., & Bluth, G. (1980). Use of top-level structure in text: Key for reading comprehension of ninth-grade students. *Reading Research Quarterly, 16*(1), 72–102.

National Commission on Excellence in Education. (1983). *A nation at risk: The imperative for educational reform.* Washington, DC: Author.

Nelson, J., & Herber, H. (1982). Organization and management of programs. In A. Berger & H. Robinson (Eds.), *Secondary school reading.* Champaign, IL: ERIC Clearinghouse on Reading and Communication Skills.

Ngandu, J. (1976). What do remedial high school students do when they read? *Journal of Reading, 2*(3), 231–234.

Rieck, B. (1977). How content teachers telegraph messages against reading. + Journal of Reading, 20, 646–648.

Rumelhart, D. (1976). *Toward an interactive model of reading* (Technical Report no. 46). San Diego: University of California, Center for Human Information Processing.

Scribner, S., & Cole, M. (1978). Unpackaging literacy. *Social Science Information, 1*(1), 19–40.

Seifert, M. (1978–1979). High schools where scores haven't declined. *Journal of Reading, 2*(2), 164–166.

Shafer, R. (1978). Will psycholinguistics change reading in secondary schools? *Journal of Reading,* 21(4), 305–316.

Shultz, J. (1979). It's not whether you win or lose, it's how you play the game. In O. Garnica & M. King (Eds.), *Language, children, and society.* Oxford: Pergamon.

Silliman, E. (1984). Interactional competencies in the instructional context: The role of teaching discourse in learning. In G. Wallach & K. Butler (Eds.), *Language learning disabilities in school age children.* Baltimore: Williams & Wilkins.

Simon, H. (1971). Reading comprehension: The need for a new perspective. *Reading Research Quarterly, 6,* 340–363.

Singer, H. (1983). A century of landmarks in reading and learning from text at the high school level: Research, theories, and instructional strategies. *Journal of Reading, 2*(4), 332–342.

Sirotnik, K. (1982). *What you see is what you get: A summary of observations in over 1000 elementary and secondary classrooms* (report no. 29). Los Angeles: University of California, Graduate School of Education, Laboratory in School and Community Education. (ERIC Document Reproduction Service No. ED 214 897)

Smith, F. (1973). *Psycholinguistics and reading.* New York: Holt, Rinehart, & Winston.

Smith, F. (1975). Comprehension and learning: A conceptual framework for teachers. New York: Holt, Rinehart and Winston.

Smith, F., & Feathers, K. (1983). The role of reading in content classrooms: Assumption vs. reality. *Journal of Reading, 27*(3), 262–267.

Smith, F., & Goodman, K. (1971). On the psycholinguistic method of teaching reading. *Elementary School Journal, 71,* 177–181.

Spearritt, D. (1972). Identification of subskills of reading comprehension by maximum liklihood factor analysis. *Reading Research Quarterly, 8,* 92–111.

Spiro, R. (1980). Constructive processes in prose comprehension and recall. In R. Spiro, B. Bruce, & W. Brewer (Eds.), *Theoretical issues in reading comprehension.* Hillsdale, NJ: Erlbaum.

Stallard, C. (1976). *Objective-based reading programs: A comparative analysis.* Madison, WI: Development Center for Cognitive Learning and Instruction.

Stevens, K. (1980). The effect of background knowledge on reading comprehension of ninth graders. *Journal of Reading Behavior, 12*(2), 151–154.

Teaching of writing gets new push. New York Times. Winter Education Survey, January 8, 1984.

Tierney, R., & Lapp, D. (Eds.) (1979). *National assessment of education progress in reading.* Newark, DE: International Reading Association.

Vogel, M. (1981). A comparison of basic concept formation performance and verbal concept performance of ninth graders grouped according to reading ability. *International, 42*(2), 637A.

Whiteman, M. (1980). What can we learn from writing research. *Theory Into Practice, 19*(3).

Whiteman, M. (Ed.). (1981). *Variation in writing: Functional and linguistic-cultural differences.* Hillsdale, NJ: Erlbaum.

Wiig, E., & Semel, E. (1975). A preliminary study of productive language abilities in learning disabled adolescents. *Journal of Learning Disabilities, 8,* 578–586.

Wiig, E., & Semel, E. (1976). *Language disabilities in children and adolescents.* Columbus, OH: Merrill.

Wiig, E., & Semel, E. (1980). *Language assessment and intervention for the learning disabled.* Columbus, OH: Merrill.

Author Index

Subject Index